BALLET AND THE ARTS
DAS BALLETT
UND DIE KÜNSTE
25 JAHRE / 25 YEARS
INTERNATIONALE SOMMERAKADEMIE
DES TANZES KÖLN

BALLETT-BÜHNEN-VERLAG KÖLN

Dieses Buch wurde mit der freundlichen Unterstützung der BAYER AG, Leverkusen, gedruckt.
This book has been generously supported by BAYER AG, Leverkusen, Germany.

Darüber hinaus gilt den nachfolgenden Förderern Dank für ihre Hilfe. In addition, our grateful acknowledgement for their help goes to the following sponsors.
Deutsche Ballett-Bühne e.V., Köln · Fruttagent De Decker, Köln · Gerling-Konzern Zentrale Vertriebs-Aktiengesellschaft, Köln · Kreissparkasse Köln · Renate Russ, Köln · Johannes Schmitz-Krahé, Köln · Rudolf Walker, Köln

Impressum: Horst Koegler, Jens Wendland, Jochen Schmidt et al. Das Ballett und die Künste/Ballet and the Arts

Herausgegeben von der Internationalen Sommerakademie des Tanzes in Zusammenarbeit mit dem Ballett-Bühnen-Verlag Rolf Garske, Köln.
Edited by the Internationale Sommerakademie des Tanzes Köln in cooperation with Ballett-Bühnen-Verlag Rolf Garske, Cologne.

Verlegt im/Published by Ballett-Bühnen-Verlag Rolf Garske, Köln/Cologne.

Fotos: Holger Badekow, Achim Balon, Dieter Bauer, Eriks H. Berkmanis, Bert, G. Bieberstein, Marcus Blechman, Karsten Bundgaard, Daniel Cande, Tom Caravaglia, Costas, John Dady, Detlef Dorn, Siegfried Enkelmann, A. Epstein, Jorge Fatauros, Lois Greenfield, Annemarie Heinrich, Detlef Herchenbach, George Hoyningen-Huene, John R. Johnsen, Hannes Kilian, Fred Kliché, James Klosty, Pieter Kooistra, Hendrik Koßmann, Jürgen Kranich, Lesley Leslie-Spinks, Annelise Löffler, Sue Martin, Stefano Massimo, Herbert Migdoll, Dieter Milster, Mira, Jack Mitchell, Tony van Muyden, J.-M. Neukom, New York Public Library – Dance Collection, Stefan Odry, Andrew Oxenham, Standfotos aus dem Film „The Royal Ballet" mit freundlicher Genehmigung der Rank Organisation Limited, London/Stills of the Film "The Royal Ballet" by courtesy of The Rank Organisation Limited, London, Houston Rogers, Leslie E. Spatt, Wolfgang Strunz, Martha Swope, Charles Tandy, Nathaniel Tileston, Jens Waechter, Gert Weigelt, Ridha Zouari, Ballett-Bühnen-Verlag- und Kompanie-Archive/and company archives. © Fotos Jack und/and Linda Vartoogian bei/by Jack und/and Linda Vartoogian.

„Artisans of Space" von/by Marcia B. Siegel. Nachdruck mit freundlicher Genehmigung von/Reprinted by permission from The Hudson Review, Bd./Vol. XXXIV, No. 1 (Frühjahr/Spring 1981). Copyright © 1981 bei/by The Hudson Review, Inc. · „From Diaghilev to Cunningham". Copyright © 1981 bei/by David Vaughan.

Coverfotos © Tom Caravaglia, New York. Cover: TRIBE, Ch: Alwin Nikolais, Nikolais Dance Theater, 1975. Back Cover: HOOPLA, Ch: Murray Louis, Murray Louis Dance Company, 1972.

Redaktion/Editorial Staff: Dr. George-Roman Cunningham, Birgit Kirchner, Norbert Servos.
Übersetzungen/Translations: Stewart W. Lindemann, Marion von Rautenstrauch.
Layout: Geissler Design, Bergisch Gladbach.
Lithos: LAP Light Art Production, Köln.
Gesamtherstellung/Production: J. P. Bachem GmbH & Co KG, Köln.
Printed in the Federal Republic of Germany · ISBN 3-922224-02-4 · Ballett-Bühnen-Verlag Rolf Garske, Postf./P.O.Box 270 443, D-5000 Köln 1.

Inhalt/Contents

SCHWANENSEE/
SWAN LAKE,
Ch: Erik Bruhn (Petipa/Iwanow),
Veronica Tennant,
National Ballet of Canada,
Foto: NBC-Archiv

Man braucht nur einige der großen Ballett-
daten des 19. Jahrhunderts denen der anderen Künste zur gleichen Zeit gegenüberzu-
stellen; die Titel sprechen für sich:

1830/31

BALLETT
Filippo Taglionis Nonnenballett in Robert
der Teufel, große Oper von Giacomo Meyerbeer, L: Eugène Scribe, UA: Opéra, Paris
1831.
ANDERE KÜNSTE
Rot und Schwarz. Chronik des 19. Jahrhunderts, Roman von Stendhal, d. i. Henri Beyle,
ersch. 1830.
Die Freiheit führt das Volk an, Gemälde von
Eugène Delacroix, 1830.

1832

BALLETT
La Sylphide, Ballett in 2 Akten, L: Adolphe
Nourrit, Ch: Filippo Taglioni, M: Jean-Made-
leine Schneitzhoeffer, UA: Opéra, Paris 1832.
ANDERE KÜNSTE
Oberst Chabert, Roman von Honoré de Bal-
zac, ersch. 1832.
Symphonie fantastique. Episodes de la vie
d'un artiste (= Phantastische Sinfonie. Epi-
soden aus dem Leben eines Künstlers) von
Hector Berlioz, 1832.

1840/41

BALLETT
Giselle oder Die Wilis, phantastisches Bal-
lett in 2 Akten, L: Vernoy de Saint Georges,
Théophile Gautier und Jean Coralli, Ch: Co-
ralli und Jules Perrot, M: Adolphe Adam, UA:
Opéra, Paris 1841.
ANDERE KÜNSTE
Ein Held unserer Zeit, Roman von Michail
Lermontov, ersch. 1840.
I. (Frühlingssinfonie) und IV. Sinfonie (in er-
ster Fassung als II. Sinfonie) von Robert
Schumann, beide 1841.

1868/69

BALLETT
Don Quixote, Ballett mit Prolog, 4 Akten und
8 Bildern, L und Ch: Marius Petipa, M: Lud-
wig Minkus, UA: Bolschoi-Theater, Moskau
1869.
ANDERE KÜNSTE
Die Meistersinger von Nürnberg, Oper in 3
Aufzügen, L und M: Richard Wagner, UA:
Königl. Hof- und Nationaltheater, München
1868.
Krieg und Frieden, Roman in 4 Bänden von
Leo N. Tolstoi, ersch. 1868/69.
L'Education sentimentale. Histoire d'un jeu-
ne homme (Lehrjahre des Gefühls. Ge-
schichte eines jungen Mannes), Roman von
Gustave Flaubert, ersch. 1869.
Ehepaar Sisley, Gemälde von Pierre-August
Renoir, 1868.

VERSUCHE ÜBER DAS REALISMUS-PROBLEM IM BALLETT DES 19. JAHRHUNDERTS

1870/72

BALLETT
Coppélia ou La Fille aux yeux d'émail, Ballett
in 3 Akten, L: nach E. T. A. Hoffmanns Der
Sandmann von Charles Nuitter und Arthur
Saint-Léon, Ch: Saint-Léon, M: Léo Delibes,
UA: Opéra, Paris 1870.
ANDERE KÜNSTE
Die Walküre, erster Tag aus dem Bühnen-
festspiel Der Ring des Nibelungen, UA
(unautorisierte): Königl. Hof- und National-
theater, München, 1870.
Wolga-Treidler, Gemälde von Ilja Efimovic
Repin, 1872.

1876/77

BALLETT
Schwanensee, Ballett in 4 Akten, L: V. P. Be-
gitschew u. W. Geltzer, Ch: Julius Reisinger,
M: Peter Iljitsch Tschaikowsky, UA: Bolschoi-Theater, Moskau 1877.
ANDERE KÜNSTE
Die Stützen der Gesellschaft, Schauspiel in
4 Akten von Henrik Ibsen, UA: Odense, Dänemark, 1877.
Der Absinth, Gemälde von Edgar Degas,
1876.

1890/91

BALLETT
Dornröschen, Ballett mit Prolog in 3 Akten u.
4 Bildern, L: Marius Petipa u. Iwan Wsewo-
loschki, Ch: Marius Petipa, M: Peter Iljitsch
Tschaikowsky, UA: Maryinsky-Theater, St.
Petersburg 1890.
ANDERE KÜNSTE
Hedda Gabler, Schauspiel in 4 Akten von
Henrik Ibsen, UA: Hoftheater, München,
1891.
Cavalleria rusticana, Melodram in 1 Akt nach
Giovanni Vergas gleichnamigem Volks-
stück von Giovanni Targioni-Tozetti u. Guido
Menasci, M: Pietro Mascagni, UA: Teatro Co-
stanzi, Rom 1890.
Moulin Rouge, Plakatentwurf von Henri Tou-
louse-Lautrec, Paris 1890.
Kartenspieler, Gemälde von Paul Cézanne,
1885–90.

1892/93

BALLETT
Der Nußknacker, Ballett in 2 Akten und 3 Bil-
dern, L: Marius Petipa, Ch: Lew Iwanow, M:
Peter Iljitsch Tschaikowsky, UA: Maryinsky-
Theater, St. Petersburg 1892.
ANDERE KÜNSTE
Die Weber, Schauspiel aus den vierziger
Jahren, soziales Drama von Gerhart Haupt-
mann, ersch. 1892, UA: Neues Theater, Ber-
lin, 1893.
Falstaff, Lyrische Komödie in 3 Akten (nach
Shakespeare) von Arrigo Boito, M: Giusep-
pe Verdi, UA: Teatro alla Scala, Mailand
1893.

1897/99

BALLETT
Raymonda, Ballett in 3 Akten und 4 Bildern,
L: Lydia Paschkowa und Marius Petipa, Ch:
Marius Petipa, M: Alexander Glasunow, UA:
Maryinsky-Theater, St. Petersburg, 1898.
ANDERE KÜNSTE
Onkel Wanja. Szenen aus dem Landleben,
Schauspiel in 4 Akten von Anton Tsche-
chow, ersch. 1897, UA: Künstler-Theater,
Moskau, 1899.
La Bohème, Oper in 4 Bildern nach Henri
Murgers Roman Scènes de la vie de Bo-
hème, L: Luigi Illica u. Giacomo Giacosa, M:
Giacomo Puccini, UA: Teatro Regio, Turin,
1896.

Man kann es natürlich auch von der Gegen-
seite her betrachten:

1836

ANDERE KÜNSTE
Woyzeck, ein als Bruchstück hinterlassenes
Drama von Georg Büchner.
BALLETT
La Sylphide, Ballett in 2 Akten, L: Adolphe
Nourrit, Ch: August Bournonville, M: Her-
mann von Løvenskjold, UA: Königl. Däni-
sches Ballett, Kopenhagen, 1836.

1848

ANDERE KÜNSTE
Die Kameliendame, Roman von Alexandre
Dumas fils, ersch. 1848.
BALLETT
Die vier Jahreszeiten, Ballett-Divertissement
in 1 Akt, Ch: Jules Perrot, M: Cesare Pugni,
UA: Her Majesty's Theatre, London 1848.

1862/63

ANDERE KÜNSTE
Väter und Söhne, Roman von Iwan S. Tur-
genjew, ersch. 1862.
BALLETT
Diavolina, Ballett von Arthur Saint-Léon, UA:
1863.

1880/81
ANDERE KÜNSTE
Nana, Roman von Emile Zola, ersch. 1879/80.
BALLETT
Excelsior, ein aufwendiges und spektakuläres Ballett in 6 Akten und 12 Bildern, Ch: Luigi Manzotti, M: Romualdo Marenco, UA: Teatro alla Scala, Mailand 1881.

1888/89
ANDERE KÜNSTE
Fräulein Julie. Ein naturalistisches Trauerspiel, Einakter von August Strindberg, ersch. 1888, UA: Kopenhagen 1889.
BALLETT
Der Talisman, Ballett von Marius Petipa, UA: 1889.

Mit anderen Worten: das Ballett, zu Beginn des 19. Jahrhunderts zumindest noch im „Schlepptau" der Künste seiner Zeit (Gluck, Mozart und Beethoven hatten nach anfänglicher Aufgeschlossenheit jeglichen Ballettehrgeiz aufgegeben) hat sich auf seinem Weg durch das Jahrhundert immer weiter ins Abseits der herrschenden geistigen Strömungen und Richtungen begeben. Es würde den Versuch lohnen zu untersuchen, warum das Ballett gerade zur Zeit der Restauration (1815–1848) seinen eigentlich verspäteten romantischen Höhepunkt erlebte – ob man nicht sogar behaupten kann, es sei in seiner Rückwärtsorientierung und seinem Eskapismus die spezifische künstlerische Ausdrucksform des Metternich-Zeitalters gewesen.

Sieht man sich die Liste der zwischen 1830 und der Jahrhundertwende entstandenen Ballette an, so scheint es, als hätten Hegel und Marx, der Eisenbahningenieur Stephenson und der Erfinder der drahtlosen Telegraphie, Marconi, Balzac und Tolstoi, Ibsen, Strindberg und Hauptmann, Wagner und Verdi, Cézanne, Repin und van Gogh nie existiert.

Wofür diese Namen stehen, kann zusammengefaßt werden unter dem Begriff des Realismus. Das 19. Jahrhundert war das Zeitalter des Realismus, doch an den großen Debatten über die Funktion des künstlerischen Realismus (besonders heftig in der Literatur seit Balzac und Stendhal, in der Malerei seit der Schule von Barbizon, verstärkt in den Salons der Impressionisten und in der Musik insbesondere bei den Neudeutschen um Liszt sowie im Umkreis des russischen Mächtigen Häufleins), an ihnen war das Ballett nicht beteiligt. Das Kernproblem jenes Zeitalters, das den rapiden Fortschritt von Technik und Industrie mit wachsender sozialer Unruhe bezahlte, war, wie denn die sich so unaufhaltsam verändernde zeitgenössische Gesellschaft künstlerisch in den Griff zu bekommen sei,

und wie sie angemessen reflektiert werden könne, so daß das Publikum sich in den Kunstwerken wiedererkennen könne; wo denn die Realität aufhöre, und wo die Kunst anfinge. Dies alles scheint Tänzer, Choreographen und Ballettpädagogen kaum interessiert zu haben.

Giuseppe Verdi immerhin erklärte 1853: „Ich will neue, schöne, große, abwechslungsreiche, kühne Stoffe. Kühn bis zum äußersten, neu in der Form, und bei all dem gut komponierbar... In Venedig will ich die Dame aux camélias aufführen, sie wird vielleicht La Traviata heißen. Es ist ein Stoff unserer Zeit. Ein anderer hätte das vielleicht nicht komponiert wegen der Kostüme, wegen der Zeit, wegen tausend anderer dummer Hemmungen. Ich tat es mit besonderem Wohlgefallen." Als Verdis Traviata dann 1853 bei ihrer Uraufführung in Venedig die Zeitgenossen durch den ungewöhnlichen Realismus ihrer musikalischen Charakterzeichnung schockierte (mehr jedenfalls als durch ihren Handlungsrealismus, dessen übriggebliebener Rest an Sozialkritik sich gegenüber dem Original von Dumas fils reichlich verwässert und sentimentalisiert ausnimmt), brachte Joseph Mazilier an der Pariser Opéra gerade sein Ballett Aelia et Mysis heraus, ein antikes Eifersuchtsdrama mit einem mythologischen Divertissement, dem Théophile Gautier bescheinigte: „Hier ist die Antike in all ihrem unergründlichen Geheimnis."

Der Verlust des Balletts an ästhetischer und theoretischer Substanz im 19. Jahrhundert ist erschreckend. Hervorgegangen aus der Diskussion von Akademikern am Hofe Ludwigs XIV., die im Ballett und seinen allegorischen und symbolischen Perspektiven eine vollkommene Widerspiegelung der absolutistischen Ordnung sahen, befand sich das Ballett bis ins beginnende 19. Jahrhundert hinein durchaus im Einvernehmen mit den anderen Künsten. Daß so wenige seiner historischen Choreographien überlebt haben, scheint mir nicht so sehr auf einen generellen Mangel an künstlerischer Qualität, sondern eher auf das Desinteresse an der Entwicklung eines allgemeinverbindlichen choreographischen Notationssystems zurückzuführen zu sein. Bis zu Salvatore Viganò waren die großen Choreographen durchweg gebildete Künstler, die auch als Theoretiker ihren Mann standen. Auf anderer Ebene ist die heftige Auseinandersetzung zwischen Jean-Georges Noverre und Gasparo Angiolini zu Beginn der 70er Jahre des 18. Jahrhunderts durchaus mit dem Pariser Buffonistenstreit zwischen den Anhängern Glucks und Piccinis 20 Jahre früher zu vergleichen.

Man kann nur mutmaßen, welchen anderen Verlauf die Ballettgeschichte genommen hätte, wenn August Bournonville in Paris geblieben und nicht 1830 nach Kopenhagen

zurückgekehrt wäre. An choreographischer Kreativität seinen zeitgenössischen Kollegen zumindest ebenbürtig, wenn nicht überlegen, dürfte er sie als universal gebildeter Künstler, der mit wachen Sinnen und klarem Verstand seine Umwelt wahrnahm und seine sehr eigene Meinung dazu auch zu artikulieren verstand, alle überragt haben. In Kopenhagen arbeitete er in der Isolation, auf verlorenem Posten. Immerhin legen die realistischen Episoden in seinen so durch und durch bürgerlichen Balletten wie Napoli, Kirmes in Brügge und Das Freiwilligen-Corps auf Amager die Vermutung nahe, daß er sich in Paris, in der unmittelbaren Nachbarschaft zu Balzac, Stendhal und Eugène Sue, zu dem großen realistischen Choreographen entwickelt hätte, den uns das 19. Jahrhundert schuldig geblieben ist.

Es ist bemerkenswert, daß wir von Bournonville als einzigem Choreographen des 19. Jahrhunderts nach Viganò eine ungefähre Vorstellung seiner Persönlichkeit und seiner Denkweise haben, während alle anderen, inklusive Filippo Taglioni, Jean Coralli, Jules Perrot, Joseph Mazilier, Arthur Saint-Léon, Marius Petipa und Lew Iwanow, die den künstlerischen Weg des Balletts im 19. Jahrhundert bestimmten, bloße Chiffren bleiben. Man vergleiche nur einmal die Memoiren Bournonvilles mit denjenigen Petipas, um sich nicht nur des enormen intellektuellen Abstands, sondern speziell auch des unterschiedlichen Grades an Realitätsverständnis und Realitätbegreifen beider Choreographen bewußt zu werden. Nur daß Bournonville das Pech hatte, in Kopenhagen zu wirken, dessen Ballettkompanie außerhalb Dänemarks kaum bekannt war, während Petipa den richtigen Instinkt hatte, in das gerade zur Ballettkapitale der Welt aufstrebende St. Petersburg zu gehen, ohne sich im mindesten über die dortigen Vorgänge außerhalb der engen Pariser Ballettkolonie bewußt zu sein, mit welch einer Heftigkeit in der Tschernyschewsky-Nachfolge insbesondere in dem Kreis um den Kritiker Stassow und im Mächtigen Häuflein über die ästhetischen und sozialen Beziehungen der Kunst zur Wirklichkeit nachgedacht und diskutiert wurde.

Nicht auszudenken, was geschehen wäre, wäre nicht Petipa, sondern Bournonville als Botschafter des französischen Balletts in St. Petersburg mit Männern wie Tschernyschewsky, Stassow, Balakirew, Mussorgsky, Borodin und Rimsky-Korsakow – von Tschaikowsky gar nicht zu reden – zusammengetroffen!

Doch ausgerechnet 1830, im Jahr der Julirevolution, als das Ballett in Paris sich zu seinem, gegenüber den anderen Künsten verspäteten, romantischen Höhenflug anschickte, kehrte Bournonville – wie gesagt – in seine dänische Ballettprovinz zurück. Und überließ das Pariser Ballett Théophile Gautier, dem einzigen wortmächtigen Schriftsteller, der sich überhaupt dafür interessierte. Gautier war im Gefolge Victor Hugos zweifellos eine der flamboyantesten Persönlichkeiten der französischen Romantik, der als Erfinder des l'art pour l'art-Slogans mit dem aufkommenden Realismus, der sich zunehmend gegen die sozialen Mißstände des Zeitalters engagierte, nicht das mindeste im Sinn hatte.

Als Literat und professioneller Kritiker, Amateur-Librettist und Ballerinen-Verehrer, wuchs ihm fast automatisch das Renommee eines Ideologen des romantischen Balletts zu. Da kein anderer Schriftsteller von Format, schon gar kein Ballettprofi, ihm dieses Renommee streitig machen konnte, konnte er zu der literarischen Zentralinstanz des Balletts um die Jahrhundertmitte werden, als der er bis heute gilt, und als der er damals keinen Nachfolger fand. Das Ballett, nach Gautiers Abtreten von der Szene ohne jegliche ästhetisch-theoretische Hilfestellung, fuhr nach dem ihm von Gautier diktierten Gesetz fort – kursgenau in dem romantischen Fahrwasser der Erfolgsformeln von *La Sylphide, Giselle* und *La Péri.* Wobei sein ursprünglich durchaus vorhandener romantischer Gehalt mehr und mehr versikkerte, schließlich im letzten Jahrzehnt des Jahrhunderts derart austrocknete, daß außer in den Jahren 1893 und 1897 keine Ballettpremieren an der Pariser Opéra stattfanden.

So erwies sich Gautier letzten Endes als großes Hemmnis für das Ballett, das, mit ihm als einzigem literarisch-fundierten Wegbereiter, sehr bald an die Grenzen seiner romantischen Ästhetik gelangt war, die es jahrzehntelang nicht zu überschreiten wagte – verurteilt zu endloser Wiederholung und unfruchtbarer Stagnation. Während sich die anderen Künste, gerade auch das Schauspiel und selbst die Oper (via Verdi, Puccini) zunehmend realistische Gestaltungsmittel erarbeiteten und derart die literarische Entwicklung mitvollzogen, verharrte das Ballett im Abseits seiner als quasi medium-essentiell begriffenen romantischen Attitüde, die spätestens nach 1848 auch ihres letzten künstlerischen Sinns verlustig gegangen war, lediglich im fernen St. Petersburg noch ein einziges Mal als „absolutistische Endzeit-Utopie" zu einer letzten Blüte gelangte.

Sofern das Ballett des 19. Jahrhunderts sich überhaupt auf Gegenwartssujets und -themen einließ, verblieb es meist in der Zuständigkeit einer mit aktuellen Gebrauchsgegenständen garnierten Revue – wie Katti Lanners Londoner Empire-Ballette à la *The Sports of England, The Paris Exhibition* und *On Brighton Pier* oder Luigi Manzottis Scala-Enormitäten vom Schlage *Excelsior, Amor* und *Sport.* An diesen Stücken gemessen, entpuppt sich *La Fille mal gardée* vom Jahrgang 1789 als Frühlingshauch einer veritablen realistischen Ballettkomödie des Dritten Standes, der gerade sein Selbstverständnis entdeckt hatte. (Es ist ein Jammer, daß das Ballett den hier von Jean Dauberval so überaus erfolgreich eingeschlagenen Weg zu einer *Comedy of manners* nicht weitergegangen ist, sondern gleich ins bürgerliche Rührstück à la Louis-Jacques Milons *Nina ou La Folle par amour* oder Filippo Taglionis *Danina oder Jocko, der brasilianische Affe* abgesunken ist.)

Der Ausschluß von der großen Realismus-Diskussion des 19. Jahrhunderts bildete den nicht wiedergutzumachenden Sündenfall des Balletts, an dem wir noch heute kranken. Denn als das Ballett endlich aus seinem romantischen Schlaf erwachte und sich um den Wiederanschluß an die anderen Künste bemühte, war die Schwelle zum 20. Jahrhundert bereits überschritten, hatten die Nachbarkünste ihre realistischen Lehrjahrzehnte hinter sich. Als Serge Diaghilew mit seinen Ballets Russes 20 Jahre lang das Exempel eines an Haupt und Gliedern reformierten Balletts statuierte, stand diese Reform im Zeichen von Neuromantik, Jugendstil, Expressionismus und Konstruktivismus. Wo sie sich um Realismus bemühten, etwa in den Volksszenen von *Petruschka,* herrschte das pure Chaos. Niemand hielte etwa *Jeux* schon für ein realistisches Ballett, nur weil dort drei Personen im modernen Tennisdreß auftreten.

Eine systematische Diskussion über Realismus und Ballett begann erst in den 20er Jahren unseres Jahrhunderts in der Sowjetunion, jedoch von vornherein pervertiert durch die Auflage, dieser Realismus habe sozialistisch zu sein. Seinen Nachholbedarf an realistischen choreographischen Gestaltungsmitteln deckte das sowjetische Ballett, indem es, an sich nicht unlogisch, an die Mittel des romantischen Balletts anknüpfte – mit einer Verspätung von rund einem Dreivierteljahrhundert. (Was sich im Zusammenhang mit den sich so fortschrittlich-revolutionär gebärdenden Stoffen und Inhalten naturgemäß noch anachronistischer ausnahm, als ohnehin der Fall gewesen wäre. Daher der so entsetzlich altmodische, opernhaft-pathetische, so ganz dem 19. Jahrhundert verhaftete Realismus der sowjetischen Ballette vom *Roten Mohn* über *Das Goldene Zeitalter* und *Küste der Hoffnung* bis zu *Angara.*)

Im westlichen Ballett des 20. Jahrhunderts gab es überhaupt keine grundlegende Realismus-Diskussion. Realismus im Ballett unserer Tage definiert sich immer noch vom Stoff, dem Bühnenbild, den Kostümen sowie von der Anverwandlung nicht genuin tänzerischer Alltagsbewegungen her. Das läßt die meisten Versuche einer choreographischen Übermittlung realistischer Inhalte so oberflächlich, so aufgesetzt, so forciert, so wenig tänzerisch motiviert erscheinen.

Fazit: Keine Kunstgattung kann sich auf Dauer ungestraft den künstlerischen Erscheinungsformen entziehen, die der legitime Ausdruck ihrer Zeit sind. Indem das Ballett die Realismus-Bewegung des 19. Jahrhunderts ignorierte, fiel es aus dem Gesamtzusammenhang der Künste heraus – ein Verschulden, dessen ästhetische (und qualitative) Konsequenzen bis auf den heutigen Tag spürbar sind.

One need only compare a few of the important ballets of the 19th century with the other arts of the same time. The titles speak for themselves:

1830/31

BALLET
Filippo Taglioni's ballet of the nuns in Robert le Diable, grand opera by Giacomo Meyerbeer, libr.: Eugène Scribe, first prod. 1831, Paris Opéra.
OTHER ARTS
The Red and the Black. A Chronicle from the 19th Century, novel by Stendhal i.e. Henri Beyle, publ. 1830.

Horst Koegler

MARGINAL NOTES ON THE PROBLEM OF REALISM IN THE BALLET OF THE 19TH CENTURY

Liberty Leading the People, painting by Eugène Delacroix, 1830.

1832

BALLET
La Sylphide, ballet in 2 acts, libr.: Adolphe Nourrit, ch: Filippo Taglioni, m: Jean-Madeleine Schneitzhoeffer, first prod. 1832, Paris Opéra.
OTHER ARTS
Colonel Chabert, novel by Honoré de Balzac, publ. 1832.
Symphonie fantastique. Episodes de la vie d'un artiste by Hector Berlioz, 1832.

1840/41

BALLET
Giselle, ou les wilis, fantastic ballet in 2 acts, libr.: Vernoy de Saint Georges, Théophile Gautier, and Jean Coralli, ch: Coralli and Jules Perrot, m: Adolphe Adam, first prod. 1841, Paris Opéra.
OTHER ARTS
A Hero of Our Time, novel by Mikhail Lermontov, publ. 1840.
First (Spring) Symphony and Fourth Symphony (in first version as Second Symphony) by Robert Schumann, both 1841.

1868/69

BALLET
Don Quixote, ballet with prologue, 4 acts and 8 scenes, libr. and ch: Marius Petipa, m: Ludwig Minkus, first prod. Bolshoi Theater, Moscow 1869.
OTHER ARTS
Die Meistersinger von Nürnberg, opera in 3 acts, libr. and m: Richard Wagner, first prod. Royal Court and National Theater, Munich 1868.
War and Peace, novel in 4 volumes by Leo N. Tolstoy, publ. 1868/69.
L'Education sentimentale. Histoire d'un jeune homme, novel by Gustave Flaubert, publ. 1869.
Mr. and Mrs. Sisley, painting by Pierre-August Renoir, 1868.

1870/72

BALLET
Coppélia ou La Fille aux yeux d'émail, ballet in 3 acts, libr. after E. T. A. Hoffmann's The Sandman: Charles Nuitter and Arthur Saint-Léon, ch: Saint-Léon, m: Léo Delibes, first prod. 1870, Paris Opéra.
OTHER ARTS
Die Walküre, first day of Der Ring des Nibelungen, first prod. (unauthorized): Royal Court and National Theater, Munich 1870.
Volga Boatmen, painting by Ilya Yefimovich Repin, 1872.

1876/77

BALLET
Swan Lake, ballet in 4 acts, libr.: V. P. Begitchev and W. Geltzer, ch: Julius Reisinger, m: Peter Ilyich Tchaikovsky, first prod. Bolshoi Theater, Moscow 1877.
OTHER ARTS
Pillars of Society, drama in 4 acts by Henrik Ibsen, first prod. Odense, Denmark 1877.
Absinthe, painting by Edgar Degas, 1876.

1890/91

BALLET
The Sleeping Beauty, ballet with prologue, 3 acts, and 4 scenes, libr.: Marius Petipa and Ivan Vsevolojsky, ch: Marius Petipa, m: Peter

Ilyich Tchaikovsky, first prod. Maryinsky Theater, St. Petersburg 1890.
OTHER ARTS
Hedda Gabler, drama in 4 acts by Henrik Ibsen, first prod. Court Theater, Munich 1891.
Cavalleria rusticana, melodrama in 1 act after Giovanni Verga's folk piece of the same name by Giovanni Targioni-Tozetti and Guido Menasci, m: Pietro Mascagni, first prod. Teatro Costanzi, Rome 1890.
Moulin Rouge, design for a poster by Henri Toulouse-Lautrec, Paris 1890.
The Card Players, painting by Paul Cézanne, 1885–90.

1892/93

BALLET
The Nutcracker, ballet in 2 acts and 3 scenes, libr.: Marius Petipa, ch: Lev Ivanov, m: Peter Ilyich Tchaikovsky, first prod. Maryinsky Theater, St. Petersburg 1892.
OTHER ARTS
The Weavers. Drama of the '40s, social drama by Gerhart Hauptmann, publ. 1892, first prod. New Theater, Berlin 1893.
Falstaff, Lyrical comedy in 3 acts (after Shakespeare) by Arrigo Boito, m: Giuseppe Verdi, first prod. Teatro alla Scala, Milan 1893.

1897/99

BALLET
Raymonda, ballet in 3 acts and 4 scenes, libr.: Lydia Pashkova and Marius Petipa, m: Aleksandr Glazunov, first prod. Maryinsky Theater, St. Petersburg 1898.
OTHER ARTS
Uncle Vanya. Scenes from Country Life, drama in four acts by Anton Chekhov, publ. 1897, first prod. Artists Theater, Moscow 1899.
La Bohème, opera in 4 scenes after Henri Murger's novel Scènes de la Vie de Bohème, libr.: Luigi Illica and Giacomo Giacosa, m: Giacomo Puccini, first prod. Teatro Regio, Turin 1896.

One can, of course, look at it the other way round:

1836

OTHER ARTS
Wozzeck, a fragmentary tragedy by Georg Büchner.
BALLET
La Sylphide, ballet in 2 acts, libr.: Adolphe Nourrit, ch: August Bournonville, m: Herman Løvenskjold, first prod. Royal Danish Ballet, Copenhagen 1836.

1848

OTHER ARTS
Camille (The Lady of the Camellias), novel by Alexandre Dumas fils, publ. 1848.

BALLET
The Four Seasons, ballet divertissement in 1 act, ch: Jules Perrot, m: Cesare Pugni, first prod. Her Majesty's Theatre, London 1848.

1862/63

OTHER ARTS
Fathers and Sons, novel by Ivan S. Turgenev, publ. 1862.
BALLET
Diavolina, ballet by Arthur Saint-Léon, first prod. 1863.

1880/81

OTHER ARTS
Nana, novel by Emile Zola, publ. 1879/80.
BALLET
Excelsior, a sumptuous and spectacular ballet in 6 acts and 12 scenes, ch: Luigi Manzotti, m: Romualdo Marenco, first prod. Teatro alla Scala, Milan 1881.

1888/89

OTHER ARTS
Miss Julie. A naturalistic drama, one-act-play by August Strindberg, publ. 1888, first prod. Copenhagen 1889.
BALLET
The Talisman, ballet by Marius Petipa, first prod. 1889.

In other words, at the beginning of the 19th century ballet was at least still taken in tow by the other arts of its time. (After initial interest, Gluck, Mozart, and Beethoven had given up all ballet ambitions). As the century progressed, ballet lost importance in the prevailing intellectual trends. It would be worth examining why the romantic ballet reached its belated climax during the restauration (1815–'48). Perhaps one could even argue that its retrogressive orientation and escapism best represented the specific artistic expression of the Metternich era.

If one looks at the list of ballets emerging between 1830 and the turn of the century, it appears as though Hegel and Marx, the railway engineer Stephenson, and the inventor of wireless telegraphy Marconi, Balzac and Tolstoy, Ibsen, Strindberg, and Hauptmann, Wagner, Verdi, Cézanne, Repin, and van Gogh had never existed.

These names can be grouped under the headline of realism. The 19th century was the century of realism, but ballet did not participate in the important debates concerning the function of artistic realism. Ever since Stendhal and Balzac, these subjects were vehemently discussed in the field of literature, since the Barbizon school, in painting, and in music, particularly in the New German School around Liszt and in the circle of the Russian Mighty Five. The main problem of that age, which paid for the rapid technical and industrial progress with increased social unrest, was how to reflect the constantly changing contemporary society in art, so that the public could recognize itself therein, and to see where reality leaves off and art begins. All of this, however, hardly seemed to interest dancers, choreographers, and ballet teachers.

In 1853, Giuseppe Verdi commented: "I want plots that are great, beautiful, varied, daring ... daring to an extreme, new in form and at the same time adapted to composing.... I shall have *La Dame aux Camélias* performed in Venice. It will perhaps be called *La Traviata*. A subject from our own time. Another person would perhaps not have composed it because of the costumes, because of the period, because of a thousand other foolish objections. I did it with particular pleasure."

As in 1853 Verdi's *Traviata* was first performed in Venice, it shocked his contemporaries – mainly due to the exceptional realism of its musical characterization (more, in any case, than through the realism of the action, its remaining social criticism appearing rather diluted and sentimental in face of the original work by Dumas fils). At the same time, Joseph Mazilier presented his ballet *Aelia et Mysis* at the Paris Opera, an antique drama of jealousy, including a mythological divertimento, of which Théophile Gautier declared: "Here is antiquity in all its unfathomable mystery".

The deplorable loss of aesthetic and theoretical substance suffered by ballet during the 19th century is appalling. Having emerged out of the discussions of academicians at the court of Louis XIV, who saw in ballet with its allegoric and symbolic perspectives a perfect reflection of absolutism, ballet was consistent with the other arts until the early 19th century. The fact that so few choreographies have survived throughout history is, in my opinion, not due to a general lack of artistic quality but rather to a disinterest in the development of a valid and binding system of choreographic notation. Up to the time of Salvatore Viganò, most of the famous choreographers were cultivated artists who could also hold their own as theorists. On another level, the vehement discussion between Jean-Georges Noverre and Gasparo Angiolini in the early '70s of the 18th century is quite comparable to the Buffonist dispute between the followers of Gluck and Piccini 20 years earlier.

One can only guess at the course ballet history would have taken had August Bournonville remained in Paris instead of returning to Copenhagen in 1830. In choreographic creativity, he was at least equal, if not superior to his contemporaries. Possibly, he would have surpassed them all, for he was a universally educated artist as well as a man who registered everything that went on around him with an alert and clear mind, holding very definite opinions which he was also able to articulate. In Copenhagen he worked in isolation. For all that, the realistic episodes in his thoroughly bourgeois ballets, such as *Napoli, The Kermesse in Bruges*, and *The Life Guards on Amager* leads one to speculate that in Paris, in the close vicinity to Balzac, Stendhal, and Eugène Sue, he would have developed into the great realist choreographer missing in the 19th century.

It is remarkable that Bournonville is the only 19th century choreographer, after Viganò, of whom we have an approximate idea about his personality and way of thinking, whereas all the others, including Filippo Taglioni, Jean Coralli, Jules Perrot, Joseph Mazilier, Arthur Saint-Léon, Marius Petipa, and Lev Ivanov, who determined the artistic trends of 19th century ballet, remain merely as names. One need only compare Bournonville's memoirs with Petipa's to realize not only the enormous superiority of the former's intellectual capacity, but particularly the varied degree of his understanding and grasping of reality. Bournonville had the bad luck to be working at the Copenhagen Royal Danish Ballet, the existence of which was hardly known outside Denmark. Petipa, on the other hand, had the right instinct to go to St. Petersburg, which had just set out to become the ballet capital of the world. While there, he was not in the least aware of what went on outside the tight Paris ballet colony. He did not realize at all with what vehemence the circle around the St. Petersburg critic Stassov and the Mighty Five considered and discussed the aesthetic and social relationship of art to reality. Unthinkable what would have happened if Bournonville instead of Petipa had encountered, as ambassador of French ballet in St. Petersburg, men like Tchernichevsky, Stassov, Balakirev, Mussorgsky, Borodin, Rimsky-Korsakov, not to mention Tchaikovsky.

Instead, just at the moment when ballet in Paris began rising to its delayed romantic climax in 1830, the year of the July revolution, Bournonville went back to his Danish ballet province. He left the Paris ballet to Théophile Gautier, the only powerful writer who showed any interest in ballet. Gautier, after Victor Hugo, was undoubtedly one of the most flamboyant personalities in French romanticism. As the author of the l'art pour l'art slogan, he had not the least bit of interest in the rising realism which was increasingly engaged in fighting the social misery of the day.

As a man of letters and professional critic, amateur librettist and admirer of ballerinas, he almost automatically became known as an ideologist of romantic ballet. Since there was no one else of his stature, to say nothing of a ballet savant who could compete with his personality, Gautier came to be the central literary figure of ballet at the middle of the century, and as such is still recognized today. During his time he had no successor. Ballet, left without any aesthetic-theoretical support following Gautier's exit from the scene, continued according to the principles he had dictated – navigating full course ahead in the romantic waters with success formulas like *La Sylphide, Giselle* and *La Péri,* whereby the original, pure, romantic content ebbed away and dried out to the point that (with the exception of 1893 and 1897) there were no ballet premieres at the Paris Opera during the last decade of the century. So, in the end, Gautier proved to be a great hindrance to ballet, which had depended on him as the only pioneer versed in literature. It soon arrived at the limit of its romantic aesthetics, beyond which it did not dare go for decades, condemned to constant repetition and fruitless stagnation. While the other arts, especially drama and even opera (through Verdi and Puccini), worked more and more with the principles of realism, thus keeping step with literary development, ballet stubbornly stood apart, in its quasi essential-to-the-medium romantic attitude, which after 1848, at the latest, also lost its remaining artistic purpose and solely in distant St. Petersburg had its one last flowering as absolutistic end-of-time utopia. In as far as 19th century ballet allowed itself to deal with contemporary subjects and themes at all, it remained for the most part in the category of a revue garnished with the latest trends, as for example Katti Lanner's creations for the London Empire Ballet *The Sports of England, The Paris Exhibition,* and *On Brighton Pier,* or Luigi Manzotti's La Scala spectacles *Excelsior, Amor* and *Sport.* Compared to these, *La Fille mal gardée* (1789) reveals itself as a breath of spring, a truly realistic ballet comedy, with the newly acquired self-assurance of the lower classes. It is lamentable that ballet did not continue on Jean Dauberval's successful path towards a *comedy of manners,* but instead sank into sentimental, middle class pieces, such as Louis-Jacques Milon's *Nina, ou la Folle par Amour,* or Filippo Taglioni's *Danina or Jocko the Brazilian Monkey.*

The failure to participate in the important realism discussion of the 19th century was a contributing factor to the fall of ballet, a fall from which to this day it has never recovered. When ballet finally woke up from its romantic sleep and tried to reconnect with the other arts, the threshold of the 20th

oben/above
LA PERI,
Ch: Jean Coralli,
Carlotta Grisi, Lucien Petipa,
Lithographie/Lithograph:
Marie-Alexandre Alophe
unten/below
EXCELSIOR,
Ch: Luigi Manzotti,
La Scala, Milano

century had been crossed and the other arts had their learning decades of realism behind them. When Serge Diaghilev with his Ballets Russes established the example of a from top to bottom reformed ballet, this reformation was under the influence of neo-romanticism, art nouveau, expressionism, and constructivism. Where, for instance, it dealt with realism, in the folk scene in *Petrushka,* it turned out to be pure chaos. No one would consider *Jeux* to be a realistic ballet merely because three people appear in modern tennis dress.

A systematic discussion of realism and ballet first began in the '20s of our century in the Soviet Union, but, from the start, it was perverted through the assumption that realism had to be socialist. The Soviet ballet quite logically met the pent-up demand for realistic subjects by using the means of romantic ballet, with a three-quarter of a century delay. (This, of course, turned out to be even more anachronistic in connection with its progressive-revolutionary themes. That explains the so frightfully old-fashioned, operatic realism of Soviet ballet clinging to the 19th century, from *Red Poppy* through *The Golden Age,* and *Shore of Hope* to *Angara.*

In western 20th century ballet there has been no fundamental discussion of realism. Realism in ballet today still defines itself through subject matter, décor, and costumes as well as through the assimilation of everyday movements not common to dance. That makes most choreographic attempts at transmitting realistic content appear so superficial, so put on, so forced, so little motivated by dance.

The conclusion: no art form can go forever unpunished when it cuts itself off from the artistic mainstreams which are the legitimate expression of the time. Since ballet ignored the 19th century realism movement, it lost relevance to the other arts; a sin, the aesthetic (and qualitative) consequences of which are felt to this day.

LA SYLPHIDE,
Ch: Filippo Taglioni,
Marie Taglioni,
Lithographie/Lithograph
oben/above
Achille Devéria,
Henri Grevedon
nach/after August Barre
unten/below
John Templeton *nach/after*
Alfred Edward Chalon

oben/above
SCHWANENSEE/SWAN LAKE,
Ch: Marius Petipa/Lew Iwanow,
Szene aus der Originalproduktion/
from the original production,
Foto: Dieter Milster
unten/below
SCHWANENSEE/SWAN LAKE,
La Scala, Milano

oben/above
LA BAYADERE,
Ch: Natalia Makarowa (Petipa),
American Ballet Theater,
Foto: ABT-Archiv
Mitte/middle
DORNRÖSCHEN/
THE SLEEPING BEAUTY,
Ch: Michail Baryschnikow (Petipa),
Martine van Hamel,
American Ballet Theater,
Foto: Martha Swope
unten/below
GISELLE,
Ch: Michail Baryschnikow
(Coralli/Perrot/Petipa),
American Ballet Theater,
Foto: Mira

rechts/right
SCHWANENSEE/SWAN LAKE,
Ch: Rudolf Nurejew (Petipa/Iwanow),
Margot Fonteyn, Rudolf Nurejew,
Ballett der Wiener Staatsoper/
Vienna State Opera Ballet,
Foto: Archiv

LE SPECTRE DE LA ROSE,
Ch: Michail Fokine
unten/below
Tamara Karsawina,
Vaslav Nijinsky,
Foto: Bert

rechts/right
Nadia Potts, Raymond Smith,
National Ballet of Canada,
Foto: Andrew Oxenham

oben/above
SCHEHERAZADE,
Ch: Frederic Franklin (Fokine),
Virginia Johnson, Eddie Shellman,
Dance Theater of Harlem,
Foto: Jack Vartoogian
unten/below
SCHEHERAZADE,
Ch: Murray Louis,
Michael Ballard,
Murray Louis Dance Company,
Foto: Lois Greenfield

L'APRES-MIDI D'UN FAUNE,
Ch: Vaslav Nijinsky,
Joffrey Ballet
oben/above
Charlene Gehm, Gregory Huffmann,
Foto: Herbert Migdoll
unten/below
Charlene Gehm, Rudolf Nurejew,
Foto: Jack Vartoogian

ERWARTUNG,
Ch: Erich Walter,
Bühnenbild von/décor by
Heinrich Wendel,
Monique Janotta, Falco Kapuste,
Ballett der Deutschen Oper am Rhein
Düsseldorf-Duisburg/
Ballet of the German Opera
on the Rhine Düsseldorf-Duisburg,
Foto: Fred Kliché

Jens Wendland

EINE GEFANGENE KUNST

WACHSTUMSPROBLEME DES WESTDEUTSCHEN BALLETTS

Ist das wirklich eine verwegene, angesichts des stolzen Jubiläums vielleicht ganz abwegige Spekulation: Was würde jetzt, nach 25 Jahren ziemlich unangefochtenem Aufbau und längst routiniertem Betrieb aus der Internationalen Sommerakademie des Tanzes, wenn ihre Initiatoren, ihre Begründer und „Betreiber" (aus welchen Gründen auch immer) resignierten? Welche Bestandskraft hätte dann diese freie, vom verschleißenden Ballettbetrieb glücklicherweise unabhängige und wahrscheinlich gerade deshalb so einflußreiche „Institution"? Wie weit, und nur insofern sei hier der Erfolg der Sommerakademie in Frage gestellt, ist aus einer freien Initiative auch eine bestandskräftige Institution geworden? Wie weit ist sie ins Bewußtsein derer gerückt, die kulturpolitisch Verantwortung tragen? Und mit einem nur auf den ersten Blick kühnen Gedankensprung vom Besonderen dieser Tanz-Trainingsinitiative aufs Allgemeine des Ballettbetriebs gefragt: Provoziert nicht gerade eine so von Personen getragene, in relativ freier Initiative entfaltete Einrichtung, etwas grundsätzlichere Gedanken über die institutionelle Absicherung des Balletts hierzulande?

Wird einem nicht doch etwas bange, wenn man die Widersprüchlichkeit dieser Tanzszene bedenkt. Widersprüchlich erscheint mir dies: Das Ballett hat, grob gesagt seit John Crankos historischem Stuttgarter Werk, seine überaus engen Grenzen gesprengt, seinen ästhetischen Elfenbeinturm erstaunlich weit verlassen – jedenfalls innerhalb des Kulturbetriebs. Es ist sogar mittlerweile regelmäßiger im Fernsehen vertreten, dient als Gala-Gebinde zu Festtagen. Seine Protagonisten werden – neben den Autoritäten des Schauspiels, der Oper – als Partner anerkannt. Eine Neumeier-Premiere, zumal, wenn sie einem Monument abendländischer Kultur wie der *Matthäus-Passion* gilt, ist ein Medienereignis. Und die thematische Spannweite des Tanzes hat durch einen Zugewinn an realistischen Stoffen, selbst Bereichen alltäglichster Bewegungsformen, viel gewonnen. Es bildet sich sogar schon eine Vielzahl von freien Gruppen, die mittlerweile mit einer gewissen, vielleicht wachsenden Berechtigung meint, auch auf Dauer ohne die Bindungen des verfestigten, subventionierten Theaterapparats auszukommen. Und eine durchaus bis in Ballettformen reichende Schauspiel- und Opernchoreographie ist an der Tagesordnung des avancierten subjektiven Regietheaters: Auffällig und oft weit über die kritischen Ambitionen der Ballettleute reicht der phantastisch freie, ästhetisch schlagfertige Umgang der Schauspiel- oder Opernregisseure mit tänzerischen Formen (siehe nur als ein beliebiges, herausragendes Beispiel die diversen trivialen und schneidend parodistischen Tanzzitate in Hans Neuenfels' provokanter Frankfurter *Aida*). Wahrscheinlich kann man sogar behaupten, der Tanz habe nicht nur innerhalb des Kulturbetriebs einen neuen Stellenwert gewonnen, er scheint auch eine weiter gehende, breitere gesellschaftliche Bedeutung zu erlangen, indem er von dem Versuch profitiert, die Entfremdungen unserer spätindustriellen Zivilisation durch den Rückgewinn eines (neuen?) Körpergefühls einzuholen. Diese abstrakte Aussage läßt sich in ziemlich konkrete einzelne Beobachtungen kleiden: Beispielsweise scheinen sich in Deutschland amerikanische, schon vor Jahren von den dortigen Medien gewürdigte Erfahrungen zu wiederholen. Der Kultur-Bürger, der etwas auf sich und seine Kinder hält, schickt diese zunehmend nicht mehr zum Klavierunterricht, sondern in Ballettschulen (wobei auf einem anderen Blatt steht, was deren Versprechungen bringen, außer dauerhaften Haltungsschäden).

Aber selbst bei so manchem Wildwuchs ließe sich natürlich folgern: Wenn der Tanz, über sich selbst hinaus wachsend, mittlerweile einen solchen Reichtum bietet, nicht mehr von Klüngeln betrieben wird, von Esoterik gezeichnet ist, dann könnte Zufriedenheit, Stolz herrschen, die Kritik einmal aussetzen. Trotzdem, man muß bei Widersprüchen bleiben. Der äußerliche Boom hat keine innere Festigung des Tanzbetriebs bewirkt. Der Bühnentanz leidet unter seinen alten „Haltungsschäden", seinen historischen Hypothesen, und leider ist da eine ebenso lange Meßlatte anzulegen wie bei den Erfolgsmeldungen, mit denen sich der Tanzbetrieb schmücken darf. Vom herkömmlichen Ballettbetrieb ausgehend, kann man diese Hypotheken nach ihrer historischen, organisatorischen Rangordnung förmlich herunter deklinieren: Die großen, der Oper angegliederten Ballettkompanien, in denen noch das „übliche" Repertoire kultiviert wird, darben – in einigen prominenten Fällen, Berlin oder München, ist schon die Klassifizierung „Repertoire" gelinde euphemistisch. Und wenn es schon nicht darum geht, Defizite und künstlerische Unfreiheiten des Tanzes allein auf eine kurzatmige Tagesform zurückzuführen, so findet man doch in der Zusammenschau aller Tagesformen der letzten Jahre die Gleichförmigkeit der Krisen – Berlin hangelt sich von Namen zu Namen, München laboriert und leistet sich Katastrophen. In Hamburg überglänzt noch der Name John Neumeier, daß dieser Choreograph mit immer größeren Versprechungen – zuletzt wie gesagt mit der *Matthäus-Passion* – überdecken muß, wie schwach noch sein persönlicher Stil ist. Stuttgart leistet sich, eingedenk der mehr und mehr belastenden Cranko-Legende, eben nicht den radikal anderen, für den langfristigen Bestand dieser Kompanie unerläßlichen Persönlichkeitsstil – auch wenn es einer gefährlichen, aber notwendigen Durststrecke bedürfte. Nicht, daß in Stuttgart nicht konsequent genug versucht würde, neue Ansätze zu finden. Aber in dem Versuch liegt auch immer wieder die Gefahr, daß der Betrieb bröckelt, und folgerichtig muß in regelmäßigen Erschlaffungsmomenten ein „Highlight" wie eine Publikums-Droge nachgeschoben werden. Düsseldorf, eine andere größere, melancholisch gepflegte Kompanie, spielt in immer neuen Variationen dasselbe Stück ohne erlösendes Happy End – Dornröschen ohne den aufweckenden Kuß …

Zweite Stufe in der Liste der Hypotheken: Hier wird man leider in unmittelbarer Nachbarschaft der Jubilarin fündig, die bedauerlich wenig von ihrer Freiheit (gleichsam als Bazillus) in den Theaterbetrieb einschleusen konnte. Der Weg des Kölner Tanz-Forum ist mittlerweile – Wunder werden dankbar erhofft – als eine typische Resignation des neueren Ballettbetriebs zu bezeichnen. Und dabei geht es nicht um Personen, sondern vor allem um Formen, um eine Institution und ihre Produkte. Am Anfang stand der Versuch, per Mitbestimmung, sogar mit Option für eine Beteiligung der Tänzer, den Tanzbetrieb zu verändern. Am gegenwärtigen Ende, das zwar noch durch regelmäßige Premieren prolongiert, aber dennoch absehbar ist, stehen meist von einem Autor verantwortete, in allein-direktorialer Gestaltung routiniert verfestigte abendfüllende Mischungen, auf denen Opernballett und Tanzexperiment vor Jahren ein problematisches, doch offenbar dauerhaftes Verhältnis gründeten. Sie wollen vorderhand unterhalten und dahinter belehren – beide Intentionen schwächen sich, und das Ergebnis ist meist verkorkst. Um die kurze, in monomanen Persönlichkeitsstilen (wie dem von Hans Kresniks aggressiven Polit-Revuen) noch konservierte Form des neueren Tanztheater-Experiments zu markieren: Nur wer die Verweigerung des herkömmlichen Balletts demonstrierte, hatte eine ganz eigene Perspektive gewonnen, die wohl die Bewegung ästhetisch verficht, jedoch nichts mit dem Ballettbetrieb zu tun haben möchte (und das gilt natürlich auch für Pina Bausch mit ihren Fluchtversuchen ins Schauspiel oder ihren Unterhaltung zuletzt förmlich verweigernden Minimal-Revuen). Jedenfalls gilt diese Tendenz für Westdeutschland, wohingegen in anderen Ländern, den Niederlanden zum Beispiel, Tanz und Experiment, platt gesagt, eine wirklich fruchtbare Ehe eingegangen sind. Zwar gibt es neben dem Theaterbetrieb, wie genannt, eine Vielzahl kleiner Gruppen, deren Aktivitäten von den neuen Freiheiten des alten Tanzes zeugen sollen. Doch sind diese sogenannten freien Gruppen offenbar nicht als wirkliche Alternative zu verstehen. Sie bilden mit Sicherheit nicht die Spitze eines Eisbergs, einer ganz großen freien Tanzbewegung. Oft tragen sie den Stempel des Sektierertums, kultivieren das dilettantische Gehabe und beerben in dieser Hinsicht eher den Ausdruckstanz der 20er und beginnenden 30er Jahre als das moderne tänzerische Experiment amerikanischer Herkunft.

Gegenwärtig stimmt allerdings die Tatsache pessimistischer, daß die Spitzen eines neuen freieren Tanzes innerhalb unseres herkömmlichen Ballett-, sprich Theatersystems, nahezu abgebrochen sind. Die Entwicklung, die sich etwa vor 15 Jahren abzeichnete, scheint zum Stillstand gekommen. Damals hatte die Krise der Institutionen dieser zweiten deutschen Republik auch die klassischen Kulturträger erfaßt, vor allem das Schauspiel. Sie berührte auch das Ballett und zunächst schien es, als gäbe es in Zukunft jede Menge Tanz-Beispiele für die kritische Bewegung der späten 60er Jahre.

Die deutsche Ballett-Wirklichkeit wurde auf einmal zweigeteilt. Neben den herkömmlichen opernabhängigen Kompanien entstand eine neue Form des Bewegungstheaters, das sich nicht nur in der Veränderung der Tanzstoffe und choreographischen Formen manifestierte. „Tanzforum" oder „Tanztheater" lauteten die Titel dieser Unternehmen in Köln, Bremen, Wuppertal, ja sogar zeitweise an einem mittleren Staatstheater wie Darmstadt. Es waren überwiegend ehemalige Spielwiesen für jüngere Choreographen, die, wie Gerhard Bohner, Hans Kresnik oder Pina Bausch, mit dem alten Opernballett und seinen Tanzmärchen nichts im Sinn hatten.

Die Entwicklung dieser an sich mobileren, solistisch von Persönlichkeiten geprägten, kleineren Kompanien ist hinlänglich bekannt. Ihre Expansionsversuche gingen ins Strukturelle. Man versuchte, die Demokratisierung der künstlerischen Arbeit meist im Schlepptau progressiver Schauspiele nachzuvollziehen. Das Kölner Tanz-Forum sah ein Dreier-Direktorium vor, und auch

Bohners Darmstädter Theater war durch kollektive Bemühungen geprägt. Gerade dieser mutigste Versuch erhielt schnell einen sichtbaren Riß. Darmstadts Tanztheater war in sich überfordert, der Freiraum im mittleren Staatstheaterbetrieb zu begrenzt. Das Kölner Tanz-Forum hat von seinen Gründerzeit-Träumen sehr schnell Abschied nehmen müssen. Am ehesten haben sich noch die Kompanien gehalten, deren alleinverantwortliche Leiter einen unverwechselbaren persönlichen Stil radikal und einigermaßen kompromißlos, wenn auch immer noch in Opernhäusern, verfochten. Gemeint sind Hans Kresnik, erst in Bremen, dann in Heidelberg, und die Wuppertalerin Pina Bausch.

Dies heißt auch: Die Krise der Institutionen hat das Ballett in Wirklichkeit nur partiell berührt. Eine tiefgreifende Strukturreform wurde verpaßt oder verpatzt. Die Unabhängigkeitserklärung des neueren Bühnentanzes fiel deshalb halbherzig aus, weil alle Kompanien in den kameralistischen Theaterbetrieb eingepfercht bleiben. Diese Krisen eines neueren Tanztheaters haben sich mittlerweile mit den Schwächen der großen alten Opernballettkompanien gepaart. Von den Freiheiten, die der Tanz einmal meinte, ist für die Entwicklung einer beständigen Tanzkultur zu wenig übriggeblieben. Und die Frage ist, warum unsere eigentlich so pluralistische, sich in vielerlei Tanzaktivitäten auch verlierende Ballettkultur auf diese Weise nicht oder nur in Ansätzen über historische Modelle und Organisationen hinausgelangt ist.

Man muß es bei Stichworten bewenden lassen, bei einigen Thesen. Das westdeutsche Ballett hat das Korsett des deutschen Theaterbetriebs für sich nicht sprengen können, weil es in beinahe jeder Beziehung diesem Betrieb nachgeordnet blieb. Dies wird immer dann erschreckend deutlich, wenn ein deutscher Theaterintendant in offenbar zunehmender Hektik nach neuen Choreographen sucht und dabei mehr auf Namen setzt als auf eine sachlich begründete Ballettarbeit an seinem Theater. Es geht immer mehr um die Frage, wer die Leitung übernehmen soll, immer weniger um die Frage nach dem Konzept. Die deutschen Theaterintendanten sind offenbar nicht sonderlich tanzkundig, und sie sind es – trotz weniger Ausnahmen von dieser Regel (Walter Erich Schäfer in Stuttgart) – in all den Jahren auch nicht geworden.

Die Tatsache, daß der westdeutsche Bühnentanz auf diese Weise zu viele falsche Bindungen eingegangen ist, daß das Ballett, das lange Entwicklungen braucht, in den kurzatmigeren Theaterbetrieb eingepfercht ist, hängt natürlich an seiner eigenen historischen Schwäche. In anderen Ländern, in denen sich autonome Tanzkulturen

langfristig entwickelt haben, gab es auch nicht die Hypotheken, die den deutschen Tanz immer noch belasten. Da ist einmal die Tatsache, daß eine Gründerzeit im deutschen Tanz nach dem Zweiten Weltkrieg nicht richtig stattgefunden hat. Zu lange hat man mit einer verengten, falschen historischen Alternative gelebt, das eigene Erbe, den deutschen Ausdruckstanz, als ideologisch verworfen und sich an klassische Leihgaben aus Frankreich, dann an den Neo-Klassizismus der Amerikaner gehalten. Choreographen wie Gerhard Bohner oder Pina Bausch und junge Begabungen des Essener Folkwangballetts, in dem der deutsche Ausdruckstanz zum Teil konserviert wurde, haben hier wenige Korrekturen anbringen können.

Zum anderen ist die Frage, ob diese Tanzkultur „regelrecht" begründet worden ist. Das ist ganz wörtlich gemeint: Sind unsere Tanzschulen wirklich die richtige Schule fürs Ballettleben geworden? Eine Sommerakademie des Tanzes kann hier zwar Maßstäbe setzen, aber nicht Geburtsfehler der westdeutschen Tanzschulen beseitigen. Immer noch gibt es ein Defizit an Theorie-Fächern in der Tanzausbildung, wird zu oft (oder auch zu wenig) standardisiert, das vordergründige Technik-Bedürfnis der Ballettarbeit bedient, was unter anderem zur Folge hat, daß das Bild des Choreographen und seiner professionellen Eignung innerhalb des Ballettbetriebs immer noch zu schwach, wenn nicht oft falsch ist.

Es sind nur zwei hauptsächliche Gründe, die allerdings dazu geführt haben, daß eine Bildung von unabhängigen Kompanien nicht als kulturpolitische Notwendigkeit angesehen wurden. Die Kulturpolitiker halten die Einordnung des Balletts im Theaterbetrieb wohl immer noch für angemessen. Zwar gab es diese oder jene Überlegung (beispielsweise in einem Theaterreform-Papier in Nordrhein-Westfalen), selbständige moderne Kompanien zu gründen oder aus dem Theaterverband zu lösen, aber bei diesen vagen Andeutungen neuer Projekte ist es denn auch geblieben. Das gilt nicht nur für die „alternativen", die experimentellen Tanztheater. Die große Chance, aus dem seinerzeit besten deutschen Opernballett, dem Stuttgarter Ballett, eine große selbständige, nationale Kompanie zu begründen, ist zu Zeiten John Crankos vertan worden. Die Widersprüche zwischen dem glänzenderen Erscheinungsbild und der viel zu schwach abgesicherten Organisation des westdeutschen Tanzes sind gefährlich. Der Reichtum dieser Tanzaktivitäten hängt noch zu sehr von Personen ab, deren Schwächen sich allzu leicht im Bestand der jeweiligen Tanzunternehmung, wie der gesamten Ballettkultur niederschlagen.

Jens Wendland

ART IN CAPTIVITY

GROWTH PROBLEMS OF BALLET IN
WEST GERMANY

Is it really a bold and, in the light of this proud anniversary, perhaps a completely erroneous speculation: What, after 25 years of relatively uncontested growth and long established routine in operations, would now become of the International Summer Academy of Dance if its initiators, its founders and its "managers" were (regardless of the reasons) to resign? What existential force would this free "institution", luckily independent of the attrition common to the established ballet system and probably therefore so influential, then exhibit? To what extent (and only here should the achievements of the Summer Academy be questioned), has a stable institution been developed from a free initiative? How far has it penetrated into the consciousness of those responsible for politico-cultural affairs? And, to make a sudden, only at first sight daring change of subject from the special character of this dance training initiative to the ballet system in general, one would ask: Doesn't just such an institution, dependent on individuals and developed in relatively free initiative, provoke one to reconsider the institutional security of ballet in this country?

Are the contradictions within this dance scene not reason enough to cause anxiety? Put roughly, it seems to me contradictory that, since John Cranko's historical work in Stuttgart, ballet has burst out of its completely narrow limits, has wandered amazingly far afield of its aesthetic ivory tower – at least within the institutionalized cultural world. It is now even found regularly in television, serving as a gala bouquet for festive occasions. Its protagonists are recognized as serious partners – on the same level as the authorities in theater and opera. A Neumeier premiere, particularly when dedicated to a monument of western culture such as the *St. Matthew Passion,* is a media event. And the thematic range of dance has gained much through incorporating realistic subjects, even drawing from most common, day-to-day forms of movement. There are even being formed large numbers of free groups, their members having come to believe, with a certain and perhaps growing justification, that they can survive on a permanent basis without the strictures of the rigid, subsidized theater apparatus. And theater and opera choreography, making use of ballet forms, is on the regular agenda of generally accepted, subjective directing: The fantastically free, aesthetically quick-witted way in which theater and opera directors deal with the forms of dance is striking, often reaching far beyond the critical ambitions of ballet professionals. (See, as only one random, but excellent, example, the diverse trivial and cuttingly parodistic dance quotations in Hans Neuenfels' provocative *Aida,* in Frankfurt.) One can probably even claim that

dance has gained a new rank not only within the established cultural world; it appears to have achieved a further-reaching, broader social significance, profiting from the attempt to make up for the alienation in our overly industrialized civilization by regaining a (new?) consciousness of the body. This abstract statement can be supported by individual, concrete observations. For example, American experiences, honored years ago by the media there, seem to repeat themselves here in Germany. The pretentious culturally oriented, who think something of themselves and their children, send them less and less to piano lessons, but rather to ballet schools (although it is quite another question as to what results from their promises, except for permanent posture damage).

But even considering such cultural undergrowth, there are of course consequences. If dance, expanding beyond itself, has come to offer such richness that it is no longer pursued by cliques and branded as esoteric, then self-satisfaction and pride could prevail, doing away with criticism. In spite of this, contradictions do remain. The external boom has not effected any internal stability in the dance establishment. Dance still suffers from its old "posture damages", its historical mortgages. And regretfully here, too, one has to use just as long a yardstick as the one for reports of success with which professional dance feathers its hat. Considering the conventional ballet system, one can literally set up a "declination" of these mortgages in a historical and organizational hierarchy: The large companies associated with an opera house, in which the "standard" repertoire is cultivated, wither – in some prominent cases, such as Berlin or Munich, the term "repertoire" is mildly euphemistic. And even if it is not intended to lay blame für the deficits and artistic restrictions of dance only on a short-winded daily condition, one still finds in a survey of all the "daily conditions" of recent years a congruity in the crises – Berlin lunges from one name to the next, Munich labors and rewards itself with catastrophes. In Hamburg the name John Neumeier outshines the fact that this choreographer is forced to cover up the weakness of his personal style with ever larger promises – the most recent, as mentioned, being the *St. Matthew Passion.* Considering the ever more strained Cranko legend, Stuttgart has not found its

way free to engage another radical personal style, imperative for the long-term existence of this company even if it means a dangerous, but necessary "long, dry spell". Not that there is a lack of perseverance in Stuttgart, in the search for new approaches, but in the attempt there is always the danger that the company begins to crumble. Consequently, a highlight has to be conjured up during the regular slack phases, as a drug for the public. Düsseldorf, another large, melancholically tended company, plays the same piece, over and over, in new variations but never with the liberating happy end – *Sleeping Beauty* without the awakening kiss.

Second in the list of mortgages: Here one will regrettably strike paydirt in the immediate neighborhood of the 25-year-old, who has unfortunately been able to inject little of its freedom (like a bacteria, as it were) into the theater system. The path followed by the Cologne Tanz-Forum has in the meantime – wonders will be accepted with great thanks – come to be seen as typical for the resignation of the newer ballet companies. Here it is not a matter of persons, but primarily of forms, of an institution and its products. Initially there was the attempt to modify the conventional dance system by co-determination, even with an option for participation by the dancers. At the present juncture in the demise of this experiment, which may be prolonged by regular premieres but still foreseeable, there appear evening-length mixtures, usually the responsibility of a single author, created in a practiced, single-director process, mixtures on which the opera ballet and experimental dance years ago founded a problematic but apparently durable relationship. They want to entertain in the foreground and at the same time instruct – the two intentions weaken each other and the result is usually muddled. To mark the short-lived form of the newer dance theater experiment, still preserved in monomaniac personal styles (such as that of Hans Kresnik's aggressive political revues): Only one who demonstrably rejected conventional ballet has gained his own perspective, which does in fact maintain the movement aesthetically while not having anything to do with the organized ballet world. (And this, of course, also applies to Pina Bausch with her attempted escapes into theater or her minimalist revues, which literally refuse to entertain.) This tendency is in any case applicable to West Germany, whereas in other countries, the Netherlands, for example, dance and experiment have entered into a truly fruitful marriage.

In addition to the established theater system there is, as previously mentioned, a multitude of smaller groups, the activities of which should testify to the new freedoms of the old dance. But these so-called free groups are apparently not to be taken as a real alternative. They certainly do not represent the tip of an iceberg – of a large and free dance movement. Often they carry the stamp of sectarianism, cultivating a dilettantish posture, inheriting in this respect more the *Ausdruckstanz (dance of expression)* from the '20s and at the beginning of the '30s than the modern experimental dance of American origin.

At the present, however, a more pessimistic view is promoted by the fact that the tip of a new, freer dance within our conventional ballet (read: theater) system has almost melted away. The development which emerged some 15 years ago seems to have come to a standstill. At that time the institutional crisis in this second German Republic had also gripped the classical cultural institutions, drama above all. The crisis touched ballet as well and initially it appeared that there would be any number of dance examples in the future for the critical movement of the late '60s.

German ballet reality was suddenly split in two. Parallel to the conventional, opera-dependent companies there arose a new form of theater of movement, which manifested itself not only in the modification of the dance subjects and choreographic forms. *Tanz-Forum* or *Tanztheater* were the names chosen for these undertakings in Cologne, Bremen, Wuppertal, and at times even in a medium-sized municipal theater such as that in Darmstadt. They were predominantly the former playgrounds for younger choreographers who – like Gerhard Bohner, Hans Kresnik or Pina Bausch – had no interest in the old opera ballet and its fairy tales.

The development of these smaller, more mobile companies, their character molded by individual personalities, is sufficiently well-known. Their attempts at expansion penetrated into the structural realm. Attempts to democratize artistic work were usually in the tow of a more progressive drama theater. The Cologne Tanz-Forum planned a triumvirate in the directorship, and Bohner's Darmstadt theater was characterized by collective efforts. And it was in just this most courageous of attempts that the first fissures appeared. Darmstadt's dance theater was in itself overtaxed, the freedom of movement in a medium-scale municipal theater system being too limited. The Cologne Tanz-Forum, too, had to take quick leave of the dreams of its founding period. The companies which best endured were those whose director, bearing sole responsibility, maintained an unmistakable personal style, radically and generally uncompromisingly, even though within

opera houses. Meant here are Hans Kresnik, first in Bremen, then in Heidelberg, and Wuppertal's Pina Bausch.

But this also means: The crisis of the institutions had in reality touched ballet only partially. A more thoroughgoing structural reform was either missed or messed up. The declaration of independence of the newer dance was only half-hearted because all the companies remained cooped up in the cameralistic theater system. These crises of a younger dance theater have in the meantime mated with the weaknesses of the large, old opera ballet companies. There is too little left over of the freedoms, which dance once meant, for the development of a durable dance culture. The question is why our so very pluralistic ballet culture, which also loses itself in a multitude of dance activities, has not been able to free itself at all (or only rudimentally) from the restraints of historical models and organizations.

One will have to make do with clues, with a few theses. West German ballet has not been able to split the corset of the German theatrical system, because it is in virtually every respect in a subordinate position. This always becomes shockingly apparent when a German theater manager pursues an obviously and increasingly hectic search for new choreographers, in doing so paying more attention to names than to any pertinently founded ballet work in his theater. It is increasingly a question of who is to take over the directorship, and ever less a question of concept. Generally speaking, German theater managers are not particularly knowledgeable in the area of dance, and aside from a few exceptions to this rule (Walter Erich Schäfer in Stuttgart), they have not become so through the years. The fact that dance in West Germany in this way has entered into too many wrong commitments and the fact that ballet – which requires long periods of development – has been wedged into the quicker tempo of the spoken theater, is, of course, due to its own historical weakness. In other countries, in which over long periods of time, autonomous dance cultures have developed, there were not those mortgages, which still burden German dance. There is first the fact that a period of renewal in German dance following the Second World War never really took place. One lived too long with a limited and false historical alternative, rejecting one's own heritage, German *Ausdruckstanz,* as being ideological and looking to cultural loans from France and later to the neoclassicism of the Americans. Choreographers such as Gerhard Bohner or Pina Bausch and younger talents of the Folkwang ballet in Essen, where German *Ausdruckstanz* has in part been preserved, have been able to achieve only a few corrections.

The other question is whether this dance culture has been "properly" founded. This means quite literally: Are our ballet schools really the proper schools to prepare for a life of ballet? A summer academy of dance can, of course, set standards, but cannot correct all the birth defects of the West German ballet schools. There is still a deficit in theoretical subjects in dance education; standardization is encountered too often (or too little), the empty use of technique for ballet works is too often served, the result of which has been that the image of the choreographer and his professional qualification within the ballet system is still too weak, if not often erroneous.

There are only two main reasons which have caused the formation of independent companies not to be seen as necessities of cultural policy. The cultural policymakers still feel it appropriate to organize ballet within the framework of normal theater operations. There has in fact been one insight or the other (for example in a paper on theater reform in North Rhine-Westphalia), directed toward establishing independent, modern companies or to release them from the normal theater system, but other than these vague implications of new projects all remained the same. This applies not only to the "alternative", the experimental dance theaters. The great chance to form a large, independent, national company out of the best German opera ballet of that time, the Stuttgart Ballet, was missed during John Cranko's time. The contradictions between the glowing appearance and the much too weakly supported organization of West German dance are dangerous. The richness of these dance activities is still too much dependent on persons, whose weaknesses can all too easily be reflected in the existence of the particular dance venture and in ballet culture in general.

SOLO MIT SOFA/SOLO WITH SOFA,
Ch: Reinhild Hoffmann,
Reinhild Hoffmann,
Foto: Gert Weigelt

UNKRAUTGARTEN/
WEED GARDEN,
Ch: Reinhild Hoffmann,
Bremer Ballett/Bremen Ballet,
Fotos: Gert Weigelt

ZWEI GIRAFFEN TANZEN TANGO/
TWO GIRAFFES DANCE THE TANGO,
Ch: Gerhard Bohner,
Bremer Ballett/Bremen Ballet,
Fotos: Gert Weigelt

BILDER EINER AUSSTELLUNG/
PICTURES FROM AN EXHIBITION,
Ch: Gerhard Bohner,
Bremer Ballett/Bremen Ballet,
Fotos: Gert Weigelt

oben/above
DEUTSCHE SUITE/
GERMAN SUITE,
Ch: Birgitta Trommler,
Tanz-Projekt München/
Dance Project, Munich,
Foto: G. Bieberstein
unten/below
MUDANZA,
Ch: Marilén Breuker,
Folkwang-Tanz-Studio, Essen/
Folkwang Dance Studio, Essen,
Foto: Ridha Zouari

gegenüber/opposite page
oben/above
FRAUENBALLETT/
WOMEN'S BALLET,
Ch: Susanne Linke,
Folkwang-Tanz-Studio, Essen/
Folkwang Dance Studio, Essen,
Foto: Ridha Zouari
unten links/below left
WIEGENLIED/LULLABY,
Ch: Immo Buhl,
Immo Buhl, Hannele Vuorimaa,
Imotion Dance Company, Fürth,
Foto: Dieter Bauer

unten rechts/below right
PERSEPHASSA,
Ch: Birgitta Trommler,
Raumgestaltung: Judith Vassallo,
Barbara Hampel, Bonger Voges,
Tanz-Projekt München/
Dance Project, Munich,
Foto: Achim Balon

Jochen Schmidt

Wer sich auf das Glatteis einer Vorhersage über die zukünftige Entwicklung der Künste (oder auch einer speziellen Kunstform) begibt, hat jede Chance, kräftig auf die Nase zu fallen, und kann froh sein, wenn er sich dabei nicht Hals und Glieder bricht. An Seriosität ähnelt eine solche Prognose einer Prophezeiung aus dem Kaffeesatz – mit dem bemerkenswerten Unterschied, daß sich ein Kaffeesatzorakel wenigstens auf eine in sich gleiche Grundsubstanz stützen kann. Dagegen sind die Daten, auf die sich eine sinnvolle Aussage über längerfristige Trends und Perspektiven in den Künsten stützen könnte, derart heterogen, daß ein Faktum das andere dementiert, von den widersprüchlichen Interpretationen, die sie zulassen, ganz zu schweigen.

Wer zu Beginn der 70er Jahre vorauszusagen gewagt hätte, daß die Ballettszene dieses Jahrzehnts zumindest im westlichen Europa dominiert sein würde von einem bislang unbekannten Boom des abendfüllenden Balletts, hätte vermutlich nur ein Lächeln geerntet angesichts der Dominanz eines abstrakten, kurzatmigen Neoklassizismus, dessen stromlinienförmige Uniformität die Spielpläne von Glasgow bis Wien, von Stockholm bis Lissabon prägte. Weit eher als diese Konjunktur des Abendfüllers (die in manchen Spielzeiten mühelos zwei bis drei Dutzend Novitäten unterschiedlichster Couleur, Struktur und Qualität hervorbrachte), wäre vor einem Jahrzehnt eine Überwindung des tänzerischen Neoklassizismus durch jene Mittel denkbar gewesen, wie sie der Holländer Hans van Manen und sein amerikanischer Kompagnon Glen Tetley mit dem Nederlands Dans Theater (NDT) sich erarbeitet hatten. Doch während van Manen über das, was er bei seiner Trennung vom NDT im Jahre 1970 an choreographischem Rüstzeug bereits erworben hatte, in der Folgezeit noch ein gutes Stück hinauswuchs, brach die positive Entwicklung Tetleys beinahe augenblicklich ab: ein Beispiel dafür, welch starken Einfluß Imponderabilien wie die Auflösung eines Vertrags- und Arbeitsverhältnisses zwischen einem Künstler und einer ihn inspirierenden Gruppe auf ästhetische Entwicklungen haben können. Das soll nicht heißen, daß die Entwicklung des europäischen Tanztheaters mit Sicherheit anders verlaufen wäre, wenn van Manen und Tetley ihre Arbeit mit dem NDT gemeinsam fortgesetzt hätten (oder wenn etwa John Cranko heute noch lebte und das Stuttgarter Ballett leitete). Es soll nur zeigen, von welchen Unwägbarkeiten Entwicklungen abhängig sind, im Positiven wie im Negativen.

Ebenso wichtig wie persönliche Konstellationen (oder auch Schicksale) sind objektive Bedingungen, die den Rahmen einer Entwicklung setzen und von den Künstlern selbst so gut wie nicht zu beeinflussen sind. Die wichtigste Bedingung dieser Art ist die Ausstattung der öffentlichen Hand mit finanziellen Mitteln sowie der Anteil, den die Gesellschaft den Künsten daran zubilligt. Tanzbühne, Ballett und generell die Theaterkünste könnten hier auf doppelte Weise in Schwierigkeiten geraten, die sich schließlich sogar als existentielle erweisen könnten. Denn einerseits hat die schlechte wirtschaftliche Entwicklung dazu geführt, daß – zum erstenmal seit dem Ende des Zweiten Weltkriegs – die öffentlichen Einnahmen stagnieren und zum Teil sogar zurückgehen. Andererseits wachsen die Kosten auch der Theater und Ballettensembles überproportional (was auch, jedoch nicht allein, auf ihre nicht rationalisierbare Arbeitsintensität zurückzuführen ist). So ist der Tag vorherzusehen, an dem sich die westlichen Gesellschaften ein subventioniertes Theater im bisherigen Umfang nicht mehr leisten können (oder, was in seinen Auswirkungen auf das Theater keinen Unterschied macht, leisten wollen). Schon sind am Horizont die ersten Anzeichen von Sturm zu erkennen. In den USA beginnt die Reagan-Administration bereits, die unter Mühen erreichten Anfänge staatlicher Kunstförderung zurückzuschneiden, und auch im alten Europa setzen die Sparkommissare den Rotstift mit Vorliebe bei den Kulturetats an. Daß speziell in der Bundesrepublik das Ballett als traditionsloseste aller Bühnenkünste von Sparmaßnahmen stärker betroffen würde als Oper, Schauspiel oder selbst die Operette, ist wohl keine Frage.

Eine Kürzung der öffentlichen Mittel für Ballett (was in dieser Argumentation zunächst einmal umfassend alles das bezeichnet, was sich, wie auch immer tanzend, auf einer Bühne bewegt) hätte zunächst natürlich vor allem quantitative Konsequenzen. Ensembles müßten aufgelöst werden, gerieten in Schrumpfungsprozesse, könnten Produktionen nicht durchführen. Sie würden in ihren Auftrittsmöglichkeiten eingeschränkt, könnten Tourneen nicht mehr durchführen,

BARFÜSSIGE EXPEDITIONEN IN ZERKLÜFTETE TRAUMLANDSCHAFTEN?

VERSUCH ÜBER EIN REALISTISCHES TANZTHEATER SOWIE ÄSTHETIK UND ZUKUNFT DES BALLETTS IN EUROPA

wodurch einmal der internationale Kulturaustausch litte, dann aber auch die Ensembles und Choreographen selbst an Erfahrungsmöglichkeit einbüßten.

Es bedarf keines Propheten um zu erkennen, daß aus diesen zunächst quantitativen Einschränkungen qualitative sich sogleich ergeben. Ein eingeschränkter Tournee- und Gastspielbetrieb, eine verminderte Mobilität der Produktionen, bewirkt automatisch eine Einschränkung der ästhetischen Anregungen. Die vergleichsweise geringe Verbreitung des Bournonville-Stiles steht in direktem Zusammenhang mit der geringen Neigung des Königlich Dänischen Balletts zu ausgedehnten Gastspielen. Der große ästhetische Einfluß, den seit den späten 60er Jahren zunächst die Arbeiten von Hans van Manen und Glen Tetley, neuerdings die von Jiří Kylián, auf die jüngeren europäischen Choreographen ausüben, erklärt sich zu einem nicht geringen Teil mit der ausgedehnten Gastspieltätigkeit des NDT. Es hat durch sein Beispiel die europäische Ballettszene stärker verändert als jede andere künstlerische Kraft innerhalb oder außerhalb Europas.

Eventuelle Etatkürzungen würden allerdings die Ästhetik des Balletts nicht nur auf diese indirekte Art beeinflussen; sie nähmen auch direkten Einfluß, etwa über das Bühnenbild, das für viele der wichtigeren Tanztheaterproduktionen der letzten Jahre (von den abstrakten Choreographien Merce Cunninghams bis zu den realitätsgesättigten Stücken der Pina Bausch) eine bedeutende Funktion und Rolle gespielt hat.

Die Bühnenbildaskese des Neoklassizismus, zumal der Spielart eines George Balanchine, war ja nicht nur Tugend, sondern auch Not. Nicht nur, daß Balanchine zu bestimmten Zeiten das Geld fehlte, um eine Choreographie durch Kostüme und prachtvolle Prospekte aufzuputzen. Ihm fehlten – und fehlen noch heute – im Grunde auch die Bühnenbildner, die ihm einen Rahmen für seine Choreographien gebaut hätten, der das stilbildende Blau hinter schwarzen oder weißen Tuniken und Trikots ästhetisch übertraf. Was immer auch Karinska, Rouben Ter-Arutunian oder David Hays an Dekors für Balanchine-Ballette entwarfen: es blieb weit hinter dem Markenzeichen-Blau zurück, das den strengen Arbeiten von Mr. B. nicht nur Hintergrund, sondern auch Halt gab.

Um zu erkennen, daß dieser spezifische Balanchine-Stil, gerade auch in Bühnenbild und Kostüm, nicht nur eine Stärke, sondern auch eine Schwäche ist, muß man sich nur die Bühnen vergegenwärtigen, die Jean-Paul Vroom über rund zwanzig Jahre und vor allem seit 1970 für Hans van Manen gebaut hat. Von *Situation* bis zu den *Fünf*

Tangos, von *Twilight* bis *Sacre du printemps* geben diese Bühnenbilder den Choreographien nicht nur den festen, unverwechselbaren Rahmen und damit eine Stütze; sie stimulieren die Choreographie förmlich zu neuen, unkonventionellen Lösungen. Aber sie ähneln den Bühnenbildern der Balanchine-Stücke immer noch insofern in der Struktur, als sie im Grunde nach wie vor überwiegend aus einem Hintergrundprospekt plus Lichtdesign bestehen, die Tanzfläche freihalten und den Raum als solchen eher suggerieren als wirklich strukturieren (von Ausnahmen wie *Keep Going* mit seiner sich allmählich öffnenden Tiefe einmal abgesehen oder *Essay in der Stille,* bei dem Vrooms Zweit-Dekoration die Rückwand als schallschluckenden Teppich bis unter die Füße der Tanzenden zieht).

Auch jene durchaus stilbildenden Bühnen mit modernistischen Stahlskelettstrukturen, die Nadine Baylis unter anderem für Glen Tetley baute und mit Tänzern in changierenden Glanztrikots bevölkerte, unterscheiden sich, strukturell, noch nicht sehr stark von der (neo)klassischen Ballettbühne – eher schon John F. MacFarlanes zuweilen nahezu gehäuseartigen Entwürfe, wie beispielsweise für Jochen Ulrichs Arbeiten am Kölner Tanz-Forum.

Doch die Bühne als Ballettinnenraum, nicht nur als freigehaltene Fläche fürs Tanzen mit atmosphärischer Garnierung: das haben – läßt man die genialen Sonderfälle der Rauschenberg-, Warhol-, Stella- oder Morris-Bühnen für Merce Cunningham außer Betracht – erst jene Bühnenbildner erreicht, die den Stücken eines neuen, freien Tanztheaters ihre realistischen oder visionären Environments schufen. Da wäre an erster Stelle der Name des 1980 viel zu früh gestorbenen Rolf Borzik zu nennen, dessen geniale Räume für die Stücke von Pina Bausch zwischen *Orpheus und Eurydike* und *Keuschheitslegende* (etwa die Rutschbahn für *Komm tanz mit mir,* die Wasserbühne für *Arien,* die mit Stühlen zugestellte Fläche des *Café Müller)* ihn zuweilen fast schon als Co-Autor der Bausch erscheinen ließen. Aber auch die Räume, die sich Johannes Schütz für Reinhild Hoffmann ausgedacht hat *(Hochzeit, Unkrautgarten),* oder manche Bühne für die furiosen Affekthandlungen des Hans Kresnik (VA Wölfls Kachelinterieur für *Magnet)* erfüllen diese neuen Funktionen: eine Fläche nicht nur freizuhalten für eine beliebige Art von Tanz, sondern einen Raum zu konditionieren für eine ganz bestimmte Art von Choreographie, ja sogar: diese Choreographie vorzuprägen in einem ganz bestimmten Sinn. (Auf der Wasserbühne bewegt man sich notgedrungen anders als auf festem Boden; der Torf, den Borzik für Pina Bauschs *Sacre* auf den Boden ge-

schüttet hat, würde den Stil der Danse d'école einfach nicht zulassen.)

Natürlich meint das nicht, daß sich die Räume ihre Stücke gesucht hätten, die Bühnenbildner ihre Choreographen. Es waren die Choreographen, die die Richtung angaben – und diese Richtung hieß: weg von der Abstraktion, hin zu einem neuen Realismus. Die Bewegung ging Hand in Hand mit einer neuerwachten Neigung zum abendfüllenden Ballett, und mit letzter Sicherheit ist nicht auszumachen, was in diesem Fall früher war: das Ei oder die Henne. Daß die neue Lust an der Realität als ihr gemäßen Ausdruck das abendfüllende Ballett wählte (und nicht umgekehrt das abendfüllende Ballett eine Hinwendung zum Realismus zur Folge hatte), dafür spricht die Einbindung der Bewegung in eine allgemeine Entwicklung der Künste. Den Vorreiter machte die bildende Kunst, speziell die Malerei, die über die monochrome, dann weiße Fläche, schließlich den leeren Rahmen nicht mehr hinauskam. Mit vergleichsweise geringer Verzögerung folgten die Literatur (Verlagsthese von Suhrkamp: „Achtung, es wird wieder erzählt"), der Film (mit der Abkehr von Symbolismen nach Art von Ingmar Bergmans *Schweigen)* und das Schauspieltheater, das zumindest in der Bundesrepublik als Neo-Kulinarismus (etwa durch die Bühnenbilder von Wilfried Minks, Erich Wonder oder Karl-Ernst Herrmann) das zögernde Tanztheater nachhaltig beeinflußte.

Was unter Realität auf der Tanzbühne zu verstehen sei: das ist gewiß keine ganz leichte Frage. Die Antwort ist zu verschiedenen Zeiten und unter verschiedenen Ideologien unterschiedlich ausgefallen; dem sozialistischen Realismus waren, mitten im 2. Weltkrieg, noch tragische Liebesgeschichten wie *Romeo und Julia* oder Märchen wie *Cinderella* Realität genug. Solche Stücke in klassischer Technik, im Grunde tief in der Ästhetik des 19. Jahrhunderts verwurzelt, sind natürlich auch auf der europäischen Tanzszene noch anzutreffen; als Klassiker-Revisionen oder -Reproduktionen beherrschen sie sogar die Spielpläne. Die Aufführungsstatistik der Spielzeit 1979/80 sieht solche Stücke in der Bundesrepublik eindeutig an der Spitze; *Der Nußknacker,* ausgerechnet, führt vor *La Fille mal gardée* und *Romeo und Julia, Don Quixote* nimmt vor *Dornröschen* den vierten Platz ein, und auch *Coppélia, Schwanensee* und *Sylvia* liegen auf den Plätzen 10 bis 12 gut im Rennen, unmittelbar gefolgt von John Neumeiers *Kameliendame,* die im Grunde demselben Geist entspringt, allerdings schlechter choreographiert ist als die meisten der auf klassische Originale zurückgreifenden Konkurrenten.

Stücke dieser Art müssen wohl sein, können von einem zeitgenössischen Bewußt-

sein aber kaum als „realistisch" empfunden werden. Die Realität, die die Choreographen des neuen Tanztheaters, zumal in der Bundesrepublik, in ihre Stücke einbringen, ist jedoch nicht die eines ungebrochenen „realistischen" Erzählens, sondern die einer schmerzlichen Reibung an bestimmten Verhältnissen, die der Tanzstückautor nicht mehr als gegeben akzeptiert. Eine solche Haltung setzt die Aufgabe der klassischen Traditionen, von der unreflektierten Technik der Danse d'école bis zur konventionellen Stückform, grundsätzlich voraus. Pina Bauschs Aussage, sie interessiere sich nicht dafür, *wie* sich Menschen bewegten, sondern wolle erfahren, *was* die Menschen bewegt, ist sozusagen das Glaubensbekenntnis eines neuen Tanztheaters, das den Tänzer nicht als technisch perfekte Kunstfigur, sondern als denkendes und fühlendes Individuum begreift und einsetzt.

Praktisch alle Tanzstücke Pina Bauschs, zweifellos eine Schlüsselfigur dieses neuen realistischen Tanztheaters, sind stilistisch definiert durch eine starke Reibung an Normen und Sachverhalten, ein Anrennen gegen die Mauern der Konvention (was etwa in *Blaubart* buchstäblich erfolgt), ein Zerbröckeln der Formen und Zerstören der planen Abläufe. Das Tanztheater der Pina Bausch, gescholten und verrissen von den Anhängern der klassischen Tanzkunst, gehätschelt von den Kritikern eines unkonventionellen Schauspieltheaters, läßt nicht allein die Frage hinter sich, ob etwas, was auf seiner Bühne geschieht, „Tanz" sei (weil es den Definitionen und Verabredungen, die Tanz auf einen bestimmten ästhetisch-historischen Standard festlegen wollen, mißtraut). Es läßt auch die Grenze zwischen Kunst und Trivialität absichtsvoll verschwimmen – und zwar nicht etwa deshalb, weil es die Trivialität adelte, sondern indem es sie ausstellt und akzeptiert.

Dabei hat die Zertrümmerung der überkommenen Formen eine neue Dramaturgie und neue Form längst entwickelt. Vom frühen Einakter *Ich bring dich um die Ecke* über den Brecht-Weill-Abend *Die Sieben Todsünden, Kontakthof, Arien, Keuschheitslegende, 1980* bis zu *Bandoneon* hat die Bausch sich langsam und stetig vorgetastet zu einem Prinzip der Montage, das auf der Grundlage der Revue die disparatesten Einzelteile miteinander verschmilzt. Eine Dramaturgie des Kontrastes, die die Wiederholung und quasimusikalische Variation eines Grundmusters zum Stilprinzip gemacht hat und die ihre stilistisch-ästhetischen Wechselbäder ebenso verwegen wie perfekt ausbalanciert, paart Hektik mit Ruhe, Trubel mit Einsamkeit, Fröhlichkeit mit Jammer, Lautstärke mit Leisem, Helligkeit mit Bühnendunkel, Spaß mit Frustration, Solo mit Ensemble, Statik mit Tanz – und bringt bei alledem noch das Kunststück fertig, ihre Stücke gleichzeitig satirisch scharf und träumerisch sanft zu machen, bitter und süß, kritisch und glänzend.

Es ist dieses Tanztheater des Unkonventionellen mit seinen barfüßigen Expeditionen in zerklüftete Traumlandschaften des Unbewußten, seinen komplexen Erkundungen menschlicher Verhaltensweisen und seiner sehnsüchtigen Suche nach einer neuen, überall verstandenen Körpersprache, von dem auch in den 80er Jahren die wesentlichen künstlerischen Erfahrungen auf dem Gebiet des Balletts (als umfassende Bezeichnung für jede Art von Bühnen- oder Podiumstanz) zu erwarten sind. Die Stagnation, die viele Kritiker in Pina Bauschs beharrlichem Festhalten an bestimmten Themen, Formen und Verfahrensweisen sehen möchten, vermag ich nirgends festzustellen; nur ein stetiges, wenn auch nicht gleichmäßiges Voranschreiten in einem Gelände, das längst noch nicht künstlerisch vermessen ist.

Mittlerweile freilich steht die Bausch nicht mehr allein – und wenn man die Perspektive nicht national oder auch europäisch verkürzte, tat sie das nie. Reinhild Hoffmann, wie Pina Bausch aus dem Tanzstudio der Essener Folkwang-Hochschule stammend, geht mit Stücken wie *Solo mit Sofa, Fünf Tage, fünf Nächte, Hochzeit* oder *Unkrautgarten* einen verwandten, gleichwohl ganz eigenen Weg, der ein wenig näher an der Tradition (des Modern Dance) entlangführt. Und auch Hans Kresnik, Jochen Ulrich, Gerhard Bohner und, unlängst, Susanne Linke sind Stücke geglückt, die mindestens partienweise jene neue, eminent politische Seh- und Verfahrensweise vorführten, die sich nicht mit der Darstellung eines Sachverhalts begnügt, sondern die Analyse mitzuliefern sucht, ohne daß die Stücke deshalb zu soziologischen Oberseminaren mit obligater Bewegung würden. Daß solche Stücke kein typisch deutsches Phänomen sind, zeigen vor allem auch gewisse amerikanische Erscheinungen, etwa die Arbeiten von Meredith Monk und, in gewissem Sinn, Twyla Tharp, wohingegen andere wichtige Strömungen der amerikanischen New Dance-Szene eher eine Gegenposition zum neuen deutschen Tanztheater verraten. Wo Bausch, Hoffmann, Linke vom Interesse am Menschen zu einem ästhetischen Neuansatz mit gesellschaftskritischen Auswirkungen kamen, gleichzeitig aber aus Zweifeln an der Möglichkeit ungebrochener Tanzformationen die Bewegung immer mehr einfroren, führte bei Choreographinnen wie Trisha Brown, Lucinda Childs oder Laura Dean eine Ausgangsposition der ästhetischen Verweigerung (das Reduzieren der Formen und der Bewegungsmenge aufs

äußerst Mögliche im Minimal Dance), zum Teil verbunden mit dem politischen Standpunkt der Frauenbewegung, nach einer Phase großer Erstarrung zurück zu einer Virtuosität, die der Schaulust des Publikums auf eine noch vor zehn Jahren fast undenkbare Weise entgegenkam. Die Rückkehr der Virtuosität ins neue Tanztheater (in Stücken wie *Brahms-Paganini* oder *Baker's Dozen* von Twyla Tharp längst Tatsache, in *Dance* von Lucinda Childs zumindest annonciert) könnte einer jener Trends der 80er Jahre sein, dem neben dem zärtlichen, um Menschen bemühten Montagetheater der Pina Bausch die nachhaltigsten Eindrücke zu verdanken sein könnten.

In gewissem Sinn liegt hier die einzige Parallele zur Entwicklung des klassischen Tanzes. Generell zwar ist die Karte der Virtuosität im klassischen Tanz längst ausgereizt. Daß zusätzliche Höchstschwierigkeiten nach dem Vorbild der Eiskunstläufer (nach den Double tours die Triple tours en l'air, wie sie Cranko in *Der Widerspenstigen Zähmung* verlangt) das Tanzen als Kunst nicht weiterbringen, hat sich im letzten Jahrzehnt herumgesprochen (wenn auch nicht überall; Amerika wird, als Folge der Emigration von Nurejew, Baryschnikow, Panow und Godunow, von einer neuen Welle des Höchstschwierigkeitstanzes überschwemmt). Doch just solche Choreographen (wie Hans van Manen), die in den späten 60er und frühen 70er Jahren die Virtuosität und das Tanztempo wesentlich reduziert hatten, sind in den letzten Jahren sukzessive zu höherem Tempo und größerer Virtuosität zurückgekehrt – obwohl nicht dorthin, wo sie einmal begonnen hatten.

Der Name van Manen markiert, wie immer sich Amerika an Jiři Kylián begeistern mag, der vorerst eher ein virtuoser Assimilator von Vorhandenem ist als ein wirklicher Neuerer –, der Name van Manen markiert, auch zu Beginn der 80er Jahre, das Optimum dessen, was europäisches Tanztheater auf klassischer Basis zu bieten hat. Seit Mitte der 60er Jahre, seit seine *Metaphoren* mitten im Satz aufbrachen, um den Neoklassizismus George Balanchines zu überwinden, setzt der heute 49jährige Holländer die ästhetischen Trends und künstlerischen Wegmarken. Von *Squares* bis *Lieder ohne Worte, Situation* bis *Fünf Tangos, Große Fuge* bis *Live, Adagio Hammerklavier* bis *Klaviervariationen I, Four Schumann Pieces* bis *Grand Trio* hat niemand in gut einem Jahrzehnt mehr Meisterstücke und „Geniestreiche" hervorgebracht als er, George Balanchine eingeschlossen. Die 70er Jahre, zumindest in ihren ersten zwei Dritteln, waren das Jahrzehnt van Manens als wichtigstem Choreographen seiner Zeit.

Im Gegensatz zu Choreographen wie John

Neumeier, den man sich unschwer als Petipa-Kompagnon am Petersburger Zarenhof des 19. Jahrhunderts vorstellen könnte, ist die vorstechendste Eigenart van Manens tatsächlich seine Zeitgenossenschaft. Er versteht sich gleichsam als Ingenieur der Tanzkunst und ist der festen Überzeugung, was immer man auf der Tanzbühne mache, müsse unter rationalen und logischen Gesichtspunkten nachprüfbar sein. Seine Choreographien freilich sind, fast durchweg, mehr als nur klar und logisch, nämlich schlechthin schön, von einer fast schmerzhaften Harmonie, die die Widersprüche und schmerzlichen Erfahrungen nicht mit Heile-Welt-Floskeln überkleistert, sondern ihnen ein utopisches Menschenbild entgegensetzt.

Im Ausdruck, nicht in der Technik, wirken van Manens Choreographien so „klassisch", wie Ballett heute nur wirken kann. Doch ist er eher ein Neuerer als ein Traditionalist: im Grunde der Gegenpart der anarchischen Pina Bausch, deren Schaffen sich von rückwärts mit dem des Holländers berührt. Noch in den konventionellsten Arbeiten van Manens stecken mehr Innovationen als in vielen als avantgardistisch gepriesenen Stücken seiner Konkurrenten.

Vom Balanchineschen Neoklassizismus, aus dem sie erwuchs, unterscheidet sich van Manens neue, aus der Auseinandersetzung mit dem Modern Dance gehärtete Klassik weniger durch ein verändertes Bewegungsrepertoire (das zweifellos auch vorhanden ist) als durch eine veränderte Haltung. Rollenverständnis und Partnerschaftsverhältnis sind in van Manens Balletten neu definiert (nicht nur dadurch, daß van Manen erstmals Männer mit Männern und Frauen mit Frauen zum Pas de deux zusammenbrachte). Der Tanz bezieht sich bei ihm weniger auf die imaginäre vierte Wand der Guckkastenbühne als auf das Gegenüber des Tanzenden auf der Bühne, den Partner, den man nicht nur stützt, sondern dem man sich zuwendet, den man anschaut und völlig neu wahrnimmt. Dadurch wird nicht nur eine neue Plastizität des Tanzens erreicht, sondern vor allem eine neue Humanisierung des Mediums, die im Neoklassizismus schließlich verlorengegangen war an das tänzerische Ornament – eine Gemeinsamkeit mit dem Werk der Pina Bausch, die unmittelbar einleuchten sollte.

Die Entwicklung van Manens verlief nicht ganz bruchlos, doch im Wesentlichen stetig, bis in die späten 70er Jahre. Dann geriet sie in eine Krise, die einen allgemeinen Wendepunkt in der Entwicklung des klassischen Balletts andeuten könnte. Van Manen, der mehr als ein Jahrzehnt lang wie aus dem vollen zu schöpfen schien und beinahe in jeder Spielzeit drei neue Stücke heraus-brachte, die sich nach Farbe und Charakter unterschieden, geriet plötzlich ins Stocken – und das vermutlich aus objektiven, nicht-persönlichen Gründen. Er hatte das Terrain abgeschritten, das sich nach der Überwindung des Neoklassizismus vor ihm auftat, hatte erprobt, was zu erproben war, und lief nun Gefahr sich zu wiederholen.

So brach er mit dem Schubert-Ballett *Grand Trio* eine Entwicklung gleichsam auf ihrem Höhepunkt ab, legte eine fast einjährige schöpferische Pause ein und knüpfte, mit seinen wesentlichen Stücken vor und nach dieser Atempause (einem Strawinsky-Ballett und einer Bach-Dallapiccola-Choreographie) an einem Punkt an, an dem er schon mehr als ein Jahrzehnt früher begonnen, dann aber einen anderen Weg eingeschlagen hatte.

Die neuen van Manen-Stücke sind (gewissermaßen „ein Rückblick auf morgen") kühler und unromantischer als die großen Ballette der 70er Jahre. Das Formenmaterial, das in Choreographien wie *Adagio Hammerklavier* oder *Four Schumann Pieces* erarbeitet wurde, erscheint hier gehärtet und kondensiert: als habe man es zerhackt und zerkleinert und in einem Teilchenbeschleuniger zu einer neuen Substanz verfestigt. Die Stücke sind sachlich, klar in der Form, im Innenleben gleichsam vollelektronisch. Doch geben sie deshalb die Humanität, das Interesse am Menschen, nicht auf; sie sind allenfalls skeptischer geworden gegenüber dem Glauben an die rasche Realisierung der Utopien vom freien, zärtlichen Miteinander der Menschen, denen sie gleichwohl noch anhängen.

Da trifft sich dann van Manen nicht nur mit Pina Bausch, sondern – in der Organisation seines Materials, in der Stückstruktur, im Lebensgefühl – auch mit Twyla Tharp. Diese drei stellen die Alternativen dar, die es – betrachtet man sie als Chiffren für künstlerische Standpunkte und Entwicklungen – nach meiner Auffassung für das Tanztheater der 80er Jahre gibt. Immer vorausgesetzt, es geht diesem Tanztheater nicht um leere kunstgewerbliche Betriebsamkeit, sondern um Kunst: um schmerzhafte Auseinandersetzung mit Normen und Tabus also, um die Ausdehnung und Erweiterung von Möglichkeiten, um persönliches Risiko der Autoren. Denn nur, wer sich mit jeder neuen Arbeit selbst aufs Spiel setzt, wie Pina Bausch oder Hans van Manen, treibt künstlerische Entwicklungen voran.

Anyone venturing onto the slippery ice of predictions concerning future developments in the arts (or even in a particular art form) has every chance of falling flat on his face, and can be thankful if he does not break his neck and both arms in the undertaking. The seriousness of such an attempt is similar to reading tea leaves – with the remarkable difference that the fortune teller at least has a coherent substance on which to base his forecasts. On the other hand, the data which might be suited for supporting a valid statement concerning longterm trends and perspectives in the arts are so very heterogenous, that one fact negates the other, to say absolutely nothing of the contrary interpretations which these facts allow.

At the beginning of the '70s, anyone who had dared to predict that this decade's ballet world, at least in Western Europe, would have been dominated by a previously undreamed-of boom in evening-length ballet would probably have garnered only a smile, considering the dominance of an abstract, shortwinded neoclassicism, the streamlined uniformity of which molded repertories from Glasgow to Vienna, from Stockholm to Lisbon. A decade ago, a much more likely prospect than this upswing in evening-length pieces (which in some seasons effortlessly produced two to three dozen novelties of the most widely differing character, structure, and quality) would have been overcoming neoclassicism in dance through those means which Holland's Hans van Manen and his American colleague Glen Tetley developed in the course of their work with the Nederlands Dans Theater (NDT). While van Manen continued to grow, ultimately well beyond the choreographic capacities which he had acquired up to the time of his departure from the NDT in 1970,

Jochen Schmidt

BAREFOOTED EXPEDITIONS INTO FISSURED DREAMSCAPES?

ATTEMPTS AT A REALISTIC DANCE THEATER — ALONG WITH THE AESTHETICS AND FUTURE OF BALLET IN EUROPE

Tetley's positive development virtually broke off at the moment he left: an example of the strong influence which imponderables, such as the termination of a contractual and working relationship between an artist and the group which inspires him, can have on aesthetic developments. This should not be interpreted to mean that the progress of European dance theater would surely have taken another course if van Manen and Tetley had continued their mutual efforts with the NDT (or if perhaps John Cranko were still living and directing the Stuttgart Ballet today). It is intended only to show the unfathomable factors upon which developments, both positive and negative, depend. Just as important as personnel structure (and perhaps fate) are those objective conditions which set the framework for development and which are virtually outside the sphere of influence of the arts and the artists themselves. The most important of this type of condition is the financial means available to public institutions and the share of these funds which the society allocates to the arts. There are two possibilities by which dance, ballet, and theatrical arts in general can run into difficulties here, difficulties which could

finally prove to threaten their very existence. On the one hand, the lagging development of the economy has brought about – for the first time since the end of World War II – a stagnation of public receipts and in some cases even a decline. On the other hand, the rise in expenses of theater and ballet companies tends to be overly proportional (due, in part, to the fact that the highly intensive nature of theater work makes cost-cutting difficult). Thus the day is foreseeable when the western societies will no longer be able to afford subsidized theater on the present scope (or – and this makes no difference in the effect on theater – will not want to afford such subsidies). Already the first signs of the storm have been sighted on the horizon. In the U.S.A., the Reagan Administration has begun to cut back public subsidies for the arts, funding granted only after years of great effort; and in old Europe, too, the cost-cutting commissioners have a particular fondness of aiming their red pencils at the arts. There is no question that, particularly in Germany, ballet, as the performing art enjoying the shortest tradition, will be harder hit by cutbacks than the opera, theater, or even operetta.

A reduction in public funds for ballet would, of course, initially have above all quantitative consequences. (For the purposes of this discussion, ballet is defined comprehensively as being everything which however dancing moves on a stage.) Ensembles would have to be dissolved, would slide into a period of shrinkage, would not be able to carry out productions. They would be limited in their opportunities to perform and to go on tour, whereby international cultural exchange would suffer, as well as the companies and the choreographers themselves who would lose out on occasions to gather experience.

One need not be a prophet to realize that these initially quantitative restrictions would necessarily be followed by limitations of a qualitative nature. Limited touring and guest engagements – a reduction in mobility for the productions – would at the same time place restrictions on aesthetic stimulus. The comparatively limited dissemination of the Bournonville style stands in direct proportion to the limited inclination of the Royal Danish Ballet to undertake extensive guest appearances. The great aesthetic influence which the work of Hans van Manen and Glen Tetley initially and, more recently, of Jiři Kylián, has exercised on younger European choreographers since the late '60s is due in no mean part to the extensive guest performances of the Nederlands Dans Theater. It set an example, which has changed the European ballet scene to a greater extent than any other artistic force inside or outside of Europe.

Possible budget cuts would, however, affect the aesthetics of ballet not only in this indirect manner. They would also exert a very direct influence – on stage settings, for example, which have exercised a significant function, playing a major role in many of the more important dance theater productions of recent years, from the abstract choreographies of Merce Cunningham to the reality-saturated pieces by Pina Bausch.

The scenic asceticism of neoclassicism, particularly the variety of George Balanchine, was not only a matter of virtue, but of necessity as well. Not only that Balanchine at certain times lacked the money to touch up a choreography with costumes and majestic backdrops, he also lacked – and still lacks today – the set designers who would have constructed a framework for his choreographies, who would have surpassed aesthetically the style-setting blue behind black or white tunics and tricots. Whatever even Karinska, Rouben Ter-Arutunian or David Hays may have designed as décor for Balanchine ballets, it always limped far behind the trademark blue which gave Mr. B's severe works not only a background, but also support.

In order to recognize that this specific Balanchine style, particularly in set design and costume, is not only a strength, but a weakness as well, one need only visualize the sets which Jean-Paul Vroom has created over a period of more than 20 years and especially since 1970 for Hans van Manen. From *Situation* to the *Five Tangos,* from *Twilight* to *The Rite of Spring,* not only do these set designs provide the dance compositions a firm, unmistakable frame and thus a support; they stimulate the choreography literally to new and unconventional solutions. But yet they resemble in structure the set design for the Balanchine pieces to the extent

that they basically still consist, for the most part, of a backdrop plus lighting design, keeping the dancing area free and more suggesting than actually structuring the space itself (disregarding however such exceptions as *Keep Going* with its gradually receding depths or *Essay in Silence,* in which Vroom's second set draws the backdrop right down under the dancers' feet in the form of a sound-absorbing carpet).

Even those style-setting designs with modernistic steel skeleton structures which Nadine Baylis created for Glen Tetley, among others, and populated with dancers in ever-changing, glancing tricots, do not differ greatly in a structural sense from the (neo)-classical ballet stage – more likely candidates are John F. MacFarlane's occasional, almost box-like designs, such as those for Jochen Ulrich's work at the Cologne Tanz-Forum.

But the stage as a ballet interior, not only as a surface uncluttered for dance and trimmed with atmospheric decoration (if we disregard the ingenious special cases represented by the Rauschenberg, Warhol, Stella or Morris sets for Merce Cunningham) was first achieved by those set designers who created their realistic or visionary environments for the pieces of a new, free, dance theater. First place would be occupied by the name of Rolf Borzik, who died, much too soon, in 1980, and whose inventive spaces for the works of Pina Bausch – from *Orpheus and Eurydice* to *Keuschheitslegende/Celibacy Legend* (such as the slide for *Komm tanz mit mir (Come Dance with Me),* the flooded stage for *Arien,* the dance floor of *Café Müller,* filled with chairs) – have made him appear on occasion virtually as co-author with Bausch. But also those spaces, which Johannes Schütz thought out for Reinhild Hoffmann *(Hochzeit/Wedding, Unkrautgarten/Weed Garden)* or some of the settings for Hans Kresnik's furious acts of passion (VA Wölfl's tiled interior for *Magnet),* fulfill these new functions. Not only keeping a space clear for any desired dance form, but conditioning a space for a very particular type of choreography, and even to pre-impose a quite special sense on the choreography. (Movement on a stage flooded with water is of absolute necessity different from that on a solid floor; the peat which Borzik strewed on the boards for Pina Bausch's *Rite of Spring* would simply not allow execution in the style of the danse d'école.)

Of course this does not mean that spaces would have searched for a piece or set designers for choreographers. It was the choreographers who set the direction – and this direction was: away from abstraction, towards a new realism. This movement went hand in hand with a newly revived inclination

towards evening-length ballet, and it cannot be positively established in this case which was first, the chicken or the egg. The ties between this movement and general developments in the arts speak for the presumption that this new passion for reality chose evening-length ballet as its fitting expression (and not the reverse – that evening-length ballet inspired a turn to realism). The visual arts were the forerunners, in particular painting, which failed to advance beyond the first monochrome, then white surfaces and finally the empty frame. This new trend was taken up with comparatively little delay by literature (as the publishing house Suhrkamp noted: "Careful! They're telling stories again"), film (the break with symbolism represented by Ingmar Bergman's *Silence),* and spoken theater, which at least in Western Germany in its neo-culinarism (the sets by Wilfried Minks, Erich Wonder or Karl-Ernst Herrmann) exerted a permanent influence on the hesitating dance theater.

What is to be understood by the phrase "reality" on the dance stage is certainly no simple question. The answer has been different at varying times and under varying ideologies; in the midst of the Second World War tragic love stories such as *Romeo and Juliet* or fairy tales such as *Cinderella* were reality enough for socialist realism.

Such pieces, couched in classical technique and basically rooted deep in the aesthetics of the 19th century, are of course still to be found on the European dance scene; as classical revisions or reproductions they even dominate some seasons. The performance statistics for the 1979/80 season in Western Germany show such pieces clearly occupying top positions. *(The Nutcracker,* of all things, leads *La Fille mal gardée* and *Romeo and Juliet; Don Quixote* takes fourth place, trailed by *Sleeping Beauty;* and even *Coppélia, Swan Lake* and *Sylvia* in positions 10 to 12, are well up in the race, followed immediately by John Neumeier's *Lady of the Camellias,* which is basically of the same spirit, although more poorly choreographed than most of the competitors who drew upon the classical originals.)

Pieces of this type, it seems, have to exist, but can hardly be called "realistic" by contemporary standards. The reality which the choreographers of the new dance theater, at least in West Germany, bring into their pieces is, however, not that of an unbroken "realistic" story-telling, but that of painful abrasion with particular relationships which the author of the piece no longer takes as being a given. Such an attitude fully presupposes the task of the classical traditions, from the unreflected technique of the danse d'école to its conventional structure. Pina Bausch's statement – that she is not interested in *how* people move, but rather in *what* moves people – is a confession of faith for a new dance theater, which understands the dancer to be not a technically perfect, artificial figure, but rather a thinking, feeling individual, and utilizes him as such.

Virtually all the pieces by Pina Bausch, doubtlessly a key figure in this new, realistic dance theater, are defined stylistically by severe friction with standards and prevailing circumstances, an attack on the walls of convention (which happens literally in *Bluebeard*), a crumbling of forms and destruction of smooth sequences. Pina Bausch's dance theater, scorned and torn to shreds by devotees of the classical dancing arts, coddled by critics of an unconventional spoken theater, not only leaves behind it the question of whether what happens on its stage is "dance" (since it mistrusts the definitions and conventions which would tie dance to a certain aesthetic-historic standard). It also blurs, intentionally, the frontier between art and triviality – not to ennoble triviality, but rather to expose and accept it. In so doing, the destruction of the traditional forms had long since developed a new dramaturgy and new form. From the early one-act piece *Ich bring dich um die Ecke,* through to the Brecht-Weill evening *The Seven Deadly Sins, Kontakthof, Arien, Keuschheitslegende, 1980,* and through to *Bandoneon,* Bausch has slowly and persistently felt her way towards a "montage" principle, based on the variety revue, which melts together the most disparate of individual components. A dramaturgy of contrast, which has made repetition and quasi-musical variation of a basic pattern to a principle of style and which has made her stylistic and aesthetic abrupt plunges into hot and cold baths just as daring as they are perfectly balanced, pairing frenzy with tranquility, hubbub with solitude, cheerfulness with misery, volume with quiet, brightness with black-outs, fun with frustration, solo with ensemble, static and dance – and in the midst of all this, masters the trick of making its pieces at once satirically sharp and dreamily soft, bitter and sweet, critical and glossy.

For the '80s, too, it is this dance theater of the unconventional – with its barefooted expeditions into the fissured dreamscapes of the subconscious, with its complex soundings of human behavior patterns and its longing search for a new and universally understood body language – that the essential artistic experience in dance (as a comprehensive designation for every type of stage dancing) is to be expected. While some critics would like to discern stagnation in Pina Bausch's persistent adherence to certain themes, forms, and procedures, I have nowhere detected this, but only a continuous, if not

always uniform, striding forward into uncharted artistic territory.

In the meantime, Bausch indeed no longer stands alone – and if the perspectives are not foreshortened to national or even European dimensions, she never really did. Reinhild Hoffmann, emanating, like Pina Bausch, from the dance studio of the Folkwang College of Fine Arts in Essen, in pursuing with pieces such as *Solo mit Sofa, Fünf Tage, fünf Nächte (Five Days, Five Nights), Hochzeit* or *Unkrautgarten* a related but at the same time individual path, which follows a bit nearer along the tradition (of modern dance). And also Hans Kresnik, Jochen Ulrich, Gerhard Bohner and, more recently, Susanne Linke have registered success with pieces which, at least in stretches, presented that new and eminently political point of view and procedure which are no longer satisfied with the representation of a state of affairs, but which attempt to supply the analysis as well, without the pieces becoming sociological graduate seminars with obligatory motions. That such pieces are not a typical German phenomenon is demonstrated above all by select American manifestations, such as the works of Meredith Monk and, in a certain sense, those of Twyla Tharp, while other significant currents in the American New Dance scene reveal rather a counterposition to the new German dance theater. Where Bausch, Hoffmann and Linke advanced from an interest in people to an aesthetically new approach with socio-critical consequences, while at the same time, doubting the possibility of unbroken dance formations, increasingly froze the movement, choreographers like Trisha Brown, Lucinda Childs, or Laura Dean started from a point of aesthetic non-acceptance (the reduction of the forms and of motion to the extreme minimum in minimal dance), linked in part with the political standpoints of the women's liberation movement; following a phase of rigidity, this starting point led the way back to a virtuosity, which met the curiosity of the public in a way which would have been almost unthinkable ten years ago. In addition to the tender montage theater of Pina Bausch, devoted to humankind, our most tenacious impressions of the '80s may well be indebted to the return of virtuosity to the new dance theater (in pieces like *Brahms-Paganini* or *Baker's Dozen* by Twyla Tharp, an established fact, in *Dance* by Lucinda Childs, at least announced).

Here lies, in a certain sense, the only parallel to developments in classical dance. The trump of virtuosity has, indeed, been played too often in classical dance. Word has gotten around in the last decade that additional superlatives in difficulty of execution, following the figure skaters' example (after the double

tours, the triple tours en l'air, required by Cranko in *The Taming of the Shrew*), do nothing to advance dancing as art (even if this is not the case everywhere; as a result of the emigration of Nureyev, Baryshnikov, Panov and Godunov, America is being flooted with a new wave of high-difficulty dancing). But just such choreographers (like Hans van Manen) who in the late '60s and early '70s had far reduced the level of virtuosity and dance tempo, have in recent years returned successively to faster tempi and greater virtuosity – even though they have not arrived at the point where they once began.

However highly America may be enthused about Jiři Kylián – at the present more a virtuoso assimilator of the existing than a real innovator – the name van Manen marks, at the start of the '80s as well, the optimum of that which European dance theater has to offer on a classical basis. Since the middle of the '60s, since his *Metaphoren* broke off in "mid-sentence" to overcome George Balanchine's neoclassicism, the 49 year-old Dutchman has been marking blazes and setting aesthetic trends. From *Squares* to *Songs without Words, Situation* to *Five Tangos, Große Fuge* to *Live, Adagio Hammerklavier* to *Piano Variations I, Four Schumann Pieces* to *Grand Trio,* no one has brought forth, within the course of a decade, more masterpieces and „strokes of genius" than he, George Balanchine included. The '70s, at least in their first two thirds, were van Manen's decade, his as the most important choreographer of his time.

In contrast to choreographers like John Neumeier (whom one could without great difficulty imagine to be a nineteenth-century associate of Petipa in the Czar's court at St. Petersburg), van Manen's most prominent feature is in fact his contemporaneity. He understands himself to be, as it were, an engineer of the art of dance and is of the firm conviction that whatever one does on the stage must be verifiable in accordance with rational and logical points of view. Almost all of his choreographies are, of course, more than just clear and logical; they are purely and simply beautiful, possessed of an almost painful harmony which does not plaster over contradictions and dolorous experience with flowery, "best-of-all-possible-worlds" phraseology, but rather counters them with a utopian concept of the human race.

It is in expression, not in technique, that van Manen's choreographies appear so "classical", as only today's ballet can appear. But he is in fact more an innovator than a traditionalist, basically the counterpart of the anarchistic Pina Bausch, whose creation makes contact with that of van Manen's back to back. Even in the most conventional of van Manen's works there is more inno-

vation than in many of his competitors' pieces, hailed as avant-garde.

Hardened by the confrontation with modern dance, van Manen's new classic differs from Balanchine's neoclassicism (out of which it arose) less through a modified repertoire of motion (which doubtlessly also exists) than through a modified attitude. The understanding of roles and partnerships are newly defined in van Manen's ballets (not only by the fact that van Manen for the first time paired men with men and women with women in pas de deux). His dance is related less to the imaginary fourth wall of the proscenium stage than to the dancer's partner, whom one not only supports, but to whom one turns, whom one sees and perceives in a totally new way. This brings forth not only a new plasticity of dancing, but above all a new humanization of the medium, which ultimately had been lost to the ornament of dance in neoclassicism, this new humanization being a factor shared in common with the work of Pina Bausch, which should be obvious.

The course of van Manen's development was not completely free of interruptions, but essentially steady through to the late '70s. Then the development ran into a crisis which could imply a general turning point in the development of classical ballet. Van Manen, who appeared to have drawn on unlimited resources for more than a decade, creating three new pieces almost every season, differing in color and character, suddenly faltered – and this presumably due to objective, non-personal reasons. He had paced off the terrain which opened up to him after overcoming neoclassicism, had tested everything there was to be tested and now ran the danger of repeating himself.

Thus, with the Schubert ballet *Grand Trio,* he broke off a development at its high point, undertook a creative intermission of almost a year, and went on – together with his most important pieces before and after this breather (a Stravinsky ballet and a Bach-Dallapiccola choreography) – from the point at which he had begun more than a decade before, but whence he had turned down another path.

The new van Manen pieces (to a certain degree a "retrospect of tomorrow") are cooler and less romantic than the grand ballets of the '70s. The form materials which were worked out in choreographies such as *Adagio Hammerklavier* or *Four Schumann Pieces* seem here to have been hardened and condensed, as though chopped and pulverized and then solidified in a particle accelerator to form a new substance. The pieces are pertinent, clear of form, their inner spirit fully electronic, so to speak. But this has not forced them to give up their humanity, the interest in mankind; at the outside they have become more skeptical towards faith in an early achievement of utopias of free, gentle interaction among humans, which they nonetheless hang on to.

There van Manen meets not only with Pina Bausch, but also – in the organization of his material, in the structure of the pieces, in his awareness of life – with Twyla Tharp. These – if one considers them as ciphers for artistic points of view and developments – are the three alternatives which, in my opinion, are open to the dance theater of the '80s. Always provided that in this dance theater it is not a matter of empty artistic activity, but rather of art: of painful confrontation with standards and taboos, of the expansion and extension of possibilities, of the authors' personal risk. Only putting oneself on the line with every new work, as does Pina Bausch or Hans van Manen, only this gives impetus to artistic advancement.

*Fotos auf den
vorangegangenen Seiten/
Photos on the preceding pages*
SITUATION,
Ch: Hans van Manen,
Nederlands Dans Theater
Foto S. 42/Photo p. 42
Leon Koning, Chris Frey,
Foto: Gert Weigelt
Fotos S. 43/Photos p. 43
unten links/bottom left
Rachel Beaujean, Rob van Woerkom
*rechts von oben nach unten/
right, top to bottom*
Ensemble,
Mea Venema (vorn/in front),
Rachel Beaujean und/and Rob van Woerkom,
Mea Venema und/and Simon de Mowbray,
alle Fotos auf S. 43 von/
all photos on p. 43 by Jorge Fatauros

*Fotos auf dieser Seite/
Photos on this page*
KONTAKTHOF,
Ch: Pina Bausch
oben/above
Josephine Anne Endicott
(links/left), Meryl Tankard
unten/below
Mari Di Lena
Wuppertaler Tanztheater/
Dance Theater, Wuppertal,
Fotos: Gert Weigelt

Fotos S. 45/Photos p. 45
BANDONEON,
Ch: Pina Bausch,
Wuppertaler Tanztheater,
Dance Theater, Wuppertal,
Fotos: Gert Weigelt

Hans Werner Henze

Hans Werner Henze ist einer der wenigen profilierten Komponisten, die sich für Ballett, für Tanzkompositionen eingesetzt haben. Angesprochen auf sein Verhältnis zu dieser Kunstgattung sagt er:

Das Ballett hat nicht meinen Einsatz benötigt, sondern nur (gelegentlich) Musik für seine Bedürfnisse. Ballett ist etwas Wunderbares, es ist für mich die Theaterform, in der sich die Beziehungen zwischen dem menschlichen Körper und der Musik am reinsten und am klarsten manifestieren. Diese Beziehung kann reichen von den einfachsten Formen der Folklore bis in das verfeinerte Zusammenspiel von Bild, Farbe, Bewegung, Philosophisch-Literarischem und den Geheimnissen der *Musique savante*. Ich stelle mir vor, daß das Ballett den Musikern, aber auch den Malern, den Schneidern wie auch den Dichtern und Denkern zuweilen ein Behälter für eine ganz bestimmte Ausdruckskategorie wird: Ich denke, daß dabei die Vorstellung physischer Schönheit eine besondere Anziehungskraft besitzt für alle, die sich dieser Kunstform auf die eine oder die andere Weise nähern möchten. Es wäre hypokritisch, das wegleugnen zu wollen. Im Gegenteil, es ist sicherlich diese Anziehungskraft, der wir die Ballettmusiken von Tschaikowsky, Debussy, Ravel, Strawinsky, de Falla, Prokofiew, Britten und Henze verdanken, die Dekors von Tschelitschew, Bakst, Benois, Cocteau, Picasso, De Nobili und Ter-Arutunian. In den Ballettpartituren, in den Ballettlibretti, in den Malereien und Kostümen für das Ballett stellt sich jeweils – und in immer neuen Erfindungen – das vom Eros beflügelte Schönheitskonzept des Künstlers dar.

Wenn wir uns darüber einig sind, daß die Beziehungen zwischen der besonderen Physis unseres Gegenstandes und der Musik von Fall zu Fall, von Gegebenheit zu Gegebenheit sich ändern können, sollen und müssen wir zugeben, daß es – jedenfalls in unserer Zeit – in der Produktion einen mittleren Breitstreifen gibt, auf dem sich routiniert und wirkungslos eine Konvention angesiedelt hat, in der die Rolle der Musik und der Charakter der Beziehung zwischen dieser und dem Choreographen immer gleichförmiger, oberflächlicher und daher fragwürdiger und veränderungsbedürftig geworden ist.

Die Musik ist nicht daran schuld, besonders diejenige nicht, die für das Tanzen gar nicht gedacht war, deren Thematik auf ganz andere Inhalte bezogen war und ist, als man ihr und dem Publikum nun plötzlich weismachen will. Es ist schon ganz schön ärgerlich für die Musiker, mitansehen zu müssen, wie Werke, große Werke der großen Musikliteratur, Werke der

TANZ UND MUSIK

Aufklärung, des religiösen Realismus, der späte Beethoven, Bach, denkende, wissende Musik mit den zierlichen Füßchen unserer Ballerinen und Knaben getreten werden. Für mich sind solche Übergriffe das sicherste Zeichen dafür, daß den Übergreifenden das Gefühl für Maß fehlt, und daß bei den Theaterleutchen nicht mehr darüber nachgedacht wird, was die künstlerische Aufgabe denn wohl sein könnte, und wo die Grenzen zwischen den einzelnen Gedankenfeldern der Künste denn wohl liegen könnten. Es wäre mir angenehm, die Choreographen würden ihre Finger von der Musik lassen, die nicht für sie gedacht ist. Es gibt ausreichend Tanzmusik und tanzbare Musik (was immer das sei), es muß also nicht immer gleich die Große Fuge sein und auch nicht immer gleich die Bach-Kantate. Wer sich nicht zurückhalten kann bei den Meisterwerken, kommt mir ziemlich *camp* vor (ich denke dabei an die obligatorische Amateurhaftigkeit der *campness*) und ganz offensichtlich mit einer mangelhaften ästhetischen Erziehung versehen, und ein bißchen unverschämt vielleicht auch.

Andererseits gibt es natürlich auch den Übergriff der Musik auf die Physis des Tanzes: Das beste Beispiel dafür ist *Le Sacre du printemps*. Das ist eine Musik, bei der sich jeder Hörer, dank der Genauigkeit der dieser Partitur innewohnenden semiotischen Zeichen, seine eigenen lebhaften, für ihn selbst absolut zutreffenden Vorstellungen machen kann, Vorstellungen von Farben, Formen, realen Vorgängen, Bewegungsabläufen aus einer eigenen psychischen Welt. Vielleicht ist das der Grund, daß so ein Werk bei seiner choreographischen Realisierung immer wieder die bekannten Schwierigkeiten hervorruft, so viele Probleme aufwirft und doch nie hilft, eine wirklich zufriedenstellende Lösung zutage zu fördern. Strawinsky hat sich beim Komponieren dieses Stücks offensichtlich alle Bewegungsabläufe, Farben, Formen, physisch Reales ausgiebig vorgestellt. Er hat das Tanzen mitkomponiert, hat die Bewegungen, die Schwankungen, die Sprünge, die Abgründe und die zutiefst verwurzelte Emotion seines Eros in tönende Formen, Bewegungsabläufe und psychische Realität verwandelt. Somit ist er es praktisch überflüssig gemacht, daß eine Einzelperson, ein Choreograph mehr zu sehen, zu hören, zu schmecken vermeinen muß als Igor Fjodorowitsch selbst, und jeder

Mensch kann beim Anhören von *Sacre,* ganz wie bei der Beethovenschen *Siebenten,* seine eigene unerhörte Choreographie im Köpfchen entwickeln. Übergriffe von einer Kunstform in die andere gibt es ja auch, wenn Filmemacher sich über die große Literatur hermachen und ein solches *Embarrassment* erzeugen wie Luchino Visconti bei seinem peinlichen Auftritt mit Thomas Manns *Tod in Venedig.* (Ein gütiges Schicksal hat uns davor bewahrt, daß der Meister seinen Plan, das große Proustsche Epos von 13 Gallimard-Bänden zu einem Kinostück zu machen, noch realisieren konnte.) Die Übergriffe aber, von denen ich hier spreche – nicht nur das häufige phantasielose Heranziehen der großen Literatur (das etwas von Alibi-Beschaffung hat), sondern auch die kriterienfreie Art, mit der man mit der Musik umspringt, diese Sorglosigkeit im Umgang mit Kunst – das sind eben die Dinge, die mir das heutige generelle Ballettdenken so fremd und suspekt machen. Ich bin halt altmodisch, ich halte es mit Frederick Ashton und George Balanchine. Von beiden könnten die jungen Herren zumindest das Gefühl für Maß lernen, die künstlerische Korrektheit. Vielleicht gehören diese Leute, beide mit der Diaghilewschen Ästhetik vertraut und beide in einer Zivilisation bewußt verankert, in eine Zeit und in einen Zusammenhang, den es nicht mehr gibt. Immerhin gehen solche Leute nicht in den Schallplattenladen, um sich dort den Zufallsfund für den nächsten Mißbrauch zu ergattern. Ein Mann wie Balanchine kann Partituren lesen. Er sucht sich, mit einem untrüglichen Geschmack ausgestattet, die richtige musikalische Antwort auf ein choreographisches Problem, das ihm im Kopf herumgeht. Er kennt die Musik, er weiß, was von ihr zu erwarten ist, er weiß, wie man auf der Bühne ihre im Notenbild verborgenen Schönheiten hervorbringen, widerspiegeln, in den menschlichen Gliedern fortsetzen kann. Er ist auch ein *Könner,* denn er beherrscht alle Genres des Balletts: Die wichtigsten Charakteristika seines Stils sind die Reichweite seiner Mittel, die Eleganz und ästhetische Korrektheit, mit der er die Probleme gelöst hat. Man kann nicht sagen, daß Balanchine sich jemals wiederholt hätte oder daß er sich jemals in der Wahl der Musik vergriffen hätte.

Ich meine mit alledem durchaus nicht, daß der Balanchinesche Weg der einzige ist, den man sich heute vorstellen kann. Wir haben es gerade mit den ersten Zeichen einer facettenartigen Evolution oberhalb oder abseits von dem oben erwähnten Breitstreifen zu tun, und es ist wichtig, daß die jungen Choreographen weitergehen.

Aber eben deshalb: Warum studieren sie die Musik nicht besser, diese jungen Choreographen? Warum macht es ihnen nichts aus, daß sie die musikalischen Zusammenhänge nicht begreifen? Warum befragen sie nicht ihre in großer Zahl und Qualität vorhandenen gleichaltrigen Komponisten-Kollegen, laden sie in die Ballett-säle ein und führen sie bei der Gelegenheit in die offenen und versteckten Geheimnisse der Kunstform Ballett ein? Jeder kann von jedem lernen.

Hans Werner Henze

DANCE AND MUSIC

Hans Werner Henze is one of the few prominent composers devoting efforts to composition for the dance. Asked about his relationship to this art form, he responded: Ballet had no need of my efforts, but rather only (occasionally) of music to meet its requirements. Ballet is something wonderful; for me, it is the theatrical form representing the purest and clearest manifestation of the relationship between the human body and music. This relationship can range from the simplest forms of folk dance through the refined interplay of optics, color, motion, the philosophical-literary and the mysteries of *musique savante*. I sometimes imagine ballet to be for musicians – but also for painters, tailors, as well as for poets and philosophers – a vessel for a very particular category of expression: I think that the idea of physical beauty has a particular drawing power for everyone who would like to get closer to this art form in one way or another. It would be hypocritical to try to deny this. On the contrary, it is surely this attractive force to which we owe our gratitude for the ballet music of Tchaikovsky, Debussy, Ravel, Stravinsky, de Falla, Prokofiev, Britten and Henze, for the sets designed by Tchelitchev, Bakst, Benois, Cocteau, Picasso, De Nobili, and Ter-Arutunian. It is in the ballet scores, in the ballet librettos, in the sets and costumes respectively that – in ever new inventions – the artist's concept of beauty, given wing by Eros, is represented.

If we are in agreement that the relationship between the special physis of our object and the music can change from case to case, from one given situation to the next, then we should and indeed must admit that there is in the production, at least in our time, a broad strip down the middle on which a routine and ineffective convention has taken foothold, a convention in which the role of music and the character of its relationship to the choreographer has become ever more uniform and superficial, thus more questionable and needful of change.

The music is not at fault here, and in particular that music which was not conceived for dancing at all, a music whose subject matter was and is based on a completely different content than that of which one is now suddenly trying to convince the music and the public. The musician finds it most annoying to have to observe the manner in which the great works of the great music literature – works of the Enlightment, of religious

realism, late Beethoven, Bach, thinking, knowing music – are trampled with the delicate little feet of our ballerinas and ballerinos. For me, such encroachments are the surest sign that the trespasser lacks all sense of proportion, and that among theater people there is no longer any thought being given to what the nature of the artistic mission might be and to where the borders between the several fields of thought in the arts might lie. I would be most pleased if choreographers would keep their hands away from music which was not conceived for them. There is a sufficient volume of dance music and danceable music (whatever that might be); it need not, therefore, always be the great fugue nor the Bach cantatas. Anyone who cannot restrain himself with the masterworks seems to me to be rather camp (and I am thinking of the obligatory amateurism of campness); such artists have quite obviously been equipped with a deficient aesthetic education, and are perhaps a bit impertinent as well.

On the other hand, there is, of course, also the infringement of music into the physis of the dance; the best example of this is *The Rite of Spring*. This is music to which every listener, thanks to the accuracy of the semiotic symbols inherent in the score, can formulate his own vivid and, for him, absolute correct images, images of color, shapes, real events, sequences of movement from his own, psychic world. Perhaps that is the reason why such a work as this prompts again and again the same familiar difficulties by its choreographic realization, posing so many problems, never helping to promote a really satisfactory solution. During the composition of this piece Stravinsky apparently had an extensive concept of all the sequences of motion, colors, shapes and physical reality. He composed the dancing along with the music, transforming the movements, the swings, the leaps, the chasms, the deeply rooted emotion of his eros into acoustical forms, sequences of movement and physical reality. Thus he made it practically superfluous that an individual, that a choreographer feel the need to see, to hear, to taste more than Igor Fedorovich himself. And, just

as with Beethoven's *Seventh,* everyone can develop his own, unprecedented choreography in his mind's eye when listening to *The Rite of Spring.* Incursions of one art form into another are also to be found when filmmakers attack great literature, generating such an embarrassment as that of Luchino Visconti with his awkward presentation of Thomas Mann's *Death in Venice.* (Benevolent fate has protected us from the master's realizing his plan to transform the great Proustian epic of 13 Gallimard volumes into a cinematic event.) But the incursions of which I am speaking here – not only the frequent and unimaginative adaptation of great literature (which has something of an alibi character), but also the uncritical way in which one deals with music, the carelessness in handling art – these are things which make the general strain of current thought in ballet so foreign and suspicious to me. I am indeed somewhat old-fashioned, something I share with Frederick Ashton and George Balanchine. The younger generation could learn from both of them at least a sense of dimension, of artistic propriety. Perhaps these men, both familiar with the Diaghilevian aesthetic and both consciously anchored in a particular civilization, belong to an era and a context which no longer exist. At any rate, such people do not wander into the nearest record shop to acquire an accidental discovery for the next round of abuse. A man like Balanchine can read a score. Equipped with undeceivable taste, he searches for the correct musical answer to a choreographic problem circling in his head. He knows the music, what to expect of it. He knows how to elicit on the stage the beauty hidden among the written notes, to reflect and continue that beauty in human limbs. He is also an *expert,* a master of every genre of the ballet: the most important characteristic of his style is the breadth of its means, the elegance and aesthetic correctness with which he has solved the problems. One cannot say that Balanchine has ever repeated himself or that he has ever erred in selecting his music. But with all this I do not intend to imply at all that Balanchine's way is the only one conceivable today. We are dealing just at the moment with the first signs of a facet-like evolution above or beyond the broad strip mentioned above, and it is important that the younger choreographers continue to push forward. But it is just for this reason that I ask

UNDINE/ONDINE,
Ch: Frederick Ashton,
Margot Fonteyn, Michael Somes,
Royal Ballet Covent Garden, London,
Fotos: Houston Rogers
aus dem Film/from the film
„The Royal Ballet" von/by
The Rank Organisation Limited, London

why these young choreographers do not study the music more carefully. Why are they indifferent to the fact that they do not grasp the musical contexts? Why not ask the composers of their own generation, who exist in great numbers and quality? Why not invite them into the ballet studio, using the occasion to introduce them to both the open and the hidden mysteries of the art form called ballet? Then, one could only learn from the other.

ORPHEUS,
Ch: William Forsythe,
Birgit Keil, Richard Cragun,
Stuttgarter Ballett/
Stuttgart Ballet,
Foto: Charles Tandy

ORPHEUS,
Ch: William Forsythe,
Birgit Keil, Richard Cragun
(vorn/in front),
Stuttgarter Ballett/
Stuttgart Ballet,
Foto: Charles Tandy

DER WUNDERBARE MANDARIN/
THE MIRACULOUS MANDARIN,
Ch: Jochen Ulrich
oben/top
Monika Montiva, François Passard,
Mitte und unten/middle and bottom
Monika Montiva, Ralf Harster,
Tanz-Forum Köln/Cologne,
Fotos: Gert Weigelt

David Vaughan

VON DIAGHILEW BIS CUNNINGHAM

ZEITGENÖSSISCHE KÜNSTLER ARBEITEN FÜR DAS BALLETT

Im 19. Jahrhundert wurde das Bühnenbild, das in der Zeit der Renaissance und des Barock in den Aufgabenbereich der Künstler und Architekten fiel, immer mehr in die Werkstätten der Kulissenmaler verlegt, die Innen- und Außenszenen bis ins kleinste Detail auf Leinwand und Kulisse übertragen konnten. Der Beitrag, den etwa Pierre Ciceri für das romantische Ballett leistete, sollte nicht unterschätzt werden. Er entwarf das Bühnenbild für *La Sylphide* (1832) und *Giselle* (1841). In der zweiten Hälfte des Jahrhunderts wurden die Ballette in Paris und Rußland häufig in Gemeinschaftsarbeit ausgestattet, wie etwa *Coppélia* (Paris 1870) von Charles Cambon, Edouard Despléchin und Antoine Lavastre, oder *Dornröschen* (St. Petersburg 1890) von Heinrich Levogt, Iwan Andrejew, Michail Botscharow, Konstantin Iwanow und Matwej Schischkow. Einige dieser Bühnenbilder mögen Details der Zeit pedantisch genau wiedergegeben, ja sogar einen gewissen Charme besessen haben. Es fehlte ihnen jedoch die poetische Atmosphäre, die durch die kreative Phantasie eines mit dem Librettisten, Komponisten und Choreographen gleichberechtigt zusammenarbeitenden Künstlers hätte geschaffen werden können.

Die Wiederbelebung des Bühnenbildes begann in Rußland Ende des 19. Jahrhunderts; insbesondere in den Opernproduktionen, die der Moskauer Fabrikant und Mäzen Sawa Mamontow finanzierte, und deren Bühnenbilder von Malern wie Konstantin Korowin, Isaak Levitan, Valentin Serow und Michail Vroubel stammten. Diese bemerkenswerten Produktionen beeinflußten die Qualität der Bühnenbilder in den Kaiserlichen Theatern von St. Petersburg und Moskau, wo Dekors einiger dieser Künstler erschienen. Nachhaltiger noch beeinflußten sie Serge Diaghilew und die Gruppe von Malern um seine Zeitschrift *Mir Iskustwa (Welt der Kunst)*. 1899 berief man Diaghilew für besondere Projekte an die Kaiserlichen Theater, und er legte einen Plan für eine Wiederaufnahme des Balletts *Sylvia* von Léo Delibes vor, das von Mitgliedern der Gruppe entworfen werden sollte: der erste Akt von Alexandre Benois, der zweite Akt von Konstantin Korowin und der dritte von Eugène Lanceray mit Kostümen von Léon Bakst und Valentin Serow – insgesamt eine Gruppe ganz unterschiedlichen Niveaus. Die Annullierung dieses Projekts führte zu Diaghilews Entlassung, aber als er seine eigene Ballettkompanie nach Westeuropa führte (angefangen mit der ersten Saison in Paris 1909), bestand das Repertoire überwiegend aus Werken, die nach dem Prinzip geschaffen (oder dazu neu aufgenommen) waren, daß ein Ballett ein geschlossenes Werk sei, in dem Choreographie, Musik und Bühnenbild ein gemeinsam vereinbartes Konzept aufzeigen sollten.

Die meisten Ballette der ersten Spielzeiten der Ballets Russes statteten Benois und Bakst aus, die ebenfalls häufig die Libretti lieferten. Sie waren zudem in hohem Maße für die Festlegung des ästhetischen Konzepts der Kompanie verantwortlich, demzufolge ein Ballett ein *Gesamtkunstwerk* sein habe. (So nannte es Richard Wagner, zu dessen Lebzeiten diese Forderung allerdings nie voll verwirklicht wurde, eben gerade darum, weil es an entsprechenden Bühnenbildnern fehlte.)

Durch diese Art künstlerischer Zusammenarbeit entstanden Meisterwerke wie *Petruschka* (1911) – Libretto von Alexandre Benois und Igor Strawinsky, Choreographie von Michail Fokine und dem Dekor von Benois mit seiner berühmten Darstellung des St. Petersburger Fastnachtsjahrmarkts aus der Zeit um 1830 – und *Le Carnaval* (Fokine/Schumann, 1910) mit Baksts zarter Beschwörung des Biedermeier. Baksts persischer Harem für *Scheherazade* (Fokine/Rimsky–Korsakow, 1910) mit seinen grellen Farbzusammenstellungen übte enormen Einfluß auf Mode und Inneneinrichtungsstil der Zeit aus.

Obwohl ein Großteil der Arbeiten aus dieser ersten Zeit der Ballets Russes im Vergleich zu dem Ballett der Pariser Oper oder des Maryinsky Theaters in St. Petersburg innovativ war, war er im Vergleich zu zeitgenössischen Entwicklungen der Malerei und Bildhauerei in vieler Hinsicht rückständig. Bereits 1909 war der Kubismus etabliert, aber in den frühen Diaghilew–Balletten lag die Betonung noch in Ort und Zeit der Handlung auf dem Exotischen (auf dem Orient, dem antiken Griechenland, dem heidnischen Rußland), auf nostalgischer Beschwörung des Barock *(Le Pavillon d'Armide)* oder auf der Romantik des 19. Jahrhunderts *(Les Sylphides, Le Carnaval, Le Spectre de la rose)*.

Niemand wußte das besser als Diaghilew selbst, der solcher Stücke wie *Scheherazade* und *Cléopâtre* bald überdrüssig wurde – obwohl wirtschaftliche Überlegungen ihn zwangen, sie im Repertoire zu behalten – und der die Ballets Russes mit der Avantgarde von Malerei und Musik zusammenbringen wollte. In der Musik hatte er die Unterstützung von Igor Strawinsky, der die Musik für *Feuervogel* und *Petruschka* für

ihn komponiert hatte und der begierig war, experimentelle Kompositionsformen weiterzuentwickeln. Michail Fokine, erster Choreograph der Kompanie, lag nichts an derartigen Bestrebungen, und deshalb wandte sich Diaghilew bei seiner Suche nach choreographischen Neuerungen an Vaslav Nijinsky. Nijinsky erfüllte diese Erwartungen mit *L'Après-midi d'un faune* (1912), *Jeux* (1913) und *Le Sacre du printemps* (1913). *Faune,* das bei seiner Uraufführung wegen seines Inhalts, dem sexuellen Erwachen einer primitiven Kreatur, einen Skandal provozierte, zeigte ebenfalls eine radikal neue Beziehung zwischen Tanz und Musik auf (die Schritte stimmen nicht zwangsläufig mit dem Takt der Musik überein). *Jeux,* zu einer Auftragskomposition von Claude Debussy, beschäftigte sich gleichfalls mit sexuellen Bräuchen – erstmalig im modernen Ballett in zeitgenössischem Rahmen. *Sacre* entwickelte die in *Faune* eingeführte Umkehrung der klassischen Technik weiter, stellte in der Behandlung seines Themas prähistorischer Riten eine Hinwendung zur Abstraktion her. Die Uraufführung am 29. Mai 1913 ist ein Schlüsselereignis zeitgenössischer Musikgeschichte.

Was die Ausstattung betrifft, stellten Nijinskys Ballette keine Abkehr von Grundsatz und Praxis der frühen Ballets Russes dar. Bakst entwarf *Faune* und auch *Jeux,* ersteres noch in seiner idealisierten Visionen des antiken Griechenland, das zweite ein von Mondlicht durchströmter Garten à la Watteau. Nicolas Roerichs Bühnenbild für *Sacre* erschien wie die Nachbildung einer heidnisch–russischen Landschaft aus seinen Bildern. Den ersten Schritt zu größerer Modernität der Dekorationen taten Natalia Gontscharowa und Michail Larionow, zwei Maler der Moskauer Avantgarde, deren Bildwelten, Folklore und primitiver Malerei entstammten, in ihren Augen Bezug zum Kubismus und Fauvismus hatten. Ihre Arbeiten erschienen zum ersten Mal auf der Ballettbühne in dem Opernballett *Le Coq d'or* (Fokine/Rimsky-Korsakow/Gontscharowa, 1914) und *Le Soleil de nuit* Massine/Rimsky-Korsakow/Larionow, 1915).

Die zweite Periode der Ballets Russes begann erfolgreich mit der Pariser Produktion von *Parade* (18. Mai 1917). Als *realistisches Ballett* bezeichnet, mit einem Thema von Jean Cocteau, der Musik von Erik Satie, dem Bühnenbild und den Kostümen von Pablo Picasso und in der Choreographie von Léonide Massine, versuchte man hier, Elemente des Kubismus, wie parallelen Ablauf der Bilder, Collage und Zerstückelung der Form, in Bewegung zu übertragen. Früher im gleichen Jahr hatte Diaghilew bereits in Rom in einem Gemeinschaftsprogramm mit Strawinskys *Feux d'artifice* ein futuristisches Multi-Media-Stück ohne Tanz

55

herausgebracht, das von Giacomo Balla ausgestattet wurde, und hatte einen anderen Futuristen, Fortunato Depero, beauftragt, das Bühnenbild für Strawinskys *Le Chant du rossignol* zu entwerfen, daß jedoch nie benutzt wurde (statt dessen schuf Henri Matisse schließlich das Dekor).

Von da an wählte Diaghilew seine Bühnenbildner meistens aus der Pariser Schule und anderen Avantgarde-Strömungen. Picasso entwarf weitere Bühnenausstattungen, vor allem für *Der Dreispitz* (Massine/de Falla, 1919) und *Pulcinella* (Massine/Strawinsky, 1920). Robert und Sonja Delaunay entwarfen ein neues Dekor für *Cléopâtre* (1918), André Derain für *La Boutique fantasque* (Massine/Rossini–Respighi, 1919). Nach der aufwendigen Wiederaufnahme von *Dornröschen* 1921 in London, ausgestattet von Bakst, arbeiteten als einzige Bühnenbildner der Anfangszeit der Ballets Russes auch weiterhin Gontscharowa und Larionow für die Kompanie. Darüber hinaus beauftragte Diaghilew Maler wie Juan Gris, Marie Laurençin, Georges Braque, Maurice Utrillo, Joan Miró, Max Ernst, Giorgio de Chirico und Georges Rouault, für die das Ballett-Bühnenbild ein Weg war, die Bildwelt ihrer Gemälde in einem großflächigeren Maßstab realisieren zu können. In den meisten Fällen wurden die Kulissen traditionell auf Leinwand gemalt (die Skizzen der Künstler wurden von Kulissenmalern wie Prinz Scherwadschidze und Vladimir Polunin übertragen.

Andere Ballette führten die Experimente weiter bis hin zu einer wirklichen Umwandlung des Bühnenraumes. So wurde etwa *La Chatte* (Balanchine/Sauguet, 1927) mit Konstruktionen von Naum Gabo und Antoine Pevsner unter Verwendung neuer Materialien wie Plastik und Wachstuch ausgestattet; *Le Pas d'acier* (Massine/Prokofiew, 1927) war ein „bolschewistisches" Ballett, das in einer Fabrik spielt, mit Dekorationen, die dem Westen den kinetischen, konstruktivistischen Stil präsentierten, der damals in den sowjetischen Theatern, wie dem von Wsewolod Meyerhold in Moskau, gängig war, und sogar für Neuproduktionen vorrevolutionärer Opern und Ballette gestattet wurde. Eine noch erfindungsreichere Neuerung boten die Dekorationen für *Ode* (Massine/N. Nabokow, 1928) von Pawel Tschelitschew, die Lichtprojektionen und einen Film einschlossen, der in Zusammenarbeit mit Pierre Charbonneau entstanden war. Es war sogar ursprünglich beabsichtigt Neonlicht zu gebrauchen, doch erwies sich dies als nicht durchführbar.

Diaghilews Rivalen und Nachfolger führten erweitert seine Praxis fort, Bühnenbild und Kostüme bei berühmten Malern in Auftrag zu geben. Die Ballets Suédois unter der Leitung von Rolf de Maré existierten nur fünf

LE SACRE DU
PRINTEMPS
Ch: Vaslav Nijinsky,
Ballets Russes
Kostüme von/costumes by
Nicolas Roerich,
Foto: Ballets Russes

Jahre, von 1920 bis 1925, mit einem Repertoire von fast ausschließlich neuen Balletten, von denen einige sogar die Diaghilews in ihrem Avantgardismus übertrafen. Ihr schwächster Punkt waren sicherlich die Choreographien von Jean Börlin, die von den Dekorationen der Maler in den Schatten gestellt wurden – von Malern wie Pierre Bonnard (eine Neufassung von *Jeux*), Fernand Léger (*La Création du monde,* inspiriert von afrikanischen Skulpturen und *Skating Rink*), Gerald Murphy (dessen Prospekt für *Within the Quota* zu Musik von Cole Porter aus einer gigantischen Vergrößerung der Titelseite einer Boulevardzeitung mit dem Titel „Unbekannter Bankier kauft Atlantik" bestand) und Francis Picabia (der das Dada-Stück *Relâche* zu Musik von Erik Satie und einem filmischen Zwischenakt von René Clair konzipierte und das Dekor entwarf). Nach *Relâche* löste sich die Kompanie auf, die die Bilderstürmerei (wie es damals schien) bis zum Äußersten getrieben hatte. 1924 brachte Comte Etienne de Beaumont seine Reihe von *Soirées de Paris* heraus, die Arbeiten von Massine einschloß, der sich von Diaghilew getrennt hatte. Das experimentellste Werk dieser Reihe, *Mercure,* das Diaghilew später übernahm, bestand aus einer Abfolge von *Poses plastiques* zur Musik Saties und dreidimensionalen Kulissen Picassos, die die tänzerische Bewegung auf ein Minimum reduzierten. Auch nach Diaghilews Tod 1929 und der sich daraus ergebenden Auflösung seiner Kompanie blieb sein Einfluß bestehen und wurde durch seine Mitarbeiter weiter verbreitet. Den größten Teil des Repertoires übernahmen die Ballets Russes-Kompanien, die nacheinander von Colonel de Basil, René Blum und Serge Denham geleitet wurden und für die Michail Fokine, Léonide Massine, Bronislawa Nijinska und George Balanchine auch weiter Ballette kreierten. Balanchine und Boris Kochno, der persönliche Sekretär Diaghilews in seinen letzten Jahren, gründeten später Les Ballets 1933, eine neue Kompanie, so up to date, wie es der Name andeutet. Serge Lifar wurde Ballettdirektor der Pariser Oper. Sie alle führten Diaghilews Praxis fort, die Bühnenbilder von Kunstmalern arbeiten zu lassen, vielfach von denjenigen, die auch für Diaghilew tätig waren. So wählte Massine Joan Miró, dessen Bühnenbild für *Jeux d'enfants* (1932) aus beweglichen, abstrakten Formen bestand (inklusive eines auf und ab springenden Balls), André Masson für *Les Présages,* dem ersten seiner „sinfonischen" Ballette (zu Tschaikowskys Fünfter) und Raoul Dufy für *Beach* (beide 1933), während Balanchine Derain für *La Concurrence* nahm, Benois für *Le Bourgeois gentilhomme* und *Cotillon,* dem dritten der Ballette, die er 1932 für das Ballet Russe de Monte Carlo schuf.

Außerdem zog er Christian Bérard hinzu, einen unbedeutenderen Maler, jedoch ein großer Bühnenbildner dank seines außergewöhnlichen Instinkts, die poetische Essenz eines Balletts mit einfachsten Mitteln auszudrücken. Bérard entwarf später zwei weitere „sinfonische" Ballette für Massine, *Symphonie fantastique* von Hector Berlioz (1936) und die *Siebte Sinfonie* von Ludwig van Beethoven (1938). *Labyrinth* (zu Schuberts *Neunter*) wurde von Salvador Dali 1941 ausgestattet.

Auf Einladung von Lincoln Kirstein ging Balanchine 1934 in die USA und nahm die Ausstattungen der inzwischen aufgelösten Ballets 1933 von Bérard, Derain und Tschelitschew mit (aber anscheinend nicht Caspar Nehers Bühnenbild für *Die Sieben Todsünden der Kleinbürger,* ein Ballett mit Gesang von Bertolt Brecht und Kurt Weill). In New York gründeten Balanchine und Kirstein die School of American Ballet und die (mit dieser verbundenen) verschiedenen Kompanien American Ballet, Ballet Caravan, Ballet Society und das heutige New York City Ballet. Wohl keine zeitgenössische Kompanie außerhalb der Sowjetunion hat einen so geringen Beitrag für Ballettausstattung geleistet wie das New York City Ballet, aber in den früheren Jahren versuchte Kirstein es Diaghilew gleichzutun, indem er junge amerikanische Maler als Bühnenbildner heranzog. Pawel Tschelitschew, der zu dieser Zeit in den USA lebte, entwarf mehrere Produktionen von Balanchine; besonders die berühmte Fassung von Christoph Willibald von Glucks *Orfeo* (an der Metropolitan Opera 1936) mit seinen phantastischen Bildwelten, wie auch Eugene Berman (dessen erste Ballettarbeit Frederick Ashtons *Devil's Holiday* 1939 für das Ballet Russe de Monte Carlo war). Die Ballet Society, eine Abonnementsgesellschaft, die sich der Produktion neuer Ballette widmete, brachte in ihrem ersten Programm *The Four Temperaments* (1946) von Balanchine/Hindemith mit Bühnenbildern und Kostümen von Kurt Seligmann heraus, einem Künstler, der sich mit okkulten Themen befaßte. Kostüme, die die Bewegung fast völlig verdeckten, wurden später durch schwarze, ärmellose Trikots für die Mädchen und weiße T-Shirts für die Männer ersetzt – beinahe eine Uniform in den Balletten Balanchines. Die Ballet Society zeigte auch zwei Arbeiten des japanisch-amerikanischen Malers Isamu Noguchi, der seit Mitte der 30er Jahre mit Martha Graham zusammenarbeitete: *The Seasons* (Cunningham/Cage, 1947) und *Orpheus* (Balanchine/Strawinsky, 1948).

In England wurde die Lücke, die durch die Auflösung von Diaghilews Ballets Russes entstand, vorübergehend von der Camargo Society geschlossen, deren Programm

zum Teil neue Ballette enthielt. Maler wie Augustus John, Vanessa Bell, Duncan Grant, John Armstrong und Edward Burra wurden für die Bühnenbilder herangezogen (John war nicht in der Lage, den Auftrag für die Ausstattung von Ashtons *Pomona* auszuführen, so daß ein weiterer Bloomsbury-Maler, John Banting, die Arbeit übernahm).

Die Camargo Society führte auch Diaghilews Brauch weiter, besondere Vorhänge anfertigen zu lassen, die bei Orchesterwerken zwischen den einzelnen Balletten gezeigt wurden. Die Gesellschaft wurde aufgelöst, als sich das Sadler's Wells Ballet fest etabliert hatte; diese Kompanie war im ganzen nicht so unternehmungsfreudig bei der Wahl ihrer Bühnenbilder, obwohl die Ausstattung des Plakatmalers E. McKnight Kauffer für *Checkmate* (de Valois/Bliss, 1937) hervorstach, wie auch die von Rex Whistler nach William Hogarth für de Valois' *The Rake's Progress* (1935) und für Ashtons *The Wise Virgins* (1940), letztere eine exquisite Barock-Vision. Während des Zweiten Weltkrieges entwarf Graham Sutherland Innenlandschaften als Hintergrundvorhang für Ashtons psychologisches Ballett *The Wanderer* (Schubert, 1941); und John Pipers topographischer Stil wurde auf die Bühnenbilder für Ashtons *The Quest* nach Edmund Spensers *The Faerie Queene* zu Musik von William Walton (1943) übertragen. Ashtons fruchtbarste Zusammenarbeit war die mit Sophie Fedorowitsch, einer engen Freundin, deren Beitrag zu seinen Balletten sich nicht allein im Bühnenbild erschöpfte, so schön dieses auch wirkte, wie zum Beispiel für *Horoscope* (Lambert, 1938), *Dante Sonata* (Liszt, 1940) und *Symphonic Variations* (Franck, 1946).

Mehrere Avantgarde-Strömungen des 20. Jahrhunderts dehnten ihre Aktivitäten auf das Theater aus, das eine erweiterte Anwendung ihrer Ideen ermöglicht – in szenischen Entwürfen, in der Theaterarchitektur, oder sogar durch Eigenauftritte, wie etwa die Konstruktivisten in Rußland unmittelbar vor und nach der Revolution (etwa Kasimir Malewitsch, El Lissitzky, Vladimir Tatlin, Alexandra Exter und Ljubow Popowa), das Bauhaus im Deutschland der 20er Jahre (vor allem Oskar Schlemmer, in dessen *Triadischem Ballett* es um die Umgestaltung der menschlichen Form ging), die Dadaisten in Frankreich, der Schweiz und Deutschland (Tristan Tzara, Francis Picabia, Robert und Sonja Delaunay, Hans Arp, Kurt Schwitters waren alle an den verschiedenen Dada-Aufführungen beteiligt). Diese können hier nicht im Detail beschrieben werden, aber sie sind eindeutig Vorläufer ähnlicher theatralischer Erscheinungen (Happenings und anderen Formen der Performance Art), die von amerikanischen Malern unserer Zeit erdacht wurden. Einige von ihnen befaßten sich durch die Zusammenarbeit mit Merce Cunningham unmittelbar mit dem Tanz.

Merce Cunningham und John Cage, sein musikalischer Mitarbeiter seit den ersten unabhängigen Choreographien in den frühen 40er Jahren bis in die heutige Zeit, kamen zu einer neuen Beziehung zwischen Tanz und Musik, in der diese beiden Künste zwar unabhängig voneinander, aber gleichzeitig nebeneinander bestehen. Cage begann seine Kompositionen auf Zufallsprozesse zu gründen, die Cunningham für seine eigenen choreographischen Ziele übernahm. Unter diesen Umständen war eine konventionelle Zusammenarbeit sichtlich unmöglich und der Gedanke der Unabhängigkeit übertrug sich auch auf seine künstlerischen Mitarbeiter. Cunningham gewöhnte sich an, seinen Mitarbeitern nur minimale Erläuterungen seiner Ideen für ein neues Tanzstück zu geben, dem Komponisten etwa nur die vorgesehene Dauer des Stücks und dem Bühnenbildner die räumlichen Begrenzungen. Choreographie, Musik und Dekorationen entstehen dann separat und werden erst in einer späten Phase der Probenarbeit zusammengebracht, oder sogar erst bei der Aufführung.

Von 1954 bis 1964 war Robert Rauschenberg der ständige Bühnenbildner der Merce Cunningham Dance Company (gegründet 1952). Er entwarf 1954 das Bühnenbild für *Minutiae* (Musik von John Cage, Kostüme von Remy Charlip), ein frei stehendes, dreidimensionales Objekt, durch das hindurch, unter dem und um das herum sich die Tänzer bewegen konnten. Gelegentlich gab Cunningham einen etwas genaueren Umriß seiner Ideen, wie zum Beispiel in *Antic Meet* (Cage, 1958), das er in einem Brief an den Künstler als „eine Reihe sich überlappender Varieté-Szenen" beschrieb, ihm dabei aber die Freiheit ließ, diesen Vorschlag frei zu interpretieren. Im gleichen Brief schrieb Cunningham über ein anderes Ballett das er plante, *Summerspace* (Musik von Morton Feldman), es sei „wie der Blick auf eine riesige Landschaft, und man könne die Handlung nur in einem bestimmten Ausschnitt davon sehen". Rauschenbergs Umsetzung dieses Einfalls war sein berühmter, abstrakt-pointillistischer Hintergrundprospekt, der theoretisch über die Grenzen des Bühnenraums hinaus in die Unendlichkeit hätte ausgedehnt werden können, mit Kostümen, die ähnlich bemalt waren und als „Tarnung" dienten, wenn die Tänzer ruhig verharrten.

Rauschenbergs Entwürfe waren fast nie aufdringlich. Sein Prinzip war, den Tänzern soviel Bewegungsfreiheit wie möglich zu gewähren. Seine Kostüme bestanden fast immer in Varianten einfacher Trikots, und er plazierte keine Hindernisse im Bühnenbereich. Dennoch wirkte das Bild der Bühne als Ganzes wie ein Gemälde Rauschenbergs, besonders in *Story* (1963), wo das Dekor bei jeder Vorstellung aus Gegenständen bestand, die er im Theater zusammensuchte. In einer Reihe von vier Vorstellungen in London 1964 bestand die „Dekoration" einfach darin, daß Rauschenberg auf der Bühne ein Bild malte. Am Ende der letzten Vorstellung war auch das Bild fertig, das heute in der Art Gallery von Toronto, Kanada hängt. Rauschenberg verließ die Kompanie 1964, kehrte aber 1977 zurück, um wieder mit Cunningham und Cage in *Travelogue* zusammenzuarbeiten, dessen dekorative Elemente das spiegelten, womit er sich gerade auseinandersetzte, etwa die segelartigen Fahnencollagen, die seiner kürzlich entstandenen Serie *Jammers* ähneln.

Rauschenbergs Freund und Kollege Jasper Johns, seit 1967 künstlerischer Berater der Kompanie, wurde mit der Aufgabe betraut, Maler für Ausstattungen auszuwählen, gelegentlich selbst das Dekor zu übernehmen. In dieser Zeit waren die Bühnenbilder viel komplizierter, drangen oft in den eigentlichen Bühnenraum ein. Frank Stellas Entwurf für *Scramble* (1967) formte sich aus einer Anzahl Leinenstreifen verschiedener Länge in den Grundfarben, die an beweglichen Rahmen von unterschiedlicher Höhe befestigt waren, so daß die Tänzer sie während des Tanzes verschieben und ihre Gestalt verändern konnten. Andy Warhols Dekor für *RainForest* (1968) war eine Adaption seiner als Raumkunst für eine Galerie geschaffenen *Silver Clouds,* eine Anzahl heliumgefüllter Silberkissen, manche frei schwebend, manche am Boden verankert, aber dennoch beweglich. Für *Canfield* (1969) entwarf Robert Morris einen vertikalen Balken, der sich vorn am Bühnenrand hin und her bewegte und Licht auf den Hintergrundvorhang warf. Bruce Naumanns Ausstattung für *Tread* (1970), eine Reihe schwerer, laufender Industrieventilatoren, stand ebenfalls zwischen den Tänzern und dem Publikum.

Marcel Duchamp, eine Art Schutzpatron der Cunningham Company, arbeitete indirekt an *Walkaround Time* mit (1968), als Johns sein (Duchamps) *Large Glass* (im Philadelphia Museum) veränderte, indem er die Bilder im Siebdruckverfahren auf aufblasbare Plastikteile übertrug, die am Ende des Tanzes in einer dem Original ähnelnden Form arrangiert wurden (Duchamps einzige Auflage). Für *Second Hand* kleidete Johns die zehn Tänzer in Kostüme, die ein Spektrum bildeten, als sie sich am Ende in einer Reihe dem Schlußapplaus stellten; darüber hinaus gab es keine weiteren Dekorationen. Das abendfüllende Werk *Un Jour ou deux* wurde 1973 für das Herbstfestival der Pariser Oper bei Cunningham, Cage und Johns in Auftrag gegeben. Johns bezog den ganzen Raum der riesigen Opernbühne ein und teilte ihn nur durch einen grauen Gazevorhang, hinter dem das Licht die Tiefe der Bühne schattenhaft sichtbar werden ließ. Johns' Assistent bei diesem Ballett war der britische Maler Mark Lancaster, der daraufhin ständiger Bühnenbildner der Cunningham Company und 1980 Johns' Nachfolger als künstlerischer Berater wurde. Lancaster, wie auch Rauschenberg, schwört darauf, die Tänzer so einfach wie möglich zu kleiden. Er liebt, „wenn Dinge so aussehen, wie sie wirklich sind". In Squaregame (1976) legte er die Bühne bis auf die Brandmauern frei, behielt die Lichtbrücke in voller Sicht und markierte die Tanzfläche durch ein weißes, mit Streifen grünen Kunstrasens umrandetes Bodentuch. Sein „Dekor" für Tango (1978) bestand aus einem Fernsehapparat, auf dem irgendein Programm eingeschaltet war.

Obwohl, wie bereits erwähnt, die Zusammenarbeit mit Cunningham keine langen Beratungen erfordert, wie bei Diaghilew, geschieht es oft – zufällig oder absichtlich –, daß die verschiedenen Elemente sich zu einem atmosphärischen oder sogar dramatischen Gesamteindruck zusammenfinden, wie etwa bei RainForest oder Sounddance

(1975), zu der apokalyptischen Musik von David Tudor und dem Bühnenbild von Mark Lancaster, einer zeltartigen Struktur aus Gummilaken, aus denen die Tänzer nacheinander hervortreten und in denen sie am Ende wie eingesogen verschwinden. Bei Inlets (1977) konnte Cunningham sich seinen langgehegten Wunsch erfüllen, mit dem aus dem Nordwesten der USA stammenden Maler Morris Graves zusammenzuarbeiten, dem er und Cage 40 Jahre früher in Seattle begegnet waren. Graves' zauberisches Bühnenbild mit einer großen Silberscheibe, die langsam am Hintergrund vor einem Gazevorhang vorbeizieht, durch den man – undeutlich zunächst – den Ablauf der Handlung sieht, beschwört glaubhaft das Klima und den Charakter der Landschaft dieses Teils der USA herauf – ebenso wie Cages „Wassermusik". 1978 kehrte Johns zurück, um das Bühnenbild von Exchange zu kreieren, ein Werk von epischem Ausmaß, dessen düster graue Dekorationen und Kostüme durch rußige Farbflecke aufgehellt wurden, die gemeinsam mit David Tudors rauher Musik eine Stadtlandschaft heutiger Zeit suggerieren. In diesen und anderen Werken definierte Cunningham die Vorstellung eines integrierten Kunstwerks, wie Diaghilew es geschaffen hatte, in einer zeitgenössischen

Sprache neu. Zwar ist die Basis der Mitarbeit Gleichberechtigung, jedoch nach einem Prinzip, das Cunningham „eine Art Anarchie" nannte. Auch andere zeitgenössische Tänzer arbeiteten mit Malern zusammen; erwähnt seien die Stücke des verstorbenen James Waring mit einem Künstler wie George Brecht, von Paul Taylor mit William Katz oder von Lucinda Childs mit Sol LeWitt. Die besondere Qualität der so entstandenen Werke macht es um so bedauerlicher, daß im amerikanischen Ballett von heute diese Art künstlerischer Zusammenarbeit so selten zu finden ist, überwiegend aufgrund der Einschränkungen durch die Bühnengewerkschaften. Ironischerweise ist das amerikanische Ballett heute wieder an dem Punkt angelangt, wo es sich vor dem Auftreten Diaghilews befand. Die wenigen Gelegenheiten, bei denen ein Maler aufgefordert wird ein Dekor zu entwerfen – wie vor kurzem, als Joe Brainard einen lustigen Collage-Vorhang für Robert Joffreys Satie-Ballett Postcards schuf, oder als David Hockney das hinreißende Parade ausstattete, das (gemeinsam mit einer Neuversion des gleichnamigen Satie-Werks) im Februar 1981 an der Metropolitan Opera gezeigt wurde – machen nur allzu deutlich was einem entgeht.

David Vaughan

FROM DIAGHILEV TO CUNNINGHAM
CONTEMPORARY ARTISTS WORK WITH DANCE

During the 19th century, theatrical design, which had been the province of artists and architects during the Renaissance and the Baroque period, was increasingly relegated to the workshops of the scene painter, who executed interior and exterior scenes in meticulous detail on canvas cloths and flats. The contribution to the Romantic ballet of such a designer as Pierre Ciceri, who designed the scenery for both La Sylphide (1832) and Giselle (1841) should not be underestimated, but by the latter part of the century in both Paris and Russia ballets were frequently designed by committee, as it were – for instance, Coppélia (Paris, 1870) by Charles Cambon, Edouard Despléchin, and Antoine Lavastre, and The Sleeping Beauty (St. Petersburg, 1890) by Heinrich Levogt, Ivan Andreyev, Mikhail Bocharov, Konstantin Ivanov, and Matvey Shishkov. While some of these décors may have been pedantically authentic in period detail, and even possessed of a certain charm, they lacked the poetic atmosphere that might have been created by the imagination of an artist who collaborated on equal terms with the ballet's librettist, composer, and choreographer.

The revitalization of stage décor began in Russia at the end of the 19th century; particularly in the opera productions sponsored by

the Moscow manufacturer and patron of the arts, Sava Mamontov, which had scenery by such painters as Konstantin Korovin, Isaac Levitan, Valentin Serov, and Mikhail Vroubel. These distinguished productions had an effect on the quality of design at the Imperial Theaters in St. Petersburg and Moscow, where décors by some of these artists began to appear. Even more profoundly, they influenced Serge Diaghilev and the circle of painters associated with his review, Mir Iskustva (World of Art). In 1899 Diaghilev was attached to the Imperial Theaters to work on special projects, and submitted a plan for a revival of Léo Delibes's ballet Sylvia, to be designed by members of the group: Act I by Alexander Benois, Act II by Konstantin Korovin, Act III by Eugène Lanceray, with costumes by Léon Bakst and Valentin Serov – a committee of a very different caliber. The cancellation of this project led to Diaghilev's dismissal, but when he took his own ballet

company to Western Europe, beginning with the first Paris season in 1909, the repertory consisted for the most part of works made (or newly revised for the occasion) on the principle that a ballet should be an integrated spectacle in which choreography, music, and design would all illustrate an agreed concept.

The two painters who designed the scenery and costumes, and often provided the librettos, for most of the ballets in the early seasons of the Ballets Russes were Benois and Bakst. They were in fact largely responsible for defining the company's aesthetic: a ballet should be a Gesamtkunstwerk (Richard Wagner's term, though his ideal had never been fully realized in his lifetime precisely for the lack of an adequate designer).

This collaborative method produced such masterpieces as Petrushka (1911) – libretto by Alexander Benois and Igor Stravinsky, choreography by Mikhail Fokine, and décor by Benois, with its famous recreation of the St. Petersburg Shrovetide fair in the 1830s – and Le Carnaval (Fokine/Schumann, 1910), with Bakst's delicate evocation of the Biedermeier period. Bakst's setting of a Persian harem for Sheherazade (Fokine/Rimsky-Korsakov, 1910), with its barbaric colorscheme, had a tremendous influence on couture and interior decoration.

Although much of the work of this first period of the Ballets Russes was innovative in comparison with the ballet of the Paris Opera or the Maryinsky Theater in St. Petersburg, it was in many ways backward-looking in comparison with contemporary developments in painting and sculpture. By 1909 Cubism was established, but in the early Diaghilev ballets the emphasis was still on exoticism of time and place – the Orient, ancient Greece, pagan Russia – or on nostalgic evocations of the Baroque (*Le Pavillon d'Armide*) or of 19th century Romanticism (*Les Sylphides, Le Carnaval, Le Spectre de la rose*).

No one was more aware of this than Diaghilev himself, who soon tired of such ballets as *Sheherazade* and *Cléopâtre* (though commercial considerations obliged him to retain them in the repertory) and wanted to ally the Ballets Russes with the avant-garde in both painting and music. In music, he had the support of Igor Stravinsky, who had composed *The Firebird* and *Petrushka* for him and was eager to pursue experimental forms of composition. Mikhail Fokine, the company's first choreographer, was not in sympathy with such aspirations, and accordingly Diaghilev looked to Vaslav Nijinsky for the kind of choreographic innovations he sought. Nijinsky supplied them in *L'Après-midi d'un faune* (1912), *Jeux* (1913), and *Le Sacre du printemps* (*The Rite of Spring*) (1913). *Faune,* which caused a scandal at its first performance because of its subject matter, the sexual awakening of a primitive creature, also proposed a radically new relationship between dance and music (the steps are not invariably tied to the musical meter). *Jeux,* with a commissioned score by Claude Debussy, was similarly concerned with sexual mores, and for the first time in modern ballet the setting was contemporary. *Sacre* carried to further lengths the inversion of classical ballet technique introduced in *Faune* and also represented a move towards abstraction in the handling of its theme of prehistoric ritual. Its first performance on May 29, 1913 is of course a key event in contemporary musical history.

In terms of design, Nijinsky's ballets did not represent a departure from early Ballets Russes principle or practice. Bakst designed both *Faune* and *Jeux*, the first another of his idealized visions of ancient Greece, the second a moonlit garden that was almost Watteauesque. Nicolas Roerich's sets for *Sacre* were in the vein of recreating pagan Russian landscape as he explored in his paintings. The first step toward a greater modernism in design came with the advent of Natalia Goncharova and Mikhail Larionov, two avant-garde Moscow painters whose imagery, derived from Russian folk and primitive art, was related in

their eyes to Cubism and Fauvism, and first appeared on the ballet stage in the opera-ballet *Le Coq d'or* (Fokine/Rimsky-Korsakov/Goncharova, 1914) and *Le Soleil de nuit* (Massine/Rimsky-Korsakov/Larionov, 1915).

The second period of the Ballets Russes began effectively with the production of *Parade* in Paris (May 18, 1917) termed a *ballet réaliste*, with theme by Jean Cocteau, music by Erik Satie, décor and costumes by Pablo Picasso, and choreography by Léonide Massine that attempted to translate into movement such elements of Cubism as simultaneity of images, collage, and fragmentation. Earlier in the same year, Diaghilev had presented in Rome a Futurist "mixed media" spectacle, without dancing, designed by Giacomo Balla to accompany Stravinsky's *Feux d'artifice (Fireworks),* and had commissioned designs from another Futurist, Fortunato Depero, for Stravinsky's *Le Chant du rossignol* (*Song of the Nightingale*) that were never used – in the event, the ballet was designed by Henri Matisse. From then on, Diaghilev chose most of his designers from the School of Paris and other avant-garde art movements. Picasso designed further ballets, notably *Le Tricorne* (*The Three-Cornered Hat*) (Massine/de Falla, 1919) and *Pulcinella* (Massine/Stravinsky, 1920). Robert and Sonia Delaunay designed a new version of *Cléopâtre* in 1918, André Derain *La Boutique fantasque* (Massine/Rossini-Respighi, 1919). After the sumptuous London revival of *The Sleeping Beauty* in 1921, designed by Bakst, the only designers from the first period who continued to work for the Ballets Russes were Goncharova and Larionov. Otherwise, Diaghilev commissioned sets from easel painters like Juan Gris, Marie Laurençin, Georges Braque, Maurice Utrillo, Joan Miró, Max Ernst, Giorgio de Chirico, and Georges Rouault, for whom ballet décor was a means of treating the imagery of their paintings on a larger scale; in most cases, the sets were constructed of painted flats and cloths in the traditional way (the artists' sketches were realized by scenic artists like Prince Shervadshidze and Vladimir Polunin).

In other ballets, experiment was carried further, involving the actual modification of the stage space. Thus, *La Chatte* (Balanchine/Sauguet, 1927) was decorated with constructions by Naum Gabo and Antoine Pevsner that used new materials like clear plastic and oilcloth. *Le Pas d'acier* (Massine/Prokofiev, 1927) was a "Bolshevik" ballet set in a factory, with décor that brought to the West the kinetic, constructivist style then current in Soviet theaters such as Vsevolod Meyerhold's, in Moscow, and even permitted in state theaters for new productions of pre-revolutionary operas and ballets. Still

more innovative were the decorations for *Ode* (Massine/N. Nabokov, 1928), by Pavel Tchelitchev, which involved light projections and a film made in collaboration with Pierre Charbonneau – it was even intended originally to use neon lighting, but this proved impractical.

Diaghilev's competitors and successors continued and extended his practice of commissioning sets and costumes from distinguished painters. The Ballets Suédois, under the direction of Rolf de Maré, existed for only five years, from 1920 to '25, with a repertory consisting almost entirely of new ballets, some of which outdid Diaghilev in avant-gardism. Their choreography by Jean Börlin was certainly the weakest element, overshadowed by décors designed by such painters as Pierre Bonnard (a new version of *Jeux*), Fernand Léger (*La Création du monde*, inspired by African sculpture, and *Skating Rink*), Gerald Murphy (whose backcloth for *Within the Quota*, with music by Cole Porter, was an enormous blow-up of the front page of a tabloid newspaper, with the headline "Unknown Banker Buys Atlantic"), and Francis Picabia (who conceived and designed the Dadaist spectacle *Relâche*, with music by Erik Satie and a cinematographic entr'acte by René Clair). After *Relâche* the company folded, having pushed iconoclasm to what seemed then its furthest extreme. In 1924, the Comte Etienne de Beaumont presented his series of *Soirées de Paris,* including ballets by Massine, who had left Diaghilev. The most experimental of these, *Mercure,* was later taken over by Diaghilev – a series *of poses plastiques* with music by Satie and three-dimensional sets by Picasso that reduced the possibilities for dancing to a minimum.

After Diaghilev's death in 1929 and the consequent disbanding of his company, his influence persisted, spread by his surviving collaborators. Most of his repertory was taken over by the Ballets Russes companies directed at various times by Colonel Vassily de Basil, René Blum, and Serge Denham, for whom Mikhail Fokine, Léonide Massine, Bronislava Nijinska, and George Balanchine also made new ballets. Balanchine and Boris Kochno, Diaghilev's personal secretary in the last years of his life, later joined Les Ballets 1933, a new company as up-to-date as its name suggests. Serge Lifar became the ballet director of the Paris Opera. All of these continued the Diaghilev practice of commissioning décors from easel painters, in many cases the same ones who had worked for Diaghilev. Thus, Massine used Joan Miró for *Jeux d'enfants* (1932), for which the décor consisted of mobile abstract shapes (including a ball that bounced up and down), and turned to André Masson for *Les Présages,* the first of his "symphonic" ballets (to Tchaikovsky's *Fifth*) and to Raoul Dufy for *Beach* (both 1933), while Balanchine used Derain for *La Concurrence,* Benois for *Le Bourgeois gentilhomme,* and for *Cotillon,* the third of the ballets he made for the Ballet Russe de Monte Carlo in 1932, brought in Christian Bérard, a minor painter but a great stage designer with an extraordinary instinct for expressing the poetic essence of a ballet by the simplest means. Bérard later designed two of Massine's further "symphonic" ballets, Hector Berlioz's *Symphonie fantastique* (1936) and Ludwig van Beethoven's *Seventh Symphony* (1938) *Labyrinth* (to Schubert's *Ninth*) was designed by Salvador Dali (1941).

In 1934 Balanchine went to the United States at the invitation of Lincoln Kirstein, taking with him décors from the now defunct Ballets 1933 by Bérard, Derain, and Tchelitchev (but not, apparently, Caspar Neher's set for *Les Sept péchés capitaux* (*The Seven Deadly Sins*), a ballet-cantata by Bertolt Brecht and Kurt Weill. In New York, Balanchine and Kirstein founded the School of American Ballet and the various performing companies associated with it – the American Ballet, the Ballet Caravan, Ballet Society, and the New York City Ballet of today. Probably no contemporary company outside the Soviet Union has such an undistinguished record in design as the New York City Ballet, but in the earlier years Kirstein attempted to emulate the Diaghilev method and recruited young American painters as designers. Pavel Tchelitchev, by then resident in the United States, designed several productions for Balanchine, notably the famous version of Christoph Willibald von Gluck's *Orfeo* (at the Metropolitan Opera in 1936) with its fantastic imagery, as did Eugene Berman (whose first work for ballet was Frederick Ashton's *Devil's Holiday* for Ballet Russe de Monte Carlo, 1939). Ballet Society, a subscription organization devoted to the production of new ballets, included in its first program the Balanchine/Hindemith *The Four Temperaments* (1946), with décor and costumes by Kurt Seligmann, an artist preoccupied with occult subject matter, that almost completely obscured the movement; later they were replaced by what has become almost a uniform for Balanchine ballets – black tights with leotards for the women, white T-shirts for the men. Ballet Society also presented two works designed by the Japanese/American sculptor Isamu Noguchi, who had been collaborating with Martha Graham since the middle 30s: *The Seasons* (Cunningham/Cage, 1947) and *Orpheus* (Balanchine/Stravinsky, 1948). In Britain, the gap left by the dissolution of the Diaghilev Ballets Russes was filled temporarily by the Camargo Society, with programs consisting partly of new ballets. Painters like Augustus John, Vanessa Bell, Duncan Grant, John Armstrong, and Edward Burra were brought in to design scenery (John was unable to fulfill the commission to design Ashton's *Pomona,* which was designed by John Banting, another Bloomsbury painter). The Camargo Society also followed Diaghilev's practice of commissioning special drop curtains to be displayed during the playing of orchestral works between ballets. The Society was dissolved once the Sadler's Wells Ballet had been firmly established; that company was on the whole less enterprising in its choice of designers, though the poster artist E. McKnight Kauffer's designs for *Checkmate* (de Valois/Bliss, 1937) were distinguished, as were Rex Whistler's for de Valois's *The Rake's Progress,* after William Hogarth (1935) and for Ashton's *The Wise Virgins* (1940), the latter an exquisite Baroque fantasy. During World War II, Graham Sutherland designed the interior landscapes that served as back-cloths for Ashton's psychological ballet *The Wanderer* (Schubert, 1941), and John Piper's topographical style was adapted for the sets of Ashton's *The Quest,* after Edmund Spenser's *The Faerie Queene,* with music by William Walton (1943). Ashton's most fruitful collaboration was with Sophie Fedorovich, a close personal friend who contributed far more to his ballets than just her designs, beautiful as these were, for such ballets as *Horoscope* (Lambert, 1938), *Dante Sonata* (Liszt, 1940), and *Symphonic Variations* (Franck, 1946).

Various avant-garde movements in 20th century art have extended their activities into the theater, where an enlarged application of their ideas was possible, through the design of scenery or theater architecture, or even through actual performance – the Constructivists in Russia immediately before and after the Revolution (including Kasimir Malevich, El Lissitzky, Vladimir Tatlin, Alexandra Exter, and Liubov Popova), the *Bauhaus* group in Germany in the '20s (notably Oskar Schlemmer whose *Triadic Ballet* was concerned with the transfiguration of the human form), the Dadaists in France, Switzerland, and Germany (Tristan Tzara, Francis Picabia, Robert and Sonia Delaunay, Hans Arp, Kurt Schwitters were all involved in various kinds of Dada performances). These cannot be described in detail here, but they are clearly forerunners of similar theatrical manifestations (*Happenings,* and other forms of performance art) devised by contemporary American painters, some of whom have become directly involved with dance through collaboration with Merce Cunningham.

Merce Cunningham and John Cage, his musical collaborator from his first independent choreographies, in the early '40s, until the present time, arrived at a new relationship between dance and music, in which the two arts exist independently though simultaneously. Cage began composing with chance processes, which Cunningham adapted for his own choreographic purposes; in these circumstances, collaboration on orthodox lines was clearly impossible, and the notion of independence was extended to his artistic collaborators as well. It became Cunningham's habit to give his collaborators only minimal indications of his ideas for a new dance – the composer is told the planned duration, and the designer of any spatial limitations. Choreography, music and design are then created separately and brought together only at a late stage in rehearsals or even at the time of the performance.

From 1954 to '64, Robert Rauschenberg was resident designer of the Merce Cunningham Dance Company (formed in 1952). In 1954 he designed the set for *Minutiae* (music by John Cage, costumes by Remy Charlip), a free-standing, three-dimensional object around, through, and under which the dancers could move. Occasionally Cunningham would give a slightly more detailed outline of his ideas, as with *Antic Meet* (Cage, 1958), which he described in a letter to the artist as being "like a series of vaudeville scenes which overlap", leaving him free to interpret his suggestions as he wished. In the same letter Cunningham wrote of the other dance he was preparing, *Summerspace* (music by Morton Feldman), that it was "like looking at part of an enormous landscape and you can only see the action in this particular portion of it". Rauschenberg's interpretation of this idea was his famous abstract, pointillist backcloth, which could theoretically have been extended beyond the confines of the stage into infinity, with costumes similarly painted that would act like camouflage when the dancers were at rest.

Rauschenberg's designs were almost never self-assertive; his principle was to give the dancers as much freedom of movement as possible. Nearly all his costumes were variations on basic leotards and tights, and there were no obstacles in the performing area. Even so, the stage picture sometimes did look like a Rauschenberg painting, particularly in *Story* (1963), for which the décor was assembled at each performance from materials he found around the theater. At one series of four performances in London in 1964, the "décor" consisted of Rauschenberg actually making a painting on stage; when the last performance was finished, so

PARADE,
Ch: Léonide Massine,
Ballets Russes
Die Manager/The Managers,
Kostüme von/Costumes by
Pablo Picasso

was the painting, which now hangs in the Art Gallery of Toronto, Canada.

Rauschenberg left the company in 1964 but returned in 1977 to collaborate again with Cunningham and Cage on *Travelogue*, in which the decorative elements reflected his current preoccupations, as in the sail-like collage banners which resemble his recent series of works entitled *Jammers.*

In 1967 Rauschenberg's friend and colleague Jasper Johns became the company's artistic advisor, entrusted with the choosing of painters to design works as well as doing so himself on occasion. At this time the sets became much more elaborate and frequently invaded the actual stage space. Frank Stella's set for *Scramble* (1967) took the form of a number of canvas strips in primary colors, of various lengths, mounted on movable frames at various heights so that the dancers could move them around during the dance and alter their configuration. Andy Warhol's set for *RainForest* (1968) was an adaptation of his gallery installation piece *Silver Clouds*, a number of helium-filled silver pillows, some of them free-floating and others anchored yet still mobile. For *Canfield* (1969) Robert Morris designed a vertical beam that moved back and forth across the front of the stage, throwing light on to the back-cloth. Bruce Nauman's set for *Tread* (1970), a row of heavy industrial fans, all of them in operation, also stood between the dancers and the audience.

Marcel Duchamp, a kind of "patron saint" of the Cunningham Company, collaborated indirectly on *Walkaround Time* (1968), for which Johns adapted his *Large Glass* (in the Philadelphia Museum), silk-screening the images on to a number of plastic inflatables that were assembled into an approximation of the original at the dance's end (Duchamp's only stipulation). For *Second Hand* Johns dressed the ten dancers in costumes that formed a spectrum when they lined up across the stage for their final bows. There was no other décor. In 1973 the full-length work, *Un Jour ou deux*, was commissioned from Cunningham, Cage, and Johns by the Paris Autumn Festival for the ballet of the Paris Opera. Johns used the entire space of this enormous stage, dividing it by a grey scrim; when the lights went up behind this the shadowy depths of the stage were revealed.

Johns's assistant on this ballet was the British painter Mark Lancaster, who subsequently became resident designer of the Cunningham Company and 1980 succeeded Johns as artistic advisor. Lancaster, like Rauschenberg, believes in dressing up the dancers as little as possible – he likes things "to look the way they really are". In *Squaregame* (1976) he stripped the stage down to the bare walls, with lighting instruments in full view and the dancing area defined by a white floorcloth outlined with strips of green Astroturf. His "set" for *Tango* (1978) consisted of a television, tuned in to whatever program was playing.

Although, as has been noted, Cunningham's collaborations do not involve prolonged consultation as in the Diaghilev company, it often happens, accidentally or by design, that the various elements do contribute to a total atmospheric or even dramatic effect: *RainForest* or *Sounddance* (1975), with its apocalyptic score by David Tudor and Mark Lancaster's tent-like set made of rubber sheeting from which the dancers emerge one by one and into which they disappear at the end, as though sucked in.

For *Inlets* (1977) Cunningham was able to realize a long-held ambition to collaborate with Morris Graves, the painter from the Northwest whom he and Cage had met in Seattle 40 years before. Graves's mysterious set, featuring a large silver disk that slowly passes across the backdrop, behind a gauze front curtain through which the action is seen, dimly at first, palpably evokes the climate and geography of that part of America, as does Cage's aqueous score.

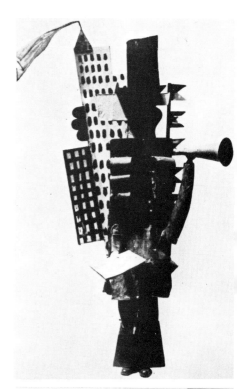

Johns returned in 1978 to design *Exchange*, a work on an epic scale, with set and costumes in somber greys, relieved by touches of sooty color, suggestive, in conjunction with David Tudor's abrasive score, of a contemporary urban landscape. In these and other works Cunningham has redefined in contemporary terms the notion of an integrated spectacle established by Diaghilev. The collaborators still cooperate on a basis of equality, but the principle is one which Cunningham has called "a kind of anarchy".

Other contemporary dancers have also collaborated with painters – one may mention the late James Waring's work with such artists as George Brecht, Paul Taylor's with William Katz, Lucinda Childs's with Sol LeWitt. The distinction of the works that have resulted makes it all the more regrettable that such collaborations seldom occur in American ballet today, chiefly because of theater union restrictions. Ironically, the situation in American ballet has reverted to that which existed before the advent of Diaghilev. The rare occasions when a painter is called in to design a décor – as happened recently when Joe Brainard designed a witty collage drop curtain for Robert Joffrey's Satie ballet *Postcards* or when David Hockney designed the ravishing spectacle presented in February 1981 at the Metropolitan Opera under the title *Parade* (including a new version of Satie's ballet of the same name) – show what one is missing.

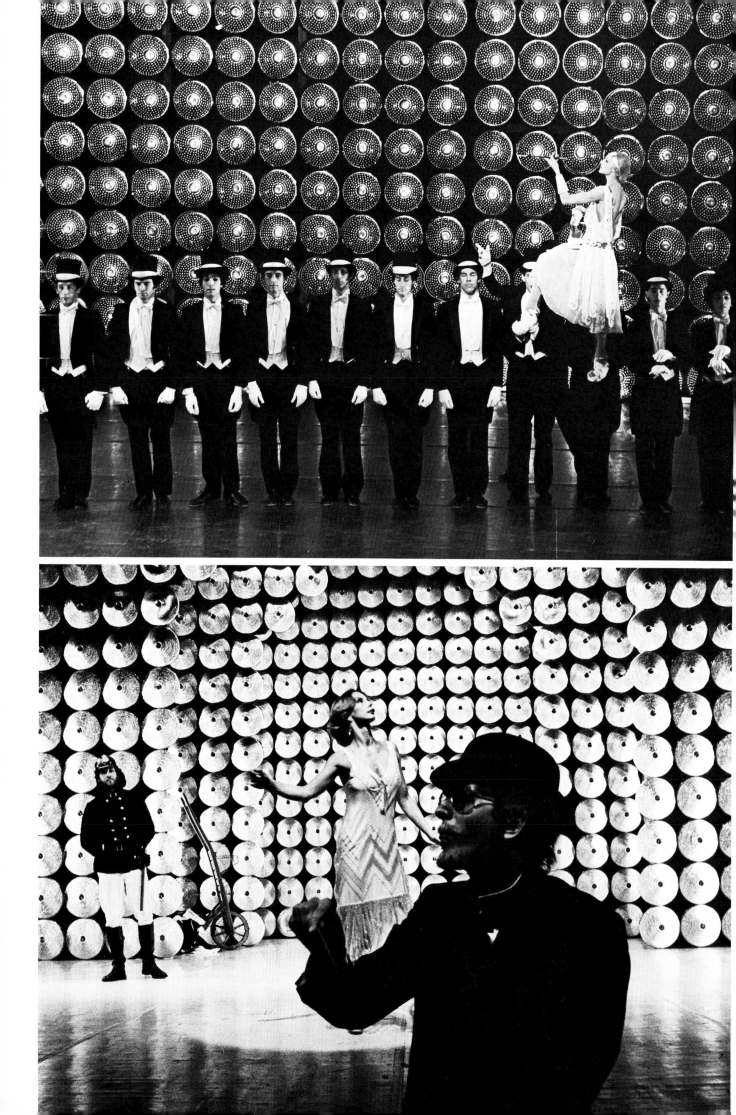

links/left
RELACHE,
Ch: Jean Börlin
Ausstattung von/décor by
Francis Picabia
oben/above
Joffrey Ballet
Neueinstudierung/
New Production,
Foto: Lois Greenfield
unten/below
Knete Kompanie,
Köln/Cologne
Neueinstudierung/
New Production,
Foto: Gert Weigelt

diese Seite/this page
rechts/right
oben/top
PRESENCE,
Ch: John Cranko,
Ausstattung von/décor by
Jürgen Schmidt-Oehm,
Marcia Haydée, Reid Anderson,
Stuttgarter Ballett/
Stuttgart Ballet,
Foto: Charles Tandy
Mitte/middle
DEUCE COUPE,
Ch: Twyla Tharp,
Bühnenbild, bei jeder
Vorstellung „live" kreiert/
décor, created "live"
at each performance
von Mitgliedern der/
by members of the
United Graffitti Artists,
Harlem,
Twyla Tharp Dance Company/
Joffrey Ballet,
Foto: Herbert Migdoll
unten/bottom
ASTARTE,
Ch: Robert Joffrey,
Ausstattung von/décor by
Thomas Skelton
mit Filmprojektionen von/
with projected films by
Nancy Robinson,
Christian Holder,
Joffrey Ballet,
Foto: Herbert Migdoll

oben/above
NOCTURNES,
Ch: Merce Cunningham,
Ausstattung von/décor by
Robert Rauschenberg,
Merce Cunningham and
Dance Company,
Foto: Cunningham Company
unten/below
WALKAROUND TIME,
Ch: Merce Cunningham,
Ausstattung von/décor by
Jasper Johns nach/after
Marcel Duchamp's „Large Glass",
Merce Cunningham and
Dance Company,
Foto: James Closty

TRAVELOGUE,
Ch: Merce Cunningham,
Ausstattung von/décor by
Robert Rauschenberg,
Merce Cunningham
(oben/above),
Merce Cunningham and
Dance Company,
Fotos: Lois Greenfield

DANCE,
Ch: Lucinda Childs,
visuelle Effekte von/
visual effects by
Sol LeWitt,
Lucinda Childs Dance Company,
Fotos: Nathaniel Tileston

oben/above
TIGER RAG,
Ch: Louis Falco,
Shelley Freydont, Juan Antonio,
Louis Falco Dance Company
unten/below
THREE EPITAPHS,
Ch: Paul Taylor,
Kostüme von/costumes by
Robert Rauschenberg,
Paul Taylor Dance Company,
Fotos: Jack Vartoogian

TRIADISCHES BALLETT/
TRIADIC BALLET
Ch: Oskar Schlemmer,
Rekonstruktion von/
Reconstruction by
Gerhard Bohner,
Colleen Scott, Ivan Liska
(unten/below),
Fotos: Gert Weigelt

Marcia B. Siegel

Der Zweite Weltkrieg setzte der fruchtbaren und populären Linie des modernen Tanzes, die sich über zwei Jahrzehnte in Deutschland und Osteuropa entwickelt hatte, ein Ende. Die antideutschen Gefühle während des Krieges, das Elend von Vertreibung und Zerstörung und der darauf folgende wirtschaftliche Aufschwung verwischten, was auch immer noch an Spuren aus der Tanzentwicklung dieser Zeit fortbestand. Heute erscheinen sie unter der Bezeichnung Deutscher Expressionismus, die von vornherein nicht sehr exakt war. Obwohl die Deutschen für den modernen Tanz den Begriff *Ausdruckstanz* verwandten, konnten sich nicht alle Fachleute darauf einigen. Einige nannten ihn freien Tanz, andere neuen künstlerischen Tanz. Als ich anfing, mich mit dem Tanz der 20er und 30er Jahre intensiv zu beschäftigen, entdeckte ich, daß zumindest zwei Betrachtungsweisen vorherrschten, die zwar durch ein gemeinsames kulturelles Umfeld verbunden, in anderer Hinsicht aber sehr verschieden waren.

Während Tänzer, die wir als Expressionisten bezeichnen (wie Mary Wigman, Kurt Jooss und Harald Kreutzberg) Tanzformen zu entwickeln suchten, die den Gefühlen der politischen und psychischen Kämpfe der Zeit Ausdruck verliehen, arbeiteten andere mehr theoretisch, indem sie die Funktion des menschlichen Körpers in seinem physischen Element, im Raum, zu definieren suchten. Sowohl Rudolf von Laban, wichtigster Lehrer von Mary Wigman und anderen, als auch Oskar Schlemmer, Leiter der Bauhaus-Bühne, versuchten die Eigenschaften der Bewegung zu verstehen und deren Bildwelt zu erweitern. Wenn sie sich überhaupt klassifizieren lassen, so waren sie Anti-Expressionisten, da sie an eine Bedeutung des Tanzes glaubten, die jenseits der persönlichen Ausstrahlung des einzelnen Tänzers oder in subjektiven, post-romantischen Ausflügen in die Seele der Gesellschaft liege.

Die naturwissenschaftlichen und technischen Entdeckungen des 19. Jahrhunderts hatten Europa aus seinen ländlichen, christlich-monarchistischen Verankerungen gerissen. Kraft der vorausgesetzten Beziehung zu einem allmächtigen Gott, glaubte sich der Mensch auf dem Gipfelpunkt der Entwicklung. Aber Darwin, Freud und Einstein nahmen dem Menschen das Vertrauen in seine unbeschränkte Herrschaft. Der Erste Weltkrieg bewies, dem Theaterdirektor Erwin Piscator zufolge, daß der „bürgerliche Individualismus endgültig begraben war. Die aus dem Krieg zurückkamen, hatten keinerlei Beziehung mehr zur Größe des Menschen, die als Symbol für die Ewigkeit der göttlichen Ordnung in den Salons der Vorkriegsgesellschaft gedient hatte." Während die Künstler zu Beginn des 20.

KÜNSTLER DES RAUMES

Jahrhunderts nach neuen Zusammenhängen suchten oder die Ordnung durch ihre futuristische Wut noch weiter zerstörten, ging die Kunst der 20er Jahre auf die Maschine ein. Es galt nicht mehr, sich an den rostigen Ankern der Vergangenheit festzuhalten, oder Ersatzgötter zu finden, sondern sich an eine industrialisierte Welt anzupassen.

Walter Gropius entschied sich, mit der Welt Frieden zu schließen, die nun für immer jenseits der Herrschaft des Menschen stand: „Die alte dualistische Weltanschauung, die das Ich im Widerspruch zum Universum sah, verliert schnell an Bedeutung. An ihrer Stelle kommt die Idee einer universellen Einheit auf, in der alle widerstrebenden Kräfte sich in einem Zustand absoluten Gleichgewichts befinden." Das Bauhaus, das Gropius 1919 gründete, versuchte die Technik mit der Kunst und dem Handwerk zu vereinen, neue Symbole für ein neues Bewußtsein zu schaffen und festzustellen, welche Aktivitäten in einer vorgefertigten Umgebung möglich seien. Die Bauhaus-Künstler, wie auch die Kubisten und Konstruktivisten, die an anderen Orten Europas wirkten, lehnten den Ästhetizismus als Prämisse ihrer Arbeit ab; dies bedeutete keine Weltflucht, auch wenn es ihrer bisherigen Auffassung von Bewegung, Geschwindigkeit, Zeit, Entfernung und Kontinuität widersprach. Sie wollten ihre Werke in den offensichtlich unausweichlichen Rahmen neuer Realitäten einbringen.

Wenn man sich die kubistischen Bilder Picassos, die zerrissenen Bühnenbilder der Russen oder die Mosaikmuster der Art Deco-Objekte ansieht, bemerkt man, wie sehr die bildenden Künstler mit diesen neuen Störungen der geltenden Ordnung rangen. Die Form ist zerbrochen, zersplittert und in Einzelteile zerstreut. Die Gewißheit der Horizontalen und ihrer vertikalen Koordinaten sind aus ihren Verankerungen gerissen, gekippt, aus dem Lot gebracht. Die repräsentative Gestalt vor einer Landschaft ist nicht mehr Gegenstand der modernen Malerei; der Künstler arbeitet mit starken Veränderungen von Linie, Komposition und Farbe, von keinem Zierat überladen. Die Farbharmonien Kandinskys, die schwebenden Formen Calders und Arps, die optischen Studien von Albers, die strengen, formalen Grafiken Mondrians, die entkörperten aber genauestens plazierten Formen Malewitschs und Moholy-Nagys, sie alle stellen ein Verlangen nach dem Wesentlichen und nach Wahrheiten dar, die tief genug sind um standzuhalten. Indem er die menschliche Figur vorsichtig in diese geometrischen Formen stellt, kann der Künstler möglicherweise aus dem verwirrenden Universum Sinn schöpfen.

Die Konstruktivisten, die am Theater arbeiteten, bauten komplizierte, nicht realitätsgetreue Räume, die Schauspieler und Tänzer zwangen, sich in ungewohnter Weise zu bewegen und die von den Ausführenden in neue Konfigurationen verwandelt werden konnten. Es war buchstäblich ein Theater der Struktur, wo das Publikum ermuntert wurde, den inneren Mechanismus der Bühne wie auch seine magische äußere Erscheinung zu sehen. Einige der konstruktivistischen Dekorationen wirkten derart überladen, als ob der Künstler sagen wollte, daß eine immer kompliziertere, immer vielfältigere oder zunehmend zersprengte Welt immer noch real sein könne und immer noch kräftig genug, um Aktivitäten zu tragen. Die Tatsache, daß diese Epoche die Verbreitung des Flugzeugs, des Autos, des Aufzugs, der Fotografie oder des Films brachte, die alle uns zwingen, die Eigenschaften des Raumes in neuer Weise wahrzunehmen, erklärt wahrscheinlich, zumindest teilweise, wieso der Schauspieler in einen so merkwürdig veränderten Bühnenraum gestellt wurde.

Pawel Tschelitschews *Ode* (1928) für Serge Diaghilews Ballets Russes, in der Choreographie von Léonide Massine, wandte verschiedene reale und illusionistische Kunstgriffe an, um ungewöhnliche räumliche Beziehungen herzustellen. Das Grunddekor bestand aus einem Netz von Streifen, die sich von einer zentralen, vertikalen Stütze strahlenförmig ausbreiteten, und einer Reihe von in falscher Perspektive angeordneten Puppen, denen sich dann die gleichgekleideten Tänzer zugesellten. An einer Stelle des Balletts wanden die Tänzer die Streifen und bewirkten, was der englische Kritiker A.V. Coton „eine geometrische Bewegungsfolge euklidischer Formen" nannte, „um welche die Figuren eine komplementäre Aufzeichnung von Raumbildern woben." Zu diesem Zeitpunkt interessierte Tschelitschew besonders das Licht, und in *Ode* gab es viele Effekte durch Schatten, Farben und Projektionen und sogar einen Tanz auf vollkommen dunkler Bühne (ein Nicht-Raum), in dem die Tänzer winzige Taschenlampen auf dem Kopf trugen. Ebenso war ein Film mit Vergrößerungen von Blumenbildern Teil dieser Produktion. Um die Klarheit dieser Dekorationen zu verstärken, konzentrierte sich Massine auf unkomplizierte, lineare Bewegungen der Tänzer. Der Kritiker Cyril Beaumont sah in *Ode* „eine Art bildliche Bloßlegung der funktionierenden Intelligenz".

Am anderen Ende dieses konzeptionellen

Weges befinden sich diejenigen, die den Theaterraum von allem, außer der Grundstruktur, befreien wollten, damit sich ein plastischer Fluß der einzelnen Tänzer und konzentrierten Gruppen herstellen ließ. Ohne eigenen stilistischen oder symbolischen Bezug zum Stück trennten die Kulissenelemente einfach den Raum ab, machten ihn sichtbarer als ein Bilderrahmen oder ein Fenster. Das bekannteste Bühnenbild dieser Art ist die Jessner-Treppe, nach dem Berliner Intendanten Leopold Jessner benannt, eine sich staffelnde Reihe von Ebenen, die irgendwo auf der Bühne plaziert und auf denen die Schauspieler in variablen Gruppen arrangiert werden konnten. Die Stufen eigneten sich vorzüglich für die Intentionen der deutschen Choreographen, die sie dazu benutzten, Höhen- und Tiefenstruktur in ihre Gruppenarrangements zu bringen. Eine frühe Anwendung der Stufen in den USA konnte man 1930 in Irene Lewisohns Produktion von Charles Martin Loefflers *Pagan Poem* mit Martha Graham und Charles Weidman in den Hauptrollen sehen. Ein paar Jahre später entwickelten Doris Humphrey und Weidman die Idee von ungeschmückten Schachteln und Plattformen zu szenischen Grundmodellen für alle Stücke der Kompanie.

Schließlich gab es, besonders am Bauhaus, ein Interesse am Theater als Raum für Publikum und Darstellende. Schlemmers Bauhaus-Bühne in Dessau war eine vielseitige Spielfläche, ein bescheidener praktischer Anfang dessen, was die Bauhaus-Künstler als totalen Raum dachten, innen und außen, in dem das Spiel mit Raum, Körper, Linie, Farbe, Licht und Ton in einer neuen Perspektive vom Publikum erfahren werden konnte. Schlemmer sah auch das Gebäude des Dessauer Bauhauses mit seinen glatten Glas- und Mauerflächen, seinen Flachdächern und vorspringenden Balkonen als potentielle Bühne, und nahm damit den Tanz im urbanen Environment vorweg, das in den USA 40 Jahre später auftauchte. Schlemmer war Maler und Bildhauer, aber schon vor seinem Wirken am Bauhaus ab 1920 hatte er eine frühe Fassung seines berühmtesten Werkes, das *Triadische Ballett* geschaffen. Schlemmer sah die Bühne wie eine Komposition auf Leinwand und den Tänzer darin als zeichnerisches Arrangement aus Formen, Farben, Linien und Volumen, den Gesetzen des Raumes und den inneren Gesetzen des menschlichen Körpers unterworfen. Er wollte durch diese greifbaren Rohmaterialien Abstraktionen schaffen, und er schlug vier Grundarten vor, in denen Naturgesetze zur Verwandlung des menschlichen Körpers eingesetzt werden konnten. In schachtelähnliche Konstruktionen gehüllt, wurde der menschliche Körper zur „wandelnden Architektur". Wenn die Grundkonturen und Einteilungen des Körpers betont wurden, stellte er sich eine Marionette vor. Die Möglichkeiten der Bewegung im Raum, die Fähigkeit des Körpers zu Drehung, Richtung und Schneiden des Raumes konnten einen „technischen Organismus" schaffen. Und schließlich konnte die Vorstellung einer „Entmaterialisierung" erreicht werden, die er in symbolischen Assoziationen von Körperformen sah, wie etwa die Form des Sterns in der ausgestreckten Hand oder des Kreuzes zwischen Schultern und Rückgrat.

Auch Kostüme, die diese Eigenschaften verstärkten, konnten den Menschen nicht gänzlich von den Gesetzen der Schwerkraft befreien, aber Schlemmer befürwortete jedes technische Mittel im Theater, das die Illusion einer solchen Freiheit erzeugen konnte, was die Nutzung mechanischer Figuren einschloß. In seinen Theaterexperimenten wandte er sowohl das Konzept der *Übermarionette* wie der *Kunstfigur* an. Er und die anderen Mitglieder des Bauhaus-Theaters verwirklichten ihre Theorien vor allem durch die Kostüme. Die echte Persönlichkeit des Darstellers verschwand hinter verformtem, verdrehtem, ausgestopftem und aufgetürmtem Material, das an den Körper angebracht war und dem Tänzer erlaubte, durch Bewegung abstrakte Formen und Effekte zu erzielen. Requisiten und Masken konnten die Größe und Reichweite des Körpers zusätzlich verstärken. Beleuchtung und Projektionen veränderten die Stimmung und die Umgebung selbst.

Mensch und Kunstfigur, ein bemerkenswerter deutscher Film aus dem Jahre 1968, verbindet neun rekonstruierte, kurze Schlemmer-Tänze mit einigen unaufdringlichen aber passenden filmischen Tricks, die seine Ideen, die irdische Raumerfahrung zu überschreiten, unterstützten. Wenn es hier auch wenig konventionellen Tanz gibt, so muß der Darsteller sich doch sehr bewußt sein, wie er sich im Raum bewegt und darstellt, auch in Beziehung zu den anderen Tänzern. Die Bildwelt besitzt einen beträchtlichen Spielraum, auch in diesen einfachen Stücken. Manche sind richtig satirisch. In *Gestentanz* spielen drei maskierte, wattierte Personen eine minimale Konversation, sie verändern die emotionalen Implikationen durch Kippen des Körpers oder Neigen des Kopfes oder das Ausstrecken oder Zurückziehen einer Hand. In *Formentanz* scheint die Absicht mehr im Abstrakten zu liegen, indem die Figuren verschiedene Requisiten (wie Stangen, eine große weiße Kugel und einen kleinen Metallball) in Stellungen bringen, die den Bildern eines anderen Lehrers und häufigen Mitarbeiters des Bauhaus-Theaters, Laszlo Moholy-Nagy, ähneln. In anderen Stücken scheint der Körper völlig zu verschwinden. Schwarz gekleidet, auf einem schwarzen Hintergrund bewegt der Tänzer eine Handvoll weißer Reifen gestaffelter Größe, um entkörperte Op-Art-Formen zu schaffen *(Reifen-Tanz),* oder lange Stangen, die an seinen Gliedern befestigt sind, um bewegte geometrische Muster zu gestalten *(Stocktanz,* den Schlemmer „Lied der Gelenke" nannte).

Wenn man Schlemmers Werk betrachtet, mit seinen Schlagzeugen, präpariertem Klavier und synthetischen Klängen, mit seinem unheimlichen doch konkreten Zusammenspiel von Formen und leerem Raum, kann man sich Phantasien hingeben oder sich einfach von Sinneswahrnehmungen unterhalten lassen. Ein Schüler der Bauhaus-Bühne, Alfredo Bortoluzzi, erinnerte sich Jahre später, es sei das Ziel gewesen, „Bewegung und Bild in eine feste, harmonische Beziehung zu bringen".

Rudolf von Laban, der andere große Raum-Theoretiker, dachte überhaupt nicht an Bilder, obwohl auch er mehr von der bildenden Kunst als vom Tanz her kam.

Laban arbeitete vom Inneren des Menschen her nach außen. Wenn der Raum ein uns umgebendes, unbegrenztes Etwas ist, das mit anderen Menschen und Objekten erfüllt ist, die durch Größe, Entfernung und Proportion mit uns in Beziehung stehen, dann verändert sich der Raum selbst so, wie wir uns in ihm bewegen. „Raum ist ein verborgener Teil der Bewegung und Bewegung ist ein sichtbarer Aspekt des Raums", schreibt Laban in der Einführung zu seinem Buch *The Language of Movement* über die Theorie des Raumes.

Ausgehend von der vertikalen Struktur des Körpers mit Vorder- und Rückseite, bestimmte Laban den Raum, der den Körper umgibt – eine ausdehnbare Hülle, Kinesphäre genannt – je nach den verschiedenen Ausrichtungsmöglichkeiten. Die reinen vertikalen, horizontalen und sagittalen Achsen entsprechen der Bewegung von oben nach unten, von Seite zu Seite und von vorne nach hinten. Die diagonalen Neigungen zwischen diesen reinen Dimensionen könnten zu einem Kubus schematisiert werden, indem die Endpunkte der ausgebreiteten Arme durch Geraden verbunden werden. Andere Richtungselemente könnten in der gleichen Weise entworfen und in andere gedachte geometrische Strukturen gebracht werden. Laban erarbeitete Bewegungsabläufe durch diese kristallinen Formen (Skalen, Kurven und Spiralen), die die Bewegung wie Ballettexercises formalisierten, die Bewegung aber stets an dem Raum außerhalb des Körpers orientierten, anstatt wie im Ballett die inneren Bezugspunkte der Körperachse zu berücksichtigen, so die Stellung der Glieder, des Kopfes. Ebenfalls interessierte Laban die Dynamik der Bewegung – die Quelle und die Dosierung des Energieflusses, der Bewegung erzeugt und individuelle Ausdrucksweise und Aktionsmuster hervorbringt. Er glaubte, daß gewisse dynamische Strömungen zu Raumströmungen in Beziehung stehen, so daß zum Beispiel das Vorangehen im Raum normalerweise mit den aggressiven Eigenschaften von Kraft und Geschwindigkeit assoziiert wird, während das Zurückweichen eine Affinität zu den nachgebenden Eigenschaften von Langsamkeit und der Ausbreitung von Energie besitzt. Selbst wenn man diese Theorie der Affinitäten nicht teilt, wird der Tänzer durch Labans Erklärungen des Bewegungsablaufes als eines Dialoges zwischen Körper und Raum fast zu expressivem Ausdruck gezwungen.

Laban sprach von räumlicher Spannung, die im Körper entsteht, wenn er sich aus der vertikalen Achse in die unsichere seitwärtige oder rückwärtige Diagonale bewegt, und er baute in seine Abläufe verschiedene Möglichkeiten ein, um die Spannungen zu vermindern oder zu erhöhen. Wenn Paare oder Gruppen zusammenwirkten, erhielt die räumliche Spannung eine kollektive Dynamik; sie konnte gesteigert werden, wenn viele Menschen sie gemeinsam spürten, oder es konnte ein kontrastierendes Element durch gegenläufige Bewegungsströmungen eingebracht werden. Ein weiteres dynamisches Element bringt der Rhythmus. Mit anderen Worten, Laban versuchte die gleichen theatralischen Effekte zu erreichen, wie es die Theaterleute immer getan haben, aber er ging fast ausschließlich von dem bewegten Körper als Quelle der Gefühle aus, und interessierte sich weniger für das, was das Publikum sehen würde.

Obwohl er auch für die Bühne choreographierte, setzte Laban seine Ideen am wirk-

samsten in seinen Bewegungschören ein. Diese bestanden aus einer Gruppe, oft Laien oder Kinder, die sich gemeinsam bewegten, um ein Thema zu entwickeln. Das Ziel war nicht, eine rein formale uniforme Technik oder Choreographie zu zeigen, sondern jeder Teilnehmer sollte den kollektiven Antrieb dadurch verstärken, daß er mit seinen eigenen Bewegungen das Motiv und den Grundgedanken ausdrückte.

Es scheint mir, als ob die Bewegungschöre aus einer nationalen Leidenschaft für körperliche Tätigkeit auf einer breiten sozialen Ebene entstanden mit Gymnastik, Sport, Volkstänzen oder Wandergruppen, die sich ebenfalls im Deutschland der 20er und 30er Jahre ausbreiteten. Die Nazis bemächtigten sich dieser Manie für ihre eigenen Zwecke, indem sie sogar den Tanz durch Einsetzung mit dem Regime sympathisierender Leiter politisierten. Es ist kaum zu verstehen, wie ein Humanist wie Laban den wachsenden Militarismus und die Unterdrückung ignorieren konnte, doch anscheinend war er sich bis kurz vor der Olympiade in Berlin 1936 des Propagandawertes der „Bewegungsbewegung" nicht bewußt.

Laban organisierte den gewaltigen Aufmarsch zur Eröffnung der Spiele 1936, bei dem 10.000 Jugendliche eine Massenverherrlichung deutscher Ideale, wie Mutterschaft, körperliche Gesundheit, Heldentum und Vaterlandsliebe demonstrierten. Vielleicht sah er es nur als den größten Bewegungschor aller Zeiten. Laban begriff die politische Absicht in letzter Minute und zog sich zurück, bevor der Aufzug stattfand, arbeitete aber weiter in Deutschland bis 1938 und ging dann nach England. Auch Schlemmer zögerte, seine Heimat zu verlassen. Seine Arbeit wurde als entartet erklärt, und er wurde 1933 vom Bauhaus entlassen, kurz bevor

die Nazis dieses Institut schlossen. Von da an arbeitete er fast in Vergessenheit geraten und starb 1943 in Baden-Baden.

Alle diese kreativen Aktivitäten schwemmte der Zweite Weltkrieg mit sich fort, und viele der Kunstwerke wurden entweder von den Nazis beschlagnahmt oder durch Kriegseinwirkung zerstört. Nach dem Wiederaufbau Deutschlands in den 50er Jahren, erhielt das Ballett einen neuen, aber konservativen Platz in den Opernhäusern. Die Neugier, der Idealismus und die Abenteuerlust, aber auch die Unzufriedenheit, die den Ausdruckstanz beflügelt hatten, schliefen ein. Es sah so aus, als ob die Deutschen an die Experimente ihrer eigenen Vergangenheit nicht einmal erinnert werden wollten.

Laban setzte seine Arbeit im Exil fort, befaßte sich mehr und mehr mit der Analyse der Arbeitsbewegung, und seine sehr aktiven Erben in England und den USA beschäftigen sich statt mit den Theatertheorien mit der Weiterführung seiner Theorien der Tanzerziehung und der Bewegungsanalyse. Paradoxerweise ist der wichtigste Erbe Schlemmers und Labans Alwin Nikolais. Von Mary Wigmans Schülerin Hanya Holm in Amerika ausgebildet, übernimmt er seine Betrachtungsweise der Bewegung von Laban, seine Theatermethoden aber von Schlemmer. Nikolais spricht oft von seiner Absicht, den Menschen als „Verwandten des Universums" zu zeigen, und sein Totaltheater mit seinen „entmenschlichten" Tänzern, die sich in die durch Lichtprojektionen, Requisiten und elektronischen Klängen entstandenen phantastischen Environments einfügen, sind die Fortführung der Reise in das Territorium, das Schlemmer entwarf, mit den technischen Hilfsmitteln eines Raumzeitalters, von dem selbst Schlemmer nicht zu träumen wagte.

Marcia B. Siegel

ARTISANS OF SPACE

World War II put an end to the fruitful and popular strain of modern dance that had grown up in Germany and Eastern Europe over two decades. The anti-German feeling that accompanied the war, and the pains of dispersion, destruction, and economic recovery that followed it, have blurred whatever traces remained of that period's dance discoveries. Now they all come under the label of German Expressionism, which was never very accurate in the first place. Although the Germans had a term, *Ausdruckstanz* (dance of expression), even its practitioners could not all agree on it. Some called it the free dance, some the new artistic dance. When I started studying the 1920s and '30s intensively, I realized that at least two approaches to dance prevailed, approaches related by their common cul-

tural environment but quite different in other respects.

While the dancers we think of as Expressionists – like Mary Wigman, Kurt Jooss, Harald Kreutzberg – were trying to devise dance forms to project the feelings arising out of the political and psychic struggles of the time, others were working more theoretically, trying to define how the human body works within its physical element, space. Both Rudolf von Laban, the chief teacher of Wigman and the others, and Oskar Schlemmer, head of the Theater of the Bauhaus, tried to understand the prop-

erties of movement and extend its imagery. They were, if anything, anti-expressionists, in that they thought dancing could have meaning beyond the power exerted over it by the individual dancer's personality or by subjective, post-romantic delvings into the soul of society.

The 19th century's discoveries in science and technology had torn Europe from its rural, Christian-monarchist moorings. By virtue of his presumed relationship to an all-powerful God, man had imagined himself at the top of the evolutionary heap. But Darwin and Freud and Einstein took away this confidence in man's ultimate control. World War I, according to theater director Erwin Piscator, proved that "bourgeois individualism was finally buried. … Those who returned no longer had any relationship to the greatness of man which had served as the symbol of the eternity of divine order in the parlors of pre-war society." While the artists of the early 20th century had been casting about for new connections or further disrupting order with their futuristic rages, by the 1920s, art was beginning to come to terms with the machine. The question no longer was how to hang on to the rusty anchorages of the past, or how to find substitute gods, but how to habituate oneself to an industrialized world.

Walter Gropius chose to make peace with this world now forever beyond man's domination: "The old dualistic world concept which envisaged the ego in opposition to the universe is rapidly losing ground. In its place is rising the idea of a universal unity in which all opposing forces exist in a state of absolute balance." The Bauhaus school, which Gropius founded in 1919, attempted to unify technology with the arts and crafts, to create new symbols for a new consciousness, and to see what activity was possible within a fabricated environment. The Bauhaus artists, like the Cubists and the Constructivists who were working elsewhere in Europe, rejected aestheticism as a premise; they did not want to flee this world even if it defied their previous perceptions of motion, velocity, time, distance, continuity. They wanted to incorporate their product into what was clearly an inescapable set of new realities.

If we look at the Cubist paintings of Picasso, at the exploded theater designs of the Russians, at the mosaic patterns of art deco objects, we see how visual artists were wrestling with these new dislocations of accepted order. Form is fractured, splintered, and blown into scattered fragments. The certitudes of the horizon line and its perpendicular coordinates have been shaken loose, tilted, sprung out of plumb. The representational figure against a landscape is no longer the subject of modern painting; the artist is working with manipulations of line, composition, and color, unencumbered by ornament. The color harmonies of Kandinsky, the floating shapes of Calder and Arp, the optical studies of Albers, the severe, formal graphics of Mondrian, the disembodied but meticulously placed forms of Malevich and Moholy-Nagy all represent a hunger for basics, for truths that are deep enough not to give way. By carefully placing the human figure within these geometries, the artist might make reason out of a confusing universe.

Working in the theater, the Constructivists made intricate, nonliteral environments that would force actors and dancers to move in unaccustomed ways, and that could be manipulated by the performers into new configurations. It was literally a theater of structure, where the audience was encouraged to see the inner mechanisms of the stage as well as its magical outer appearances. Some of the Constructivist designs actually look overbuilt, as if the artists were saying that a universe increasingly complicated, multiplied, or blasted apart could still be real, could still be substantial enough to support activity. The fact that this period saw the widespread use of aircraft, automobiles, elevators, photography and motion pictures, all of which cause us to perceive the properties of space in new ways, probably explains, at least in part, how the actor came to be placed in such strangely altered theatrical spaces.

Pavel Tchelitchev's *Ode,* produced in 1928 for Serge Diaghilev's Ballets Russes, with Léonide Massine as choreographer, employed several real and illusionary devices to create unusual spatial relationships. The basic set was a web of tapes radiating from a central vertical support, and a row of dolls constructed in false perspective which were later to be joined by live dancers dressed the same way. In one section of the ballet, dancers plied the tapes to make what the English critic A. V. Coton called "a geometric succession of moving, Euclidean forms about which the figures wove a complementary notation of space-images". At this period, Tchelitchev was especially interested in light, and *Ode* had many effects created by shadows, colors, projections, and even a dance on a blacked-out stage (a non-space) where the dancers wore tiny flashlights on their heads. Film was also a part of this production, including blown-up images of flowers. To enhance the clarity of these designs, Massine concentrated on uncluttered, linear movement for the dancers. To the critic Cyril Beaumont, *Ode* "suggested a kind of visual 'laying bare' of the intelligence at work".

At the other end of this conceptual track were those who tried to clear the theater space of everything except the basic architecture for a plastic flow of individuals and massed groups of performers. Having no stylistic or symbolic relationship to the play in themselves, these scenic elements simply offset the space, made it more visible, as a picture frame or a window does. The Berlin theater director Leopold Jessner's most notable of many such designs was the so-called Jessner Stairs, a graduated series of levels that could be placed anywhere on stage and on which the actors could be ranged in varied groupings. The stairs were well-suited to the intentions of German choreographers, who used them to add height and depth to their group designs. An early use of the stairs in the USA was seen in Irene Lewisohn's 1930 production of Charles Martin Loeffler's *Pagan Poem,* with Martha Graham and Charles Weidman in the leading roles. A few years later, Doris Humphrey and Weidman adopted the idea of unadorned boxes and platforms as the basic scenic modules for all their company's dances.

Finally, there was an interest, particularly at the Bauhaus, in the theater as a space for the audience as well as the performers. Schlemmer's Bauhaus Stage at Dessau was a flexible producing space, a modest, practical beginning to what the Bauhaus designers visualized as a total space – indoors and out – in which the play of space, body, line, point, color, light, and sound could be experienced in new perspectives by the audience. Schlemmer even saw the Dessau Bauhaus building, with its clean planes of masonry and glass, its flat roofs and projecting balconies, as a potential stage – anticipating the urban environmental dance that took place in the USA 40 years later.

Schlemmer had been trained as a painter and sculptor, but even before he began his association with the Bauhaus in 1920 he had produced an early version of his most famous work, the *Triadic Ballet.* Schlemmer viewed the stage as a composition on canvas, and the dancer within it as a draftsman-like arrangement of forms, colors, lines, and volumes, obedient to the laws of space as well as the internal laws of human functioning. He wanted to create abstraction from this tangible set of raw materials, and he suggested four basic ways in which natural laws could be applied to transforming the human body. Encased in boxlike constructions it could become "ambulant architecture". If the body's basic shapes and divisions were emphasized, he imagined a marionette. The possibilities for motion in space, the body's capacity for rotation, direction, and cutting through space, could produce a "technical organism". And images could be developed from the symbolic associations he saw in the body's form, such as the star shape of the spread hand or the cross of shoulders on spine, creating "dematerialization".

Even costumes that extended these properties could not completely free man from the laws of gravity, but Schlemmer advocated any technical means in the theater that would create the illusion of such freedom, including the use of mechanical figures. In his theater experiments he utilized both the concept of the *Übermarionette,* the mechanical doll, and of the *Kunstfigur,* the human figure used as art object.

He and the other theater workshop members at the Bauhaus put these theories into action first of all by the use of costume. The literal, personifying aspects of the performer were hidden under molded, twisted, padded and built-up materials that were fitted to the body so that the dancer, by moving, could create superhuman shapes and effects. Props and masks could further exaggerate the size and reach of the body's parts. Lighting and projections could change the mood and even the environment itself.

Mensch und Kunstfigur (Man and Mask), a remarkable film made in Germany in 1968, combines nine reconstructed, brief Schlemmer dances with some understated but apt cinematic devices that further his ideas of transcending mundane spatial experience. Although there is little conventional dancing here, the performer has to be acutely conscious of how he is surrounding, penetrating, and shaping himself in space and with relation to the other performers. The imagery has considerable range, even among these simple pieces. Some are directly satirical. In the *Gesture Dance,* three masked, padded personages enact minimal conversations, changing the emotional implications with variations in the tilt of the body or head, the extending or withdrawing of a hand. In *Form Dance,* the purpose seems more abstract, as the figures place various props – poles, a large white sphere, a small metal ball – into positions that resemble the paintings of another Bauhaus teacher and frequent collaborator at the theater workshop, Laszlo Moholy-Nagy. In other pieces, the body seems to disappear entirely. Clad in black against a black background, the dancer manipulates handfuls of white hoops in graduated sizes to create disembodied op art designs (*Hoop Dance*), or moves long poles attached to his limbs to make moving geometric designs (*Stick Dance,* which Schlemmer called "a song of the joints").

Looking at the Schlemmer work, with its percussion, prepared piano and synthesized sounds, its eerie yet concrete interplay of forms and voids, one can indulge in fantasy or simply in sensory entertainment. A student of the Bauhaus stage, Alfredo Bortoluzzi, remembered it years later as having had the aim of "bringing movement and picture into a firm harmonic relationship".

Rudolf von Laban, the other great theorist of space, did not think of pictures at all, even though he too had more of a background in the visual arts than in dance. Laban worked outward from inside the person. If space is a limitless something that surrounds us and that is filled with other people and objects related to us by their size, distance, and proportions, then space itself changes according to the way we move in it. "Space is a hidden feature of movement and movement is a visible aspect of space", Laban said in the introduction to his book on space theory, *The Language of Movement.*

Starting from the physical structure of the body as a vertical being with two sides, a front and a back, Laban defined the space around the body – an expandable envelope called the kinesphere – according to different sets of directional possibilities. The pure vertical, horizontal, and sagittal axes correspond to up-down, side to side, and forward-back motion. The diagonal inclinations between these pure dimensions could be schematized to form a cube, by connecting with straight lines the arms-reach terminus of each diagonal. Other directional systems could be plotted in the same way and formed into other imaginary geometric structures. Laban then worked out progressions of movement through these crystals – scales, swings, and spirals that formalize movement much as ballet exercises do, but that orient movement always to the space outside the dancer's body rather than retaining the ballet dancer's internal reference points of body axis, position of the limbs, placement of the head and so on.

Laban was also concerned with the dynamics of movement – the source and variation of the energy flow that activates movement, and that creates individual phrasing and patterns of action. He thought that certain dynamic tendencies were related to certain space tendencies – that, for example, advancing in space is more normally associated with the aggressive properties of force and speed, while retreating has an affinity with the indulgent qualities of slowness and spreading-out of energy. Even if one does not agree with his theory of affinities, Laban's clarification of the movement process as a dialogue between the body and space almost forces the dancer into an expressive mode.

Laban spoke of spatial tension existing within the body as it moves off its vertical axis and into the more precarious sideward or backward diagonals, and he built into his scales and progressions different forms for easing or heightening these tensions. When people worked together, in pairs or groups, the spatial tension took on a collective dynamic; it could be strengthened if many bodies felt it together, or an element of contrast could be introduced with opposing movement tendencies. Rhythm could add another dramatic element. In other words, Laban worked for the same kinds of theatrical effects as theater directors always had, but he worked almost entirely from the moving body as a source of feeling, and concerned himself less about what the audience would see.

Although he did choreograph for the stage, Laban used these ideas most effectively in his movement choirs. These were groups of people, often laypersons or children, who moved together to develop a common theme. The aim was not to show a formal, uniform technique or design, but for each participant to reinforce the collective drive by expressing the motive or spirit with his own movement. It seems to me the movement choirs grew out of a national passion for physical activity on a large social scale – gymnastics, sports, folk dancing and hiking groups also spread over Germany during the 1920s and '30s. The Nazis turned this craze to their own account, even politicizing dance groups with sympathetic leaders. It is hard to understand how a humanitarian like Laban could have ignored the growing militarism and repression, but apparently until just before the Berlin Olympics he was unaware of the propaganda value the "movement movement" could have for the Nazis. It was Laban who engineered the stupendous pageant that opened the 1936 Games, in which 10,000 youths created a mass celebration of teutonic ideals: motherhood, physical health, heroism, and love of the fatherland. Perhaps he merely saw it as the most fabulous movement choir of all. Realizing its political intent at the last minute, Laban withdrew before the pageant was presented, but he continued to work in Germany until 1938, when he left for England. Schlemmer too was reluctant to leave his homeland. His work was declared decadent and he was dismissed from the Bauhaus in 1933, shortly before the Nazis closed that institution. From then on he worked in semi-obscurity, and died in 1943 at Baden-Baden.

World War II swept away all of this creative activity, and many of its artifacts were either confiscated by the Nazis or destroyed in the fighting. After Germany had rebuilt its land and its economy in the '50s, the dance gained a new but conservative foothold in the opera houses. The curiosity, the idealism, and the adventurousness – and the dissatisfactions – that had prompted the *Ausdruckstanz* went dormant; it seems the Germans did not even want to be reminded of the experiments of the recent past.

Laban continued to work in exile, turning his attention more and more to analysis of work movement, and his very active heirs in England and the USA are pursuing his theories in dance education and movement analysis rather than theater. The most important legatee, paradoxically of both Schlemmer and Laban, is Alwin Nikolais. Trained by Mary Wigman's disciple in America, Hanya Holm, he inherits his movement approach from Laban, but his theatrical methods are all Schlemmer. Nikolais often speaks of his intention to show man as "kinsman to the universe", and his total theater pieces, with their "dehumanized" dancers blending into fantasy environments created by lighting projections, props and electronic sound, are a continuing journey into the territory laid out by Schlemmer, employing the technical resources of a space age even Schlemmer may not have imagined.

8 Честни, Матрос

Внимательный рабочий.

3 Сторожий

links/left
Entwürfe zu/sketches for
VICTOIRE SUR LE SOLEIL,
Inszenierung von/
Staged by
Kasimir Malewitsch

Fotos auf dieser Seite/
Photos on this page
oben/top
HOFFMANNS ERZÄHLUNGEN/
THE TALES OF HOFFMANN,
von/by Jacques Offenbach,
Skizze von/Drawing by
Laszlo Moholy-Nagy
Mitte/middle
L'EPHEMERE EST ETERNEL,
von/by Michel Seuphor,
Bühnenbild von/décor by
Piet Mondrian
unten/bottom
SKATING RINK,
Ch: Jean Börlin,
Ballets Suédois,
Bühnenbild von/décor by
Fernand Léger

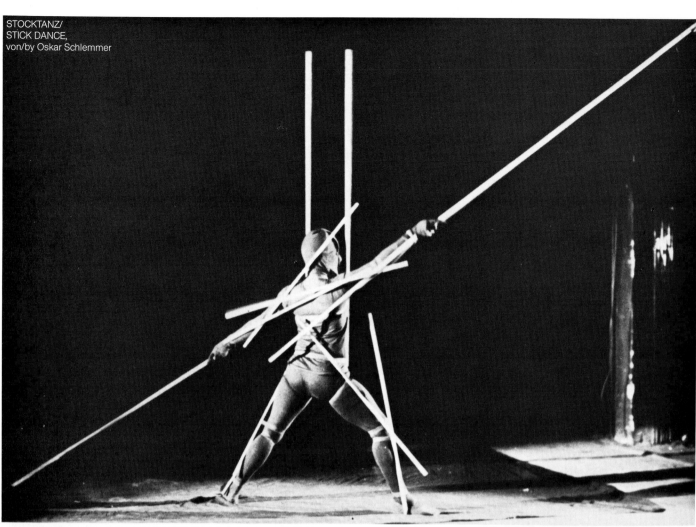

STOCKTANZ/
STICK DANCE,
von/by Oskar Schlemmer

DER MENSCH IM RAUM/
MAN IN SPACE,
von/by Oskar Schlemmer

Jsidora Duncan — Wiener Photo-Kurier

Neue Wigman-Gruppe — Phot. Volwahsen

Palucca — Phot. Jacobi

Mary Wigman — Phot. Rudolph

Neue Wigman-Gruppe — Phot. Renger

Hanya Holm — Phot. Rudolph

Rudolf von Laban — Phot. Becker & Maass

Frühere Wigman-Gruppe — Phot. Rudolph

Lotte Goslar — Phot. Rudolph

Phot. Robertson

Laban-Schule — Phot. John Thiele, Hamburg

Palucca-Schule — Phot. Rudolph

Phot. Robertson — Yvonne Georgi

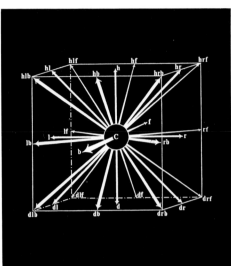

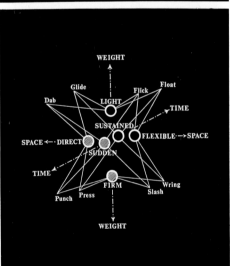

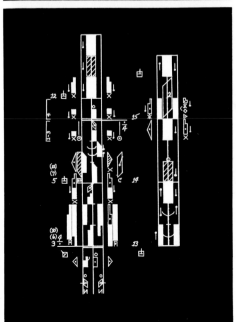

GUIGNOL,
Choreographie, Ausstattung
und Beleuchtung von/
choreography, décor and
lighting by
Alwin Nikolais,
Nikolais Dance Theater,
Foto: Caravaglia

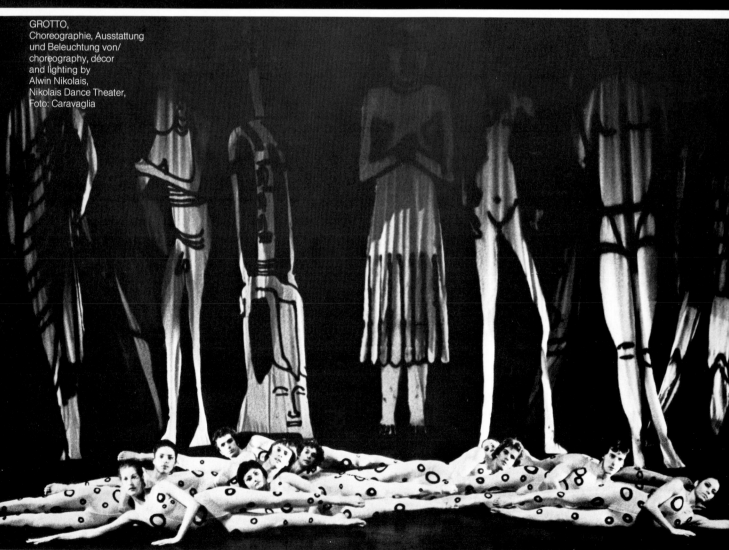

GROTTO,
Choreographie, Ausstattung
und Beleuchtung von/
choreography, décor
and lighting by
Alwin Nikolais,
Nikolais Dance Theater,
Foto: Caravaglia

SCHEMA,
Choreographie, Ausstattung
und Beleuchtung von/
choreography, décor
and lighting by
Alwin Nikolais,
Nikolais Dance Theater,
Foto: Daniel Cande

STOOLGAME,
Ch: Jiři Kylián,
Mea Venema, Nils Christe,
Nederlands Dans Theater,
Foto: Gert Weigelt

Jiři Kylián/Helmut Scheier

BALLETT UND DIE ANDEREN KÜNSTE

„Alle Künste bieten einander die Hand … Eine jede nimmt zwar ihren besonderen Weg, denn eine jede hat ihre eigenen Grundsätze; aber dem ohngeachtet finden sich doch gewisse Züge, eine gewisse Art von Ähnlichkeit, die ihre genaue Verbindung verraten und genugsam zeigen, wie unentbehrlich eine der anderen ist, um sich selbst zu erweitern, zu verschönern und zu verewigen." Diesem Urteil, das Jean-Georges Noverre im fünften seiner *Briefe über die Tanzkunst* (dt. Erstausg. 1769) äußert, wird man im allgemeinen beipflichten können. Indes sind „Verwandtschaft und Übereinstimmung aller Künste" keineswegs so selbstverständlich und problemlos, wie es den Anschein hat. Schon die historische Entwicklung verläuft nicht völlig parallel. Vor allem aber gilt nur bedingt, daß eine Kunstform der anderen unentbehrlich ist, jedenfalls dann nicht, wenn sie ihr ureigenes Ausdrucksmittel rein erhält.

Wieso denn bedarf der bildende Künstler des Wortes, der Musik oder des Tanzes; zum Wesen seiner Kunst gehören sie nicht. Allenfalls kann er sich dort inspirieren lassen. Entsprechendes gilt vom Dichter, vom Komponisten. Das Wort wirkt durch sich selbst, die Musik hat ihre Absolutheit. Schauspiel und Oper sind kein Gegenbeweis, zeigen vielmehr nur, wie die einzelnen autonomen Kunstformen doch in der Lage sind, miteinander zu korrespondieren, sich wechselseitig zu durchdringen.

Zwar besitzt der Tanz, die flüchtigste aller Künste, in der stilisierten Bewegung ebenfalls ein Mittel, das nur ihr eigen ist. Jedoch erweist sich dieses Medium, verglichen mit anderen, als ungleich weniger autonom. Zunächst ist es von der natürlichen Bewegung des Tänzers abhängig und muß mit ihr den Einklang suchen. Dann aber stellt sich heraus, daß Tanz wesensbedingt auf Musik bezogen ist, auf deren Rhythmus, Melodie, Harmonie und Tonfarbe, so daß man mit vollem Recht davon reden darf, die Musik sei für ihn „unentbehrlich". Selbst zu Malerei und bildender Kunst besteht eine engere Beziehung, lebt doch eine Choreographie in entscheidendem Maß von dem Raum, der ihr geschaffen wird, zudem beide Künste sich der optisch erfaßbaren Formgebung bedienen. Auch hier also ist der Bezug notwendig. So erweist sich das Ballett als besonderer Ort wechselseitiger Inspiration und Integration der Künste – im 20. Jahrhundert mehr als je zuvor.

Dieser Beitrag, entstanden aus einem Werkstattgespräch mit Jiři Kylián, dem Chefchoreographen und künstlerischen Leiter des Nederlands Dans Theater, will keine umfassende Ästhetik dieser Zusammenhänge entwickeln. Er gibt vielmehr einen unmittelbaren Eindruck von den Möglichkeiten und Problemen, denen sich ein bestimmter Choreograph heute gegenübersieht, wenn er seine Arbeit in bewußter Korrespondenz mit den anderen Künsten anlegt. Die geäußerten Ansichten tragen persönlichen Charakter, haben ihre unverwechselbare Farbe. Kylián portraitiert sich in ihnen gleichsam selbst. Daß er zugleich Grundsätzliches formuliert, ist verständlich. Vergegenwärtigt man sich die Choreographien Jiři Kyliáns, so fällt auf, daß sie nicht allein aus dem Dialog mit einer einzigen Kunstform erwachsen. Obwohl ihre Verbindung zur Musik besonders eng ist, leidet darunter in keiner Weise der Bezug zur bildenden Kunst. Dies belegt allein die Tatsache, daß Kylián des öfteren durch die bildende Kunst zu Balletten angeregt wurde.

Das Frauenballett *Ariadne* (1977) geht auf ein Fresco aus der Villa dei Misteri in Pompeji zurück, die *Kinderspiele* (1978) knüpfen an das gleichnamige Gemälde von Pieter Breughel d. Ä. aus dem Jahre 1560 an, zu sehen im Wiener Kunsthistorischen Museum, und *Psalmensinfonie* (1978) bezieht sich auf Entwürfe von Marc Chagall. In jedem Fall integriert Kylián die bildnerischen Vorwürfe auf andere Weise, niemals aber erzählt er sie einfach inhaltlich nach.

So dient ihm der auf dem pompejanischen Fresco dargestellte Dionysos-Kult und die Beziehung Dionysos-Ariadne dazu, die Psyche der Frau, ihre Individualität und gesellschaftliche Rolle kunstvoll stilisiert zu reflektieren. Er setzt sieben Tänzerinnen ein, um die verschiedenen Aspekte in der Entwicklung Ariadnes widerzuspiegeln.

In *Kinderspiele* nutzt er zwar die Gesamtaussage des Bildes, zitiert aber zwei bestimmte Figuren, um an ihnen den Umschlag vom Spielerischen in Aggression zu verdeutlichen.

Ingeniös gelingt die Verschmelzung von graphischer Vorlage und choreographisch belebter Umformung in *Psalmensinfonie*. Hier dienen einzelne von Chagall skizzierte Körperhaltungen als Anregung von Bewegungssequenzen, die die Struktur des Balletts wesentlich prägen und eine verblüffende Einheit sowohl mit der Komposition Igor Strawinskys wie mit ihrem thematischen Gehalt und der Deutung Kyliáns bilden.

Es überrascht, daß der Choreograph derartige Verbindungen intuitiv erfaßt, die sich auf einer neuen Ebene bestätigen, „als wäre es schon immer so gewesen. Zwischen Strawinsky und Chagall sehe ich eine ganz starke Beziehung. Ich habe das nirgendwo gelesen, aber ich empfinde es so und würde mich in jedem bis aufs Messer streiten, der mir sagt, daß es da keine Beziehung gibt. Vielleicht erscheint das sonderbar, und gewiß ist das, was dann entsteht, ein Drittes, etwas Neues." Ähnliche Korrespondenzen sieht Kylián zwischen Claude Debussy und Claude Monet oder Benjamin Britten und William Turner; und er fügt hinzu: „Vielleicht hat Britten überhaupt nichts von Turner gehalten. Das aber ist mir gänzlich gleichgültig, für mich ist es so."

Anregungen von Meistern der Vergangenheit zu nehmen ist eines, mit lebenden Künstlern zusammenzuarbeiten ein anderes, was jedoch nicht immer gelingt. Gelegentlich mußte Jiři Kylián seine Stücke sogar selbst ausstatten, doch betrachtet er dies allemal als „Notlösung". „Mitunter allerdings hat man als Choreograph eine feste Vorstellung von der Bühne; da hat es keinen Sinn, einen bildenden Künstler zu zwingen, das auszuführen, was man will. So war es beispielsweise bei dem Debussy-Ballett *La Cathédrale engloutie* (1975). Bei *November Steps* (1976) habe ich jedoch Tom Schenk gebeten, das auszuführen, was mir vorschwebte. Es war eine gute Zusammenarbeit; aber so sollte man es nicht machen. Eine andere Sache war es dann mit *Elegia* und *Sinfonie in D* (beide 1976)."

Kyliáns bevorzugte Bühnenbildner sind Walter Nobbe, William Katz und in allerjüngster Zeit offensichtlich John F. MacFarlane, nicht zu vergessen Nadine Baylis. „Mit einem Bühnenbildner arbeitet man ja schon zusammen, bevor man angefangen hat zu choreographieren. Da ist es am wichtigsten, daß er die Musik liebt, die ich benutze. Bei Walter Nobbe ist das phänomenal. Er kennt die Musik mindestens so gut wie ich, kann jedes Thema singen, phantastisch, das könnte ich nicht. Ein musikalisch außerordentlich begabter Künstler, der auch hervorragend tanzen kann. Cliff Keuter wollte sogar einmal ein Stück für ihn machen." Die Zusammenarbeit mit Walter Nobbe inspiriert Kylián besonders. „Er ist ein recht einsamer Mensch, arbeitet als freischaffender Maler monatelang allein in seinem Atelier. Es ist, als speichere er in dieser Zeit seine Gedanken, und dann sprudelt es aus ihm heraus; es ergibt sich ein ständiges Geben und Nehmen." Ähnlich fruchtbar ist Kyliáns Zusammenarbeit mit MacFarlane, auch er ein ungewöhnlich begabter Maler, immer bereit mitzuarbeiten, zu geben, im Dialog das gemeinsame Werk zu schaffen. Niemals heißt es bei ihm: „Take it or leave it!"

„Ganz anderer Art ist William Katz. Er steckt voller Ideen. Er hat eine Art, Konversation zu treiben, die provoziert und ständig dazu zwingt, weiterzudenken, weiterzuarbeiten." Das besondere Problem der Zusammenarbeit des Choreographen mit seinem Ausstatter liegt darin, daß der bildende Künstler seine Arbeit nicht isoliert entwickeln darf. Andernfalls entstehen „schreckliche Komplikationen. Es gibt wunderbare Maler und Bildhauer, die sich dafür interessieren, ein Bühnenbild zu schaffen, aber nur ihr Werk ausstellen wollen. Dann kommt es zu einer Konfrontation zwischen Choreographie und Malerei. Ich aber brauche einen Entwurf, in den ich meine Choreographie integrieren kann, so daß eine absolute Einheit von Bühnenbild, Kostüm, Musik und Choreographie entwickelt werden kann. Ich bin grundsätzlich dagegen, daß man ein Kunstwerk auf die Bühne stellt, um das dann lediglich herumgetanzt wird. Schon wenn sich der Vorhang öffnet, noch kein Tänzer auf der Bühne steht, darf es nicht wie eine Ausstellung wirken. Der gestaltete Raum muß von Anfang an auf die Choreographie hinführen. Nur so kann die Choreographie ihrerseits auf das Bühnenbild antworten."

Äußerst wichtig ist für Kylián der Raum, der ihm vorgegeben wird. Er hat in seinen Balletten höchst unterschiedliche Funktionen. Erst während der Arbeit an *Psalmensinfonie* wurde ihm die Bedeutung der von vier Seiten begrenzten Bühne voll bewußt, akzeptierte er diese Begrenzung in ihrer Unabdingbarkeit. „*Alles* wird innerhalb dieses Rechtecks gelöst. Eine Beziehung zum äußeren Raum besteht nur gedanklich, gefühlsmäßig. Die gesamte Energie drängt von den Bühnenseiten in die Mitte, von hinten nach vorne und umgekehrt. Erst am Ende, wenn alle Energie schwindet, wird der Raum aufgehoben, gehen die Tänzer ins Nichts, beziehungsweise in die Vollendung. Bei *Sinfonietta* nach Leoš Janáček ist es genau umgekehrt. Man hat das Gefühl, die Tänzer tanzen weiter, auch nachdem sie die Bühne verlassen haben. Hier wird der Raum absolut nicht respektiert. *Sinfonietta* ist völlig extrovertiert entworfen, im Gegensatz zu *Psalmensinfonie*."

Wieder anders verhält es sich bei *Stoolgame* (1974). Die Choreographie spielt sich in einem geschlossenen Raum ab. „Am liebsten hätte ich so etwas wie eine Schachtel gemacht, in der die Zuschauer mit eingeschlossen sind und nicht herauskommen können." Diese spezifische Lokalisierung der Choreographie in bestimmten Räumen prägt auch das Detail der Bewegungsfolgen, unabhängig davon, daß Kylián in jedem Stück die Balance zwischen

horizontaler, vertikaler und in die Tiefe des Raumes ausgreifender Bewegung sucht; zwischen Bewegung am Boden, respektive auf den Boden zu, und in die Luft hinein; zwischen Bewegung, die den Zuschauer trifft, und die an ihm vorüberläuft.

Kyliáns Interesse gilt von jeher mehr der Malerei als der Skulptur. Zwar fühlt er sich im Pariser Rodin-Museum „unheimlich glücklich. Alles, was man dort sieht, sind wunderbare Ballette." Ebenso stark berührten ihn Michelangelos *Gefangene* in der Akademie von Florenz – „eine meiner größten Inspirationen, obwohl sie mich nie zu einem Ballett anregten." Das verwundert insofern, als Kylián etwa bis zum Jahr 1977 in seinen Choreographien häufig skulpturale Elemente verwandte.

Er selbst führt dies nicht auf eine besondere persönliche Beziehung zur Skulptur zurück. Vielmehr ergab sich das Skulpturale in seinen Choreographien stets aus dem Thema, etwa wenn er in dem John Cranko gewidmeten Ballett *Rückkehr ins fremde Land* die Todverfallenheit des Körpers, oder in *November Steps* das allmähliche Erstarren der Natur habe bezeichnen wollen.

So stark nun Jiři Kyliáns Choreographien in den bildnerischen Gesamteindruck verwoben sind, so sehr er sich wehrt, eine Prävalenz unter den ihn inspirierenden Künsten zu setzen – dennoch spielt die Musik bei ihm eine hervorragende Rolle. Mit Musik wuchs er auf, genoß am Prager Konservatorium eine besondere musikalische Ausbildung und ließ sich während seiner Studienzeit beim Royal Ballet kein Londoner Konzert entgehen, ob es nun der Tradition oder der Avantgarde verpflichtet war.

Sein Interesse richtet sich bis heute nicht nur auf Kompositionen, die er für seine Choreographien verwendet. „Ich liebe mittelalterliche Musik, Musik der Renaissance; seit meinem 15. Lebensjahr spiele ich Klavierkompositionen von Bach, aber ich kann mir nicht vorstellen, darauf zu choreographieren. Am meisten inspirierten mich Komponisten, die gegen Ende des 19. Jahrhunderts geboren sind. Der Kampf des Abschieds von der Romantik und der Beginn der sogenannten modernen Musik haben mich stets gefesselt. Es ist die Zeit, in der man der reinen Schönheit und Harmonie der Klänge zu mißtrauen beginnt, in der man eine eigenartige Schönheit sogar in dem entdeckt, was man landläufig ‚häßlich' nennt; es ist die Zeit, in der sonderbare Klänge in die Musik eingebracht werden, in der eine Epoche in ihr Endstadium tritt, zerbricht, neue Formen und Inhalte entwickelt. Das hat etwas mit Impressionismus zu tun, auch mit dem Einfluß der Natur.

So inspirieren mich Komponisten, die eine tiefe Beziehung zur Romantik haben, ihr

sich aber mit der ganzen Kraft ihrer Persönlichkeit zu widersetzen suchen: Leoš Janáček, Claude Debussy, Arnold Schönberg, die ganze Wiener Schule, Igor Strawinsky, auch Béla Bartók. Sie alle bilden keinen einheitlichen Stil." Bei Bohuslav Martinu hat Kylián gewisse Schwierigkeiten: „Er war allzu begeistert von der klassischen Form, aber in manchen Werken drängt er den Klassizismus beiseite und seine eigene Persönlichkeit kommt zum Tragen." Auch bei Benjamin Britten steht ihm allzu große Schönheit im Wege. Nur in *Sinfonia da Requiem*, 1940 unter dem Eindruck des Krieges geschaffen und Brittens Eltern gewidmet, empfindet er größere Ehrlichkeit, eine gewisse Tiefsinnigkeit.

Komponisten der 50er und 60er Jahre, die konstruktivistisch arbeiteten, blieben Kylián fremd. Ihn inspirieren Komponisten, „die zum Menschen wollen und die Verbindung von Mensch und Natur suchen", wie Arne Nordheim, Luciano Berio und vor allem Toru Takemitsu. Komponisten wie Takemitsu haben aus dem gelernt, was in der Zeit unmittelbar vor ihnen geschaffen wurde. Aus dieser Erfahrung knüpfen sie mit neuen Mitteln am Ideal der Romantik an, ohne deren Ästhetik zu wiederholen. Zu einer derartigen Musik kann Kylián Vertrauen fassen. „Das Gefühl, daß jede Note ehrlich ist, daß der Komponist es im Innersten gefühlt hat, fordert mich heraus, für jede Atmosphäre, jede Harmonie, jede Nuance, für jeden Kontrapunkt der Musik eine entsprechende Bewegung auf die Bühne zu bringen, eine Transfiguration, eine räumliche Lösung, eine Gruppierung. Die Choreographie muß der Komposition gleichsam ‚entnommen' sein, ihren Ausdruck ‚beantworten' und mit ihr eins werden. Sie muß Interpretation und Auseinandersetzung zugleich sein, muß den persönlichen Beitrag des Choreographen enthalten."

Deswegen ist Choreographie als Illustration ebenso überflüssig wie als reine Strukturanalyse.

Vielleicht liegt in diesen Prinzipien Kyliáns auch der Grund dafür, daß er es nicht für nötig hält, mit der Partitur in der Hand zu choreographieren. „Man muß das Werk so hören, wie es der Tänzer hört." Dennoch greift Kylián in gewissen Momenten auf die Partitur zurück. Als er beispielsweise mit der Arbeit an dem Janáček-Ballett *Auf verwachsenem Pfade* nicht mehr voran kam, stellte er anhand der Partitur fest, daß der Tonmeister das Werk nicht richtig geschnitten hatte.

Für Kylián muß die Bewegung im Einklang oder im Dialog mit der Musik gefunden werden. Eine Schwierigkeit liegt darin, daß jeder Tänzer seinem eigenen Bewegungs-, Atem- und Pulsrhythmus folgt, den es mit dem Rhythmus der Musik in Übereinstimmung zu bringen gilt. Nur wenn das gelingt, vermag der Choreograph der stilisierten Bewegung eine eigene Qualität zu geben. Damit sie jedoch nicht leere Figuration bleibt, sondern glaubhaften Ausdruck erhält, muß sie in sich logisch sein und auf der natürlichen Bewegung des menschlichen Körpers beruhen, selbst wenn sie etwas seltsam Verkrüppeltes darstellen soll. Sie muß Tiefenschärfe besitzen und in Beziehung zum Raum und zu der der anderen Tänzer stehen. Nur der Kontext aller Bewegungsabläufe verleiht der einzelnen Bewegung Gewicht. Linie, die allein der Schönheit dient, lediglich dem Auge gefällt, ist abzulehnen. Geht Bewegung nicht aus echtem Gefühl hervor, fehlt ihr die Ehrlichkeit, wird sie unmenschlich.

Bleibt noch zu fragen, welche Beziehung Jiři Kylián zwischen Wort und Tanz sieht. Er empfindet im Grunde jede seiner Choreographien als eine Art „Literatur", obwohl er durchweg keine „Geschichten" erzählt. Man könnte sie – ein Experiment – durchaus verbal umsetzen. Sein Menschenbild ist durch Dichtung mitgeprägt und findet in seinen Balletten seinen Niederschlag. Vor allem

fesselten ihn die russischen Romantiker und die Realisten, von Puschkin bis zu Gorki und Majakowsky. Doch nie lag ihm daran, vorgegebene Literatur choreographisch nachzuerzählen, erst recht nicht, den Tanz mit Worten zu versetzen. Darin sieht er ein Unvermögen des Choreographen, durch Bewegung den Inhalt verständlich zum Ausdruck zu bringen.

Wohl aber reizt es ihn, „literarische Geschichten von Schriftstellern choreographisch zu lösen, die sich über die Armut der Sprache beklagt haben, die Sprache einfach nicht reich genug fanden, um zu sagen, was sie bewegte, wie beispielsweise Dostojewsky."

Wie Kylián sich der direkten Umsetzung von Dichtkunst in Choreographie widersetzt, so lehnt er auch eine direkte Formulierung individueller und gesellschaftlicher Themen ab. Gleichwohl spricht er sie durch die Methode einer gleichsam indirekten Mitteilung an, die dem Zuschauer immer einen Freiraum verschiedener Deutungen beläßt.

Als Beispiel mag hier die *Psalmensinfonie* gelten, in der ein einzelnes Mädchen passiven Widerstand gegen die Gemeinschaft leistet, die Eingliederung verweigert. An

anderer Stelle kämpfen zwei Jungen aufs heftigste miteinander. Dabei wird ein ganzes Bündel von Assoziationen ausgelöst – vor allem durch eine bestimmte, an Chagall orientierte Bewegungsqualität. Und doch ergibt sich nicht die volle Eindeutigkeit, die hinter dem Werk steht: Oktober-Revolution, Vertreibung, Judenverfolgung. An anderer Stelle desselben Werkes lassen sich dergleichen Bezüge zu Religiosität und Atheismus herstellen. Und auch hier wird eine konkrete Bezeichnung vermieden. Eindeutig ist Kyliáns Bemühen nur darin, dem Menschen „ein Bewußtsein von dem zu geben, was er wirklich ist – eingeengt, beschnitten, verkrüppelt, daß er eines Tages als ein Geschöpf erscheint, das des Wortes ,Mensch' nicht mehr würdig ist." Er sieht nicht nur die Notwendigkeit, gesellschaftliche Strukturen zu ändern, sondern zugleich und zuerst den Menschen.

In seiner Offenheit für die Methode der indirekten Mitteilung, wie sie Kylián vertritt, ist das Ballett jedoch singulär und zugleich auf den Austausch mit den anderen Künsten angewiesen – ein Austausch, der nicht zuletzt für beide Seiten fruchtbar sein könnte.

Jiři Kylián/Helmut Scheier

BALLET AND THE OTHER ARTS

"Each art form extends its hand to the others … Each pursues its own path, of course, as each has its own set of principles; but in spite of this there are certain characteristics, a certain type of similarity which reveal their exact connection and illustrate sufficiently how indispensable each is to the other, so that each can expand, embellish, perpetuate itself." This judgement, given by Jean-Georges Noverre in the fifth of his *Letters on Dancing* (published 1759, dated 1760), will generally find agreement. The "kinship and concord of all arts" is nonetheless not so matter-of-fact and trouble-free as it might appear. Even the historical development does not run completely parallel. And it is above all only to a limited extent true that the one art form is indispensable to the other, at least not if it is to maintain the purity of its original form of expression.

Why, then, does the master of the fine arts require words, music or dance? They are not integral to his art. At best he can draw inspiration from them. The same applies to poets, to composers. Words speak for themselves, music has its own absoluteness. Theater and opera represent by no means a counter argument, but rather demonstrate how the individual, autonomous art forms indeed are able to interact, capable of mutual permeation.

Although dance, the most evanescent of all the arts, in its stylized movement possesses a medium all its own, this medium proves, in

comparison with the others, to be far less autonomous. First, it is dependent on the dancer's natural movement and must seek harmony with it. But then it is found that dance, by nature, is connected to music, to its rhythm, melody, harmony, and timbre, so that it is perfectly justified to state that music is "indispensable" to the dance.

There is a closer connection even to painting and sculpture, as choreography draws its vitality to a decisive extent from the space created for it; moreover, both arts make use of forms which are grasped visually. This affinity is necessary here as well. Thus, ballet proves to be a special place for mutual inspiration and integration of the arts – in the 20th century more than ever before.

This article, originating in a workshop discussion with Jiři Kylián, chief choreographer and artistic director of the Nederlands Dans Theater, does not purport to develop a comprehensive aesthetic of these correlations. It reflects much more a direct impression of the possibilities and problems faced by a particular contemporary choreographer setting the direction of his work in conscious

interaction with the other arts. The opinions expressed are of a personal character, have unmistakable color. Kylián paints a portrait of himself, so to speak. That he formulates principles in the same stroke is understandable.

If one visualizes Jiři Kylián's choreographies, it becomes quite apparent that they are not the product of a dialogue with a single art form. Although their connection to music is particularly close, the relationship to the fine arts suffers in no way from it. This is proven simply by the fact that Kylián's ballets have often been inspired by the fine arts. *Ariadne,* a ballet for women (1977), traces its heritage back to a fresco from the Villa dei Misteri in Pompeii; *Children's Games* (1978) takes its idea from the painting of the same name, created by Pieter Breughel the Elder in 1560, to be seen in Vienna's Kunsthistorisches Museum, and *Symphony of Psalms* (1978) recalls sketches by Marc Chagall. In every case Kylián integrates the subjects in other ways, never simply retelling the content.

Thus, the Dionysus cult represented in the Pompeiian fresco and the relationship between Dionysus and Ariadne serve as an elaborately stylized reflection on the psyche of woman, her individuality and social role. He utilizes seven dancers to reflect the various aspects of Ariadne's development.

In *Children's Games* he does, in fact, utilize the overall statement of the painting, but

quotes two particular figures to make clear the change from play to aggression.
Symphony of Psalms succeeds ingeniously in fusing the graphic model with the choreography animating and transforming it. Here, the body postures sketched by Chagall serve as individual stimuli for movement sequences, making an essential imprint on the structure of the ballet, and forming an astonishing unity of Igor Stravinsky's composition with the thematic content and Kylián's interpretation.

It is surprising that the choreographer registers such connections intuitively, connections which are confirmed on a new level, "as though it had always been so. I see a very strong relationship between Stravinsky and Chagall. I have never read this, but I feel it to be so and would fight to the end with anyone who claimed that there is no relationship. Perhaps this seems strange, and certainly a third entity then arises, something new. Kylián sees similar correlations between Claude Debussy and Claude Monet or between Benjamin Britten and William Turner; and he adds: "Perhaps Britten thought nothing at all of Turner. But that is completely immaterial to me; for me it is so."

Taking impulses of masters of the past is one thing, working with living artists is quite another, and it is not always successful. Occasionally, Jiři Kylián has had to provide the sets and costumes for his pieces himself, although he considers this, in all events, as a "stopgap measure". "The choreographer sometimes has a fixed image of the stage; there is no point in forcing a master of the fine arts to do something which one does not want. That is the way it was, for example, with the Debussy ballet *La Cathédrale engloutie* (1975). For *November Steps* (1976), however, I asked Tom Schenk to execute the design I had in mind. The cooperation was good, but it was not the way to do it. Then it was quite another thing with *Elegia* and *Symphony in D* (both 1976)." Kylián's preferred set designers are Walter Nobbe, William Katz and, most recently, apparently John F. MacFarlane, not to forget Nadine Baylis. "The work with the stage designer begins before one has begun to choreograph. There, it is most important that he loves the music I use. With Walter Nobbe this is phenomenal. He knows the music at least as well as I and can sing every theme. It's fantastic; I can't do that. An artist of extraordinary musical talents, who also dances excellently. Cliff Keuter once in fact wanted to do a piece for him." The cooperation with Walter Nobbe is a particular inspiration to Kylián. "He is quite a solitary person, working alone for months in his studio as a free-lance painter. It is as though in this time he stores his thoughts and then they bubble out of him; there is a continuous taking and giv-

ing." Kylián's work with MacFarlane is similarly fruitful. He, too, an unusually talented painter, always ready for collaboration, to contribute, to create a mutual work in dialogue. With him it is never a matter of "take it or leave it!"

"William Katz is a completely different type. He is full of ideas. He has a way of conversing which provokes, always pressing on to further thought, to further work."

The special problem inherent in collaboration between a choreographer and his set designer is that the fine artist must not develop his work in isolation. This can give rise to "frightful complications. There are wonderful painters and sculptors who are interested in creating a set, but who want to present only their work. Thus, there is a confrontation between choreography and painting. I, on the other hand, need a sketch into which I can integrate my choreography, so that an absolute unity of set, costume, music and choreography can be developed. I am unequivocally against setting a work of art on the stage and simply to dance. The moment the curtain rises with no dancer yet on stage, the effect should not be that of an exhibition. This shaped space must imply the choreography from the very start. Only in this way can the choreography, for its part, respond to the set."

The space which is presented to him is for Kylián of extreme importance. It has widely differing functions in his various ballets. Only during the course of work on *Symphony of Psalms* did he become fully aware of the stage being limited on all four sides, accepting this limitation in its indispensability. *"Everything* is solved within this rectangle. The relationship to external space exists only in thought, emotionally. All the energy thrusts its way from the sides of the stage towards the center, from downstage upstage, and vice versa. Only at the end, when all the energy dwindles, is the space abrogated; the dancers move into nothingness, or rather into completion."

The situation is just the opposite in *Sinfonietta*, based on a work by Leoš Janáček. The feeling here is that the dancers continue to dance, even after they have left the stage. Here the disregard of space is absolute. The idea of *Sinfonietta* is fully extroverted, in contrast to *Symphony of Psalms*.

In *Stoolgame* (1974) the situation is again completely different. The choreography transpires in a closed room. "I would have loved to build something like a box in which the audience would also have been enclosed, not able to get out." This specific localization of the choreography in certain spaces also influences the detail of the sequences of movement, independent of the fact that in every piece Kylián searches for the balance between movement thrusting into the hori-

zontal, into the vertical, and into the depth of the space; between movement on the floor or rather towards the floor and into the air; between movement which meets the viewer and that which passes him by.

Kylián's interest has always been more in painting than in sculpture. Although in the Rodin Museum in Paris he feels "tremendously happy. Everything you see there is wonderful ballet." Michelangelo's *Prisoners* in the Academy at Florence touched him just as deeply – "one of my greatest inspirations, although it never moved me to a ballet." This is amazing in so far as that Kylián often used sculptural elements in his compositions up to about 1977. He himself does not trace this back to any particular personal relationship to sculpture. It was more that the sculptural elements in his choreographies always arose out of the subject, such as when, in his ballet dedicated to John Cranko, *Return to the Strange Land,* he wanted to demonstrate the mortality of the body, or in *November Steps* the gradual petrification of nature.

As intimately as Jiři Kylián's choreographies are woven in the overall sculptural impression, as much as he defends himself against setting any priorities among the arts which are his inspiration – music plays a leading role nonetheless. He grew up with music, enjoying a particularly musical education at the Prague Conservatory and during his studies at the Royal Ballet never missed a concert in London, be it dedicated to the traditional or to the avant-garde. To this day his interests are not only in the compositions which he uses in his choreographies. "I love the music of the Middle Ages, of the Renaissance; I have played Bach's keyboard works since I was 15, but I cannot imagine choreographing one. My greatest inspirations were from composers born toward the end of the 19th century. The struggle of breaking with the romantic and the beginning of so-called modern music has always fascinated me. It is the period in which one begins to distrust pure beauty and harmony of tone, in which one discovers a strange beauty even in that which is commonly called 'ugly'; it is the time in which peculiar tones are brought into music, in which an epoch enters its terminal stage, crumbles, develops new forms and content. That has something to do with impressionism, and also with the influence of nature.

"Thus I am inspired by composers who have a deep relationship to the romantic, but who exert all the power of their personality in resisting it: Leoš Janáček, Claude Debussy, Arnold Schoenberg, the entire Vienna School, Igor Stravinsky, and Béla Bartók. They share no uniform style." Kylián has certain difficulties with Bohuslav Martinu: "He was far too enthused with the classical

form, but in some works he forces classicism aside and his own personality comes to bear." In Benjamin Britten's works, too, excess beauty gets in the way. Only in *Sinfonia da Requiem,* composed in 1940 under the impression of the war and dedicated to Britten's parents, does Kylián find greater honesty, a certain profundity.

The serial composers of the '50s and '60s remain foreign to Kylián. He is inspired by composers "who want to communicate with humankind, seeking the link between man and nature", such as Arne Nordheim, Luciano Berio and above all Toru Takemitsu. Composers like Takemitsu have learned from that which was created in the period immediately before them. From this experience they use new means to connect with the ideal of the romantic, without repeating its aesthetics. Kylián can develop trust in this kind of music. "The feeling that every note is honest, that the composer has felt it in his innermost being, this challenges me to bring to the stage a movement corresponding to every aura, every harmony, every nuance, for every counterpoint in the music – a transfiguration, a spatial solution, a grouping. The choreography must, so to speak, be 'extracted' from the composition, 'answer' its expression and become one with it. It must be interpretation and confrontation at once, must contain the choreographer's personal contribution."

It is for this reason that choreography as illustration is just as superfluous as pure structural analysis.

Perhaps the reason for his not feeling it necessary to choreograph with the score in hand is to be found in these principles. "One has to hear the work as the dancer hears it." And yet Kylián falls back on the score at certain moments. When, for example, he could not continue work on the Janáček ballet *Overgrown Path* he discovered in the score that the sound engineer had not edited the work correctly. For Kylián the movement must be found in harmony or in dialogue with the music. One difficulty is that each dancer follows his own personal rhythms of movement, breathing and pulse, and the task is to unify these with the rhythm of the music. Only when this is successful is it possible for the choreographer to impart a distinctive quality to the stylized movement. To keep it from remaining an empty figure, but rather one imbued with a credible expression, the movement in itself must be logical, based on the natural movement of the human body, even when representing something oddly crippled. It must possess depth of focus and be in proportion to the space and to the movement of the other dancers.

Only the context of all the sequences of motion lends weight to the individual movement. A line which serves only beauty, which appeals only to the eye, is to be rejected. If movement does not stem from genuine feeling, it will lack honesty, it will become inhuman.

There remains the question as to the relationship Jiři Kylián sees between the word and dance. Basically he feels that each of his compositions is a type of "literature", although he certainly tells no "stories". It would be possible – an experiment – to translate them into words. His image of humankind is also imprinted by poetry, which is found reflected in his ballets. The Russian romantics and the realists, from Pushkin to Gorky and Majakovsky fascinated him. But it was never his intention to retell a given piece of literature in choreography, and certainly not to mingle words with the dance. In such, he sees the choreographer's inability to express in movement the content understandably.

But it stimulates him, "to choreographically solve literary tales created by writers who have complained of the poverty of language, who simply did not find language rich enough to say what moved them, such as Dostoevsky."

Just as Kylián resists a direct conversion of the poetic art into choreography, just as energetically does he reject a direct formulation of individual and social themes. But, nevertheless, he touches on them through the method of an indirect message, so to speak, which always leaves the viewer leeway for various interpretations.

The *Symphony of Psalms* can be taken as an example here, in which a single girl exercises passive resistance against the community, refusing to be integrated, while at another time two boys are fighting each other fiercely. An entire spectrum of associations is triggered – above all by a certain quality of motion, oriented towards Chagall. And still the full definity behind the work is not revealed: the October Revolution, displacement, persecution of the Jews. The same relationships to religiousness and atheism can be found at another point in the same work. Here, too, a concrete representation is avoided. Kylián's efforts are only unequivocal in giving man "an awareness of what he really is – restricted, cut off, crippled, that he will one day appear as a creature which is no longer worthy of the appellation human." He sees the necessity of changing not only social structures, but first and at the same time man himself.

In its openness towards the indirect message, as promulgated by Kylián, ballet is however singular while at the same time dependent on interplay with the other arts – an exchange which could be fruitful for both sides.

*Fotos auf dieser Seite/
Photos on this page*
DIE KINDERSPIELE/
CHILDREN'S GAMES,
Gemälde von/Painting by
Pieter Breughel d. Ä./the Elder
oben/above
Szenenausschnitt/Detail

gegenüber/opposite page
KINDERSPIELE/
CHILDREN'S GAMES,
Ch: Jiři Kylián,
Nederlands Dans Theater,
Fotos: Gert Weigelt

Ulrich Tegeder

FRÜHLINGSOPFER/
THE RITE OF SPRING,
Ch: Pina Bausch,
Marlis Alt,
Wuppertaler Tanztheater/
Dance Theater Wuppertal,
Foto: Gert Weigelt

TANZ UND VIDEO

ERST DIE ENTWICKLUNG DER MODER-NEN VIDEOTECHNIK ERLAUBT DER TANZ-KUNST, IHR EIGENES MUSEUM ZU BE-GRÜNDEN UND DAMIT IN DIE ANFANGS-PHASE IHRER EIGENEN VISUELLEN GESCHICHTLICHKEIT EINZUTRETEN.

Technische, normative und vor allem öko-nomische Zwänge erlaubten bislang die theoretisch unendliche Vervielfältigung von Film- und Fernsehprodukten nur bedingt. Da aber gerade diese Medien für die soge-nannten transitorischen Künste, also die Künste, die sich zu einem wesentlichen Teil in der Dimension der Zeit vollziehen, die adäquateste Prä- und Konservationstech-nik bieten, ist ihre Nutzung seit Jahren ein Dauerthema auf internationalen Kongres-sen von Ethnologen, Musik- und Tanzwis-senschaftlern und den Medienexperten.

In den Künsten der Fläche und des Raums – also etwa der Malerei, Plastik, Baukunst – sind die Werke selbst die Manifestation ihrer Geschichte – einzeln und in ihrer Summe. Musik und Sprache, die Künste in der Zeit, haben durch die Schrift ihre unmittelbare und objektive geschichtliche Dokumenta-tion erfahren. Die Geschichte des Tanzes dagegen verfügte bis zur Entwicklung der Tonfilmtechnik nur über Sekundärdoku-mente wie beschreibende Literatur, notierte Tanzmusik; selbst die verschiedenen Tanz-notationen gleichen Geheimschriften und kommen ohne Rückgriff auf ein anderes Medium nicht aus. Tertiärdokumente aber wie Tanzkostüme oder -schuhe, Gemälde oder Plastiken sind allenfalls die Spuren der „Aura" eines Ereignisses und haben nur den Wert von Devotionalien und Fetischen.

Mit der Entwicklung der modernen Video-technik und den nahezu unbegrenzten Ver-vielfältigungsmöglichkeiten der Kassetten-systeme tritt die Tanzkunst in die Phase ihrer unendlichen Reproduzierbarkeit ein. Das Primärdokument der Tanzkunst wird ver-fügbar, abrufbar, zitierbar. Tanz erhält Aus-stellungswert, in Anthologien lassen sich Tanz und Tanzgeschichte in didaktischem Aufbau nach verschiedenen Ordnungsfak-toren vergleichen, überprüfen und durch technische Manipulationen analysieren. Die Entwicklung der Videotechnik ermög-licht darüber hinaus dem Kunsttanz, in je-nen Demokratisierungsprozeß der Kunst zu treten, wie ihn Walter Benjamin in seinem Traktat über *Das Kunstwerk im Zeitalter sei-ner technischen Reproduzierbarkeit* be-schrieben hat: „Die technische Repro-duzierbarkeit des Kunstwerks emanzipiert die-ses zum ersten Mal in der Weltgeschichte von seinem parasitären Dasein am Ritual". Das soziale und kulturelle Gefälle der Rezeption der Tanzkunst wird aufgehoben.

DER TANZ, DER DURCH DAS MEDIUM DES VIDEOBILDES AN EIN NACH MILLIO-NEN ZÄHLENDES PUBLIKUM VERMIT-TELT WERDEN KANN, WIRD SICH AUF DIESE SEINE REPRODUZIERBARKEIT HIN ORIENTIEREN UND DADURCH WOMÖG-LICH AUCH IN SEINER ÄSTHETIK BEEIN-FLUSST WERDEN.

Noch bei der höchstvollendeten Reproduk-tion aber fällt eines aus: das Hier und Jetzt des Kunstwerks – sein originäres Ereignis. Das Hier und Jetzt des Originals aber macht den Begriff seiner Echtheit aus. So „entzieht sich der gesamte Bereich der Echtheit der technischen Reproduzierbarkeit. (. . .) Man kann, was hier ausfällt, im Begriff der Aura zusammenfassen und sagen: Was im Zeit-alter der technischen Reproduzierbarkeit des Kunstwerks verkümmert, das ist seine Aura". (Benjamin) Diese Frage aber hat sich für den Tanz im Medium des bewegten Bil-des nie gestellt, selbst dann nicht, wenn Tanz wie in kommerziellen Kinofilmen nur als Unterhaltungselement benutzt wurde. Sie stellte sich nur scheinbar ein, als das Fernsehen Repertoire-Ballette, also für die Guckkastenbühne inszeniertes Tanzthea-ter zu adaptieren begann und damit den Kompromiß implizierte. Die Technik des europäischen Theatertanzes, des Balletts, entstand nach Erfindung des Proszenium-rahmens, wurde aus den stereometrischen Gesetzen des Bühnenraums auf die opti-male ästhetische Präsenz zum *Theaterpub-likum* hin entwickelt. Selbst wenn die Ka-mera den Blickwinkel des Zuschauers ein-nimmt, erscheint auf der Fläche der Lein-wand oder des Bildschirms nicht das authentische Abbild, wie es sich dem Publi-kum bietet. Die Einengung des Blickfeldes auf den Kameraausschnitt, die Verzerrung der räumlichen Dimensionen durch die ver-schiedenen Brennweiten der Objektive, die selbst die körperliche Plastizität der Tänzer verflachen, verweisen die Regisseure oder Realisatoren von Ballettfilmen auf die op-tisch-dramaturgischen Gesetzmäßigkei-ten ihres Mediums. Diese aber bedeuten „Auflösung" in verschiedene Blickwinkel, verschiedene Bildausschnitte von verschie-dener Größe und verschiedener Dauer, die wiederum bei der Montage, mittels harter Schnitte oder weicher Überblendungen zu einem Endprodukt zusammengesetzt wer-den, das sich nunmehr nach den Sehge-wohnheiten des *Film-* und *Fernsehpubli-kums* ausrichtet. Selbst bei größtmöglicher

Annäherung entsteht immer ein völlig neues Produkt, das die Kunst des Tanzes in ihrer Substanz – räumlich wie zeitlich – ver-ändert hat, und zwar unabhängig von den künstlerischen Fähigkeiten des Regis-seurs. Halsbrecherische Versuche, die cineastischen Gesetze über die choreogra-phischen dominieren zu lassen, endeten im völligen Fiasko, weil sie schließlich auch im cineastischen Sinn nicht über die negative Theologie einer „reinen" Kunst hinaus-kamen, in der nicht nur jede Bestimmung durch einen inhaltlichen Vorwurf, sondern auch jede soziale Funktion abgelehnt wird.

Es liegt also nahe, daß die Ballettautoren und Choreographen selbst das Heft in die Hand nehmen, die Mechanismen des Mediums Video erkennen und neue choreographische Möglichkeiten erproben. Das kann Veränderungen im Hinblick auf ihre Ästhetik bedeuten wie bei Birgit Cull-berg, als sie mit dem „Blue Box"-Verfahren ihre Tänzer aus ihrem originären Ambiente in eine Kunstwelt „stanzte" oder wie in ihrer neuesten TV-Produktion, *Fräulein Julie,* in der sie nicht ihre Bühnenversion auf den Bildschirm adaptierte, sondern eine Cho-reographie entwarf, die alle spezifisch cineastischen Mittel bereits berücksichtigt. Das kann aber auch bedeuten, wie bei Pina Bauschs *Sacre*-Adaption, daß nahezu der gesamte Aufnahmestab zum Zuschauer gemacht, das ganze Ballett nur durch eine Kamera aufgezeichnet und somit der Kameramann zu einem zusätzlichen En-semblemitglied umfunktioniert wird. Was hier noch ein Kunstgriff war, wurde bei Hans van Manens Produktion *Live* zum eigenen ästhetischen Prinzip. Henk van Dijk arbeite-te mit einer Videokamera, die ihm erlaubte, sich völlig aus der Zuschauerperspektive herauszunehmen, sein Kameraauge nicht Zeuge, nicht Reproduktionsmittel des Bal-letts, sondern dessen Urheber sein zu las-sen. So erhielt *Video . . . live* erst auf dem Monitorschirm seine eigentliche Form. Das Bild auf dem Schirm wurde zum Original, mit allen Insignien der Echtheit – gleichzeitig, unmittelbar und unendlich reproduzierbar, ohne die Authentizität des Kunstwerks, sein Hier und Jetzt je zu verlieren.

DER AUF VIDEOBAND ODER PLATTE KON-SERVIERTE TANZ, DER ALS WARE MILLIO-NENFACH VERVIELFÄLTIGT WERDEN KANN, KÖNNTE, WAS SEINE KONSUMIER-BARKEIT ANGEHT, ZUM BESTSELLER UNTER DEN DARSTELLENDEN KÜNSTEN WERDEN.

Die Reproduzierbarkeit der Tanzkunst birgt aber auch die Gefahr der völligen Kommer-zialisierbarkeit. Schon jetzt signalisieren die Produzenten des Kabelfernsehens einen enormen Zuwachs an Kulturprogrammen, wobei wiederum der Anteil der darstellenden Künste auf Grund ihres Unterhaltungswertes den breitesten Raum einnehmen wird. Ballett- und Tanzproduktionen aber haben, auch wegen ihres „kosmopolitischen" Inhalts, einen ökonomischen Vorteil, da sie keine Sprachgrenzen überwinden müssen. Ein Vorteil, den auch die Programmgestalter des Satellitenfernsehens nutzen werden. Diese beiden zukunftsträchtigsten Entwicklungen des Fernsehens aber werden auf dem Videokassetten-Markt eine ähnliche Entwicklung hervorrufen, wie sie die Phono-Industrie bereits erlebt hat. Die längst überfällige Regulierung des Urheber- und Leistungsschutzes für Ballettautoren, Choreographen und Tänzer, die heute nur Bruchteile der Honorare und Tan-

tiemen erhalten, die in der Musikindustrie üblich sind, wird ein weiteres Aggregat sein, den Mechanismus von Angebot und Nachfrage in Gang zu setzen, der automatisch den Konsum und damit die Produktionsraten steigert. Es liegt im Wesen des Tanzes, als ursprünglichste aller Künste, daß seine sinnliche Wahrnehmung sich nie vom originären, ersten Gebrauchswert, seiner Fundierung im Ritual gelöst hat. Dies ist der einzigartige Wert des „echten Kunstwerks". Die Fundierung im Ritual mag so vermittelt sein, wie sie will, sie ist auch noch in den profansten Formen des Schönheitsdienstes als säkularisiertes Ritual erkennbar.
Da der Kunstwert des Tanzes immer an das Medium des Tänzers gebunden bleibt, wird die „Aura der Echtheit" auch in seiner Reproduktion nicht verloren. Der Anspruch

Maurice Béjarts, daß „der Tanz die Kunst des 20. Jahrhunderts" sei, erhält durch die veränderte Vermittelbarkeit von Tanz einen neuen Beweis. Vor etwa 40 Jahren schrieb Paul Valéry in seinen *Pièces sur l'art:* „In allen Künsten gibt es einen physischen Teil, der nicht länger so betrachtet und so behandelt werden kann wie vordem; er kann sich nicht länger den Einwirkungen der modernen Wissenschaft und der Praxis entziehen. Weder die Materie noch der Raum, noch die Zeit sind seit zwanzig Jahren, was sie seit jeher gewesen sind. Man muß sich darauf gefaßt machen, daß so große Neuerungen die Technik der Künste verändern, dadurch die Invention selbst beeinflussen und schließlich vielleicht dazu gelangen werden, den Begriff der Kunst selbst auf die zauberhafteste Art zu verändern."

ONLY THE DEVELOPMENT OF MODERN VIDEO TECHNOLOGY HAS MADE IT POSSIBLE FOR THE ART OF DANCE TO FOUND ITS OWN MUSEUM AND THUS TO ENTER INTO THE EARLY PHASES OF ITS OWN VISUAL HISTORY.

Technical, normative, and above all economic restrictions had previously allowed the theoretically unlimited reproduction of film and television productions only to a limited extent. But since just these media offer the most adequate techniques for preserving and conserving the so-called transitory arts (i.e., the arts which to a major extent are realized within the dimension of time), their use has for years been a permanent topic of discussion at international congresses of ethnologists, musicologists, dance and media experts.
In the arts of surface and space – encompassing painting, sculpture, and architecture – the works themselves are the manifestation of their history – individually and as a whole.
Music and language, the arts in time, have been historically documented, directly and objectively, through writing. Until the development of sound film technology, the history of dance, on the other hand, had at its disposal only secondary documents such as written literature and annotated dance music. Even the various notation systems for the dance are something like secret codes and are not self-sufficient; they must utilize another medium. Tertiary documents such as dance costumes or dancing shoes, paintings or sculptures, are, at best, traces of the "aura" of an event, being valid only as objects of veneration and fetishes.
With the development of modern video technology and the virtually unlimited re-

Ulrich Tegeder

DANCE AND VIDEO

production possibilities of the cassette system, the art of dance enters into a phase of unended reproducibility. The primary documentation of dance is becoming available, accessible, quotable. Dance has attained exhibition value. In anthologies it is possible to compare dance in didactic structures according to various classification factors; with the help of technical manipulation, it can be examined and analyzed.
The development of video technology further made it possible for artistic dance to enter into that democratization process of the art, as described by Walter Benjamin in his treatise *The Work of Art in the Age of its Reproducibility:* "The technical reproducibility of an art work emancipates it for the first time in the history of the world from its parasitic existence in ritual." The social and cultural differences in the reception of the art of dance is thus neutralized.

DANCE, WHICH THROUGH THE MEDIUM OF THE VIDEO PICTURE CAN BE PRESENTED TO A PUBLIC NUMBERING IN THE MILLIONS, WILL ORIENT ITSELF TOWARDS THIS REPRODUCIBILITY AND THUS PERHAPS BE INFLUENCED IN ITS AESTHETICS AS WELL.

But even in the most perfect of reproductions one thing is missing – the here and now of the artwork – its original happening. The here and now of the original is the touchstone of its authenticity. Thus "the entire

range of genuineness evades technical reproducibility.... One can summarize what is missing here under the term 'aura' and say: What degenerates in the age of technical reproducibility of art works is their aura" (Walter Benjamin). Dance in the medium of the moving picture has never had to face this question, even when dance was used as an element of entertainment in commercial films. This happened apparently only as television began to adapt the ballet repertoire (i. e., dance theater produced for the proscenium stage), thus implying the compromise. The technique of the European theater dance, the ballet, arose after the invention of the proscenium as a frame; working on the basis of the stereometric laws dictated by the stage, ballet developed towards optimal aesthetic presentation to the theater audience. Even if the camera assumes the viewer's vantage point, the image on the surface of the movie or television screen is not the authentic picture as that presented to the theatergoer. The restriction to the camera's field of view, the distortion of the spatial dimensions due to the varied focal distances of lens, which even flatten the dancers' bodily plasticity, all this makes the directors or producers of ballet films aware of the limitations inherent in the optical-dramaturgical laws of their medium. This then means "resolution" into various camera angles, various takes differing in size and length, which are again compiled in the cutting room, with soft fades or sharp transitions, into a final product which from then on is oriented towards the viewing habits of the film and television audience. Even with the nearest possible approximation of the original, a completely new product is created, which has modified the substance of the dance art both temporally and

oben und Mitte/
top and middle
CIONA
unten/bottom
OCELLUS,
Pilobolus Dance Theater,
Fotos: Jack Vartoogian

spatially, regardless of the artistic ability of the director. Daring attempts to let the cinematic laws predominate over the choreographic have ended in complete fiascos because they finally, even in the cinematic sense, did not rise above the negative theology of a "pure" art, in which not only every definition of the content is rejected but every social function as well.

Thus it would seem sensible for ballet authors and choreographers themselves to take matters in hand, to recognize the mechanisms of the video medium and to try out new choreographic possibilities. This can mean changes in respect to its aesthetics, such as Birgit Cullberg experienced, as she "punched" her dancers out of their original ambience into an artificial world with the "blue box" process, or as in her newest TV production, *Miss Julie,* in which she did not adapt her stage version for the television screen, but rather drafted a choreography which took into consideration all the cinematic means from the very beginning. That can, however, also mean, as in the Pina Bausch adaptation of her *Rite of Spring,* that nearly the entire film crew is turned into viewers, where the entire ballet is recorded by only one camera, thus turning the cameraman into an additional member of the ensemble. What here was still a trick became its own, self-sufficient aesthetic principle in Hans van Manen's production *Live.* Henk van Dijk worked with a video camera which allowed him to remove himself completely from the viewer's perspective, the eye of the camera becoming not a witness to, not a means of reproduction for, but rather the originator of the ballet. Thus *Video … live* achieved its real form only on the monitor. The picture on the screen became the original, with all the insignia of genuineness – simultaneously, directly and infinitely reproducible, without losing the authenticity of the art work, its here and now.

DANCE PRESERVED ON VIDEO TAPE OR DISKS, WHICH CAN BE REPRODUCED MILLIONS OF TIMES AS A PRODUCT, COULD BECOME A BESTSELLER AMONG THE PERFORMING ARTS IN RESPECT TO ITS CONSUMER VALUE.

The reproducibility of the dance art also involves the danger of complete commercialization. Even now producers for cable television are signalling an enormous growth in cultural programs, whereby the performing arts – due to their entertainment value – will take the lion's share. Ballet and dance productions have an economic advantage also due to their "cosmopolitan" content, since they have no language barriers to overcome – an advantage of which the program managers for satellite

LIVE,
Ch: Hans van Manen,
Coleen Davis,
Het Nationale Ballet,
Foto: Jorge Fatauros

transmissions will make use. These two momentous developments in television will, however, also bring about a similar development in the video cassette market, like that which the phono industry has already experienced. The long overdue regulation of authorship and performance protection for ballet authors, choreographers, and dancers, which today prescribe only fractions of the fees and royalties which are common in the music industry, will be a further means of setting the supply and demand mechanism in motion, automatically increasing consumption and thus production rates. It is in the character of the dance, as the most primal of all arts, that its sensual perception has never freed itself from the original, initial practical value, its foundation in ritual. This is the unique value of the "genuine work of art". The foundation in ritual may be conveyed in whatever manner it will, it is still recognizable in the most profane form of service to beauty as secularized ritual.

Since the artistic value of the dance will always remain joined to the medium of the dancer, the "aura of authenticity" will also not be lost in its reproduction. Maurice Béjart's claim that "dance is the art of the 20th century" receives new proof due to the altered means of conveying dance. Some 40 years ago Paul Valéry wrote in his *Pièces sur l'art:* "In all the arts there is a physical factor which can no longer be observed and treated as it previously was; it can no longer evade the effects of modern science and practice. In the past 20 years neither material nor space nor time has been what it was before. One must be prepared for the fact that such massive innovations will change the techniques of the arts, and, in that way, influencing invention itself and perhaps finally reach a point where they change the concept of art itself – in the most magical of ways."

Ursula Borrmann

Die Begeisterung für das russische Ballett scheint keine Grenzen zu kennen. Wo immer darüber geschrieben wird, geschieht es in Superlativen. Oft genug sieht man den Grund für die ungewöhnlichen Leistungen der Russen in ihrer natürlichen Begabung für den Tanz. Selbst Anna Pawlowa sagte: „Der Tanz liegt in der Natur der Russen. Wir sind Tänzer von Natur, wie die Italiener Sänger von Natur sind."

Das mag wahr sein, aber der Ruhm der russischen Ballettkunst ist nicht nur auf eine natürliche Begabung zum Tanz zurückzuführen; er beruht auch und vor allem auf einer kontinuierlichen, professionellen Ausbildung, die vor fast 250 Jahren in Rußland begonnen wurde. Ihren Anfang nahm sie 1738 mit der Gründung der St. Petersburger Ballettschule. Der Franzose Jean-Baptiste Landé entwickelte sie aus einer Tanzschule, die Rinaldo Fossano für Töchter des Adels in St. Petersburg unterhielt. Landé war ihr erster Direktor. In der vier Jahre währenden Ausbildung gelang es ihm schon bald, die ersten russischen Solotänzer heranzubilden.

Von 1758–1764 wirkte der Österreicher Franz Anton Hilverding an der Schule, der Italiener Gasparo Angiolini in den Jahren 1762/63, 1776–1778 und 1783–1786. Neben diesen bedeutenden internationalen Persönlichkeiten, zu denen noch Giuseppe Canziani zu rechnen ist, verdient auch eine Reihe russischer Ballettmeister als Mitbegründer und Förderer der Petersburger Ballett-Tradition genannt zu werden; so Aksinja Sergejewa, Awdotja Timofejewa und Andrej Nestorow.

Nach Abschluß ihrer Ausbildung waren die Tänzer gewöhnlich zwanzig Jahre in ihrem Beruf tätig; danach stand ihnen eine Pension zu. Diejenigen, die über pädagogische Fähigkeiten verfügten, konnten als Ballettlehrer weiterarbeiten. Schülerinnen und Schüler, deren Begabung sich als nicht ausreichend erwies, blieben im Dienst des zaristischen Theaterwesens, wo sie als Näherinnen, Ballettschuster und Instrumentenstimmer eingestellt wurden.

Der erste Ballettmeister und Tanzlehrer russischer Herkunft, der großen Einfluß auf die choreographische Entwicklung erlangte, war Iwan Walberg (1766 bis 1819); ein Schüler Angiolinis und Canzianis. 1794 wurde er als Nachfolger Canzianis Ballettinspektor der Kompanie des Bolschoi-Theaters und Direktor der St. Petersburger Schule. Später reorganisierte er auch die Ballettschule in Moskau. Nachdrücklich setzte er sich für russische Tänzer ein, protegierte insbesondere die Ballerina Eugenia Kolossowa. Walberg gab sich gegenüber den Reformideen Angiolinis und Jean-Georges Noverres besonders aufgeschlossen. Selbst Choreograph, galt seine besondere Aufmerksam-

DAS WAGANOWA-SYSTEM
RUSSISCHE SCHULE

keit der Aussagefähigkeit des Tanzes und der historischen Authentizität von Bühne und Kostüm. Abgesehen von kürzeren Unterbrechungen, wirkte Walberg bis zu seinem Tode in der St. Petersburger Schule. In dieser Zeit wurde der erste einheitliche Lehrplan festgelegt, demzufolge alle Schüler verpflichtet waren, am Unterricht in Musik, Gesang, Tanz, Schauspiel und Malerei teilzunehmen.

Im Jahre 1801 kam der Franzose Charles-Louis Didelot (1767 bis 1837) nach Rußland, auch er ein Verfechter des Handlungsballetts. Auf ihn gehen die Anfänge romantischer Ballettästhetik in Rußland zurück. In seinen Choreographien verstand er es, die Poesie des Inhalts mit der dramatischen Intensität der Handlung zu verbinden. Didelot arbeitete eng mit Walberg zusammen. Er war gleichzeitig Ballettmeister, Tanzlehrer in der Truppe und in der Schule. Durch die enge Zusammenarbeit von Theater und Schule schuf er die Grundlage für eine effektive Nachwuchsförderung, bildete große russische Tänzer und Tänzerinnen heran, wie etwa Awdotja I. Istomina, Adam Gluschkowski und – wie schon Walberg – Eugenia Kolossowa, die er vor allem als Interpretin seiner Choreographien favorisierte. Er vertraute ihr sogar, als er vorübergehend Rußland verließ, die Leitung der Schule an, deren Niveau sie noch zu steigern vermochte.

Noch zahlreiche Pädagogen und Ballettmeister trugen in der Folgezeit zum Ruhm der Petersburger Schule bei, doch keiner prägte Stil und Technik stärker als der Franzose Marius Petipa (1818 bis 1910). Zwar knüpfte er an das an, was Walberg und Didelot geschaffen hatten, doch führte er das klassische Ballett erst zu der einzigartigen Brillanz, die die St. Petersburger Truppe fortan auszeichnete. Sein strenger, formbewußter, aristokratischer Klassizismus blieb bis heute maßgebend.

1917 brach eine neue Ära an. Die Sozialistische Oktoberrevolution bewirkte auch in der Tanzkunst gewaltige Veränderungen. Der neue Sowjetstaat übernahm die Aufgabe, das nationale Erbe weiter zu pflegen und zugleich neue Stile und Ausdrucksmöglichkeiten zu schaffen.

Die alte Petersburger Ballettschule wurde umbenannt in Staatliches Choreographisches Institut Leningrad, neue Lehrpläne geschaffen, die Methodik des Unterrichts

weiter vervollkommnet, und die Aufnahmekapazität erheblich erhöht. In verstärktem Maße gab man der Öffentlichkeit Gelegenheit, die Arbeit des Instituts und ihre Ergebnisse zu verfolgen.

Die Grundlagen für die heute maßgebliche Ballettausbildung legte Agrippina Waganowa (1879 bis 1951). Bereits seit 1921 als Pädagogin an der Leningrader Schule tätig, übernahm sie 1934 deren Direktion. Die von ihr entworfenen Unterrichtspläne galten als für alle Lehrkräfte verbindlich. Sie selbst bildete die an der Schule lehrenden Pädagogen aus und achtete streng darauf, daß die von ihr aufgestellten Prinzipien und Anordnungen peinlich genau eingehalten wurden.

Waganowa entwickelte ihr System aus der Summe ihrer Praxiserfahrungen, der persönlichen Arbeit mit Marius Petipa und Enrico Cecchetti und aus dem Studium der verschiedenen Systeme, die das russische Ballett im 18. und 19. Jahrhundert erarbeitet hatte. 1934 erschien ihr Buch *Die Grundlagen des klassischen Tanzes,* dessen Methodik bis zum heutigen Tage Gültigkeit besitzt, wenn auch inzwischen einige Änderungen vorgenommen wurden. Von ihr, die unermüdlich an der Weiterentwicklung ihrer Pädagogik arbeitete, stammt der Satz: „Wir pflegen sorgsam den klassischen Tanz, aber ich glaube, wenn Didelot, Taglioni oder Perrot, die ihn bei uns eingeführt haben, aus den Gräbern auferstünden, würden sie ihr eigenes Kind nicht erkennen. Die Zeit tut das ihre, alles vervollkommnet sich."

Besonders großen Wert legt Waganowa auf die Harmonie der Bewegung und die Plastizität des gesamten Körpers, auf die Koordination von Kopf und Armen. Jede Pose muß eine eigene Aussage haben, jede Bewegung Musikalität verraten. Schon in der ersten Klasse wird intensiv nach diesen Prinzipien gearbeitet. Alle virtuosen Elemente müssen sinnvoll, d. h. die Technik nur als Mittel zum Zweck, eingesetzt werden. Aus ihrem Bewegungsstil verbannt Waganowa alles Manierierte, Enge und Kokette – Eigenarten, die vor ihrer Zeit besonders im Frauentanz gepflegt wurden. Eine strenge, einfache, klare Linie, verbunden mit bis ins Detail akzentuierten Posen und eine ausladende Weite in der Bewegung sind oberstes Gebot ihrer Methodik. Sie konkretisiert alle verbindenden Bewegungen von einer Pose zur anderen, wodurch erst die tänzerische Plastizität entsteht. Ein gutes Beispiel hierfür ist, welch große Bedeutung sie dem Allongé der Arme beimißt. War es früher eine Bewegung, die den Arm und damit die Gesamtbewegung eher verkürzte, so erreichte sie durch eine bis ins kleinste Detail durchdachte Ausführung eine wirkliche Verlängerung und Größe der Bewegung. Die Tänzer unterstreichen mit kraftvollen

Sprüngen, raumgreifenden Anlaufbewegungen die Überwindung von Hindernissen – ein Ausdruck von Männlichkeit, Kraft und Mut.

Die Mädchen und Jungen beginnen am Staatlichen Choreographischen Institut Leningrad im Alter von neun bis elf Jahren ihre Ausbildung und schließen sie nach neun Jahren mit einem staatlich anerkannten Diplom und dem Abitur ab. Die Aufnahmebedingungen sind so hoch angesetzt, daß von Hunderten von Bewerbern nur wenige aufgenommen werden. Neben einwandfreien anatomischen Voraussetzungen wird bei der Eignungsprüfung auch auf rhythmisches und musikalisches Empfinden geachtet.

Die Leningrader Schüler gehen täglich nach Hause; alle anderen wohnen im Internat, wo sie auch Kleidung und Verpflegung erhalten. Die ganztägige Ausbildung ist schulgeldfrei.

Vom ersten bis dritten Ausbildungsjahr unterrichtet ein und derselbe Lehrer Jungen und Mädchen getrennt in klassischer Technik. Diese hochspezialisierten Pädagogen, die zum Teil über eine 20- bis 30jährige Praxis verfügen, sind ausschließlich in diesen Kinderklassen beschäftigt. Gleiches gilt für die Mittelstufe (vierte bis sechste Klasse). In der Oberstufe, in der die Grundlagen des klassischen Tanzes bereits gelegt sind und die Arbeit am Detail, an der Persönlichkeitsentwicklung und der Vervollkommnung der

Technik die wichtigste Rolle spielt, geben ehemalige Solisten mit langjähriger Bühnenpraxis ihre Erfahrungen und ihr Wissen weiter.

Eine besondere Rolle im russischen Ballett spielt die Folklore. Das Vokabular des russischen klassischen Tanzes ist mit den unterschiedlichsten Folkloremotiven angereichert. Elemente der russischen und ukrainischen Tänze, die Eigenart der kaukasischen, baltischen, usbekischen oder kosakischen Tänze beleben die akademische Form. Da es in der UdSSR bedeutende professionelle Folklore-Ensembles gibt, in denen zahlreiche Absolventen des Leningrader Instituts ein Engagement finden, kommt dem Unterricht in diesem Fachbereich große Bedeutung zu. Dabei werden die Schüler auch mit den Folklorestilen Europas vertraut gemacht. Besonders in den mittleren Klassen trägt dieses Fach dazu bei, Bewegungsfreiheit, Stilempfinden und Ausdruckskraft zu fördern.

Weiterhin sieht der Lehrplan Pas de deux, Rollenstudium und historische Tänze vor (in den unteren Klassen sind dies Balltänze des 19. Jahrhunderts, in den fortgeschrittenen Tänze verschiedenster Stilepochen); auch Fechten wird gelehrt. Der Klavierunterricht erstreckt sich über die ganze Ausbildungszeit, wobei die Schüler eine erstaunliche Perfektion erreichen. Ein breitgefächertes, gut abgestimmtes Unterrichtsangebot gewährleistet insgesamt ein hohes Maß an

Allgemeinwissen. Der Unterricht ist ausge sprochen praxisbezogen: durch die eng Verbindung mit dem Kirow-Theater tanze alle Schüler vom ersten Jahr ihrer Ausbi dung in den Ballettaufführungen der Kom panie mit. Die traditionellen Choreogra phien des 19. Jahrhunderts (wie *Dorn röschen, Don Quixote* und *Nußknacker* die speziell Tänze für Kinder enthalten, sin dafür besonders geeignet. Außerdem fin den alle sechs bis sieben Wochen soge nannte Schulkonzerte statt, bei denen all im Unterricht erarbeiteten Tänze vorgestell werden. Für jede Ausbildungsstufe gibt es kleine Tänze und Variationen, die genau m dem Lehrplan abgestimmt sind, die Kinde nicht überfordern, ihnen jedoch die Möglich keit geben, das im Unterricht Erlernte in tän zerischer Form auf der Bühne zu zeigen.

Höhepunkt der Studienzeit ist für den Schü ler das alljährlich veranstaltete Absolven tenkonzert, in dem jeder je nach Vermöger und Können zeigen darf, was er in neur Jahren gelernt hat. Besonders Begabte erhalten Gelegenheit, einen ganzen Akt zu tanzen. Diese Konzerte folgen nicht der Gesichtspunkten von Ausgewogenheit Publikumswirksamkeit oder choreographi scher Attraktivität, sondern dienen allein zu Vorstellung des jeweiligen Jahrgangs. Fü die begabteren Absolventen bedeutet dies die Chance, sich erstmals einem großen Publikum in einer besonderen Rolle zu präsentieren.

Ursula Borrmann

THE VAGANOVA SYSTEM
RUSSIAN SCHOOL

Enthusiasm for the Russian ballet seems to know no limits. Whatever is written about the subject is written in superlatives. Often enough the reason for the exceptional performance of the Russians is said to be found in their natural aptitude for dance. Even Anna Pavlova said, "Dance lies in the nature of the Russians. We are dancers by nature, as the Italians are singers by nature."

This may be true, but the fame of the Russian ballet is not due only to a natural talent for dance; it is also and above all due to continuous, professional training, begun almost 250 years ago in Russia. Its beginnings were in 1738 with the founding of the St. Petersburg ballet school. The Frenchman Jean-Baptiste Landé developed it out of a dancing school which Rinaldo Fossano maintained for the daughters of the nobility in St. Petersburg. Landé was its first director. In the training program which lasted four years, he soon succeeded in training the first Russian soloists.

From 1758 to 1764 the Austrian Franz Anton Hilverding was engaged at the school, the Italian Gasparo Angiolini in the periods 1762/63, 1776 to '78 and 1783 to '86. Alongside these important international personali-

ties, among whom Giuseppe Canziani must be included, a series of Russian ballet masters deserves to be named as co-founders and sponsors of the Petersburg ballet tradition – Aksinia Sergeyeva, Avdotia Timofeyeva and Andrey Nestorov.

Once their training had been completed, dancers were usually active in their profession for a period of 20 years; thereafter they were entitled to a pension. Those who showed teaching talent could continue to work as ballet instructors. Students whose talent proved not to be fully sufficient remained in the service of the czarist theater, employed as seamstresses, ballet shoemakers and tuners of instruments.

The first ballet master and dance teacher of Russian heritage to achieve great influence

on choreographic development was Ivan Valberkh (1766 to 1819); a student of Angiolini and Canziani, he became Canziani's successor as the ballet inspector of the Bolshoi Theater company and director of the St. Petersburg school. Later he reorganized the ballet school in Moscow as well. He devoted his efforts expressly to Russian dancers, sponsoring in particular the ballerina Eugenia Kolosova. Valberkh was particularly open to the reformist ideas of Angiolini and Jean-Georges Noverre. Himself a choreographer, Valberkh devoted particular attention to the expressive possibility of dance and the historical authenticity of the sets and costumes. Aside from brief interruptions, he was active at the St. Petersburg school until his death. During this period the first uniform curriculum was written, as a result of which every student was obliged to attend classes in music, voice, dance, acting and painting. In 1801 the Frenchman Charles-Louis Didelot (1767 to 1837) came to Russia, himself a proponent of the story-line ballet. The beginnings of romantic ballet aesthetics in Russia can be traced back to him. In his compositions he was skilled in combining the poetry of the content with the dramatic intensity of the plot. Didelot worked closely with Valberkh. He was at the same time ballet master and dance instructor in the company and in the school. Through the close cooperation between the theater and the school, he created the basis for effective promotion of young talent, educating great Russian dancers such as Avdotia I. Istomina, Adam Gluszkovsky and – as had Valberkh – Eugenia Kolosova, whom he favored above all as an interpreter of his choreographies. When he left Russia temporarily, he even entrusted her with the direction of the school, whose standards she was able to raise even further.

In the years following, numerous other teachers and ballet masters contributed to the fame of the Petersburg school, but none had a greater influence on style and technique than the Frenchman Marius Petipa (1818 to 1910). Although he did in fact take as a starting point the basis which Valberkh and Didelot had created, it was he who first guided classical ballet to the unique brilliance which has distinguished the St. Petersburg company from that point on. His stringent, aristocratic classicism, always aware of form, has remained authoritative to this very day.

A new era dawned in 1917. The socialist October Revolution effected far-reaching changes in the art of dance as well. The new Soviet state assumed the responsibility for tending the national heritage and at the same time for creating new styles and ways of expression.

The old Petersburg ballet school was rechristened the State Choreographic Institute, Leningrad, new curricula were formulated, the methodology of the teaching was further perfected, and capacity for admissions was increased considerably. The public was given more frequent opportunity to follow the work of the institute and its achievements.

The foundations for the ballet training program, still prevailing today, were laid by Agrippina Vaganova (1879 to 1951). Teaching at the Leningrad school as early as 1921, she assumed its directorship in 1934. The curricula which she drafted were binding for every teacher. She herself trained the instructors who were engaged by the school and monitored training carefully to see that the principles and regulations which she had laid down were strictly observed. Vaganova developed her system from the sum of her practical experience, her personal work with Marius Petipa and Enrico Cecchetti, and from her study of the various systems which the Russian ballet had developed in the 18th and 19th centuries. In 1934 her book, *Fundamentals of the Classic Dance* appeared, and the methods embodied in it remain valid to this day, even though some changes have been undertaken in the meantime. It was this educator, working untiringly on the further development of her pedagogy, who is quoted as saying: "We nurture carefully the classical dance, but I believe that if Didelot, Taglioni or Perrot, who introduced it to us, were to arise from the grave, they would not recognize their own progeny. Time does what it will; everything strives for perfection."

Vaganova placed particularly great value on the harmony of motion and the plasticity of the entire body, on the coordination of head and arms. Each pose must make a statement, each movement must give evidence of musicianship. Intensive work is devoted to these principles even in the very first classes. Every element of virtuosity must be utilized sensibly, the technique being only a means to an end. From her style of movement Vaganova banned everything affected, strained and coquettish – characteristics which up to her time had been particularly cultivated in choreography for female dancers. A stringent, simple, clear line, linked with poses accented in detail, and an expansive breadth of movement are the prime commandments of her methodology. She codified all the movements linking one pose with the next, which brings forth plasticity in dance. A good example of this is the great significance which she placed on the allongé of the arms. While it had previously been a motion which tended rather to shorten the arm and thus the entire motion, she achieved – by execution which had been worked out to the smallest nuance – an actual extension and grandeur of the movement.

The male dancers emphasize their hurdling of obstacles with powerful leaps and space-commanding approaches – expressions of virility, power and courage.

Both girls and boys begin their studies at the State Choreographic Institute, Leningrad between the ages of nine and eleven; they finish after nine years with a certificate recognized by the state along with their high school diploma. The admission requirements are so high that from hundreds of applicants only a few are accepted. In addition to perfect anatomical prerequisites, attention is paid in the selection process to rhythmic and musical sensitivity as well.

Pupils residing in Leningrad return home each day; the others live in a boarding school, where they also receive clothing and meals. No tuition is charged for the full-day classes.

During the first three years a single instructor teaches boys and girls classical technique, in separate classes. These highly specialized teachers, who in some cases can draw on 20 to 30 years of practice, are engaged exclusively in the children's classes. The same applies to the mid-level classes (fourth through sixth years). In the upper level, where the fundamentals of classical dance have already been established and work on detail, personality development, and perfection in technique are the prime goals, former soloists with many years of stage practice impart their knowledge and experience.

The vocabulary of the classical Russian dance has been enriched with widely diverging motives drawn from folk traditions. Elements of Russian and Ukrainian dances, the singularity of the Caucasian, Baltic, Usbek or the Cossack dances enliven the academic form. Since there are in the USSR renowned professional folklore ensembles, at which numerous graduates of the Leningrad Institute are engaged, great emphasis is placed on the teaching of this subject. The students are familiarized with Europe's folklore as well. This subject encourages freedom of movement, sensitivity for style and power of expression, particularly in the mid-level classes.

In addition, the curriculum stipulates the pas de deux, studying of roles, and historical dances (in the early classes these are ballroom dances from the 19th century, at the more advanced levels various period dances); fencing is also taught. Piano lessons are continued through the entire course of study, whereby the students achieve an amazing level of perfection. A wide-ranging, well balanced curriculum insures a high degree of general knowledge. The education is particularly geared to practice; due to the close connection with the Kirov Theater every student takes part in the company's ballet performances beginning with the first year. The traditional compositions of the 19th century (such as *Sleeping Beauty, Don Quixote* and *The Nutcracker*), which include dances especially for children, are particularly suitable for this purpose. Furthermore, school recitals, in which all the dances which have been learned in training are presented, are staged every six to seven weeks. There are small compositions and variations for each level, matched exactly to the curriculum, which do not overtax the children, but give them the opportunity to demonstrate on stage, what they have learned.

For the students the climax of the entire course of study is the annual graduates' recital, in which each can show, in accordance with his talents and abilities, what he has learned in nine years. Particularly talented students have the opportunity to dance an entire act. These recitals are not planned in light of balance, audience appeal or choreographic attractiveness, but serve solely to introduce the graduating class. For the more talented, this means the first opportunity to appear before a large public.

John Percival

DAS ENGLISCHE TANZ-AUSBILDUNGS-SYSTEM

Als Ninette de Valois 1926 eine Tanzschule gründete, gab sie ihr den klangvoll feierlichen Namen Academy of Choreographic Art. Im nachhinein läßt sich dies als Hinweis dafür sehen, daß sie ihr Unternehmen künstlerisch anspruchsvoller als alle anderen Ausbildungsinstitute, die bis dahin in England existierten, verstanden wissen wollte. Bis zu diesem Zeitpunkt fehlte es nicht an zum Teil exzellenten Tanzpädagogen, und schon 1904 hatte man während einer Tagung die heutige Imperial Society of Teachers of Dancing gegründet. Absicht dieser Institution war, Professionalität zu entwickeln und ein gewisses Unterrichtsniveau zu gewährleisten. Mit ihren vielen Zweigen, die die verschiedenen Bereiche von Bühnen- und Gesellschaftstanz abdecken, existiert sie noch heute als eine von mehreren Organisationen, die Prüfungen abhalten und Zeugnisse ausstellen. Unter diesen besitzt vor allem die Royal Academy of Dancing (RAD) einen hervorragenden Stellenwert, 1920 unter anderem Namen gegründet als „Verband von Experten, um Pädagogen und junge Tänzer in korrekter Balletttechnik zu unterweisen und die große Tradition unserer Kunstgattung zu wahren." (Diese Beschreibung stammt von Phyllis Bedells, eines der bedeutendsten unter den frühen Mitgliedern der RAD.) Der Ruf der Akademie spiegelt sich nicht allein darin, daß ihr 1936 durch königlichen Erlaß der Titel „Royal" zuerkannt wurde, sondern auch in dem einzigartigen Respekt, der ihren beiden bisherigen Präsidentinnen, Adeline Genée und Margot Fonteyn, von der Tanzszene und vom Publikum gezollt wurde.

Das Hauptziel dieser Organisationen war die Gewährleistung eines korrekten Unterrichts für die jugendlichen Tanzschüler. Die weitere Verwendung der einmal erworbenen Fähigkeiten war von relativ geringer Bedeutung, obwohl die RAD einen Production Club einrichtete, der als Werkstatt für angehende Choreographen diente und einigen Schülern die Möglichkeit bot, Erfahrungen durch Auftritte vor einem Publikum zu sammeln. Schon als de Valois ihre Schule eröffnete, beabsichtigte sie, ein ständiges Ballettensemble aufzubauen, dessen Arbeit ähnlich gelagert sein sollte, wie sie es als Mitglied der Ballets Russes von Serge Diaghilew kennengelernt hatte, und sie beabsichtigte, ihre Schüler daraufhin auszubilden. Infolgedessen entsprachen die Ziele ihrer Academy of Choreographic Art denen der großen Schulen in den Ballettmetropolen wie Paris, St. Petersburg und Kopenhagen. Doch wie unterschiedlich waren die Methoden.

Diese Institutionen wurden mit Mitteln des Hofes etabliert, von ihm unterstützt und auch nach dem Fall der Königreiche weiter-

hin staatlich finanziert. De Valois eröffnete ihre Schule in völliger Eigeninitiative, und sogar nach ihrem Umzug (1931) ins Sadler's Wells Theatre blieb sie von Einnahmen und Spenden abhängig, ohne jegliche Zuschüsse von seiten der Regierung auf nationaler oder regionaler Ebene. Ihr Prestige wuchs mit dem der ihr angeschlossenen Kompanie und verstärkte sich 1947, als (hauptsächlich auf Drängen des Ballettschriftstellers Arnold Haskell) der Ausbildungsplan durch die üblichen Schulfächer ergänzt wurde. Das weitere Fortbestehen der Schule war gesichert, als sie 1956 durch königlichen Erlaß integraler Bestandteil des Royal Ballet wurde, doch bis in die 70er Jahre hingen in jedem einzelnen Fall Lehr- und Unterhaltsstipendien von der Bereitwilligkeit der städtischen Behörden ab. Für die Schüler bis zum 16. Lebensjahr, die die Grundklassen besuchen, wurde diese Schwierigkeit durch eine Vereinbarung gelöst (einzig der Royal Ballet School und Yehudi Menuhins Schule für junge Musiker vorbehalten), nach der Stipendien von der Zentralregierung automatisch jedem britischen Kind bewilligt werden, das in die Schule aufgenommen wird. Doch noch heute gilt diese nicht für die höheren Klassen, so daß ein begabtes Kind Schwierigkeiten haben kann, seine Ausbildung abzuschließen.

Nicht nur in der Art ihrer Finanzierung steht die Royal Ballet School im Gegensatz beispielsweise zur Ballettschule der Pariser Oper. Selbstverständlich gibt es auch viele Ähnlichkeiten, etwa die ärztliche Beurteilung der voraussichtlichen physischen Entwicklung eines Kindes (einer der Aufnahmetests), oder auch das jährliche Aussondern der Schüler, die sich nach ihrer Aufnahme als nicht geeignet erweisen. Jedoch gestatten die höheren Finanzreserven der Pariser Oper eine gründlichere Einschätzung der Eignung. So gibt es vorbereitende Sommerkurse, in denen mehr Kinder getestet als zugelassen werden können. Die Pariser Schule ist darüber hinaus enger mit der ihr angeschlossenen Kompanie verbunden; die begabtesten Schüler werden (wie in Dänemark) in den letzten zwei Ausbildungsjahren als Eleven ins professionelle Ensemble übernommen.

In der entsprechenden Studienzeit an der Royal Ballet School steigen die Schüler in die höheren Klassen auf, die sich zwar mit der Truppe die Gebäude teilen; ihr Unterricht wie auch alle anderen Aktivitäten bleiben jedoch völlig getrennt. In diese höheren Klassen werden nicht nur die Schüler der Grundklassen übernommen, sondern auch, nach Vortanzen, die anderer in- und ausländischer Ballettschulen. Daraus ergibt sich, daß die Schule weit mehr Tänzer ausbildet, als die beiden Royal Ballet-Kompanien überhaupt aufnehmen können. Sie bildet daher einen der Hauptzulieferer für alle Ballettensembles in Großbritannien; trotzdem müssen viele ihrer Absolventen sich im Ausland ein Engagement suchen.

Die Versuche anderer Kompanien, außerhalb Londons eigene Schulen zu etablieren, blieben in ihren Ergebnissen bislang begrenzt. Das in Glasgow ansässige Scottish Ballet begann das Experiment, talentierten Schülern privater Ballettschulen wöchentlichen Unterricht anzubieten; ein geschickter Kompromiß, um das Niveau zu erhöhen, gleichzeitig das Wohlwollen der etablierten Pädagogen beizubehalten. Mittlerweile bemüht sich das Ensemble, wie das in Manchester beheimatete Northern Ballet Theatre seine eigene Schule aufzubauen.

Man könnte auf Grund der Existenz mehrerer renommierter Prüfungsorganisationen für Pädagogen und Bühnentänzer annehmen, daß der Unterrichtsstandard im ganzen Land doch immerhin recht hoch sei. Leider trifft dies nicht zu. Ein Ex-Tänzer des Royal Ballet begann eine Reihe von Seminaren in seiner Heimat Yorkshire, zu denen stets bekannte Pädagogen aus London wie auch einige aus dem Ausland eingeladen werden. Alle Schüler, die für die Seminare zugelassen werden, müssen bereits regelmäßigen Ballettunterricht nachweisen. Die Lehrer dürfen dem Unterricht zusehen. Obwohl die Seminare seit einigen Jahren stattfinden und mittlerweile eigentlich dazu beigetragen haben sollten, das dortige Niveau anzuheben, hat es sich für Gastdozenten als traurige Notwendigkeit erwiesen, in den eigentlich als Meisterklassen angesetzten Kursen sehr viel Zeit mit der Korrektur von Fehlern im Elementarunterricht zu verbringen. Nur einige Schüler erreichen ein hohes Niveau; sie bleiben jedoch die Ausnahme.

Um dem abzuhelfen, wurde vor einiger Zeit das Council for Dance Education and Training eingerichtet, dessen Hauptaufgabe es ist, eine Liste jener Unterrichtsinstitute, die seinen Kriterien entsprechen, zu veröffentlichen, und Ministerien, städtische Behörden sowie weitere interessierte Institutionen in allen Fragen im Zusammenhang mit Tanzausbildung, -unterricht und -pädagogik zu beraten. Dazu gehört, den städtischen Behörden Hinweise zu geben, welcher Bewerber am ehesten finanzielle Unterstützung erhalten sollte; aber es gibt immer noch Schwierigkeiten – wenn zum Beispiel eine städtische Behörde willkürlich eine Reduzierung der Stipendien für die führenden Schulen beschließt, die gleichzeitig die teuersten sind. Dieses Council for Dance Education and Training (wie ähnliche Verbände in Schottland und Wales) wird viel Zeit zur Verwirklichung seiner Ziele benötigen.

Zwei andere wichtige Entwicklungen der letzten Jahre, die in gewissem Sinn miteinander verbunden sind, waren die Erweiterung der Möglichkeiten, professionell Modern Dance-Techniken zu erlernen, und die Erweiterung der Tanzausbildung für jene Fortgeschrittene, die keine Tänzer- oder Pädagogenlaufbahn anstreben. Seit Beginn dieses Jahrhunderts besteht das Interesse für Modern Dance in Großbritannien. Es war Margaret Morris, die ihre eigene Technik als Reaktion auf die Konventionalität des klassischen Balletts jener Zeit entwickelte, und die 1910 ihre erste Schule gründete. Obwohl Morris ihre Schüler in ehrgeizigen Produktionen vorstellte, lag die Wirkung des Margaret Morris Movement (MMM), wie anderer Methoden des modernen oder freien Tanzes, in erster Linie in einer gesunden und befriedigenden Aktivität für die Amateure. Innerhalb von 30 Jahren entstanden in ganz Großbritannien die MMM-Schulen, deren Popularität jedoch während des Krieges schwand und danach nie wieder anstieg. Unterdessen war Großbritannien in den 30er Jahren zwei Protagonisten der deutschen Ausdruckstanzbewegung, Rudolf von Laban und Kurt Jooss, zur neuen Heimat geworden. Laban gründete gemeinsam mit Lisa Ullmann das Art of Movement Studio, aus dem das heutige Laban Centre hervorging, immer noch ein privates Unternehmen, jedoch im Gebäude und unter der Verwaltung des Goldsmiths' College der Londoner Universität (dieses College verfügt ebenfalls über eine eigene Tanzabteilung auf dem Universitätsgelände). Das Laban Centre bietet im Vollstudium Berufsausbildungskurse für Tänzer und darüber hinaus theoretisch-praktische Kurse unter anderem in Tanztechnik, Bewegungsanalyse, Choreographie, Tanzschrift, Tanzkritik und -ästhetik. Das Techniktraining basiert nicht auf einem bestimmten System, berücksichtigt allerdings Labans Prinzipien.

Das Laban Centre ist nur eines von mehreren Colleges, die Tanzausbildung auf fortgeschrittenem akademischen Niveau anbieten. Andere entwickelten sich aus der seit Beginn dieses Jahrhunderts erwachsenen Verbindung von Sport (speziell für Frauen) und Tanz. Eine vollständige Umwandlung der Modern Dance-Bewegung in Großbritannien geschah jedoch erst nach den Gastspielen der Kompanie Martha Grahams und anderer amerikanischer Modern Dance-Ensembles in den frühen 60er Jahren. Eine ihrer enthusiastischsten Bewunderer, Robin Howard, finanzierte Lehrern der Graham-Technik ihren London-Aufenthalt und ermöglichte ebenfalls britischen Tänzern das Studium in New York. 1966 gründete er die London School of Contemporary Dance (LSCD), die erste ihrer Art in Europa. Eines ihrer wichtigsten Ergebnisse war, Schüler für eine Tanzlaufbahn zu gewinnen, die sich ihrer Herkunft und ihrem Temperament nach nicht vom klassischen Ballett angezogen fühlen. Innerhalb von 15 Jahren formierten ihre Absolventen viele neue Gruppen, die im ganzen Land nicht nur in Theatern auftreten, sondern auch in weniger formellem Rahmen, in Colleges und Gemeindezentren. Kürzlich wurde eine zweite Schule in Darlington eröffnet, die Northern School of Contemporary Dance, die ebenfalls eine auf Graham basierende Technik lehrt. Und auch die führende Kompanie, die aus der LSCD erwuchs, das London Contemporary Dance Theatre, brachte jungen Leuten außerhalb Londons Erfahrungen mit Modern Dance, indem sie in anderen Städten Workshop-Programme präsentierte. Eine so gründliche professionelle Modern Dance-Ausbildung wie in Großbritannien findet man innerhalb Europas nur noch in Frankreich, wo vor kurzem Schulen eröffnet wurden, die Kurse im Stil Merce Cunninghams und Alwin Nikolais' anbieten. Zusätzlich führt die 1979 in Verbindung mit dem West London Institute of Advanced Education gegründete Rambert Academy parallel laufende Kurse in klassischem und zeitgenössischem Tanz durch, um den Bedürfnissen der Kompanien zu entsprechen (wie des Ballet Rambert in Großbritannien oder des Nederlands Dans Theater und des Kölner Tanz-Forum), deren Repertoire auf diesen beiden Tanztechniken basiert.

Dadurch sind die Möglichkeiten der Tanzausbildung in Großbritannien breiter angelegt als sonst in Europa, obwohl es beiden führenden Institutionen, der Royal Ballet School und der London School of Contemporary Dance, an finanzieller Sicherheit und Unterstützung mangelt, wie sie die staatlichen Tanzinstitute in anderen europäischen Ländern genießen. Andererseits muß man jedoch anerkennen, daß das Lehrniveau im ganzen nicht dem der amerikanischen Hauptstädte entspricht, das ebenfalls in den Arten der angebotenen Kurse eine größere Vielfalt aufweist. Die wichtigste amerikanische Schule, die School of American Ballet, ist sogar noch jüngeren Datums als die Royal Ballet School, und sie verdankt ihr Ansehen teils der Tatsache, daß George Balanchine ihr Leiter ist, teils der Entschiedenheit, mit der Lincoln Kirstein dessen Bemühungen unterstützt, teils auch der Tatsache, daß in ganz Amerika viele ehemalige Tänzer Tanzschulen professionellen Niveaus eröffneten.

Die britische Tanzausbildung ist in Europa noch in anderer Hinsicht führend. Die LSCD bietet seit ihrer Gründung (die Royal Ballet School erst in letzter Zeit) Choreographiekurse als Teil des Lehrplans an. 1975 führte die Gulbenkian Foundation einen von Glen Tetley geleiteten Sommerkurs für junge Choreographen und Komponisten als Teil eines Programms zur Förderung des Tanzes in Großbritannien durch. Ihm folgten jedes Jahr ähnliche Kurse, geleitet von Glen Tetley, Norman Morrice und Robert Cohan. Als die Gulbenkian Foundation keine Mittel mehr zur Verfügung stellen konnte (die Statuten der Stiftung gestatten nur, Projekte ins Leben zu rufen, aber nicht, sie unendlich lang zu unterstützen), wurde das Programm durch Mittel der Europäischen Gemeinschaft gefördert, und Bewerber auch aus anderen Ländern zugelassen. Ziel dieses choreographischen Sommerkurses ist es, den angehenden Choreographen die Möglichkeit zu geben, Erfahrung in der Arbeit mit Musikern und Tänzern zu sammeln, ihre Versuche dem Rat und der Kritik von professioneller Seite auszusetzen, sowie das Interesse und Verständnis junger Musiker für den Tanz zu fördern.

Eine weitere Aktivität der Gulbenkian Foundation bestand in letzter Zeit in der Untersuchung des gesamten Bereichs britischer Tanzerziehung und der Ausarbeitung von Empfehlungen zu ihrer Entwicklung und Verbesserung. Der Bericht dieses Untersuchungsausschusses, der 1980 unter dem Titel *Dance Education and Training in Britain* veröffentlicht wurde, nennt viele Errungenschaften, jedoch auch viele noch nicht erfüllte Bedürfnisse. Dank dieser Untersuchung wurden schon viele Änderungen und Neuerungen eingeführt; mit weiteren ist zu rechnen.

John Percival

THE ENGLISH EDUCATIONAL SYSTEM OF DANCE

When Ninette de Valois founded a dancing school in 1926, she gave it the pretentiously solemn name of the Academy of Choreographic Art. With hindsight, that can be seen as a way of indicating that she wanted her venture to be regarded as artistically more serious than any institute of dance education previously existing in Britain. There had been no lack of dance teachers in the past, some of them excellent, and as early as 1904 a meeting of some teachers had set up what is now the Imperial Society of Teachers of Dancing. Its intention was to safeguard and develop their professional standing and to protect standards of teaching. That body, today with many branches covering different types of stage and ballroom dancing, still exists as one of several organizations holding examinations and issuing certificates. Preeminent among such organizations is the Royal Academy of Dancing, (RAD) established in 1920 as "an association of experts to guide teachers and young dancers in the correct technique of the ballet and to preserve the great traditions of our art" (the description is that of one of its most illustrious early members, Phyllis Bedells). The reputation of the Royal Academy is reflected not only in the royal charter granted in 1936 but also in the fact that the two presidents who have, between them, held office throughout its history both enjoyed unique respect from the dancing profession and from the public, Adeline Genée and Margot Fonteyn.

The prime purpose of the examining bodies has been to ensure that children who learned to dance were taught correctly. What became of their skills, once acquired, was of comparatively little concern, although the RAD did form a Production Club to serve as a training ground for would-be choreographers and to provide some pupils with experience of performing before an audience. When de Valois set up her school, she already had the intention of forming a permanent ballet company working on lines similar to what she had observed as a member of the Ballets Russes de Serge Diaghilev, and proposed to train her pupils for that purpose. Thus, in its purpose, her Academy of Choreographic Art was like the great schools in dance capitals such as Paris, St. Petersburg and Copenhagen: but how different were the means.

Those institutions were established with the resources of the court to support them and have remained a charge on the state even when thrones toppled. De Valois began her school entirely on her own initiative, and even when it moved to Sadler's Wells in 1931 it remained dependent on what funds it could earn or beg, without any support from national or local government. Its prestige grew with that of the company it served and was enhanced in 1947 when (mainly at the urging of the ballet writer Arnold Haskell) academic studies were added to the professional curriculum. The future continuance of the school was assured when, by a royal charter granted in 1956, it became an integral part of the Royal Ballet, but until the 1970s grants towards the costs of tuition and maintenance depended on the willingness of local authorities in each individual case. For pupils up to the age of 16 attending the lower school, that difficulty was eventually resolved by an arrangement (unique to the Royal Ballet School and to Yehudi Menuhin's school for young musicians) whereby grants were automatically awarded by the central government for every British child accepted by the school, but even now that does not apply to the upper school, so that a talented child may have difficulty in completing his or her dance education.

It is not only in its financing that the Royal Ballet School may be contrasted with, for instance, the Ballet School of the Paris Opera. Naturally they have many points of similarity, such as the assessment by a doctor of a child's likely adult physique as one of the tests before acceptance, and the weeding out, year by year, of pupils who, after acceptance, prove disappointing. But the greater financial resources in Paris permit a lengthy assessment of children's aptitude for dance by the provision of a preliminary summer course at which many more children are tried out than can be accepted. The Paris school, too, is more specifically linked to the company it serves, and (as in Denmark) the most gifted pupils spend their last two years as apprentices attached to the professional company.

During the equivalent period of their education, pupils of the Royal Ballet School graduate to the upper school which shares premises with the company, but their classes and all other activities remain entirely separate. The upper school takes its pupils not only from its own lower school, but also by audition from other dance schools in Britain and overseas. Consequently, it is training far more dancers than can possibly be absorbed by the two Royal Ballet companies. In effect, it is the chief source of recruitment for all the classical ballet companies in Britain, and even so, many of its graduates have to seek employment abroad.

Attempts by other companies outside London to found their own schools have so far been limited in their results. The Scottish Ballet, based in Glasgow, instituted the experiment of offering weekly classes to talented pupils who were already attending private ballet schools; an ingenious compromise to help raise standards while retaining the goodwill of the established teachers. Now, however, the company is trying to build up its own school, as the Manchester-based Northern Ballet Theatre has already done.

It might be expected, from the existence of several reputable organizations for approving teachers and examining pupils, that the level of teaching throughout the country would be at least moderately high. Unfortunately that is not so. A former dancer of the Royal Ballet has instituted a series of seminars in his native Yorkshire, to which noted teachers from London, and some from abroad, are invited. All the pupils accepted for the seminars must already be attending regular ballet classes. Teachers are allowed to watch the classes. Although the seminars have been held for some years and should already have helped to raise standards in the region, it has proved sadly necessary for the guest teachers, at what should be master classes, to spend much of their time correcting faults in basic training. A few schools do achieve a high standard but they are the exceptions.

In an attempt to remedy this, a Council for Dance Education and Training has lately been set up, its most important activities being to draw up and publicize a list of those training establishments which meet its criteria, and to advise government departments, local authorities and other interested bodies on all matters connected with education or training for dance and for teaching dance. That includes advising local authorities on which applicants are most deserving of financial help; but difficulties still arise, for instance, because a local authority may arbitrarily decide to limit the number of awards it will make to pupils accepted for the leading schools, which also happen to be the most expensive. Clearly, it will take time for the Council, and similar bodies set up in Scotland and Wales, to achieve their intended effect.

Two other important developments in recent years, which are to some extent linked, have been the growth of opportunities for professional training in modern dance techniques, and for dance education at advanced level for persons who may not intend to pursue a performing or teaching career. There has been interest in modern dance in Britain since the early years of the century; indeed, Margaret Morris developed her own technique as a reaction against the conventional nature of classical ballet at that time, and set up her first school in 1910.

But although she herself presented her pupils in ambitious productions, Margaret Morris Movement (MMM), like other "modern" or free-dance methods, achieved its greatest impact as a way in which amateurs could enjoy healthy and satisfying activity. Within 30 years there were MMM schools all over Britain, but their popularity waned during the war and never recovered. Meanwhile, during the 1930s Britain had given a home to two leaders of the German modern dance movement, Rudolf von Laban and Kurt Jooss. Laban set up the Art of Movement Studio, in collaboration with Lisa Ullmann, from which has grown the present Laban Centre, still a private venture but based at, and under the trusteeship of, Goldsmiths' College in the University of London (the College also has its own dance department on the same campus). The Laban Centre provides full-time dance theater vocational courses and also theoretical and practical studies in technique, movement analysis, choreography, dance notation, criticism, aesthetics, and other subjects. Technical training is not confined to any one system but has regard to Laban's principles.

The Laban Centre is only one of several colleges offering dance education at an advanced academic level. Others have developed from the links that grew, also since the early years of this century, between physical training (especially for women) and dancing. However, a complete transformation of the modern dance movement in Britain came about following the visits of the Martha Graham company and other American modern dance companies during the early 1960s. One of their most enthusiastic admirers, Robin Howard, paid for Graham teachers to come to London and for British dancers to go and study in New York. In 1966, he established the London School of Contemporary Dance (LSCD), the first of its kind in Europe. One of its most important effects has been to attract into a dance career students of a background and temperament who would not have been drawn to classical ballet. In 15 years its pupils have already brought about the formation of many new performing groups who play not only in theaters but in more informal locations, colleges, and community centers, throughout the country. Lately a second school teaching a Graham-based technique, the Northern School of Contemporary Dance, has been opened in Darlington. Also, the main performing company that grew from the LSCD, London Contemporary Dance Theatre, has brought modern dance

experience to young people outside London by residencies in other towns. Only in France, where schools offering courses in the styles of Merce Cunningham and Alwin Nikolais have recently been opened, is there any opportunity in Europe for such thorough professional modern dance training as in Britain. In addition, the Rambert Academy, set up in 1979 in conjunction with the West London Institute of Advanced Education, has begun joint classical and contemporary dance courses to meet the needs of companies (Ballet Rambert in Britain, Nederlands Dans Theater and Tanz-Forum, Cologne from abroad) which base their repertory in the two forms of dance.

Thus, although the two leading institutions, the Royal Ballet School and the London School of Contemporary Dance, both lack financial security and backing such as is enjoyed by the state dance schools in other European countries, the opportunities for dance education in Britain are wider than elsewhere in Europe. On the other hand, it has to be recognized that the standard of teaching, as a whole, does not match that which can be found in the leading American cities, where also the types of courses offered are diverse. The most important American school, the School of American Ballet, is an even more recent foundation than the Royal Ballet School, and owes its eminence partly to the presence of George Balanchine as its leader, partly to the determination with which Lincoln Kirstein has supported Balanchine's efforts, and partly also to the presence in America of many former dancers who have, throughout the country, set up dancing schools based on professional standards.

British dance education leads Europe in one other respect. The London School of Contemporary Dance since its foundation, and the Royal Ballet School in recent years, have both provided courses in choreography as part of their curriculum. In 1975, as part of a program of activity to support dance in Britain, the Gulbenkian Foundation held a summer school for young choreographers and composers under the direction of Glen Tetley. It has been followed annually by similar courses led by Glen Tetley, Norman Morrice, and Robert Cohan; when Gulbenkian funds were no longer available (as the Foundation's rules allow it to initiate ventures but not to sustain them indefinitely), sponsorship was obtained from European Community funds and applicants were accepted also from other countries. The purpose of the choreographic summer schools is to allow the would-be choreographers to gain experience in working with musicians and a group of dancers and to have their attempts subjected to advice and comment from professionals; also to encourage an

interest in, and understanding of, dance among young musicians.

Another of the Gulbenkian Foundation's recent activities has been to survey the whole field of dance education in Britain and make recommendations for its development and improvement. The report by its committee of inquiry into *Dance Education and Training in Britain,* published in 1980 lists many achievements but also many needs still unmet. As a result of the inquiry many changes and innovations have already been made and others may be expected.

118

Kirsten Ralov

DIE BOURNONVILLE-SCHULE

In den letzten zwei, drei Jahrzehnten wurde die Bournonville-Schule in der Welt des Balletts berühmt. Seit Ende des Zweiten Weltkrieges fanden Bournonvilles Ballette auf internationaler Ebene zunehmend Beachtung, wohingegen sie zuvor fast ausschließlich in Dänemark aufgeführt wurden.

Es ist hier nicht die Absicht, Bournonvilles Werke, sein Leben oder seine Karriere zu beschreiben. Kurz sollte jedoch erwähnt werden, daß er 1805 in Dänemark geboren wurde, wo er bis zu seinem Tod 1879 auch den größten Teil seines Lebens verbrachte. Sein Vater Antoine Bournonville, gebürtiger Franzose, war von 1816 bis 1823 Ballettmeister des Königlich Dänischen Balletts. Er wollte, daß sein Sohn Tänzer würde. Folglich trat August Bournonville 1813 in die Schule des Königlich Dänischen Balletts ein, wo er eine hervorragende Ausbildung erhielt. Darüber hinaus ließ sein Vater ihn auch in Paris studieren. 1823 wurde August Bournonville als Tänzer an das Königlich Dänische Ballett verpflichtet; ein Jahr später kehrte er zur Fortsetzung seines Studiums nach Paris zurück, wo er unter anderem von Auguste Vestris unterrichtet wurde. 1826 debütierte er in Paris und erhielt danach ein Engagement an die Pariser Oper. Von 1830 bis 1874 arbeitete er in Dänemark als Solist, Lehrer, Choreograph und künstlerischer Direktor am Ballett des Königlichen Theaters. Seine Tänzerlaufbahn beendete er 1848, war jedoch weiterhin als Pädagoge und Choreograph tätig. Er schuf unzählige Werke; acht davon sind neben einigen Divertissements auch heute noch im Repertoire des Königlich Dänischen Balletts.

Einem seiner Nachfolger, Hans Beck, ist es vor allem zu verdanken, daß diese Ballette wie auch die Exercises seines Trainings-Programms erhalten blieben. Kurz vor Bournonvilles Tod debütierte der junge Beck in Kopenhagen. Bournonville war anwesend und bescheinigte dem Tänzer großes Talent. Hans Beck wurde 1894 zum künstlerischen Direktor des Königlich Dänischen Balletts ernannt und bewahrte Bournonvilles Werke mit äußerst umsichtiger Pflege dem Repertoire, tanzte sogar die meisten männlichen Hauptrollen selbst. Er war sich der Notwendigkeit eines ganz im Geist August Bournonvilles gehaltenen Lehrsystems bewußt, entwickelte deshalb mit seinen Kollegen sechs unterschiedliche Programme für das tägliche Training. Die Musik für den Unterricht war zumeist populär, enthielt bekannte Polkas, Walzer, Songs gängiger Revuen sowie Werke der Komponisten von Bournonvilles Balletten. Auch der Korrepetitor entwickelte eigene Stücke für einige dieser Übungen.

Das Training richtete sich nach der Methode Bournonvilles: Adagio, Port de bras, Temps de pirouette, Etudes de ballon, Temps battus. Sehr häufig wählte man Variationen seiner Ballette aus. Diese Programme wurden nach den Wochentagen benannt und waren ähnlich gegliedert. Einige Lehrer richteten ihren Unterricht nach den Wochentagen aus, andere wiederholten ihn eine Woche oder einen Monat lang. (Als Kinder hatten wir einen Tageslehrplan das ganze Jahr über; einer der Gründe dafür, daß ich mich so gut daran erinnere.) Seit Ende des vorigen Jahrhunderts bis in die 30er Jahre wurde so beim Königlich Dänischen Ballett trainiert. Es läßt sich kaum leugnen, daß es einige Lehrer gab, die kein Verständnis für die Bedürfnisse der Schüler oder für die Qualität des Stoffes aufbringen konnten. Einige Tänzer bekamen daher keinen richtigen Eindruck von dieser Methode, obwohl, alles in allem, die Tänzer die Zeit überstanden und auch die Schrittkombinationen überdauerten.

Für ein Exercise wählte man stets die gleiche Musik; einer der Hauptgründe, daß die Schritte so gut erhalten blieben. Wie in Volksliedern und -tänzen wird die Melodie zum Stichwortgeber. Leider kann das auch von Nachteil sein. Man erinnert sich etwa an einen Schritt und tanzt ihn automatisch, ohne über seinen Zweck oder die Nuancen der Technik nachzudenken, wodurch die Exercises leicht oberflächliche Routine werden. Es hat andererseits den Vorteil, daß die Auswahl der Melodien die Ausführung der besonderen Phrasierung anregt, die im Bournonville-Stil so charakteristisch ist.

Oft redet man über Bournonville und vergißt dabei seinen individuellen Gebrauch der klassischen Grundschritte wie Assemblé, Jeté, Changement, die er stets in seiner Methode nutzte und in unterschiedlichen Zusammenhängen erweiterte. Zum Beispiel finden sich oft fünf Schritte auf vier Schläge. In der Bournonville-Schule werden alle Schritte mit anderen kombiniert, das heißt, es werden nicht acht oder 16 Assemblés, Jetés oder Changements wiederholt, ohne daß eine Abfolge mehrerer Grundschritte dazwischenliegt. Viele seiner Kombinationen sind sehr lang und körperlich anstrengend. Ein Adagio in der Mitte kann leicht 96 Vierteltakte dauern und oft hohe Développés, tiefe Pliés und Sprünge beinhalten. Die sehr hohen Développés, die man heutzutage sieht, wurden in früherer Zeit nicht verwandt, höchstwahrscheinlich weil das körperliche Ideal ein anderes war. (Ich erinnere mich, daß mein besonders auf Stil bedachter Lehrer uns gern die Beine höher heben ließ als frühere Generationen. Ich bin davon überzeugt, daß Bournonville nichts dagegen hätte, vorausgesetzt, sein graziöser und müheloser Stil wäre davon nicht beeinträchtigt.)

Bournonville hat selbst viel über seine Interpretation der Tanzkunst geschrieben. Als er 1861 für kurze Zeit nicht in Kopenhagen war, veröffentlichte er *Etudes Chorégraphiques dédiées à mes élèves et à mes collègues (Choreographische Etüden, meinen Schülern und Kollegen gewidmet),* so daß seine Schüler ihr Training korrekt fortsetzen konnten. Darin gibt er zahlreiche Ratschläge und Anweisungen zu den Schritten, die ständig geübt werden sollten: „Ich stelle hier meinen lieben Schülern und verehrten Kollegen choreographische Etüden vor und erinnere sie an das oft wiederholte Wort, daß Entwicklung und Beherrschung des Stoffes nicht so sehr von der Anzahl der Übungen als von der Sorgfalt ihrer Ausführung abhängen." In seinem Buch über die wichtigsten Übungen und einfache Schrittfolgen gibt er diesen Rat: „Wie in der Natur, in der sich Vielfalt gegenseitig ergänzt, kann eine Person nicht alle künstlerische Perfektion in sich vereinen. Die Übungen sollten deshalb den Bedürfnissen des jeweiligen Schülers entsprechen. Derjenige, der mehr Kraft als Geschmeidigkeit, mehr Leichtigkeit als Aplomb besitzt, muß sich insbesondere darauf konzentrieren, seine Fehler zu beheben und seine Schwächen auszugleichen."

Es gibt eigentlich nichts wirklich Neues in der Bournonville-Schule, weil seine Choreographien so logisch und natürlich sind. Tatsächlich bediente er sich der gleichen Schritte wie Waganowa, Cecchetti und andere. Einer seiner Schüler, Christian Johannsson, ging nach Rußland, wo er auch einer der Lehrer Waganowas war. Deshalb ist die enge Verbindung des dänischen Balletts mit der französischen und russischen Schule recht offensichtlich. Unterrichtet man Bournonville im Ausland, bemerkt man allerdings einen Unterschied. Den in seiner Technik ausgebildeten Tänzern sind seine Schrittfolgen so vertraut, daß sie keine großen Schwierigkeiten haben. Es geht nur um die Frage der richtigen Phrasierung, verbunden mit schnellen Richtungswechseln und einem wesentlich einfacheren Port de bras. Die Tänzer des Königlich Dänischen Balletts vertiefen ihr Können auch dadurch, daß sie regelmäßig in seinen Werken auftreten. Daraus folgt, daß Tänzer außerhalb Dänemarks den Stil Bournonvilles erfassen sollten, um seine Ballette angemessen darzubieten.

Eines der Geheimnisse des Bournonville-Systems ist sein Programm, das aus kleinen Variationen besteht, die sich oft als Soli eignen. Die Freitagsschule basiert auf dem 1. Akt von *Conservatoire.* Wenn man diese Schritte die ganze Kindheit über ausführt, fällt es einem als Erwachsenem natürlich erheblich leichter, dieses Ballett, das zu den anspruchsvollsten Bournonvilles gehört, zu tanzen.

Als ausländische Einflüsse, wie etwa das von der russischen Schule geprägte Training Vera Volkovas, auf Dänemark übergriffen, wandte man die Bournonville-Schule nicht mehr täglich an. Das Stangenexercise hatte man bereits mit Schritten aus der französischen und der russischen Schule ergänzt, weil die Bournonvilleschen Kombinationen zu wenig und zu kurz waren. Sein Trainingsprogramm, das gegen Ende des vorigen Jahrhunderts entstand, enthält nur acht bis zehn Übungen an der Stange. Man muß zugeben, daß der Körper eine bestimmte Zahl von Exercises zum Aufwärmen benötigt. Jedoch beabsichtigte Bournonville zweifellos nie, daß die Schüler allzu vorschnell die schwierigen Bewegungsabläufe in der Mitte angingen. So sagt er: „Das Stangenexercise ist nur dafür notwendig, daß man sich ohne zu große Ermüdung auf die jeweilige Stunde vorbereiten kann."

Das Training in der Mitte ist umfangreich und ausgedehnt. Man kann zwar ein ganzes Programm in einer Unterrichtsstunde absolvieren, jedoch bleibt dann keine Zeit mehr für Korrekturen. Selbst wenn der Schüler seinen Lehrstoff völlig beherrscht, wäre es trotzdem falsch, das Material derart anzuwenden. Heute ist man dankbar dafür, daß die Methode Bournonvilles erhalten ist, aber um sie völlig auszuschöpfen, sollte man unbedingt die richtigen Übungen zur rechten Zeit ausführen. Und dies ist es, was man mit der Aufzeichnung der Lehrpläne erreichen wollte. Nach den vier Stufen der Kinderklasse, wie es sie heute im Königlich Dänischen Ballett gibt, können Lehrer wie Tänzer einen solchen Leitfaden gebrauchen, da das gesamte Bournonville-Programm nur für Fort-

geschrittene entwickelt wurde. Es gibt keinen Lehrplan, der den Schüler über Jahre hinweg dazu befähigt die Schritte zu meistern. Statt dessen empfiehlt das Buch bestimmte Schritte und Übungsteile, um die komplizierteren Abläufe zu erlernen.

Das gesamte Trainingsprogramm besteht aus kürzer und länger choreographierten, mühelos scheinenden Sequenzen. Die Schüler bekommen Gelegenheit, alle Schritte vollständig zu tanzen, was so wichtig für die Entwicklung ihres Körpers ist.

Bournonvilles Variationen für den Unterricht und für die Bühne kennen keine Schritt- oder Laufpassagen; immer führen Tanzschritte die Tänzer an ihren Ausgangspunkt zurück. Das bedeutet aber nicht, daß sie während ihrer Soli keine Atempausen hätten, denn die Choreographie ermöglicht es ihnen, während des Tanzens ihre Kräfte kontrolliert einzusetzen. Ein weiteres Charakteristikum der Werke Bournonvilles ist die Vorbereitung der Sprünge. In seiner Terminologie gibt es Chassé contre temps, das bedeutet: Stehen auf dem rechten Fuß, linker Fuß Tendu derrière, links Coupé dessous, rechts Posé en avant, springen mit gleichzeitigem Schlagen links in fünfter Position hinten, und dann sofort das linke Bein nach vorne bringen in Croisé devant und das Gewicht auf das linke Bein verlagern. Der Schritt muß leicht, nicht hoch, aber raumgreifend wirken und in der vierten Position in Croisé devant in Demi plié enden. Das Battu im Sprung darf nicht dem Charakter eines Battu in einer Cabriole entsprechen. Dieser Schritt ist im allgemeinen eine Vorbereitung auf eine Glissade grand jeté oder ein anderes Contre temps.

Es wird behauptet, daß Bournonville kein Meister der Pirouette war und sie deshalb in seinen Kombinationen fehlen. Das stimmt nicht. Fast alle seiner Variationen enthalten

Drehungen, obwohl sie sich von denen der russischen Schule unterscheiden.

Bournonville mochte einen Schritt nicht um seines Effektes willen. Er sagt: „Der Tanz kann durch Unterstützung der Musik bis zur Poesie erhoben werden, andererseits aber durch die Überbetonung des Turnerischen zum akrobatischen Kunststück absinken." Dies erklärt, warum er auch nie die 32 Fouettés einsetzte. „Zum sogenannten Schwierigen bekennen sich zahlreiche Adepten, während das scheinbar Mühelose nur von wenigen Auserwählten beherrscht wird. Wahre Begabung zeigt sich darin zu wissen, wie man die Technik hinter der Ruhe der Harmonie verbirgt, die die Grundlage der wahren Grazie ist." In den Männervariationen findet man oft Tours en l'air nach links und nach rechts. Bournonville war mit begrenzten Fähigkeiten nicht zufrieden; man mußte alles meistern können. Er setzte die Pirouetten ganz bewußt in seinen Choreographien ein und sagt dazu: „Der Effekt verlangt, die zweite Pirouette in Geschwindigkeit und Anzahl zu verdoppeln." (Zum Beispiel zwei Pirouetten à la seconde gefolgt von vier Pirouetten sur le cou de pied.)

Fälschlich nahm man an, daß Bournonville die Arme nicht einsetzte. Es ist wahr, daß sie in vielen Fällen ruhig und ungekünstelt wirken, aber es ist ein Mißverständnis zu glauben, sie sollten am Körper „kleben". Die Arme sind normalerweise während kleiner Sprünge und Pirouetten sowie nach einer Variation gesenkt. „Diese behende Grazie in den anstrengendsten Bewegungen und zugleich eine Virtuosität zu bewahren, die nur durch gutes Training erworben wird, das zur Entwicklung von Qualität und zur Korrektur von Fehlern dient, mit denen jeder ausnahmslos, auch die größten Talente, zu kämpfen hat – dies ist das große Problem des Tanzes."

Kirsten Ralov

THE BOURNONVILLE METHOD

During the last two to three decades the Bournonville method has become famous all over the world of ballet. Since the end of the Second World War, Bournonville ballets have gained an ever increasing international recognition, whereas previously they were performed almost exclusively in Denmark.

It is not intended here to describe Bournonville's works, his life or his career. Briefly it should be mentioned, however, that he was born in Denmark in 1805, where he spent most of his life until his death in 1879. His father, Antoine Bournonville, who was a Frenchman by birth, was maître de ballet at the Royal Danish Ballet from 1816–23. He wanted his son, August, to become a dancer. August Bournonville entered there-

fore the Royal Danish Ballet School in 1813, where he received an excellent education. Apart from having him trained in Denmark, his father also sent him to Paris for study in 1820. In 1823 August Bournonville became a dancer with the Royal Danish Ballet. The following year he returned to Paris for further study, one of his teachers being Auguste Vestris. In 1826 he made his debut in Paris and was afterwards offered an engagement with the Paris Opera. From 1830–74 he

worked in Denmark at the Royal Theater as a soloist, teacher, choreographer, and artistic director of the ballet. He retired from dancing in 1848, but continued to teach and to create ballets. He choreographed innumerable works, eight of which, along with a few divertissements, still remain in the repertory of the Royal Danish Ballet.

The fact that it has been possible to preserve Bournonville's ballets as well as the exercises from his training-program is, for the most part, due to one of his successors, Hans Beck. Shortly before Bournonville died, the young Hans Beck made his debut in Copenhagen. Bournonville was present and attested to the young dancer's great talent. Hans Beck was appointed ballet master of the Royal Danish Ballet in 1894 and through most careful preservation he kept Bournonville's works in his repertory, dancing most of the leading male roles himself. He was aware of the need for a training program in the true spirit of August Bournonville. So, together with his colleagues, he organized six different exercise programs to be used in the daily training. The music chosen for these exercises was generally popular and included well-known polkas, waltzes, songs from current revues, as well as music by composers of Bournonville's ballets. Even the ballet répétiteur made up melodies for some of the exercises.

Practice was directed according to Bournonville's method of training: adagio, port de bras, temps de pirouette, études de ballon, temps battus and so on. Very often, variations from Bournonville ballets themselves were selected. The exercises were named after the days of the week and they all had a similar structure. Some teachers followed suit while others used only one program during the entire week or month. (As children we had the same program throughout the year, and this consequently is one of the reasons why I remember the program so well). These programs were used by the Royal Danish Ballet from the end of the last century until the 1930s. One can hardly deny the fact that there were a few teachers who were not up to understanding either the requirements of the students or the excellence of the material. Consequently, in time, some dancers did not get the right impression of this method, although, on the whole, both the dancers and the steps have survived well.

The same musical accompaniment was always used for the same exercises, this being one of the chief reasons why the steps have been preserved. Just as with remembering folk songs and dances, the melody becomes a cue. Unfortunately, this method can also pose disadvantages. For example, one remembers a step and dances it automatically without concentrating on the purpose or the nuances of the technique, the exercises easily becoming superficial routine. On the other hand there is the advantage that the selection of melodies is useful in inspiring the performance of the special phrasing so characteristic to Bournonville's style.

Very often one refers to Bournonville forgetting his individual use of the basic ballet steps assemblé, jeté, changement and the like, which he employed repeatedly throughout his method, continuing them in different phrasings. For example, one often finds five movements on four beats. In the Bournonville method almost all the steps are intermixed. That is to say, one does not repeat eight or sixteen assemblés, jetés, or changements without an enchaînement of

several basic steps placed in between. Many of the combinations are very long and physically demanding. An adagio in the center can easily consist of 96 bars of 4/4 time and often include high extensions, deep pliés, and jumps. The very high extensions seen nowadays were not used earlier, most likely because the aesthetics were different. (I recall my teacher, whilst being very careful with the style, liked to see us lifting the legs higher than former generations. I am convinced that Bournonville would not mind seeing this provided it did not interfere with the gracious and effortless Bournonville mode.)

Bournonville himself has written much about his interpretation of the art of dance. In 1861, during his short absence from Copenhagen, he published *Etudes Chorégraphiques dédiées à mes élèves et à mes collègues (Choreographic Studies Dedicated to my Students and to my Colleagues)* so that his students could continue their training in the correct way. He gives various pieces of advice and instructions on the steps which should be practiced at all times. "These are choreographic studies which I present here to my dear students as well as to my distinguished colleagues, recalling the oft repeated saying that it is not so much the number of exercises, on which progress and competence are dependent, as it is the care used in their application." In his book dealing with the most important exercises and simple enchaînements Bournonville gives the following advice: "As in nature diversity is complementary, so it is that a single individual cannot possess total artistic perfection. The études must then be applied according to the individual need of the student. Those who possess more strength than suppleness, more agility than aplomb must give special attention to remedying the imperfections and compensating for the weaknesses."

In some ways, there is nothing really new in the Bournonville method, as his choreography is so logical and natural. In fact, he used basically the same steps as Vaganova, Cecchetti and others. One of Bournonville's students, Christian Johannsson, went to Russia where, among other things, he became one of Vaganova's teachers. Therefore, a strong link between the Danish ballet and the French and Russian schools is quite evident. Although, when one teaches the Bournonville method abroad, one does notice differences. Dancers trained in the Bournonville method are so accustomed to his combinations of steps that they have little difficulty. For them it is merely a matter of the phrasing combined with quick changes of direction and a far simpler port de bras. Dancers of the Royal Danish Ballet also gain proficiency through regular performance of

Bournonville's works. It follows that dancers outside Denmark should grasp the Bournonville style, if they are to perform his ballets properly.

One of the secrets of the Bournonville system is its program which consists of small variations often suitable for solos. The Friday class is based on the first act of *Conservatoire*. When one has executed these steps throughout one's childhood, it is obviously easier as an adult to perform this ballet – one of Bournonville's most demanding works.

The Bournonville method ceased to be used daily when such influences as Vera Volkova's teaching according to the Russian school entered Denmark. The practice at the barre had already been supplemented with steps from the Russian and French schools, as the Bournonville exercises were too few and too short. In the Bournonville training program, created late in the last century, there are only about eight to ten combinations at the barre. One must admit that the body needs a certain number of exercises to warm up. However, there is no doubt that Bournonville ever intended that students should hasten to the difficult enchaînements in the center. He says, "The exercises at the barre are necessary only to such a degree to prepare oneself for the specific lesson without too much fatigue."

The exercises in the center are numerous and prolonged. It is possible to go through an entire training program during one lesson, but then there is no time left for giving corrections. Even if students know the enchaînements perfectly, it would still be wrong to use the material in this way. Today, one is grateful that the Bournonville system has been kept intact, but to get the full benefit, it is very important to use the right exercises at the right time. That is what was intended with the notation of the curricula. Following the four levels of children's classes, as they exist today at the Royal Danish Ballet, such a "textbook" can be used by both teachers and dancers, as the entire Bournonville program is designed for advanced training only. There is no syllabus by which the student over a period of years arrives at the point of mastering the steps. The book, therefore, recommends certain steps, and certain parts of exercises as a means of learning the more complicated enchaînements.

The entire training program is arranged in long and short choreographed pieces, which seem effortless. The students get the opportunity to execute all steps in the entirety, which is so important for their physical development.

Bournonville's variations never have walking or running passages, neither in the studio nor on stage. There will always be dancing steps bringing them back to their original

diese Seite/this page
oben/above
KIRSTEN RALOV
beim Unterricht/teaching
"sur le cou de pied",
Königlich Dänisches Ballett/
Royal Danish Ballet,
Copenhagen,
Foto: A. Epstein
unten/below
MITTWOCHSSCHULE/
WEDNESDAY CLASS,
Inge Jensen,
Flemming Ryberg,
Foto: John R. Johnsen

gegenüber/opposite page
oben/above
CONSERVATOIRE,
Ch: August Bournonville
unten/below
MITTWOCHSSCHULE/
WEDNESDAY CLASS,
Königlich Dänisches Ballett/
Royal Danish Ballet,
Copenhagen
alle Fotos/all photos:
John R. Johnsen

places. This does not mean that the dancers have no breathing space during a solo, as the choreography makes it possible for the dancers to pace themselves during the performance. Another characteristic aspect of Bournonville's works is the preparation for jumps. In Bournonville's terminology there is chassé contre temps, which means: stand on the right with left tendu derrière, left coupé dessous, right posé en avant, and jump while simultaneously beating the left in fifth behind and then immediately passing left forward into croisé devant, transferring weight onto left. The quality of the step must be light, not high, but travelling and finishing in fourth croisé devant in demi-plié. The beat in the air must not have the rebounding quality of a cabriole. This step is usually a preparation for glissade grand jeté or for another contre temps.

It has been said that Bournonville himself was no master of the pirouette and consequently omitted them in his variations. This is not true. Almost all of his variations include turns, although different from those we find in the Russian school.

Bournonville himself did not like the step for the effect only. He says: "Dance can, with the help of music, raise itself even to the level of poetry, but on the other hand it could, by gymnastic excesses, equally descend to the sphere of acrobatics." That explains why he never used, for example, the 32 fouettés. "The so-called difficulty is professed by numerous adherents, whereas the apparent facility is the possession of a chosen few. The height of talent is to know how to conceal the mechanics through calmness of harmony which forms the basis of genuine grace." One frequently finds tours en l'air both to the right and left in the male variations. Bournonville was not satisfied by limited ability. One had to master everything. He used pirouettes most consciously in his choreography saying: "The effect requires that the second pirouette should be double in quickness and quantity." (For example two pirouettes à la seconde followed by four pirouettes sur le cou-de-pied.)

One has wrongly believed that Bournonville does not make use of the arms. It is correct that the arms are at ease and unaffected in many cases, but it is a misunderstanding to think that they should be "glued" to the body. The arms are normally in a lowered position during small leaps and pirouettes and after a variation. "To maintain this agile grace in the midst of the most strenuous movement and at the same time a virtuosity acquired only by means of good training appropriate for developing qualities and aiding in the correction of imperfections which each, without exception of the greatest talents, has to combat – this is the big problem of dance."

BOURNONVILLE
DIVERTISSEMENTS,
Einstudierung von/
staged by
Stanley Williams,
New York City Ballet,
Foto: Costas

LA VENTANA,
Ch: August Bournonville,
Mette Hønningen, Johnny Eliasen,
Königlich Dänisches Ballett
Kopenhagen/
Royal Danish Ballet,
Copenhagen,
Foto: John R. Johnsen

Es überrascht nicht, daß Europäer häufig durch die Vielfalt von Stilen und Techniken verwirrt sind, die unter dem Begriff *American Modern Dance* zusammengefaßt werden (eine unzulängliche Bezeichnung, die zudem viele Choreographen, auf deren Arbeit sie angewandt wird, verärgert). Noch 1975 kommentierte Lincoln Kirstein, Mitbegründer und einer der Direktoren des New York City Ballet, abwertend, daß der Modern Dance niemals ein breites öffentliches Interesse, ein zentrales System oder ein allgemeines Repertoire hatte aufbauen können. Warum sollte er? Modern Dance baute immer auf idiosynkratischen Stilen auf, und dies nötigte – bis zu einem gewissen Grad – zu einer Opposition gegen das Establishment einer Akademie. In den 20er und 30er Jahren erschien es bahnbrechend, die Betonung von Konformität und neutraler Technik des Balletts zurückzuweisen und statt dessen das individuelle Recht des Choreographen herauszustreichen, sich gemäß dem Tempo der Zeit und den Geboten seiner eigenen Sensibilität zu bewegen.

Im Zusammenhang mit Ballettchoreographen bedeutete Zeitgenossenschaft normalerweise Auswahl aktueller Themen, Kostüme, Musik, möglicherweise auch Bearbeitung alter Formeln oder Anpassung neuer Gesten an das Grundvokabular des Balletts. Es bedeutete keinen – nicht einmal für Michail Fokine – Neuaufbau von Grund auf oder ein Infragestellen der Grundformen und der Raison d'être. Jedoch machten revolutionäre „Modern Dancers" von Isadora Duncan über Martha Graham, Yvonne Rainer bis hin zu Laura Dean es sich zur Hauptaufgabe, Tanz neu zu definieren, indem sie nur jene Elemente ihres künstlerischen Erbes beibehielten, in denen sie einen Sinn sahen und alles andere verwarfen.

Mit dieser hohen Wertschätzung der Originalität trachtete jeder danach, Choreograph zu werden. Warum auch nicht? Als Tänzer konnte man ohnehin seinen Unterhalt kaum verdienen. In den späten 60er Jahren begannen höhere Subventionen und wachsende Zuschauerzahlen zumindest einigen Kompanien mehr Arbeit zu garantieren. Infolgedessen waren gute Tänzer nicht so leicht versucht, mäßige Choreographen zu werden. Für viele Choreographen – und Tänzer – war Unterricht stets eine Zusatzbeschäftigung. In den frühen Jahren des Modern Dance unterrichteten sie, um neue Bewegungsideen zu erproben und um Tänzer zu trainieren, die möglicherweise daran interessiert waren, mit ihnen für wenig oder gar kein Geld aufzutreten. Die typische Modern Dance-Kompanie gruppierte – und gruppiert sich bis heute – um das Talent eines Choreographen bzw. Lehrers, der

MISSTRAUEN GEGEN DIE AKADEMIEN
MODERNE TANZAUSBILDUNG IN DEN USA

zugleich Hauptdarsteller ist und sogar den Status eines kleinen Propheten, umgeben von Jüngern, erreichen kann. Es gibt natürlich Ausnahmen. Alwin Nikolais tanzte niemals in seiner eigenen Kompanie; Alvin Aileys Kompanie verfügt über ein erweitertes Repertoire, das auch Werke anderer Choreographen beinhaltet; Paul Taylor besaß niemals eine Schule, und es gibt keine Taylor-Technik, obwohl eindeutig ein Taylorscher Stil existiert.

Moderner – oder zeitgenössischer – Tanz setzt auch die Empfänglichkeit für Veränderungen voraus, so daß der Lehrplan in Schulen niemals gleich bleibt. Man nehme den Fall Martha Graham, die viele Jahre eine erfolgreiche Schule leitete und der allgemein zugestanden wird, eine Trainingstechnik für Tänzer und ein festgelegtes Schema für Tanzklassen kodifiziert zu haben. Aber was Graham lehrte, spiegelte immer auch ihre choreographischen Ansichten wider. Eine Graham-Klasse der 80er Jahre ähnelt kaum einer der 30er Jahre, obwohl Experten sagen, man könne das Gerüst der frühen Exercises durch die neuen hindurchscheinen sehen. Als Graham um 1925 begann, ihren eigenen Stil zu entwickeln, existierte überwiegend noch keine Auswärtsdrehung der Beine in ihren Tänzen oder Klassen, noch gab es viele hohe Développés. Bewegung entsprang dem Körperzentrum und erreichte in Gesten von immenser schlagender Kraft ihren Höhepunkt. Ab einer gewissen Zeit begann Graham an ihrer inzwischen berühmten Theorie von *Contraction and Release* zu arbeiten, einer Abstraktion und Intensivierung des Atmens. Sie experimentierte mit Stürzen, artikulierte einen oft zänkischen Dialog zwischen der Schwerkraft und dem Studioboden. Graham verwandte einiges von dem, was sie während ihrer Jahre mit Ruth St.Denis und Ted Shawn gelernt hatte, insbesondere François Delsartes Vorstellung von ausdrucksstarker menschlicher Bewegung; aber wenn sie ihre Tänzer die Oberkörper gegen die feststehenden Füße bewegen ließ, war es nicht ihr Ziel, eine dekorative Pose zu produzieren oder eine archaische Kultur anzudeuten, wie noch bei Denishawn. Vielmehr sollten damit in einem einzigen menschlichen Körper gegeneinanderwirkende Kräfte ausgedrückt werden. In Tänzen wie *Heretic* (1929) oder *Primitive*

Mysteries (1931) zeigte Graham, daß sich ihre Einsichten im Einklang mit denen der meisten zeitgenössischen Künstler und Designer in Europa und Amerika befanden. Wie diese, scheute sie – und ihr reines Frauen-Ensemble – Glanz und Ornamente. Sie betonte Stärke, klare Linien und Einfachheit.

Doch jede Entwicklung in Grahams künstlerischem Leben, jede neue Tänzergeneration wirkte auf ihren Stil und ihre Technik, die ihn unterstützte. Mit ihrem (ab 1938) beginnenden Interesse an Theaterformen und Rollenspielen entwickelte sich ihr Bewegungsstil zu größerer Komplexität, wurde durch Spiraldrehungen, Schwerpunktsverlagerungen erweitert, um die Ambivalenz und den seelischen Kampf von Heldinnen wie Medea oder Jokaste anzudeuten und den puritanischen Zwiespalt von Pflicht und Verlangen, der sie viele ihrer Tänze formte, zum Ausdruck zu bringen. Einige sehr prägnante Gesten, in sich wiederholende Bewegungsmuster gefaßt, fanden ihren Weg in den Unterricht. Als Graham älter wurde, schöpfte sie neue Bewegungen nicht mehr aus ihrem eigenen Körper. Ihre Anregungen holte sie sich nun aus der Vielzahl junger Tänzer, Tänzer mit gründlichem Ballett-Training, oftmals mit Auswärtsdrehung und hohen Développés, mit schlanken, geschmeidigen Körpern, die wenig Ähnlichkeit mit den starkgebauten Frauen der 30er Jahre hatten. Heute feiert Grahams Unterricht, wie ihre Stücke, den Tänzer als „Himmelsakrobat", feurig, intensiv. Viele der Exercises sind die gleichen wie vor 20 Jahren (die bekannte „Bodenarbeit", die Exercises auf der Stelle, die schönen Fallsequenzen, die Schritte, während man sich über den Boden bewegt), doch sehen sie nicht gleich aus. Die Schönheit einer Linie wird eher betont als der Antrieb einer Bewegung; die alte, schlagende Kraft wurde allmählich weicher, Rhythmus und Dynamik wurden schonender, leichter für den Körper.

(Obwohl ehemalige Mitglieder der Graham-Kompanie in der ganzen Welt unterrichten, entwickelt die Martha Graham School of Contemporary Dance jetzt ein System für die Anerkennung und Ausbildung von Lehrern. Und obwohl Grahams Name hierdurch vor Ausnutzung mangelhaft Ausgebildeter geschützt wird, ist es eine Ironie des Schicksals, daß viele gute Lehrer, die durch jahrelange gemeinsame Aufführungen mit ihr nachhaltig beeinflußt sind, nicht länger beanspruchen können, ihre Technik zu unterrichten.)

Ein anderer Zweig des American Dance ging von Grahams großer Zeitgenossin Doris Humphrey und ihrem Partner und Mitarbeiter Charles Weidman aus. In ihrem frühen Stadium vermied die Humphrey-

Weidman-Technik, wie die Graham-Technik, gestreckte Füße, Auswärtsdrehungen, alles, was als „ballettig" ausgelegt werden konnte. Wie Graham plädierten Humphrey und Weidman für Einfachheit, für Kraft statt Schnörkel. Auch sie untersuchten die Auswirkung der Schwerkraft auf den menschlichen Körper, statt die Erdanziehung zu leugnen. Und auch bei ihnen gab es „Bodenarbeit" und Fallsequenzen. Humphrey selbst war eine zartere, lyrischere Tänzerin als Graham; Weidman, schlaksig, kraftvoll und witzig, half viele der „männlichen" Exercises zu entwickeln, die in ihren Klassen gelehrt wurden.

Humphrey entwickelte eine Tanztheorie auf der Basis von *Fall and Recovery* und erklärte, daß Bewegung sich in der Spannweite zwischen zwei „Toden" ereignet, dem „Tod" der Stasis oder perfekter Balance und dem „Tod" des völligen Zusammenbruchs. Mit anderen Worten: der Tänzer beginnt seinen Körper aus seiner Achse zu kippen, zu werfen, zu schwingen, oder aufwärts zu stemmen, und die Dramatik der Bewegung resultiert aus der Art, wie er die Bahn der Bewegung formt, im Raum, in der Zeit, in der dynamischen Qualität. In Humphreys Kompositionsklassen und in ihrem Buch *The Art of Making Dances* legt sie durchdachte Prinzipien für angehende Choreographen dar. Sie selbst war eine Meisterin der expressiven Form. 1932 schrieb sie: „Vier abstrakte Themen, alle bewegen sich gleich und harmonisch, wie eine Fuge, die die Bedeutung der Demokratie weitaus besser vermitteln würde als eine in Rot, Weiß und Blau gekleidete Frau mit Sternen im Haar." Ihre Vorstellung vom Tanz konnte kantige Bewegungen produzieren, wie in *The Shakers* (1931), wo Mitglieder einer religiösen Zölibatssekte ihre Körper hinschleudern und wegzerren von einer auf der Bühne unsichtbaren Linie, die Männer und Frauen voneinander trennt. Andere ihrer Tänze, wie *Passacaglia* (1938) waren von tiefgründiger, erhabener Poesie, Stücke, in denen die Gesten weitausladende Bögen im Raum beschrieben und ihr Rhythmus sie im verstärkten Atmen wiederholte. Auch viele der Exercises bauten auf Rhythmus, Gewichtsimpuls und der Bahn eines Schwunges auf.

1944 mußte Doris Humphrey infolge eines Unfalls endgültig das Tanzen aufgeben, unterstützte jedoch bis zu ihrem Tod 1958 ihren Protegé José Limón als Choreographin und künstlerische Beraterin. Limóns Stil und die Technik, die er lehrte, waren – unweigerlich – eine persönliche Abwandlung der Humphrey-Weidmanschen Auffassung von Tanz. Der Mexikaner Limón war ein kräftiger Tänzer, hingezogen zu den grübelnden Helden der Literatur und Mythen. Humphrey selbst betonte diese

Qualitäten in den Tänzen, die sie für ihn choreographierte. Vielleicht beruhten die spanischen Rhythmen, die zurückgezogenen Arme, die heroischen Haltungen, die in Limóns Unterricht benutzt wurden, ebenso sehr auf Humphreys Vorstellung von Limón wie auf seiner eigenen.

Die Humphrey-Weidman-Technik wird in den USA bis heute in verschiedenen Formen von ehemaligen Mitgliedern der Kompanie unterrichtet. Nach dem Tod Limóns (1972) ging seine Kompanie weiterhin auf Tournee, unterrichtete auch Limón-Technik, doch es existiert keine wirkliche „Schule". Jennifer Muller und Louis Falco, in den 60er Jahren Mitglieder der Limón-Kompanie, setzten ihrem tänzerischen Erbe neue Akzente. In den Tänzen dieser beiden Choreographen kann man die Beschäftigung mit Schwere und Schwerkraft beobachten, die schon Limóns Arbeit charakterisierte, doch sind Muller und Falco Produkte einer anderen Gesellschaft. Tragische Helden, die Polarität von Gut und Böse, starke moralische Intentionen interessieren sie nicht. Statt dessen regiert in ihren Tänzen ein überschwenglicher Hedonismus; die Tänzer agieren amoralisch, spielerisch, selbstbezogen. Die Tanzphrasen werden nicht mehr wie bei Limón und Humphrey gestaltet. Das Grundprinzip von *Fall and Recovery* erscheint als Stürzen, Taumeln, Hochschnellen, das gelegentlich in gestreckten Positionen endet.

Eine weitere bedeutende Wegbereiterin des Modern Dance, Hanya Holm, ein Mitglied von Mary Wigmans Kompanie, kam aus Deutschland. 1931, nach Wigmans zweiter erfolgreicher Amerikatournee, gründete sie in New York eine Wigman-Schule. Obwohl sich Holms choreographischer Ruf seit den 40er Jahren in erster Linie auf ihren Beitrag zu Broadway-Musicals erstreckte, führte sie bis 1967 eine Schule unter ihrem eigenen Namen weiter, lehrte seit 1941 jeden Sommer am Colorado College und hat 1981 einen neuen Tanz für Don Redlichs Kompanie geschaffen.

Hanya Holms Methode unterschied sich immer von der ihrer amerikanischen Zeitgenossen, ihre Arbeit basierte weniger auf ihrem eigenen Körper. Sie lehrte ihre Schüler, sich gegenseitig am Schlagzeug zu begleiten und gab Improvisations- und Kompositionsklassen. Der Komponist Louis Horst, der zunächst die Mitglieder der Martha Graham-Kompanie und insgesamt rund drei aufeinanderfolgende Tänzergenerationen Komposition lehrte, gründete seine Vorstellungen auf der musikalischen Struktur, der Stimmung oder der Kultur; Holm betonte dagegen den Raum in einer Art, der Horst nicht entsprach. Das Programm ihrer Kompanie enthielt in einer ihrer frühen Lecture-Demonstrations Titel wie

Raum, der zerbirst durch die explosive Qualität der inneren Erregung des Tänzers, dessen Körper der Mittelpunkt ist oder *Die Anziehung der Tiefe.*

Die Arbeit Don Redlichs, ein Schüler von Holm (wie auch Valerie Bettis und Glen Tetley) zeigt ein ähnliches Interesse sowohl für die emotionalen Aspekte des „Menschen-im-Raum" als auch für die Klarheit des Designs. Ihr berühmtester Schüler, Alwin Nikolais, ist an ersterem weniger interessiert als an letzterem. Er meinte, die menschliche Leidenschaft sei als Thema für den Tanz zu abgenutzt, glaubte jedoch, wie Holm, an den Begriff des Raums als „eines aktiven Partners im Tanz". 1952 begann er mit der Art von Tanz, für die er heute berühmt ist – magische Farb- und Lichtwelten, in denen die Tänzer nur ein Element sind, oft kaum sichtbar hinter Wänden, unter Fabrikzelten oder durch überblendende Diaprojektionen meliert.

Um Tänzer für diese Welt zu gewinnen, mußte er in ihnen sowohl körperliche wie geistige Flexibilität entwickeln. Wie Holm bot Nikolais den Tänzern, die bei ihm studierten, immer eine umfassende Ausbildung: in Technik, Komposition, Improvisation und Pädagogik. Viele Techniken Holms paßte er seinen Zielen an. Von Anfang an, seit seine Kompanie im Henry Street Settlement House lehrte und aufführte (und welch ein Glück er hatte, ein eigenes Theater für Experimente zu haben), bestand sein Training unter anderem darin, die Tänzer zu lehren, jeden Teil ihres Körpers entweder getrennt oder zusammen mit anderen Körperpartien zum Ausdruck zu bringen. Es gibt z. B. kein Gelenk, das man nicht drehen oder diagonal ausstrecken könnte, gleichgültig wie kurz die Diagonale sein mag.

Alwin Nikolais ermutigte wie Hanya Holm seine Studenten, das im Training erlernte Bewegungsmaterial aufzunehmen und mit den zugrundeliegenden Prinzipien zu experimentieren, sowohl um Kreativität anzuregen als auch ein tieferes Verständnis des Unterrichtsmaterials zu fördern. Nicht alle nach diesem System unterrichteten Schüler nehmen Nikolais' Stil an. Er begünstigt fast immer leichte Bewegung, mit einem breiten Spektrum subtiler Abstufungen zwischen langsam und schnell, flüssig und akzentuiert. Murray Louis, eines der ersten Mitglieder von Nikolais' Kompanie und ein ausgezeichneter Lehrer, mag als beispielhaftes Produkt von Nikolais angesehen werden, mit einem Körper voller geistreicher und hintergründiger Tricks. Aufgrund Nikolais' Interesse an Pädagogik sind die jetzigen und ehemaligen Mitglieder seines Ensembles (wie etwa Murray Louis, Phyllis Lamhut und Gladys Bailin) begehrte Lehrer; 1978 wurde Nikolais von der französischen Regierung beauftragt, das Centre

National de Danse Contemporaine in Angers zu gründen.

Bevor in den späten 60er Jahren das National Endowment for the Arts begann, Tanzkompanien Zuwendungen und Unterstützung zu gewähren, hatten die Leiter der Truppen ihren Tänzern nur sehr wenig Greifbares zu bieten. Statt dessen boten sie eine Lebensart. Tänzer, die mit Humphrey, Graham oder irgendeinem anderen der sogenannten „Pioniere" des Modern Dance zusammenarbeiteten, schätzten sich glücklich, Bestandteil einer neuen Ordnung zu sein, auch wenn sie als Kellner oder Modelle für Maler, Bildhauer und dergleichen arbeiten mußten, um sich ernähren zu können. Erick Hawkins mag einer der letzten charismatischen Leiter sein, die ihren Tänzern vollkommene Ergebenheit abverlangen und dafür neben der technischen Ausbildung ästhetisches Credo bieten. Obwohl Hawkins mit Lincoln Kirsteins Ballet Caravan und mit Martha Graham als Partnerin von 1938 bis 1950 auftrat, waren seine Ideen vom Körper denen Grahams oder des Balletts diametral entgegengesetzt. Beeinflußt durch die Pionierarbeit von Mabel Ellsworth Todd (The Thinking Body/Der denkende Körper) und anderen, entwickelte Hawkins ein Trainingssystem, bei dem unnötige Muskelanspannung und überflüssiger Krafteinsatz ausgeschaltet werden sollten. Wie Isadora Duncan Jahre zuvor zog ihn die Idee an, die Natur bewege sich in Wellen; seine Technik betont eher Schleifen und Kurven als direktes Vorstoßen, einen weichen, elastischen Schritt, der weder gegen die Schwerkraft ankämpft noch sich ihr entzieht. Hawkins betont einen choreographischen Stil, der bewußt poetisch, idealistisch und verfeinert ist mit einem sehr subtilen Spektrum an Dynamik. Seine Tänze sind oft abstrakte Studien der Natur oder idyllische und sinnliche Visionen des Menschen in der Natur. Die derzeitigen und früheren Mitglieder seiner Kompanie, wie Beverly Brown oder Nancy Meehan lehren auf eine Art und Weise, die seinen Vorstellungen entspricht, ihnen teilweise widerspricht oder in ganz andere Richtungen geht.

Während einiger seiner Jahre mit Graham tanzte Hawkins oftmals als Widerpart von Merce Cunningham, der von 1939 bis 1945 bei Graham tanzte. War Hawkins der dunkle und dominierende Liebhaber, wirkte Cunningham spirtueller, ein wenig asexuell; vielleicht war er Grahams erster Entwurf eines „Himmelsakrobaten". In Deaths and Entrances war Hawkins der Dunkle Geliebte, Cunningham der Poetische Geliebte, in Appalachian Spring tanzte Hawkins den Landmann, Cunningham den fanatischen Prediger; in Every Soul is a Circus war Hawkins der strenge Zirkusdirektor, Cunningham der heitere Akrobat.

Cunninghams eigener Stil weicht ebenso von dem Grahams ab wie der von Hawkins. Er hat die zeitgenössische Auffassung von Tanz radikal verändert – und dabei den konventionellen Geschmack oft empört. Man kann argumentieren, daß Cunningham in den Tanz nur einige der formalen Neuerungen eingebracht hat, die es in Musik und Malerei bereits gab, und daß er in seinen Strukturen einige der im 20. Jahrhundert veränderten Konzepte in Wissenschaft und Philosophie widerspiegelt. Ein Cunningham-Tanz bietet dem Zuschauer kein wunderbar entworfenes Bild, mit einem zentralen Punkt und einer Hierarchie von Aktivitäten (von bedeutenden Aktivitäten im Vordergrund bis zu denen im Hintergrund). Statt dessen sind seine Tänze dichte Felder von Aktivität; die Zuschauer müssen wählen, was sie sich anschauen, da alles aufzunehmen unmöglich erscheint. Der Eindruck von Dichte erhöht sich dadurch, daß Musik, Dekoration und Beleuchtung als unabhängige, dem Tanz gleichgeordnete Strukturen gesehen werden. Obwohl die Musik, oftmals sehr laut, den Tanz nicht begleitet, beeinflußt sie die Wahrnehmung des ganzen Geschehens.

Cunninghams Behauptung, die Bedeutung ist Bewegung, seine unkonventionellen Strukturen, seine Anwendung des Zufalls in der Choreographie, sein kürzliches Experiment mit Video – all das hat ihm den bleibenden Ruf eines Radikalen eingebracht. Das Alter hat sein Denken nicht erstarren lassen. Obwohl seine Werke chaotisch und anarchistisch genannt wurden, werden seine Tänzer immer wegen ihrer Schönheit, Disziplin und Intelligenz gelobt. Verglichen mit dem dionysischen Graham-Tänzer, erscheint der Cunningham-Tänzer apollinisch; man sieht ihn nicht hin- und hergerissen in Leidenschaft oder von Gefühlen überwältigt.

Viele bezeichnen Cunninghams Stil als „ballettig", wegen des ruhigen, aufrechten Rückgrats der Cunningham-Tänzer, des kontrollierten Einsatzes des Gewichts, der aktiven und komplizierten Fußarbeit, der Tatsache, daß Bewegung ihren Ursprung mehr in den Gliedmaßen als im Zentrum des Körpers hat. Aber dieser Vergleich ist irreführend. Sein Tanz unterliegt einer radikalen Verzerrung von Form, Abfolge und Timing, die im Ballett unzulässig wäre. Trotz ihrer hohen Développés erscheinen die Tänzer seiner Kompanie nicht wie Ballett-Tänzer. Die besten unter ihnen scheinen sich stets der Zeit und des Raums klar bewußt, so wachsam wie Tiere und frei von unnötiger Spannung oder Befangenheit. Sie tanzen konzentriert, als entschieden sie, was als Nächstes zu tun wäre. Cunningham leitet eine der populärsten Schulen in New York und, unabhängig davon, wer die Stun-

de gerade leitet, fördern die Exercises diese Atmosphäre wacher Intelligenz. Die Anfangsübungen werden eher auf der Stelle stehend als auf dem Boden sitzend ausgeführt. Der Rumpf mag sich drehen, biegen oder zusammenziehen, er bringt die Tänzer jedoch nicht so aus dem Gleichgewicht, daß sie nicht wieder zurückfinden und fortfahren könnten. Vieles bei dieser komplexen Rumpfarbeit ist einer ebenso komplizierten Fußarbeit gegenübergestellt und wird manchmal derart schnell ausgeführt, daß aus den Exercises Übungen zur Koordination und im schnellen Denkvermögen werden. Oft zeichnen sich seine Klassen durch sehr lange, rhythmische, komplexe Phrasen aus, anstelle der kurzen, sich wiederholenden, durch ein musikalisches Metrum geformten Phrasen, die man in vielen Modern Dance-Klassen sieht (drei Schläge laufen, drei Schläge drehen usw.).

Während der späten 40er und 50er Jahre wurde der Modern Dance eklektizistischer. Obwohl einige ausgeprägt individuelle Choreographen hervortraten (Alwin Nikolais, Merce Cunningham, Erick Hawkins, Anna Sokolow, James Waring, Katherine Litz und andere) gaben sich viele Choreographen der „Zweiten Generation" mit der Vervollkommnung oder Wiederholung dessen zufrieden, was sie gelernt hatten. 1951 eröffnete die Juilliard School of Music eine Abteilung Tanz unter der Leitung von Martha Hill, einer bemerkenswerten Tanzlehrerin und Mitbegründerin des Bennington Festival. Begabte Schüler können von der High School of Performing Arts zur Juilliard School überwechseln, Ballett und Modern Dance studieren (ursprünglich Graham- und Limón-Techniken), Komposition, Musik und andere Kurse. Sie schließen mit einem Zeugnis oder dem Bachelor of Science ab (aber dies ist ein Thema für einen anderen Artikel). Ähnliche Fächer werden inzwischen an einigen Universitäten angeboten; Schulen wie das Alvin Ailey Dance Center bieten z. B. Jazz, Ballett und moderne Techniken.

Das Überwinden von Barrieren und Rivalitäten hatte auch eine praktische Seite. Da relativ wenige Tanzkompanien genügend hohe Gehälter zahlen oder für genügend Auftritte sorgen, um für den seelischen Ausgleich der Tänzer zu sorgen, wollen Tänzer heute, praktischer als die der 30er Jahre, in der Lage sein, in einer Vielzahl von Kompanien aufzutreten und Jobs in Musicals oder Fernsehshows anzunehmen. Heutzutage ist eine Tänzerin wie Shelley Washington durchaus nicht unüblich, die mit Walter Nicks' Jazztruppe, mit der Limón- und mit der Graham-Kompanie auftrat, bevor sie sich Twyla Tharp anschloß.

Die wachsende Vielseitigkeit der Tänzer hat

ihre Entsprechung in der Mischung der choreographischen Stile – so wie die Mischung von Ballettvirtuosität mit der Kraft und gewichtigen Thematik des Modern Dance, mit der Glen Tetley in Europa so erfolgreich war, oder Alvin Aileys zugkräftige Mischung von Ballettelementen mit Bewegungen afro-amerikanischer Herkunft und Modern Dance-Phrasen (im wesentlichen aus der Lester-Horton-Technik abgeleitet, die Ailey in seiner Jugend studierte).

Standardisierung ist weiterhin rar. Studenten, die Stunden in New York nehmen wollen, können einen Lehrer seinem Ruf entsprechend wählen oder nach seiner tänzerischen Herkunft, doch bedeutet das letztere keine Garantie. May O'Donnell, eine erfahrene Lehrerin, arbeitete mit der Graham-Kompanie während der 30er und 40er Jahre, aber ihr Unterricht ist nicht der Grahams, obwohl gewisse Ähnlichkeiten bestehen. Viola Farber und Mel Wong waren viele Jahre lang in Merce Cunninghams Truppe, aber keiner von beiden behauptet Cunninghams Technik zu lehren, obwohl einiges von ihrem Lehrstoff Cunninghams Technik ähnlich sein mag.

Doch hat dieser Eklektizismus noch eine andere Seite. In den 60er Jahren attakkierte eine andere Revolution das Tanzestablishment. Die Choreographen, Tänzer, Künstler und Musiker, die im Judson Dance Theater zusammenarbeiteten, widersetzten sich fast allem, was sie im Tanz sahen. Leute wie Lucinda Childs, Yvonne Rainer, Steve Paxton, Trisha Brown waren unerbittlich gegen die bestehende Betonung von Virtuosität, Glanz, Dramatik, Intensität und Sex als Thema. Wie Merce Cunningham und sein Partner, der Komponist John Cage, akzeptierten sie nicht, warum Tanz so strukturiert sein mußte wie ein Musikstück oder ein Theaterstück. Und sie mochten das Image des Tänzers als leidendem Helden oder Superathleten mit gestreckten Füßen und geschwelltem Brustkorb nicht.

Wie Graham und Humphrey 30 Jahre zuvor definierten diese Künstler, und andere wie Meredith Monk oder Twyla Tharp, Tanz für sich neu; und wenn das, was sie produzierten, auch einige Traditionalisten entsetzte („chaotisch", „häßlich", „Anti-Kunst", schrien die Konservativen), so klärte es die Atmosphäre und eröffnete neue und verlockende Möglichkeiten. Eine dieser Möglichkeiten war, daß ein Tänzer einfach wie ein Mensch, der tanzt, aussehen konnte statt wie ein Tänzer, und daß eine alltägliche Bewegung, oder eine mit einer alltäglichen Selbstverständlichkeit ausgeführte Bewegung, Teil eines Tanzes sein konnte. Tänzer wollten leistungsfähige, starke, widerstandsfähige, aber nicht künstliche Körper sein.

Wie trainieren Tänzer mit diesen Interessen? Paradoxerweise studieren viele Ballett. Vielleicht weil es über die Jahrhunderte als Technik eine gewisse Neutralität gewonnen hat und emotional nicht belastet ist. Man kann Schritte ausführen, ohne sich das schmückende Beiwerk einzuhandeln. Tänzer, die an den traditionellen Tanztechniken nicht interessiert waren, entdeckten interessante Alternativen. Zum Beispiel verschiedene fernöstliche Kampftechniken, wie das japanische Akkido oder das chinesische Tai Chi Chuan, die Stärke und Koordination verlangen, aber auch eine Art Zentrierung, eine Gründung in Körper und Geist. Es gibt Leute wie Elaine Summers, die eine Methodik des Körperbewußtseins lehren, Wege des Streckens, Ausrichtens und Aufwärmens des Körpers ohne jede Überstrapazierung der Muskulatur. Schulen wie das Center for Movement Research bieten Unterricht in einer Vielzahl von Arten, sich der Bewegung zu nähern. Contact Improvisation hat bereits viele Anhänger angezogen, und das Angebot der Workshops vermehrt. Contact Improvisation, angeblich erfunden von Steve Paxton, ist eine Duett-Form, zwei Menschen nähern sich und finden einen Weg Kontakt aufzunehmen. Selten benutzen sie ihre Hände, um ihren Partner anzufassen, statt dessen nutzen sie die großen Körperflächen – Rücken, Vorderseite, Schultern, Oberschenkel – um sich umeinander zu rollen und zu winden, um sich gegenseitig vom Boden zu heben. Erfahrene Praktiker können bemerkenswerte Hebewirkungen erzielen; Virtuosität ist jedoch nicht ausschlaggebend. Ziel ist vielmehr, den Bewegungsfluß aufrechtzuerhalten und – noch wichtiger – dem Partner vollkommen zu vertrauen. Contact Improvisation baut Geschlechterbarrieren ab.

Ein Contact Improvisation-Workshop ist natürlich nicht mit einer täglichen Technikstunde zu vergleichen. Es ist ein Weg Bewegung zu erfahren. Viele der hervorragenden Avantgarde-Choreographen lehren nicht Technik per se. Einige, wie Trisha Brown oder Meredith Monk, veranstalten Workshops in Komposition oder Improvisation. Laura Dean leitet Workshops im schnellen Kreiseln. Twyla Tharp (vielmehr die Mitglieder ihrer Kompanie) unterrichtet Technik (Ballett- und eine Vielzahl von Modern Dance-Techniken) während ihrer Sommerseminare, sie bietet aber auch Kompositionsstunden. Sie lehrt ihre Schüler Tanzphrasen auf unzählige Art zu verändern: sie zurückzuspulen, sie umzustellen, den Umfang oder die Akzentuierung zu verändern, ihnen neues Material „einzutrichtern", die Armgesten einer Phrase mit den Fußbewegungen der anderen zu verbinden. Es sollte erläutert werden, daß viele Choreographen, die keine eigene Schule unterhalten, an Universitäten unterrichten können, vielleicht auf einer speziellen Basis. Die meisten Tourneepläne der Kompanien beinhalten nicht nur Aufführungen, sondern auch Unterricht und Demonstrationen in Colleges, Universitäten oder Studios.

Die Rolle des Jazz in der amerikanischen Tanzszene ist kompliziert. Jazz sollte eine einheimische amerikanische Form sein, aber was versteht man unter Jazz? Der Jazz, der in verschiedenen Studios und Schulen geboten wird, ist eher Modern Jazz – eine Mischform aus Modern Dance und afro-amerikanischem Schrittmaterial. So wie er von wohlbekannten Lehrern wie Luigi gelehrt wird, ist die Technik viel aggressiver, stärker, frontaler orientiert als der altmodische Step. Es gibt Jazzkompanien, wie die von Nat Horne oder Gus Giordano in Chicago; sie führen Stücke im Stil von Musicalnummern oder Kurzballette im Jazzidiom auf. Aber die Tänzer, die ernsthaft Jazztanz studieren, wollen im allgemeinen zum Broadway oder ins Fernsehen.

Oft scheint das Ziel dieses Stils, den Tänzer als sexy und verführerisch zur Schau zu stellen, wohingegen der spezifische Jazztanz – meistens Step – sich um Tanzen dreht, um den ungebrochenen Stolz auf den eigenen Schritt. (Twyla Tharps Stil ist dem näher als die meisten Modern Jazz-Stile). Ein wiederbelebtes Interesse am Steptanz hat viele der alten Steptänzer aus dem Ruhestand zurückgeholt, um wieder aufzutreten, zu unterrichten und spezielle Workshops zu leiten. Sie schwelgen in Erinnerungen an die Tage der Wettbewerbe im Savoy Ballroom in Harlem, als Tanz sich darum drehte neue Schritte zu erfinden, oder einem alten Schritt einen neuen Pfiff zu geben, Kollegen oder das Publikum mit Geschwindigkeit, Genauigkeit oder dem Klang ihrer Füße zu beeindrucken. Diese Darsteller können spontan sein, einen Schritt plötzlich feurig aufschlagen und dann innehalten. Die Unbefangenheit dieser Art des Tanzes, die Betonung der Bewegung an sich macht ihn der Post-Cunningham-Generation sympathisch, denn sie glaubt, daß Tanzen an sich schon eine bedeutungsvolle Aktivität ist, ohne daß jemand versuchen müßte, ihm eine andere *Bedeutung* zu geben.

Was den amerikanischen Modern Dance (falls jemand immer noch glaubt, er wüßte, was das sei) als kreative Kraft lebendig hält, ist für viele sein Mißtrauen gegen die Akademien und der Kampfgeist seiner häufigen Revolutionen. Dieser Kampfgeist ist friedlich und individuell, und man muß beachten: niemand wird ausgestoßen, ersetzt oder degradiert. Ein neues Territorium wird abgesteckt, und neue Pioniere ziehen aus, um es zu erforschen. Dabei versteht es sich, daß die Gesetze, die man schafft, nur auf sich selbst und auf die, die sich entschieden einen zu begleiten, anwendbar sind.

Deborah Jowitt

It comes as no surprise that Europeans are frequently baffled by the diversity of styles and techniques grouped together under the heading *American modern dance* (an inadequate and, to many of the choreographers to whose works it is applied, distasteful term). As recently as 1975, Lincoln Kirstein, co-founder and associate director of the New York City Ballet, commented disparagingly that modern dance had never gained a mass public, a central system, or a common repertory. Why should it? Modern dance has always been predicated on idiosyncratic styles, and this has necessitated, to some degree, being against the establishment of an academy. In the 1920s and '30s, it seemed a pioneering stance to reject ballet's emphasis on conformity and a neutral technique, and instead to vaunt the individual choreographer's right to move in response to the tempo of the times and the dictates of his or her own sensibility.

With ballet choreographers, contemporaneity has usually meant the choosing of up-to-date themes, costumes, music, perhaps rewriting ancient formulas or grafting new gestures onto the basic ballet vocabulary. It has not – even to Mikhail Fokine – meant building an idiom from scratch or questioning the basic forms and raison d'être. But revolutionary "modern dancers", from Isadora Duncan through Martha Graham through Yvonne Rainer to Laura Dean have made an issue out of redefining dance for themselves, using only those elements from their artistic heritage that made sense to them, and tossing out everything else.

With such a high value placed on originality, everyone aspired to be a choreographer. Why not? To earn a living as a dancer was impossible anyway. Beginning in the late 1960s, increased subsidy and a growing audience guaranteed at least some companies more work. Consequently, good dancers were not so easily tempted to become indifferent choreographers.

For many choreographers – and dancers – teaching has always been an adjunct. In the early days of modern dance, they taught to support themselves, to try out new movement ideas, and to find and train dancers who might be interested in performing with them for little or no money. The typical modern dance company was, and is, built around the talents of a choreographer-teacher who is also the principal performer, and who may even achieve the status of a minor prophet surrounded by disciples.

There are, of course, exceptions. Alwin Nikolais never danced in his own company; Alvin Ailey's company is a modified repertory company with the works of other choreographers included; Paul Taylor has never had a school, and there is no such

MISTRUST OF ACADEMIES
TRAINING TO BE A MODERN DANCER IN THE USA

thing as Taylor technique, even though there is clearly a Taylor style.

Modern, or contemporary dance, also presupposes a susceptibility to change, so that the curricula in schools do not remain the same. Take the case of Martha Graham who has run a successful school for many years and is generally conceded to have codified a "technique" for training dancers and a format for dance classes. But what Graham taught has always reflected her choreographic concerns. A Graham class of the 1980s is not much like a Graham class of the 1930s, although experts say that they can see the bones of the early exercises glinting through the new ones. When Graham began to develop her own style around 1925, there was almost no turn-out of the legs in her dances or in her classes. Nor were there many high leg extensions. Movement originated in the center of the body and culminated in gestures of immense percussive force. At some point, she began to work on her now famous theory of "contraction and release" – a kind of abstraction and intensification of breathing; she experimented with falls – articulating an often quarrelsome dialogue with gravity and the studio floor. Graham utilized some of what she had learned during her years with Ruth St. Denis and Ted Shawn – certainly François Delsarte's ideas about expressive human movement; but when she had her dancers twist their upper bodies against firmly planted feet, her purpose was not to produce a decorative pose or to suggest an archaic culture as it would have been with the leaders of Denishawn. It was to emphasize oppositional forces within a single human body. In dances like *Heretic* (1929) or *Primitive Mysteries* (1931), Graham showed that her thinking was in tune with that of the most contemporary artists and designers in Europe and America. Like them, her work (and her all-female company) eschewed ornamentation and glamor. It emphasized strength, clean lines and simplicity.

But each development in Graham's artistic life, each new generation of dancers has had an impact on her style and on the technique that supports it. Beginning in 1938, when she became interested in theater forms and role-playing, her movement became more elaborate and acquired more of the spiralling, off-balance movements needed to suggest the ambivalence or mental struggle of heroines like Medea or

Jocasta, and to articulate the Puritan dilemma of duty versus desire that shaped so many of her dances. Some very drastic gestures, set into repeating patterns, found their way into the classwork. As Graham grew older, she ceased to draw movement from her own body. She took inspiration from new crops of young dancers – dancers with extensive ballet training, often, with turn-outs and high extensions and slim, sleek bodies very unlike those of the sturdy women of the 1930s. Today, Graham classwork, like Graham dances, celebrates the dancer as "celestial acrobat", ardent, intense. Many of the exercises are the same as they were twenty years ago – the familiar "floorwork", the exercises done standing in place, the beautiful fall sequences, the steps done moving across the floor – but they do not look the same. Beauty of line is more apt to be emphasized than the impetus of a movement; the old percussive force has gradually softened, the rhythms and dynamics have become more indulgent, easier on the body.

(Although former members of Graham's company teach all over the world, the Martha Graham School of Contemporary Dance is now instituting a system for the licensing and training of teachers. The irony is that, even though Graham's name is thereby protected from exploitation by the under-educated, many fine teachers who were profoundly influenced by their years of performing with her, can no longer claim to teach her technique.)

Another strain of American dance descends from Graham's great contemporary, Doris Humphrey, and Humphrey's partner and collaborator, Charles Weidman. In its early stages, the Humphrey-Weidman technique, like the Graham technique, avoided pointed feet, turn-out, anything that could be construed as "balletic". Like Graham, Humphrey and Weidman advocated simplicity, strength, and no frills; they too explored the effects of gravity on the human body, instead of denying that pull to the ground. They too had "floorwork" and fall sequences. Humphrey herself was a lighter, more lyrical dancer than Graham; Weidman, lanky, vigorous, and witty, helped develop many of the more "virile" exercises that were taught in their classes.

Humphrey developed a theory of dancing based on "fall and recovery", deciding that movement occurred in the arc between two "deaths" – the "death" of stasis, or perfect balance, and the "death" of utter collapse. In other words, the dancer begins to tilt or thrust or swing his or her body off its axis, or press upward from the floor, and the drama of motion results from the way he or she shapes this trajectory – in space, in time, in dynamic quality. In Humphrey's composition classes and in her book, *The Art of Making Dances,* she laid out wise principles for would-be choreographers. She herself was a master of expressive form. In 1932, she wrote: "Four abstract themes, all moving equally and harmoniously together like a fugue would convey the significance of democracy far better than would one woman dressed in red, white, and blue, with stars in her hair." Her ideas about dancing could produce jagged movements, as in *The Shakers* (1931), where members of a celibate religious sect jerk and hurl their bodies toward and away from an invisible line down the center of the stage which divides men from women. Others of her dances, like *Passacaglia* (1938) were profoundly, nobly lyrical – with the dancers' gestures describing huge arcs in space and their rhythms those of exalted breathing. Many of the classroom exercises, too, were built on the rhythm, weight impulse, and trajectory of a swing.

Doris Humphrey had to give up dancing in 1944 because of a crippling injury, but she served as choreographer and artistic advisor to the company of her protegé, José Limón, until her death in 1958. Limón's style, and the technique he taught, were, inevitably, a personal reassessment of the Humphrey-Weidman view of dance. The Mexican Limón was a powerful dancer, and drawn to the brooding heroes of literature and myth. Humphrey herself capitalized on these qualities in the dances she composed for him. Perhaps the Spanish rhythms, the pulled-back arms, and heroic postures that appeared in Limón classwork were as much due to Humphrey's vision of Limón as to his vision of himself.

The Humphrey-Weidman technique is still taught, in various forms, by former company members around the USA. Since Limón's death in 1972, his company has continued to tour and Limón classes are taught, but there is no real "school" as such. Limón company members of the 1960s, Jennifer Muller and Louis Falco, have given their dance heritage a new emphasis. In the dances of both these choreographers, one can observe the preoccupation with weight and gravity that characterized Limón's works, but Muller and Falco are products of a different society. Tragic heroes, the polarity of good and evil, strong moral purpose do not interest them. There is, instead, an exuberant hedonism to their dances; the performers look amoral, playful, self-involved. The dance phrases are not molded the way Limón's and Humphrey's were; the basic fall-and-rebound principle appears as a flinging, tumbling, bouncing that occasionally stops in stretched-out positions.

Another important modern dance "pioneer", Hanya Holm, came from Germany. A member of Mary Wigman's company, she established a Wigman school in New York. This was in 1931, after Wigman's second successful American tour. Although from the '40s on, Holm's choreographic reputation has rested primarily on her contributions to Broadway musicals, she maintained a school (under her own name) until 1967, has taught at Colorado College every summer since 1941, and now, in 1981, has just created a new dance for Don Redlich's company.

Hanya Holm's approach has always been different from that of her American contemporaries, and her work less based on her own body. She taught students to accompany each other on percussion instruments, gave sessions in improvisation as well as composition classes. Composer Louis Horst, who first taught composition to members of Martha Graham's company, and to perhaps three subsequent generations of dancers, based his ideas on musical structure and mood or culture; Holm emphasized space in a way that Horst did not. The program for one of her company's early lecture demonstrations featured studies with titles like *Space shattered by explosive quality arising from inner excitement of the dancer whose body is the focal point* or *Attraction toward depth.*

The work of Don Redlich, a pupil of Holm (so are Valerie Bettis and Glen Tetley), shows a similar concern both for the emotional aspects of man-in-space and for clarity of design. Her most famous pupil, Alwin Nikolais, is not so interested in the former as in the latter. He felt that human passion had been overused as subject matter for dance, but believed, like Holm, in the concept of space as an "active partner in the dance". In 1952, he began to make the kind of dances that he is renowned for – magical universes of color and light in which the dancers are only one element, often barely visible behind screens, or under tents of fabric, or mottled by slide projections.

In recruiting dancers for this world, he needed to develop in them a flexibility of both mind and body. Like Holm, Nikolais has always provided a complete education for the dancer who studies with him: technique, composition, improvisation, and pedagogy. He adapted much of Holm's technique to his own ends. From the early days, when his company taught and performed at the Henry Street Settlement House (and how lucky he was to have a theater of his own in which to experiment!), his training has, among other things, taught dancers to articulate every part of the body, either in isolation or in collaboration with other parts. For instance, there is no joint that cannot circle or push out on a diagonal, no matter how small that diagonal may be.

Alwin Nikolais, like Hanya Holm, encourages students to take movements learned in a technique class and experiment with the principles that underlie them, using learned material both to spark creative work and to foster a deeper understanding of the classwork. Not all those trained in this system pick up Nikolais's style. It features movement that is almost always light, with a range of subtle gradations between fast and slow, smooth and sharp. Murray Louis – one of the original members of Nikolais's company and an accomplished teacher – might be considered the paradigmatic Nikolais creature, with a body full of witty and mischievous tricks. Because of Nikolais's interest in pedagogy, his company members and former company members, such as Murray Louis, Phyllis Lamhut, and Gladys Bailin, are in demand as teachers. In 1978, Nikolais himself was commissioned by the French government to establish the Centre National de Danse Contemporaine in Angers. Prior to the late 1960s, at which time the National Endowment for the Arts began to give grants to dance companies, and before private foundations provided much support, the leaders of dance companies had very little that was tangible to offer their dancers. Instead, they offered a way of life. Those who worked with Humphrey or Graham or any of the other so-called "pioneers" of modern dance considered themselves lucky to be part of a new order, even if they did have to wait on tables or serve as models for painters, sculptors and the like in order to support themselves. Erick Hawkins may be the last of those charismatic leaders who demands complete allegiance from his dancers and offers an aesthetic credo along with technique classes. Although Hawkins performed with Lincoln Kirstein's Ballet Caravan and partnered Martha Graham from 1938 until 1950, his ideas about the body are diametrically opposed to those of Graham and ballet. Influenced by the pioneering work of Mabel Ellsworth Todd (*The Thinking Body*) and others, Hawkins developed a system of training designed to do away with unnecessary muscle tension and forcing. Like Isadora Duncan years before, he was drawn to the idea of nature moving in waves; his technique emphasizes loops and curves rather than straight thrust, a smooth, elastic stride that neither fights gravity nor evades it. The teaching reinforces a choreographic style that is consciously poetic, idealistic, refined, with a very subtle range of dynamics. Often his dances are abstracted nature studies or idyllic and sensuous visions of man-in-nature. His present and former company dancers like Beverly Brown or Nancy Meehan, teach classes that in some ways affirm his precepts, in some ways contradict them, or take off in new directions.

During some of his years with Graham, Hawkins was often cast in opposition to Merce Cunningham, who danced with Graham from 1939 to '45. Where Hawkins was the dark and domineering lover, Cunningham was more spiritual, slightly asexual; perhaps he was Graham's first draft of the "celestial acrobat". In *Deaths and Entrances*, Hawkins was the Dark Beloved, Cunningham the Poetic Beloved; in *Appalachian Spring*, Hawkins was the Husbandman, Cunningham the fanatical Preacher; in *Every Soul Is a Circus*, Hawkins was the stern Ringmaster, Cunningham the blithe Acrobat.

Merce Cunningham's own style is as dissimilar from Graham's as is Hawkins's. He has radically altered contemporary thinking about dance – often outraging conventional taste in the process. It can be argued that what Cunningham did was to bring to dance some of the formal innovations that had already taken place in music and painting, and to reflect in his structures some of the altered concepts of science and philosophy which the 20th century had spawned. A Cunningham dance does not present viewers with a neatly composed picture that has a central focus and a hierarchy of activities (ranging from very important down to background). Instead, his dances are dense fields of activity; spectators must choose what to look at, since taking it all in may be impossible. The impression of density is heightened by the fact that music, décor, and lighting are considered independent structures juxtaposed to the dance. Although the music, which is often quite noisy, does not accompany the dance, it does influence the audience's perception of the whole event.

Cunningham's insistence that the movement *is* the meaning, his unconventional structures, his application of chance procedures to choreography, his recent experimentation with video – all have earned him a continuing reputation as a radical. Age has not made him rigid in his thinking. But, although his works have been called chaotic or anarchistic, his dancers always earn praise for their beauty, discipline, and intelligence. Compared to the Dionysiac Graham dancer, the Cunningham dancer has an Apollonian look; one does not see him or her buffeted by passion or carried away by emotion.

Many label Cunningham's style "balletic", because of the calm erect spine of a Cunningham dancer, the controlled use of weight, the active and complicated footwork, the fact that movement originates more in the limbs than in the center of the body. But the comparison is misleading. His dancing is subject to radical distortions of shape, sequence, and timing that would be impermissible in ballet. Despite their high extensions,

the dancers in his company do not look like ballet dancers. The best ones always seem acutely aware of time and space, as alert as animals and devoid of unnecessary strain or self-consciousness.

They dance thoughtfully, as if they were making decisions about what to do next. Cunningham runs one of the most popular schools in New York City, and no matter who is teaching a given class, the exercises foster this air of alert intelligence. The initial exercises are done standing in place rather than sitting on the floor. The torso may twist, bend, or contract, but it does not pull the dancers so far off balance that they cannot recover and continue. And much of this complex work with the torso is set against equally complicated footwork, sometimes performed at speeds that turn the exercises into studies in coordination and quick thinking. Often his classes feature very long, rhythmically complex phrases, instead of the short repeating phrases shaped by musical meter which one sees in many modern dance classes (three counts to run, three to turn, etc.).

During the late 1940s and '50s, modern dance became more eclectic. Although some highly individual choreographers appeared (Alwin Nikolais, Merce Cunningham, Erick Hawkins, Anna Sokolow, James Waring, Katherine Litz, and others), many "second generation" choreographers were content to elaborate on what they had learned – or to repeat it. In 1951, the Juilliard School of Music inaugurated a dance department under the direction of Martha Hill, a noted dance educator and co-founder of the Bennington Festival. Gifted students can go from the High School of Performing Arts into Juilliard, study ballet, modern dance (originally Graham and Limón technique), composition, music, and other courses, and emerge with a Certificate or a Bachelor of Science degree. (Similar curricula are offered now at quite a few universities, but that is, in itself, the subject of another article.) Schools like the Alvin Ailey Dance Center offer jazz, ballet, *and* modern techniques.

This breaking down of barriers and rivalries has had a practical side to it. Since relatively few modern dance companies pay neither a living wage nor provide enough performing to feed the dancers' souls, dancers a shade more practical than those of the 1930s, want to be able to perform with a variety of companies and to pick up jobs in musicals or television shows. It is not uncommon now to see a dancer like Shelley Washington, who performed with Walter Nicks's jazz-based company, with the Limón company, and with the Graham company, before aligning herself with Twyla Tharp.

The growing versatility of dancers has had an analogue in hybrid strains of choreogra-

phy – such as the amalgam of ballet virtuosity with modern dance muscularity and heavy subject matter with which Glen Tetley has been so successful in Europe, or Alvin Ailey's showy mix of ballet feats with black vernacular material and modern dance phrases (derived largely from the Lester Horton technique that Ailey studied as a youth in Los Angeles).

Standardization continues to be rare. Students looking for classes in New York may choose a teacher by reputation or dance bloodlines, but the latter is no guarantee. May O'Donnell, a highly skilled teacher, worked with the Graham company during the 1930s and '40s, but her classwork is not Graham classwork, although there are certain resemblances. Viola Farber and Mel Wong were in Merce Cunningham's company for many years, but neither purports to teach Cunningham technique, even though some of the material they offer may be similar to his.

There is an obverse side to the eclecticism. In the 1960s, another revolution attacked the dance establishment. The choreographers, dancers, artists, and musicians who worked together under the aegis of Judson Dance Theater were opposed to almost everything they saw in the way of dance. Lucinda Childs, Yvonne Rainer, Steve Paxton, Trisha Brown were among those adamantly opposed to the prevailing emphasis on virtuosity, glamor, drama, intensity, sex as a subject. Like Merce Cunningham and his associate, composer John Cage, they did not accept that a dance had to be structured like a piece of music or like a play. They did not like the image of the dancer as a suffering hero or a superathlete, with pointy toes and a puffed-up ribcage. As with Graham and Humphrey thirty years before, these artists – and others like Meredith Monk and Twyla Tharp – were redefining dance for themselves, and if what they produced outraged many traditionalists ("chaotic", "ugly", "anti-art", yelled conservatives), it also cleared the air and opened up new and enticing possibilities. One of these possibilities was that the dancer could look like a person-who-dances instead of like a dancer. Another was that everyday movement, or movement performed with an everyday casualness, could be part of a dance. Dancers began to want their bodies to be capable, strong, resilient, but not artificial.

How do dancers with these interests train themselves? Paradoxically, many study ballet. Perhaps it is because ballet has, over the centuries, achieved neutrality as a technique and bears no emotional charge. One can do the steps without buying the decorum.

Dancers who are not interested in traditional dance techniques have discovered interest-

diese Seite/this page
oben/top
RUTH ST. DENIS
Mitte/middle
ISADORA DUNCAN
unten/bottom
DANCE INTO DEATH,
Ch: Mary Wigman,
Mary Wigman
gegenüber/opposite page
ÄGYPTISCHES BALLETT/
EGYPTIAN BALLET,
Ch: Ruth St. Denis,
Ruth St. Denis, Ted Shawn,
Foto: Archiv

ing alternatives. There are the various eastern martial arts techniques, like the Japanese Akkido or the Chinese Tai Chi Chuan, which require strength and coordination, but also a kind of centering, a grounding of body and spirit. There are those like Elaine Summers, who teach methods of body awareness – ways of stretching, aligning, warming up the body for work without any muscular melodrama. Organizations such as the Center for Movement Research offer a variety of ways to approach movement. Contact improvisation has attracted many adherents and proliferated workshops. Contact, supposedly invented by Steve Paxton, is a duet form. Two people approach each other and find a way to get into contact. Rarely do they use their hands to grasp their partner; instead they use the large surfaces of their bodies – backs, fronts, shoulders, thighs – to roll and twine around each other, to lever one another off the ground. Experienced practitioners can achieve remarkable lifts, but the point is not virtuosity. The point is to sustain the flow of movement and, even more importantly, to trust your partner completely. Contact improvisation also breaks down traditional gender barriers, since women and men support each other, and partners of the same sex work with a physical closeness unusual in conventional dance.

A Contact improvisation workshop, of course, is not like a daily technique class. It is a way of experiencing movement. Many of the prominent vanguard choreographers do not teach technique per se. Some, like Trisha Brown or Meredith Monk, give workshops in composition or improvisation. Laura Dean gives spinning workshops. Twyla Tharp, or rather members of her company, teach technique (ballet and a variety of modern dance techniques) during summer teaching residencies, but she also offers classes in composition. In her case this involves teaching students to manipulate dance phrases in innumerable ways: retrograding them, inverting them, altering scale or attack, "stuffing" new material into them, combining the arm gestures of one phrase with the foot pattern of another. It should be explained that many choreographers who do not maintain schools may teach in universities, perhaps on some special basis. Most companies' touring schedules include not only performing, but giving classes and lecture demonstrations at colleges, universities, or studios.

The role of jazz in the American dance scene is a complicated one. Jazz is supposed to be an indigenous American form, but what does one mean by jazz? The jazz that is offered in various studios and schools is likely to be *modern jazz* – a hybrid form composed of modern dance and black verna-

cular steps. As taught by well-known teachers like Luigi, the technique is much more aggressive, stronger, frontally oriented than the old-time hoofing. There are jazz companies, like those of Nat Horne, or Gus Giordano in Chicago; these perform what might be numbers excerpted from musicals, or short-story ballets in the jazz idiom. However, those who study jazz dancing seriously are usually aiming for a job on Broadway or in television.

Often the purpose of this style seems to be to display the dancer as a sexy and enticing creature, whereas vernacular jazz dancing – usually tap – is about dancing, about unabashed pride in one's steps. (Twyla Tharp's style bears more kinship to this than do most of the modern jazz styles.) A resurgence of interest in tap dancing has brought many of the old hoofers out of retirement to perform, to teach, to conduct workshops. They reminisce about the days of competitions at the Savoy Ballroom in Harlem, when dancing was about inventing a new step, or adding a new twist to an old one, about dazzling one's colleagues or the audience with one's speed or accuracy or the sound of one's feet. These performers can be oblique, offhand, suddenly nail a step down fiercely, then ease off. The unaffectedness of this kind of dancing, its emphasis on the movement itself makes it appealing to those of the post-Cunningham generation who believe that dancing is a significant enough human activity, without anyone trying to make it *mean* something else.

What keeps *American modern dance* (if one still thinks one knows what that is) potent as a creative force is, to many, its mistrust of academies and the belligerance of its frequent revolutions. The belligerance is peaceful and individual, it must be understood: no one is swept aside, supplanted, or demoted. A new territory is defined and new pioneers go out to explore it, understanding that the laws they set up apply only to themselves and those who choose to accompany them.

diese Seite/this page
oben/above
CLYTEMNESTRA,
Choreographie und Kostüme von/
choreography and costumes by
Martha Graham,
Bühnenbild von/set by
Isamo Noguchi,
Martha Graham,
Foto: Martha Swope
unten/below
LAMENTATION,
Choreographie und Kostüme von/
choreography and costumes by
Martha Graham,
Martha Graham
Foto: Archiv

gegenüber/opposite page
oben/top
A CHOREOGRAPHIC
OFFERING,
Ch: José Limón,
José Limón Dance Company,
Foto: Lois Greenfield
Mitte und unten/
middle and bottom
THE SHAKERS,
Ch: Doris Humphrey,
Kostüme von/costumes by
Pauline Lawrence,
José Limón Dance Company,
Foto Mitte/middle:
Martha Swope,
Foto unten/bottom:
Lois Greenfield

diese Seite/this page
THE SPIRIT OF DENISHAWN,
Ch: Joyce Trisler
(nach/after
Ruth St. Denis, Doris Humphrey)
oben/above
SOLO WITH SCARF,
Ann-Marie Hackett,
Joyce Trisler Danscompany,
Foto: Lois Greenfield
unten/below
SOARING,
Joyce Trisler Danscompany,
Foto: John Dady

gegenüber/opposite page
oben/above
COUNTRY DANCES,
Ch: Twyla Tharp,
Twyla Tharp Dance Foundation,
Foto: Lois Greenfield
unten/below
SUITE OTIS,
Ch: George Faison,
(v. l. n. r./left to right)
Linda Spriggs, Estelle Spurlock,
Marilyn Banks, Sarita Allen,
Maxine Sherman,
Alvin Ailey American Dance Theater,
Foto: Jack Mitchell

oben/above
MUSIC,
Ch: Laura Dean,
Laura Dean Dancers
and Musicians,
Foto: Lois Greenfield
unten/below
POLARIS,
Ch: Paul Taylor,
Paul Taylor Dance Company,
Foto: Lois Greenfield

oben/above
DANCE,
Ch: Lucinda Childs,
Lucinda Childs Dance Company,
Foto: Lois Greenfield
unten/below
GLACIAL DECOY,
Ch: Trisha Brown,
Trisha Brown,
Foto: Lois Greenfield

VOLUNTARIES,
Ch: Glen Tetley,
Mette Ida Kirk,
Linda Hindberg,
Königlich Dänisches
Ballett Kopenhagen/
Royal Danish Ballet,
Copenhagen,
Foto: Gert Weigelt

Glen Tetley/Rolf Garske

RG: Herr Tetley, glauben Sie, daß es möglich ist, jemanden zum Choreographen auszubilden?

GT: Dies ist eine sehr schwierige Frage. Es ist das gleiche wie in anderen Bereichen der Kunst: Jemanden zu lehren, ein Künstler oder kreativ zu sein, ist nicht möglich. Wir sind alle kreativ. Wir lernen mehr oder weniger, diese Kreativität freizusetzen oder zu unterdrücken. Aber jemanden tatsächlich zum Choreographen auszubilden (oder zum Dichter, Komponisten, Maler, Schriftsteller) ist – so glaube ich – unmöglich. Vor Jahren arbeitete ich mit Doris Humphrey, einer unserer Tanzpioniere. Sie war eine außergewöhnliche Persönlichkeit auf diesem Gebiet, da sie sich intensiv mit der Frage des Lehrens von Choreographie als Handwerk beschäftigte. „Choreographie ist nicht lehrbar", sagte sie, „aber man kann es lernen." Ich glaube, das ist richtig.

RG: In ihrem Buch *The Art of Making Dances* greift Doris Humphrey das Thema des Choreographierens aus verschiedenen Blickwinkeln auf und illustriert grundlegende Prinzipien choreographischer Arbeit und der Präsentation des Bühnentanzes. Zweimal haben Sie den Gulbenkian-Sommerkurs für Choreographie in England geleitet. Sie leiteten eine Gruppe junger Choreographen, denen Sie bestimmte Übungen zur Aufgabe machten. Welche Absichten verfolgten Sie dabei?

GT: Zunächst befaßte ich mich nur zögernd mit dem Gulbenkian-Projekt, gerade weil ich mich bereits einige Zeit zuvor bereiterklärt hatte, einen solchen Kurs in den Vereinigten Staaten für die National Association of Regional Ballet Companies zu leiten. In erster Linie übernahm ich den Kurs, um die Situation der regionalen Kompanien kennenzulernen. Doris Hering, die damalige Präsidentin dieser Organisation, ermutigte mich. Es war eine sehr schwierige Sache: zehn Tage an der Ostküste, zehn Tage an der Westküste und zehn Tage im Landesinneren – manchmal mit 150 Leuten unterschiedlichsten Niveaus. Man konnte nicht erwarten, viel zu erreichen. Aber die Erfahrungen, die ich dort sammelte, halfen mir, meine Vorstellungen für das Gulbenkian-Projekt zu konkretisieren. Von Anfang an beschlossen Gale Law – mit dem ich sehr eng zusammengearbeitet hatte, als er noch Tänzer, später Pressesekretär beim Nederlands Dans Theater war – und ich, daß ein sehr hoher Standard der in Frage kommenden Teilnehmer durch Vortanzen gesichert werden müsse. Sie sollten bereits eine professionelle Ausbildung haben und nicht zuletzt große Lust, mit den anderen Choreographen, Komponisten und Tänzern zusammenzuarbeiten. Eine andere Idee war, Lichtregisseure und Bühnenbildner hinzuzuziehen. Die besten Lehrer für moder-

KREATIVITÄT ODER HANDWERK
IST CHOREOGRAPHIE LERNBAR?

nen und klassischen Tanz sollten engagiert werden. Mit anderen Worten, wir wollten für die kurze Zeit von zwei Wochen bei dem Gulbenkian-Projekt so viel Anreize wie möglich bieten.

RG: Kann man Choreograph werden, ohne getanzt zu haben?

GT: Nein, natürlich nicht. Keiner kann Choreograph werden, ohne zunächst einmal Tänzer gewesen zu sein. Dies ist die einzige Möglichkeit, dies Handwerk zu erlernen. Was immer ich heute kann, habe ich durch die praktische Arbeit mit Choreographen gelernt, indem ich versuchte, ein so qualifizierter Tänzer wie möglich zu sein, und durch die enge Zusammenarbeit mit Menschen, die ich bewunderte und mit denen ich zusammenarbeiten wollte. Meine enge Beziehung zu Martha Graham war für mich wie ein ganzes Universitätsseminar. Ich beobachtete ihr intensives Bemühen um eine Choreographie, erfuhr, wohin ihre Genialität sie führte, wenn Dinge nicht funktionierten, sah, was geschah, wenn es schwierige Situationen gab, und wie sie mit ihnen fertig wurde – all das war ein gewaltiger Lernprozeß. Dies erinnert mich an einen anderen Grund, warum ich den Gulbenkian-Kurs unterrichten wollte. In unserem Fach sind wir so isoliert! Es ist seltsam, daß in der Tanzwelt die Choreographen nicht miteinander sprechen. Einfach zusammenzukommen, nicht mit dem Ziel zu lehren, sagen zu müssen, das sind die Regeln, folge ihnen und du wirst Erfolg haben – dies tun zu können, ist eine wundervolle Sache und darüber hinaus wichtig. Denn wenn Regeln überhaupt derartiges leisten könnten, wäre jedermann ein choreographisches Genie. Neunundneunzig Prozent der Zeit bricht man diese Regeln, geht seinen eigenen Weg, folgt seiner Eingebung. Ich glaubte, daß es sehr wertvoll für uns wäre, zusammenzukommen, nur um darüber zu reden, Erfahrungen auszutauschen mit jungen Tänzern, die Choreographen werden und etwas Kreatives versuchen wollten. Das ist die grundsätzliche Absicht des Gulbenkian-Kurses.

Mit derselben Hast der Welt, in der wir leben, werden professionelle Tänzer nur in Technik ausgebildet. Ich war 20, als ich nach New York kam, um mit dem Tanzen zu beginnen. Ich hatte bereits Medizin studiert. Auf der einen Seite war ich ein Romantiker, auf der anderen Seite sehr analytisch. Ich hatte gelernt, zu analysieren und Fragen zu stel-

len. Mein Glück war, daß ich, obwohl ich meine ersten Trainingsstunden in Klassisch erhielt, sofort auf Hanya Holm traf, die nach ihrer Ausbildung bei Mary Wigman zu einer weiteren Pionierin des zeitgenössischen amerikanischen Tanzes wurde. In jener Zeit kehrte man zu den Grundlagen zurück, von denen der Tanz kommt. Man fragte sich, was allen Tanzbewegungen gemeinsam ist, was ihre grundlegenden Bausteine sind. Dies war für mich genau das richtige: zu wissen, daß – analytisch wie anatomisch – ein Plié ein Plié, ein Relevé ein Relevé ist, sei es nun im indischen Tanz, im klassischen Ballett oder irgendeiner anderen Form des Tanzes.

Der Körper ist derart gebaut, daß dieses Detail zum Beispiel in allen Tänzen vorkommt. Das Studium dieser von Mary Wigman und Rudolf von Laban stammenden Theorien machte mir viele Dinge in Hinsicht auf Bewegung klar. Wir hatten Unterricht in Technik, was praktisches Training bedeutete, und Theorie, wo Dinge diskutiert und auseinandergenommen wurden. Man hatte Zeit, Fragen zu stellen. Zwei Stunden täglich hatten wir Improvisation. Das war praktisch und wesentlich für einen Choreographen. Selbstverständlich hatten wir auch Unterricht in Komposition, Musik, Tanznotation und Tanzgeschichte. Hanya Holms ursprüngliche Idee war, eine Tanzuniversität für professionelle Tänzer aufzubauen. Ich bewundere ihre unglaubliche Hochschätzung des Tanzes als ebenbürtige Kunst neben all den anderen Künsten. Ein Musiker muß Theorie und Komposition studieren. Wo stünde ein Musiker, hätte er all diese Dinge nicht studiert? Vielleicht liegt der Grund für die Situation der Choreographen in der Tatsache, daß ihnen diese Trainingsstrukturen nicht zur Verfügung stehen.

RG: Warum gibt es Leute, die sagen, es gäbe heute keine neuen Choreographen, wenngleich sich doch eine solche Explosion von Nachwuchskräften zu zeigen scheint? Wie erwirbt man den Titel „Choreograph"?

GT: Jeder kann Bewegungen zusammensetzen, jeder ist in der Lage, Klänge aneinanderzureihen, jeder kann Farbe auf eine Leinwand bringen oder ein Happening veranstalten. Wir neigen dazu, solche Leute Künstler zu nennen. Und natürlich sind sie Künstler. Aber wenn man etwas zu seiner Lebensaufgabe macht, egal was es ist, warum dann nicht für immer, warum nicht mit all der Vorbereitung, mit all der Erfahrung, mit der man das ganze Leben bestreiten kann. Ich kam zum Tanz, weil ich das Tanzen liebte. Ich hatte keine andere Wahl! Es ist das, was mein Leben lebenswert macht, und ich denke, je tiefer man sich einläßt, um so stärker muß die Basis sein, die man braucht. Es ist eine Sache, einen ersten

Talentbeweis zu erbringen, seine erste Choreographie zu machen, aber etwas anderes, weiterzumachen, sich zu entwickeln und während des ganzen Lebens etwas Neues darin zu finden. Es kommt die Zeit, da man diese Erfahrungen, umfassendes Training und so viel Information als möglich braucht.

RG: Sollten Tänzer, die an Choreographie interessiert sind, dieses breite Ausbildungsspektrum besitzen?

GT: Warum nicht? Es wird sicherlich nicht schaden. Je mehr man weiß, je mehr man gelernt, je mehr Erfahrung man durch Arbeit mit verschiedenen Choreographen gesammelt hat, je mehr Erfahrungen man durch Aufführungen bekommen hat, um so mehr Handwerkszeug hat man, mit dem gearbeitet werden kann. Die große Vielfalt an Choreographien, die es heute gibt, ist nur zu einem ganz geringen Teil interessant; der Rest ist uninteressant auf Grund seiner geringen Tragweite.

Ich liebe das technische Training des Tänzers. Ich staune immer über die außergewöhnlichen Resultate, die ein Tänzer mit gutem Training erzielen kann. Ich glaube an eine fundierte technische Ausbildung, weil die Technik dem Tänzer Freiheit gewährt, die Freiheit, alles zu tun. Ich verstehe zwar auch andere Standpunkte. Ich bin auch jemand, der Menschen beobachtet. Ich sitze gern auf einer Parkbank und beobachte Menschen. Das fasziniert mich sehr. Aber es beeindruckt mich nicht, ins Theater zu gehen und Minimal und Nichttechnisches zu erleben. Ich mag alles, was mich nicht zu sehr zwingt, mein Interesse wachzuhalten. Wenn ich in eine Tanzveranstaltung gehe, so möchte ich mich in die Gedanken des Choreographen versetzen können; ich möchte etwas Außergewöhnliches, etwas Neues erleben. Ich möchte herausgefordert werden.

Wenn ein Komponist die gesamte Geschichte der Komposition und Musik vor ihm ignorierte, wenn er alle Komponisten vor ihm ignorierte, wenn er seine Augen und Ohren verschlösse vor der Vielfalt an Stilen und Kompositionen, wo wäre dann die Musik? Sie wäre sofort wieder an ihrem Ausgangspunkt. Ich habe bis jetzt noch nicht erlebt, daß Training und Wissen jemanden behindert hätten. Ich halte nichts von Nationalismus, nichts von Rassismus, nichts von Abgrenzung und habe auch nie an künstliche Grenzen in der Kunst geglaubt. In einer Zeit, als der Modern Dance in den USA sehr stark war, stark, weil die Pioniere noch lebten, begann ich mit dem Tanzen. Ich habe mit ihnen allen eng zusammengearbeitet: mit Martha Graham, Hanya Holm, Charles Weidman, Doris Humphrey, José Limón, und, weil ich auch die andere Seite kennenlernen wollte, zum Beispiel mit Antony Tudor und Margaret Craske.

In der School of American Ballet studierte ich bei den besten der alten Kirow-Lehrer, was damals mit großem Argwohn betrachtet wurde. Entweder man war ein Vertreter des Modern Dance, oder man war es nicht. Ich konnte mich nicht zu dem bekennen, was ich als künstliche Abgrenzung empfand. Für mich war alles Bewegung, und ich war neugierig. Es war eine Auseinandersetzung mit Technik, mit Methoden, den Körper zu trainieren und ihn freizumachen, um ihn zu einem willfährigen Instrument zu machen. Natürlich, dies waren alles Probleme, eine geeignete Technik zu finden, Probleme auf der Suche nach der eigenen Kreativität und Identität als Choreograph. Das alles geht Hand in Hand mit der Ausbildung zum Tänzer, mit all den Erfahrungen, und ist – meiner Meinung nach – der beste Schritt auf dem Weg, ein guter Choreograph zu werden.

RG: Ist es für einen Tänzer schwer, diesen Schritt zu tun?

GT: Die meisten Tänzer genieren sich, dem Choreographen auch nur einen Bewegungsablauf vorzuschlagen. Sie können die hervorragendsten Tänzer der Welt sein, aber dennoch sagen: Erwarte von mir keine Aussage darüber, wie ein Bewegungsablauf sich ereignen könnte. Sie brauchen jemanden, der sie führt. Das kann ich verstehen. Was ich früher immer nur wollte, war, ein wirklich guter Tänzer zu sein; ich wollte nicht choreographieren. Allein der Gedanke erschreckte mich! Als junger Tänzer wollte ich einzig schrecklich gern Mitglied der Martha Graham Kompanie sein, ihr nahe. Auch wußte ich, daß Jerome Robbins, Agnes de Mille und Hanya Holm außergewöhnlich bedeutende Leute waren. Und ich wußte auch, daß ich ihnen ein gutes Instrument sein konnte. Ich konnte sie auf bestimmte Weise beeinflussen, weil ich mich in Improvisation entwickelt hatte. Ich wußte, daß manchmal, wenn ein Choreograph arbeitete, die Schritte allein nicht das Endprodukt darstellten; man arbeitete wie mit Ton. Alles war noch im Entstehen. Das war mir bewußt, aber die Übernahme der vollen Verantwortung war für mich eine furchterregende Sache. Die meisten Tänzer denken genauso und sind nicht willens, den Sprung ins kalte Wasser zu wagen. Das ist eigentlich schade.

RG: Sie sind sowohl mit der amerikanischen als auch der europäischen Tanzszene vertraut. Sie hatten die ungeheure Gelegenheit, mit all jenen Pionieren zu arbeiten, aber wer leistet heutzutage Pionierarbeit? Die Tanzwelt hat sich so ausgeweitet, daß es für einen Choreographen heute unmöglich ist, jedem gefällig zu sein, der daran interessiert sein könnte, mit ihm zusammenzuarbeiten. Wie wird der junge Choreograph heute damit fertig?

GT: Die Aufnahme einer Choreographie ins Repertoire ist sehr lobenswert, aber bringt den Tänzern eigentlich nichts; die individuelle Handschrift des Choreographen trägt so kaum Früchte. Als sich vor 20 Jahren das „abtrünnige" Nederlands Dans Theater neu formierte, wollte ich als junger Choreograph dorthin, um in einer Studio-Atmosphäre unmittelbar mit europäischen Tänzern zu arbeiten, die nicht meinen Modern Dance-Background besaßen. Es war eine wunderbare Zeit, weil es sich hier – glaube ich – um die erste Kompanie handelte, die versuchte, eine klassisch fundierte Tanztruppe in amerikanischen Modern Dance-Techniken arbeiten zu lassen und sich mit dieser Art choreographischer Struktur auseinanderzusetzen. Es ist merkwürdig, daß in den USA, wo so viel entstanden ist, die Grenzen immer noch viel klarer gezogen sind. Ist man ein Cunningham-Tänzer, ein Anhänger des Body Contact, ein Minimalist, oder gehört man dem New York City Ballet oder dem American Ballet Theatre an, so will man nicht unbedingt jemals andere Grundlagen der Tanzkomposition sehen, kennenlernen oder akzeptieren. Das habe ich in Europa nie erlebt! Alles war Bewegungserfahrung, alles war dort Tanzerfahrung, man hörte dort nicht: Ich will das nicht machen, weil es nicht die Technik ist, in der ich ausgebildet worden bin. In den USA war die Frage des Überlebens wahrscheinlich der Grund für diese strikte Grenzziehung. Wenn wir etwas schaffen oder ein Publikum haben wollten, so mußte man es allein durchstehen. Ich habe das in der Vergangenheitsform ausgedrückt, aber es ist immer noch so. Wie einige hundert Mal zuvor wird auch heute noch eine Kompanie gegründet – einfach so; irgendwie werden Studio und Geld gefunden; alles wird aus der eigenen Tasche bezahlt. Erst seit kurzem gibt es Subventionen der Bundesregierung in den USA, und im Zuge des jüngsten politischen Wandels werden sie vielleicht wieder gestrichen. Auf der anderen Seite gibt es in Europa feste Ensembles, die aus öffentlichen Mitteln hoch subventioniert sind. Als ich seinerzeit in Hamburg arbeitete, waren die Tänzer sehr unzufrieden, nicht genügend Aufführungen, Anreiz und neue Werke zu erhalten. Ich verstand das nicht. Ich sagte ihnen: Ihr braucht doch nicht im Theater zu bleiben. Warum gründet ihr nicht euer eigenes Ensemble, findet eure eigenen Aufführungsorte, macht was selbst? So etwas ist für euch auch als Mitglieder der offiziellen Kompanie noch möglich. Merkwürdigerweise hatten sie selbst daran nicht gedacht. Man beklagte sich, aber unternahm nichts dagegen. In den USA ergreift jeder wie selbstverständlich die Initiative, möglicherweise gebären genau diese Schwierigkeiten all jene Kreativität. Es ist ganz einfach der Kampf um die Existenz. Eigene Auftritte, die choreographischen Verpflichtungen, die Verwaltungsarbeit und die Geldsuche für meine eigene Kompanie waren einfach eine zu große Bürde. Doch dann boten mir zuerst das Nederlands Dans Theater, dann das Ballet Rambert und später andere Kompanien Probenräume, ausgezeichnete Tänzer und die Freiheit, mit jenen Designern und Komponisten zusammenzuarbeiten, die ich mir wünschte. Für einen Choreographen ist das sehr wichtig. Vorher hörte ich nämlich nur von meinem Agenten, daß ich bankrott gehen würde, wenn ich mir nicht eine kleine Kompanie (d. h. fünf oder sechs Tänzer in schlichten Trikots) und tantiemenfreie Musik leistete. Man fühlte sich wie ein Pionier in den frühen Tagen des Nederlands Dans Theater. Wichtige Veränderungen vollzogen sich. Während meiner ersten Zeit beim Ballet Rambert wurde ein neuer Tanzstil entwickelt, eine neue Art zu arbeiten, ein neues Vokabular. Für mich war das ein sehr wichtiger Lernprozeß.

RG: Was denken Sie heute über Europa, wenn Sie dort choreographieren?

GT: Es ist immer noch das gleiche. Ein Kritiker hat mir einmal gesagt: Sie choreographieren nur, aber Sie bringen den Leuten nichts bei. Ich glaube, daß das die wohl lächerlichste Behauptung war. Wenn man als Choreograph mit Tänzern arbeitet, ist man immer auch zu hundert Prozent ihr Lehrer. Andernfalls händigt man lediglich Schritte aus, die dann von den Tänzern automatisch nachvollzogen werden. Jüngst habe ich zum erstenmal in der Mailänder Scala gearbeitet, die der Prototyp einer etablierten staatlichen Kompanie mit all ihren Vor- und Nachteilen ist. Leute, die keine aufregenden Tänzer darstellten, klammerten sich an ihre Jobs, und junge Tänzer kämpften darum, in einem übermächtigen Starsystem hochzukommen. Nichtsdestotrotz war ich entschlossen, die Aufgabe auf mich zu nehmen, mühsam zu lehren, zu stimulieren, um am Ende etwas mit ihnen zustandegebracht zu haben. Das ist, wie eine Schlacht gewonnen zu haben. Man ist stolz auf den eigenen Stil des Tanzes, einen Stil, an den man glaubt. Nach kleineren zeitgenössischen Kompanien, wie das Tanz-Forum Köln, das Nederlands Dans Theater oder das Ballet Rambert, ist es etwas völlig anderes, sich mit einer großen klassischen Kompanie einzulassen, wo es zur schwierigsten Aufgabe wird, kreativ zu bleiben.

RG: Wie ordnet sich Stuttgart hier ein?

GT: Zwei der wichtigsten Dinge, auf die ich mich in meinem Leben eingelassen habe, waren, die Verantwortung für das Stuttgarter Ballett zu übernehmen und diese letztlich wieder abzugeben. In beiden Situationen habe ich unglaublich viel dazugelernt. An-

fangs habe ich lange gezögert mit Stuttgart. Ich hatte wunderschöne Erfahrungen mit seinen Tänzern gemacht, und ich liebte John Cranko. Ich wußte genau, welche Art von Kompanie es war – eine der wundervollsten Tanzmaschinerien, die ich je gesehen hatte, einfach umwerfend. Ich begann dort völlig offenherzig, vielleicht zu naiv. Viele neue Tänzer wurden engagiert. In den folgenden zweieinhalb Jahren wurden zehn Stücke für die Kompanie neu erarbeitet, und ich versuchte, das Cranko-Repertoire zu erhalten. Allerdings ist es keine einfache Sache, eine so persönlichkeitsgeprägte Kompanie zu übernehmen, noch dazu die des Gründers. Es war eine sehr eng verbundene Familie. Ich liebte sie alle, aber ich war nicht John Cranko. John und ich waren sehr verschieden voneinander. Mein Tanzstil wich sehr von seinem ab. All das zu ändern, von dem ich überzeugt war, nur um Erfolg zu haben und in Stuttgart bleiben zu können, war unvorstellbar, ein Desaster in jeder Hinsicht. In jener Zeit habe ich gelernt, wer ich bin, und ich bin dankbar für die anregende Arbeit mit wundervollen Tänzern wie Marcia Haydée, Richard Cragun, Birgit Keil und Egon Madsen – wundervolle, inspirierende Menschen. Aber es kam der Moment, wo ich alles an sie zurückgeben mußte.

RG: Sollte eine Kompanie nur mit einem Choreographen arbeiten? Träumt jeder Choreograph davon, seine eigene Gruppe von Tänzern zu haben?

GT: Nein, ich glaube nicht. Das ist nur eine Möglichkeit. Man formiert sich zu einem Ensemble mit nur einem Choreographen aus reiner Notwendigkeit, weil man die Kosten für ausgezeichnete Gastbeiträge nicht aufbringen kann. Ich glaube aber, daß jemand sich sein eigenes Zuhause suchen soll. Ich rate keinem jungen Choreographen, seine ersten Schritte in einer der großen Truppen zu versuchen. Das könnte zu einem völligen Nervenzusammenbruch führen, was oft genug selbst gestandenen Choreographen passiert ist. Später, wenn man mehr Erfahrungen gesammelt hat, wird man eher in der Lage sein, dem Arbeits- und Konkurrenzdruck zu widerstehen und mit Menschen zu arbeiten, die man erst noch für sich einnehmen muß, weil sie möglicherweise kein eigenes Interesse an der Sache mitbringen. Außerdem muß man in der Lage sein, sehr schnell zu produzieren; denn auch das gehört zur Professionalität.

RG: Ich habe zwei große Kompanien beobachtet, die junge Choreographen forcieren, nachdem sie gerade erste Talentbeweise geliefert haben. Eine dieser Kompanien ist Stuttgart. Nach Ihrem Weggang begann man dort mit einer neuen Politik, mit dem Ziel, junge Choreographen aus den eigenen Reihen zu entwickeln, ein ganzes Re-

pertoire auf deren Arbeit aufzubauen. Die andere Truppe – in geringerem Maße – ist das New York City Ballet, das Peter Martins als großes Nachwuchstalent zu präsentieren sucht.

GT: Ich würde mir nicht herausnehmen, jemandes Politik zu kritisieren. Ich war immer auf der Seite der jungen Choreographen. Als ich nach Stuttgart kam, wurde einem jungen Corps de ballet-Tänzer ein erster größerer Auftrag erteilt, und das war Jiři Kylián. Ich stand auch hinter William Forsythe. Es ist unabdingbar, choreographische Workshops anzubieten, auch in großen Kompanien. Das kann niemals eine schlechte Politik sein, selbst wenn alles völlig danebengeht.

RG: Ist es für einen Anfänger ratsam, den Stil eines gestandenen Choreographen zu kopieren?

GT: Eine außerordentlich kreative Persönlichkeit scheint den Boden um sich herum zu verbrennen, scheint wie ein Baum zu sein, der zu hoch gewachsen ist und auf alles um sich herum tiefe Schatten wirft. Die Tatsache, daß eine Kompanie durch die Vorstellungskraft einer Persönlichkeit zusammengebracht wird, schließt jede entgegengesetzte Einflußnahme aus. Das trifft mit Sicherheit auf George Balanchine und Martha Graham zu. Die Art, wie man bei Martha Graham etwas über Choreographie lernte, war, sie zu beobachten, wie sie mit ihrer wunderbaren Tanzsprache umging. Aber um Gottes Willen, man darf sie nicht kopieren, niemals ihre Sprache verwenden! Man benutze niemals Balanchines choreographisches Rezept! Die einzige Möglichkeit, Choreograph zu werden, ist, etwas Eigenes zu finden; andernfalls bleibt alles nur kommerzielle Anbiederei, ein Kurzschluß. Diese Art geborgter Werke mag manchem solider erscheinen, aber tatsächlich haben sie keinen Bestand. Wenn man ehrlich arbeitet, kommt immer etwas anderes dabei heraus. Unterschiede werden sofort sichtbar, weil jeder Mensch einen individuellen Rhythmus, eine vollständig andere Weltsicht, einen eigenen Sinn für Formen besitzt und ein Empfinden für die Integration der Dinge – all das ist einmalig. Dieser kleine Unterschied, der ist so aufregend.

RG: Glauben Sie, es ist zuträglich oder abträglich für junge Choreographen, mit großen Stars zu arbeiten?

GT: Ich mag das Starsystem nicht. Ich mag keine „Stars". Ich glaube nicht an Galas oder Gala-Stücke. Ich möchte jetzt nicht allzu ernsthaft klingen; denn ich bin es nicht. Aber ich glaube an Tänzer. Wenn ein Tänzer eine vorzügliche Bewegungsqualität besitzt, wunderbar! Aber maßgeschneiderte Arbeit für einen Star? – Das wäre Prostitution.

RG: Was halten Sie von Wettbewerben für angehende Choreographen?

147

GT: Ich habe die Schule nie gemocht. Mir waren Tests, Wettbewerbe und Bewertungssysteme ein Greuel. Jeder, der mit den richtigen Motiven dabei ist, kann an Wettbewerben, Preisverleihungen oder guten Kritiken kein Interesse haben. Das einzig Gute, das für choreographische Wettbewerbe spricht, ist die Ermöglichung einer Bühnenaufführung. Das ist sehr wichtig. In unserem Beruf ist es nicht mit dem Herumsitzen im Wohnzimmer getan. Eine Bühne und Tänzer sind notwendig. Ein junger Choreograph könnte einen Wettbewerb nutzen, sein Werk auf die Bühne zu bringen.

RG: Was halten Sie von Zusammenarbeit?
GT: An eine Zusammenarbeit zwischen Choreographen kann ich nicht recht glauben. Ich glaube, Choreographieren ist eine sehr persönliche Äußerung. Zwei Menschen können keine gemeinsame persönliche Aussage machen. Allerdings bin ich immer von Musik angeregt worden, noch bevor ich anfing zu choreographieren. Ich habe Tänze geschaffen, zum Teil ohne

Musik (das ist jedoch ein anderer Aspekt), aber einen inspirierenden Komponisten zu treffen, sich mit ihm zu unterhalten und mit ihm ein Werk zu gestalten, ist außergewöhnlich erregend, vielleicht das Aufregendste. Die Arbeit mit einem guten Bühnenbildner ist ebenfalls richtig spannend. In dem Augenblick, da man sich auf einen Dialog einläßt, wird ein kreativer Prozeß in Gang gesetzt; die Gedanken nehmen Wege, die sie niemals allein beschritten hätten. Wir streben etwas Neuem zu, keiner Kopie, nicht nur einer sauberen Arbeit, keinem adäquaten Versuch, sondern wir suchen nach etwas, das mit aller Kraft der optischen Sprache und der besonderen Kommunikation spricht, die Tanz und Design geben können. Als ich zum erstenmal Werke von Martha Graham sah, empfing ich eine Botschaft. Und obgleich ich nicht genau wußte, was es war, wußte ich doch, daß ein Geheimnis dahintersteckte. Es ist wunderbar zu wissen, daß das Leben solche Geheimnisse besitzt und daß es Augenblicke gibt, in denen ein Mensch den Schlüssel dazu findet und die

Möglichkeit, diese in so gewaltiger Weise auszudrücken. Diese sehr tiefe religiöse Erfahrung hinterließ in mir einen außerordentlichen Eindruck. Tanz hat natürlich mehrere Seiten, aber ich habe nie gefühlt, daß er nur Unterhaltung ist. Es ist nicht genug, einfach nur das Auge anzusprechen. Ich möchte vollkommen einbezogen werden, ich möchte bezaubert werden, doch gleichzeitig immer auch wissen, daß allem eine tiefere Wahrheit zugrundeliegt. Unter den Künsten war der Tanz für mich immer das stärkste Mittel zur Kommunikation. Das ist der Grund, warum ich mich mit ihm einließ, warum ich immer noch dabei bin, warum ich heute mich noch damit auseinandersetze. Und zum Glück existiert im Tanz kein Generationskonflikt. Nichts gibt einem eine größere Bestätigung, als in ein Studio zu gehen und in engem physischen, emotionellen und geistigen Kontakt mit jüngeren Menschen zu stehen. Das ist eine ungeheure Verpflichtung und ein gewaltiger Anreiz. Es ist ein Teil der Schönheit unserer Kunst.

Glen Tetley/Rolf Garske

CREATIVITY OR CRAFT
LEARNING TO BE A CHOREOGRAPHER?

RG: Mr. Tetley, do you think it is possible to train someone to become a choreographer?
GT: This is a very difficult question. It is the same as in any branch of the fine arts: To teach someone to be an artist or to be creative is not possible. All of us are creative. We learn, more or less, how to release this creativity or how to hide it. But to actually teach someone to be a choreographer or a poet or a composer or a painter or a writer is, I think, impossible. Years ago, I worked with Doris Humphrey who was one of our dance pioneers; she was an extraordinary person in the field because she was very concerned with this question of teaching choreography as a craft. She was an enormously generous person, but she always said that it is impossible. "One cannot be taught choreography", she said, "but one can learn it." I think that is true.

RG: In her book The Art of Making Dances Doris Humphrey tackles the theme of choreographing from various angles and illustrates basic principles of constructing and presenting dances on stage. On two occasions, you have conducted the Gulbenkian choreographic summer course in England. You led a group of young choreographers whom you gave certain exercises. What was your intention?
GT: At first, I was very reluctant to go into this Gulbenkian project, having remembered my acceptance sometime before to teach such a course in the United States for the National Association of Regional

Ballet Companies. I wanted to teach it in order to see first hand what was going on with the regional ballet companies. Doris Hering, who was the president of this organization, encouraged me. It was a terribly difficult thing: ten days on the East Coast, ten days on the West Coast, and ten days in Central U.S.A., sometimes with 150 people from all levels of dance experience. One could not expect to accomplish very much. However, the experience I gained there helped to form ideas for setting up the Gulbenkian project. From the beginning, Gale Law, with whom I had worked very closely when he was a dancer and later when he was press secretary with the Nederlands Dans Theater, and I decided that to insure a very high standard potential participants would have to be auditioned. They would have to have been professionally trained, not to mention the fact that they would have to possess a tremendous desire to work with other choreographers, composers and dancers involved. Another idea was to include people from the field of lighting and design. The very best teachers of modern and classical dance were also to be engaged. In other words, we wanted to provide as much stimulus as possible for the very short two-week period.

RG: Can one be a choreographer without having danced?
GT: Of course not. No one can be a choreographer without first having been a dancer. That is the only way to learn the craft. I learned whatever I have learned by dancing for choreographers, trying to be the most competent dancer I could, and by working closely with people whom I admired and with whom I wanted to collaborate. My close association with Martha Graham was an entire university course for me. Watching her struggle to make a ballet, observing where her genius took her when things did not work, what happened when there were difficult moments, and how she dealt with them – all this was an enormous learning experience. This reminds me of another reason why I wanted to teach the course. In our field, we are so isolated. It is strange that in the dance world, choreographers do not talk to each other! To come together not for the purpose of teaching, not to say that these are the rules, follow them and you will succeed – to be able to do this is a wonderful thing and, moreover, very important. Anyway, if rules could do it, everyone would be a choreographic genius. Ninety-nine percent of the time one is breaking the rules, going one's own particular bend, following one's own imagination. I thought it was a very valuable thing for us to get together just to talk about it, to share experiences with young dancers who want to become choreographers and want to try something creative. That is the general intention

of the Gulbenkian choreographic summer course.

With the speed of the world we live in, professional dancers are being trained only in technique. I was twenty years old when I came to New York to start dancing. I was already trained as a medical student. I was on the one hand a romantic and on the other hand very analytical. I had been trained to analyze and to ask questions. The good fortune was that, although my very first training was in classical ballet, I immediately encountered Hanya Holm who, through her background with Mary Wigman, was another of the American pioneers in contemporary dance. It was during that period that people were going down to the bases from which dance comes. They were wondering what was inherent in all dance movement, what were the basic building blocks of it. This was exactly right for me: to know analytically and anatomically that a plié was a plié, that a relevé was a relevé whether it was Indian dance or classical ballet or any other form of dance. The body is constructed in such a way that this detail, for example, occurs in all dances. Studying these theories, which came from Mary Wigman and Rudolf von Laban, clarified many things for me as far as movement was concerned. We had a technique class which meant training the body, then a theory class in which we discussed things and broke them down. One had time to ask questions. Then, for two hours a day we had improvisation, which was practical and essential for a choreographer, and, of course, we had composition, music, dance notation, and history classes. Hanya Holm's original concept was to build a university of dance for professionals. I admire so much her incredible estimation of dance as being on a par with all the other creative arts. A musician has to study theory and composition. Where would a musician be if he had not studied all these things? Perhaps the reason that some choreographers are as they are, derives from the fact that these training structures are simply not available.
RG: Why do some people say there are no new choreographers today, when there seems to be such an explosion of them? How does one merit the title choreographer?
GT: Anyone can put movement together; anyone can put sounds together or anyone can put paint on a canvas or make a happening. We tend to call such a person an artist. They are artists, of course. But when one goes into whatever one's life's work is, why not go into it forever, why not want to have all the preparedness, all the experience that will sustain one for an entire life? I went into dancing because I loved it. It was

no choice for me! It is the primary thing that makes my life worth living. And I think the deeper one goes, the stronger the base one needs. It is one thing to do an *initial* work, a first choreography, and another to go on, to continue, to develop and find something new in it throughout a whole life span. There comes the time when one needs to have had this experience, this training, to get as much information as one can get.
RG: Dancers who are interested in choreography should have then this broad spectrum of education.
GT: Why not? It certainly will not hurt. The more informed one is, the more one has learned, the more experience one has had working with different choreographers, the more performing experiences one has had, the more one has inside as tools with which to work. The large variety of choreography we see today is only interesting in very small sections; the rest is not of any interest because of its puny range.
I love the technical training of a dancer. I wonder at the extraordinary ends a dancer can reach with good training. I believe in a strong technical background, because technique gives a dancer freedom, freedom to do anything. I do, however, understand all the other view points. I am also a people watcher. I like to sit on a park bench and watch people. It is very fascinating to me. But I am not fascinated to go to the theater and watch the minimal and non-technical. I like something that is not going to make me work too terribly hard at keeping up my interest. When I go to see a dance program, I want to enter into the choreographer's mind; I want to experience something different, something new. I want to be challenged.
If a composer ignored all the history of composition and music, if he ignored all the composers before him, if he closed his ears and eyes to the enormous vocabulary and library they accumulated, where would music be? It would be right back at a minimal level. I have never yet found that training and knowledge inhibited someone. I have never believed in nationalism, I do not believe in racism, apartness, and I have never believed in building artificial walls in the art world either. I began with dance during a period when modern dance was very strong in this country, strong because the pioneers were still there. I worked intimately with all of them – Martha Graham, Hanya Holm, Charles Weidman, Doris Humphrey, José Limón, and, because I wanted the other thing, with Antony Tudor and Margaret Craske.
At the School of American Ballet I studied with the best of the old Kirov teachers, which was very much frowned upon. Either

one was modern or one was not. I could not acknowledge what I felt as artificial walls. To me all was movement, and I was curious. It was an exploration of technique, of how one trained the body and released it to become an instrument. Of course, these were all problems of finding a technique of discovering how to be creative or how to be a choreographer. That all goes along with being a trained dancer with a lot of experience and is, to my mind, the best step towards becoming a good choreographer.
RG: Is it difficult for the dancer to make that step?
GT: Most dancers are embarrassed even to suggest a movement to the choreographer. They can be the most wonderful dancers in the world, but they say, "Do not expect me to determine how the movement should happen." They need someone to guide them. This I understand. I wanted to be a fine dancer; I never wanted to choreograph. The thought terrified me! I knew, when I was a young dancer, how terribly much I wanted to be inside the Martha Graham Company, to be close to her. I knew that Jerome Robbins, Agnes de Mille, and Hanya Holm were extremely important people. I also knew that I could be a good instrument for them. I could lead them, in a way, because I had developed in improvisation. I knew that sometimes when a choreographer was working, the steps were not the final thing; one was working with the clay. It was to become something else. I knew that, but to take over the total responsibility was a very terrifying thing. Most dancers do not want to do this, are not willing to take the plunge. It is a pity.
RG: You are familiar with both the American and the European dance scene. You have had the tremendous opportunity to work with all those pioneers, but who are the pioneers of today? The dance world has become so large that it seems impossible for a choreographer to accommodate all of those who may be interested in working with him or her. How does the young would-be choreographer deal with this situation nowadays?
GT: To take a ballet from a choreographer and put it into a repertoire is very commendable, but it does not really teach; it does not really put seeds into the ground. Twenty years ago, when the renegade Nederlands Dans Theater was formed, I wanted to go there, as a beginning choreographer, to work directly in a studio setting with European dancers who had not had the modern background that I had. It was a wonderful time because it was, I think, the first company that tried to have a basically classical oriented company work in American modern dance techniques

and concentrate on that sort of choreographic structure. The very strange thing is that in the U.S.A. where so much was spawned and created, the lines are still very strongly drawn. If one is a Cunningham dancer, a body contact dancer, a minimalist, if one is a member of the New York City Ballet or American Ballet Theatre, he or she does not necessarily ever see, or want to see or accept, another basis of dance composition. I did not find that in Europe at all! Everything was movement experience. Everything was dance experience. People were not saying, "I do not want to do that because it is not the technique in which I was trained." In America, survival was probably the reason why these walls were so strong. If one wanted to create something and have an audience, he or she had to go it alone. I have put it in the past tense, but it is still true. As hundreds have done, a company is formed somehow, the studio and the money are found for it; everything is paid for out of one's own pocket. It is only recently that we have had U.S. Government subsidy for the arts, and with the recent political change, even this may disappear. On the other hand, in Europe there are stable companies which are highly government supported. When I was working in Hamburg some time ago, the dancers were very unhappy about not getting enough performances, enough stimulation and new works. This I did not understand. I said to them: "You do not have to remain in the theater. Why not form your own company, find your own space, do something on your own? This is possible even while you are a part of a company." Strangely enough, they had not thought of it themselves. They were complaining, but they were not doing anything about it. In America everyone takes the initiative as a matter of course. Perhaps it is precisely the difficulties in the United States which breed so much creativity. It is simply fighting against having nothing. Performing in, choreographing for, administering, and funding my own company was just too much of a burden to bear. First, Nederlands Dans Theater, then Ballet Rambert, and other companies offered studios, excellent dancers, and liberty to use the designers and composers I wanted. This was very important for a choreographer. Before that, I was constantly hearing from my agent that unless I used a small company (that is to say five or six dancers in body tights) and public domain music, I would go bankrupt. It felt like pioneering in those early days of the Nederlands Dans Theater. There were important changes taking place. My early days at Ballet Rambert brought a new style of dancing, a new way of working, a new

vocabulary, and a very important learning period for me.

RG: How do you feel about Europe today?
GT: It is still the same. A critic once said to me, "You only choreograph, you don't teach." I thought that was the most ridiculous statement. As a choreographer working with dancers one is teaching 100 percent of the time. Otherwise, one is simply giving out steps, and the dancers are doing them automatically. Recently, I was working for the first time at La Scala in Italy, which is the prototype of fixed state companies with all the pros and cons. People who were not very exciting dancers were holding on to jobs and young people were struggling to rise in a crushing star system. Even so, I was still willing to take on the job, as it were, of laboriously teaching, stimulating, and having something finally emerge. That is like a battle won. One was proud of the kind of dancing in which one believes. It is an entirely different thing, after smaller contemporary companies such as Tanz-Forum Köln, Nederlands Dans Theater or Ballet Rambert, to deal with a very large classical company where it is the hardest thing in the world to do something creative.

RG: Where does the Stuttgart Ballet fit in?
GT: Two of the most important things I have ever done in my life were accepting responsibility for the Stuttgart Ballet and relinquishing it. I learned tremendously from both. I was very hesitant about Stuttgart. I had a beautiful experience with their dancers and I had loved John Cranko. I knew exactly the kind of company it was – one of the most wonderful dancing machines I had ever seen, just thrilling. I entered it with an open heart, perhaps too naively. Many new dancers were brought in. Within two and a half years, ten works were created for the company. I tried to maintain the Cranko repertoire. However, to take over a company which has been a one-person company, a founder's company, is no simple matter. It was such a tight family. I loved them all, but I was not John Cranko. John and I were very different. My sort of dancing was very different from his. Changing what one believed in order to succeed and remain in Stuttgart was inconceivable, a disaster on all sides. I learned exactly who I am, and I am grateful for the invigorating time of working with wonderful dancers like Marcia Haydée, Richard Cragun, Birgit Keil und Egon Madsen – wonderful, inspiring people. But the moment came when it was time for me to hand it back to them.

RG: Is it preferable to be a one-choreographer company? Does the choreographer dream of having his own group of dancers?

GT: No, I don't think so. That is a formula. People become a one-choreographer company out of necessity; they cannot pay the fees for top-rate choreography. I think if anyone is going to be a choreographer, he should find some place he can call home. I would not advise any young choreographer to attempt his or her first work in a large major company. It could lead to a total nervous breakdown, which has happened many times, even with established choreographers. Later on, when one becomes more experienced, one will be able to withstand the pressure of working in a highly competitive situation and with people who have to be won over, because they may not be interested. One must also produce material very quickly.

RG: I have observed two companies which are pushing young choreographers who have shown bits of talent. One of them is Stuttgart. Following your departure, they set up a new policy, which aims to develop young choreographers out of their own group, to base the whole repertoire on their works. The other company is, to a lesser extent, the New York City Ballet which pushes Peter Martins as its up-and-coming choreographer.

GT: I would not presume to criticize anyone's policy. I have always been for the young choreographer. When I took over Stuttgart, there was a young corps de ballet dancer who was given his first major commission. That was Jiři Kylián. And I was absolutely behind William Forsythe. It is crucial to have choreographic workshops in the big companies as well. This is never bad policy, even if it fails completely.

RG: Would it be advisable to begin by copying the style of established choreographers?

GT: A strongly creative person seems to burn the ground around him or her, such as a tree does that grows too tall thus casting a shadow over everything around. The fact that a company is being formed in one image rules out any opposing image. This is certainly the case with George Balanchine and Martha Graham. The way one learned about choreography with Martha Graham was by observing the way she worked with her wonderful language. But for God's sake do not copy her, do not use her language! Do not use Balanchine's formula for choreography. The only reason one becomes a choreographer is to find something of his or her own; otherwise, it is just a business proposition, a short-cut. Such borrowed work may seem to have more solidity, but in fact, it has none. If one works honestly, the results are always different. Changes are immediately apparent because each person has an individual rhythm, a completely different view of the world, a sense of form and of how things connect that is unlike anybody else's. That slight difference is what is so exciting.

RG: Do you think it is fruitful or destructive for young choreographers to work with great stars?

GT: I do not like the star system, I do not like "stars". I do not believe in galas or gala-pieces. I do not mean to seem overly serious, because I am not. I believe in dancers. If the dancer has a superb quality of movement, wonderful, but to do a tailor-made work for a star, that would be prostitution.

RG: What do you think about competitions for aspiring choreographers?

GT: I never liked school. I hated tests and competitions and grading systems. Anybody who is in it for the right reasons is not interested in competitions or being awarded prizes and good reviews. The only thing good that could be said for choreographic competitions is that it gives another stage. That is very important. In our profession, one cannot do it sitting in the living room. A stage and dancers are needed. A young choreographer could use a competition as a means of getting his work on stage.

RG: What about collaboration?

GT: I do not really believe in collaboration between choreographers. I think choreographing is a very personal statement. Two people cannot make a joint personal statement. However, I have always been stimulated by music even before I started to choreograph. I have done dances which were, in part, in silence (that is another aspect), but to meet an inspiring composer, to talk to him and to create a work together is terribly exciting, perhaps the most exciting thing.

To work with a good designer is also tremendously exciting. The moment one begins a dialogue, creative things happen; one's mind goes in directions it would never have taken had one been alone. We aim for something new, not a copy, not just a good job, not an adequate trial, but something which speaks with all the power of the optical language and the special communication that dance and design can give. When I first saw the works of Martha Graham, they explained something to me. Although I did not know exactly what it was, I knew that there was a mystery there. It is so wonderful to know that life has this mystery and that for a moment someone has the key to it and is explaining it in such a powerful way. This very deeply religious experience made an extraordinary impact on me. Dance has many sides, of course, but I have never felt that it is merely entertainment. It is not enough to simply keep the eye involved. I want to be totally involved, to be mystified, but at the same time

to know that there is a deep underlying truth in what is being done. Dance, to me, has always been the most powerful means of communication in the arts. That is why I went into it, why I am still in it, why I am still trying. And fortunately, in dance, the generation gap is non-existent. There is nothing so reaffirming as to go into a studio and to be in close physical, emotional, and spiritual contact with younger people. It is a tremendous bond and stimulus. That is part of the beauty.

diese Seite/this page
DER STURM/
THE TEMPEST,
Ch: Glen Tetley
Ausstattung von/décor by
Nadine Baylis
oben/above
Ketil Gudim,
Norwegisches Nationalballett/
Norwegian National Ballet,
Foto: Karsten Bundgaard
unten/below
Ballet Rambert,
Foto: Gert Weigelt

gegenüber/opposite page
LE SACRE DU PRINTEMPS,
Ch: Glen Tetley,
Ausstattung von/décor by
Nadine Baylis
American Ballet Theater,
Foto: Martha Swope

diese Seite/this page
DANCES OF ALBION,
Ch: Glen Tetley
oben/above
Stephen Beagley,
Lesley Collier,
Stephen Jefferies,
unten/below
Rosalyn Whitten,
Wayne Eagling
Royal Ballet London,
Fotos: Leslie E. Spatt
gegenüber/
opposite page
CONTREDANCES,
Ch: Glen Tetley,
Natalia Makarowa,
Anthony Dowell,
American Ballet Theater,
Foto: Sue Martin

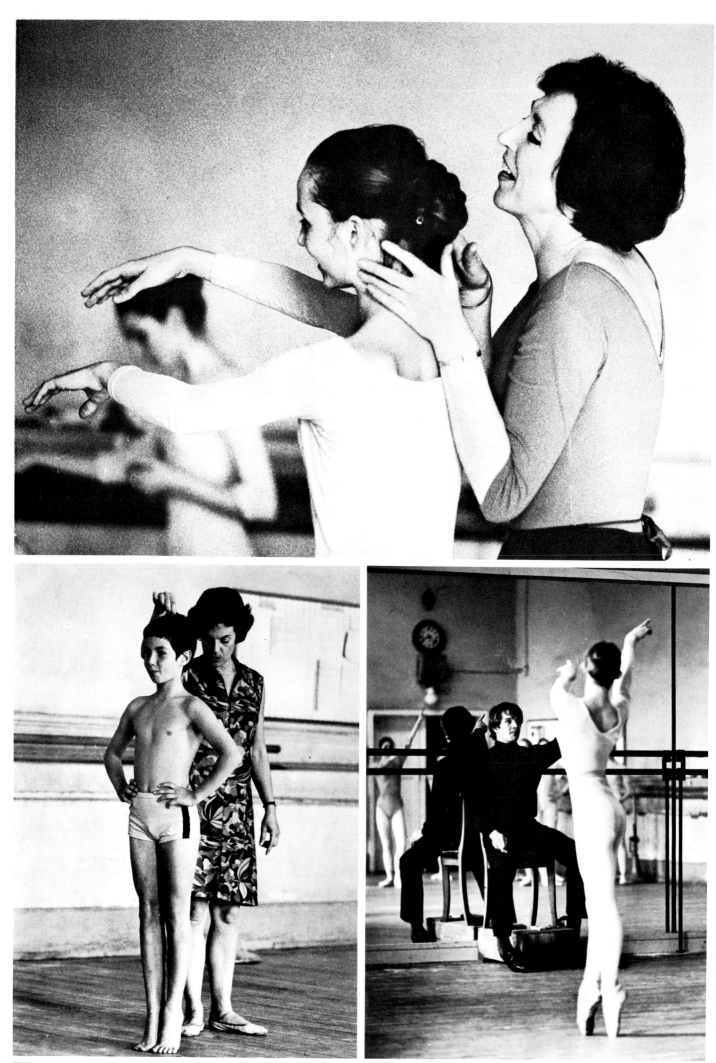

oben/above
ANNE WOOLLIAMS
unten links/below left
ANNETTE CHAPPELL
unten rechts/below right
ALAN BEALE,
Unterricht in der/teaching in
John Cranko-Schule, Stuttgart,
Fotos: Hannes Kilian

Hartmut Regitz

SOZIALE ASPEKTE DES TÄNZER-BERUFES

Es gibt wenige Berufe, bei denen zwischen Wunsch und Wirklichkeit ein solches Mißverhältnis besteht wie bei dem des Tänzers. Denn der Eindruck, den jedes Ballett erweckt, sofern es den selbstgestellten Ansprüchen aller Ausführenden genügt, der Eindruck offensichtlicher Leichtigkeit, kultivierter Bewegung und körperlicher Schönheit: er scheint das Berufsbild all jener nachhaltig zu prägen, die sich keine Vorstellung machen können von der Anstrengung, die sich hinter jeder Aufführung schamhaft verbirgt, von der kräfteverschleißenden Vorbereitung, die sie erst ermöglicht, ja überhaupt von der Mühsal der körperlichen Disziplinierung, die sich über Jahre hinweg ständig verstärkt. Und gerade dieser falsche Eindruck scheint, so paradox das auch klingen mag, für tänzerischen Nachwuchs zu sorgen. Ohne diese Fehleinschätzung wären jedenfalls kaum so viele Jungen und Mädchen willens, diesem Eindruck ihr Leben zu opfern.

Doch an Paradoxien ist der Tänzerberuf ohnehin reicher als andere. Das hängt vor allem mit der Tatsache zusammen, daß man ihn zu einem Zeitpunkt wählen muß, an dem man noch gar nicht reif genug ist, diese folgenreiche Wahl zu treffen: möglichst im Alter von acht, zehn Jahren. Besucht man nicht von frühester Jugend an eine gute Ballettschule, kann man die Technik, die letztlich Vorbedingung allen Tanzes ist, kaum noch in erforderlichem Maße erlernen. Sie bleibt wohl oder übel Stückwerk, fehlerhaft.

Aus diesem Grund muß mit der Erziehung früh begonnen werden – und so sind es in erster Linie die Eltern, die den Berufswunsch artikulieren. Sie sind es, die oft genug Tänzer werden wollten, nun aber zu alt dafür sind und ihren Berufswunsch an die Tochter oder – weit seltener – an den Sohn delegieren. Sie sind es, die in ihrem Kind das verwirklicht wissen wollen, was ihnen selbst verwehrt blieb. Sie sind es, Anne Woolliams hat es 1973 in ihrem lesenswerten Buch *Ballettsaal* bildhaft beschrieben, die in ihrem Sprößling ein Wesen sehen wollen, erhaben über Staubsauger und Waschmaschine, verwöhnt von einem Leben voller Glanz und Gloria, Reichtum und Reisen.
Wenn Anne Woolliams ergänzend meint, daß es wohl keinen Beruf gäbe, "der mehr Jünger im Alter von zehn Jahren anzieht und zehn Jahre weiter mehr Enttäuschte ausstößt", ist sicher diese Stellvertreterrolle mit daran schuld, die die Kinder vielfach erfüllen müssen. Schuld daran ist zum großen Teil zweifellos auch die biologische Entwicklung, die sie während der Pubertät nehmen. Ihnen blieben viele soziale Schwierigkeiten in ihrem späteren Beruf erspart, hätte man rechtzeitig Vorsorge getroffen. Rechtzeitig heißt in diesem Falle natürlich in der Ballett-schule. Denn betrachtet man die Karriere eines künftigen Tänzers nicht einfach als Vabanquespiel, als unkontrollierbares Zusammenspiel von Begabung, Glück und Zufall, läßt sich das Risiko mindern, das sie in sich birgt. Beispielsweise, indem man von vornherein die Ausbildung so ausrichtet, daß jederzeit Berufskorrekturen möglich sind, falls schwindende Neigungen oder körperliche Veränderungen dies notwendig erscheinen lassen. Eine Ausbildung "bis zum bitteren Ende", wenn die Voraussetzungen nicht mehr stimmen, wäre das letzte, was man sich wünschte.
Wie diese "Vorsorge" auszusehen hätte, kann man sich unschwer vorstellen. Ein Bildungsprogramm, so umfassend und vielseitig, daß jederzeit neue Interessen entwickelt werden können, sollte als soziale Sicherung eigentlich selbstverständlich sein.

Jedes gute Ballettinstitut des In- und Auslandes, das sich nicht mit dem pädagogischen Augenblickserfolg zufrieden gibt, hat denn auch ein pluralistisches Erziehungsprogramm ausgearbeitet, das Eventualitäten vorbeugt und dem Schüler soviel Wissen an die Hand gibt, daß er sich – zumindest in einem verwandten Metier – eine neue Existenz aufbauen kann.
Wie wichtig diese "Vorsorge" nicht nur für "Aussteiger", sondern gerade auch für den Tänzer sein kann, zeigt sich schon zu Beginn seiner Laufbahn. Selbst so anerkannte Ausbildungsinstitute wie die Stuttgarter John-Cranko-Schule können keinesfalls eine Beschäftigung garantieren. Vom Stuttgarter Ballett werden pro Spielzeit allenfalls zwei Absolventen der Akademie übernommen. Andere wiederum gehen beispielsweise nach Hamburg, München oder Ulm. Den meisten von ihnen aber bleibt die Anstrengung jahrelanger Engagementsuche nicht erspart – sei es bei der monatlichen Ballettbörse der Zentralen Bühnen-, Fernseh- und Filmvermittlung (ZBF) der Bundesanstalt für Arbeit in Frankfurt, sei es bei individuellen Vortanzterminen der größeren und kleineren Kompanien. Die Konkurrenz, nicht zuletzt die des Auslands, ist groß, die Kapazität der 53 Musiktheater der Bundesrepublik Deutschland begrenzt. Da kann es mitunter hilfreich sein, nicht unbedingt auf eine Tänzer-Stelle angewiesen zu sein.

Selbst wenn man einen Vertrag in der Tasche hat, kann diese Art Vorsorge nicht schaden. Die befristeten Verträge, die in der Bundesrepublik nicht zuletzt aus künstlerischen Erwägungen üblich sind, können in der Regel in der ersten Hälfte der Spielzeit ohne sonderliche Schwierigkeit wieder gekündigt werden. Zwar sind darüber hinaus die Gagen mittlerweile erheblich angehoben worden, doch nicht derart, daß man in den 20 Jahren, die einem bestenfalls im Beruf bleiben, große Reichtümer anhäufen könnte: Mehr als 3000 Mark brutto verdient auch ein Ensemblemitglied der Deutschen Oper Berlin selten.
Daß unter diesen Voraussetzungen an eine finanzielle Zukunftssicherung kaum zu denken ist, ist offensichtlich. Und doch ist gerade die Sicherung in einem Beruf unabdingbar, dessen Ende mit 35, 40 Jahren naht. Indes, wer hätte je im Zusammenhang mit dem Ballett von "Weiterbildung", gar von "Bildungsurlaub" gehört? Die Bühnengenossenschaft als zuständige gewerkschaftliche Vertretung mag dies in ihren tarifpolitischen Forderungen vertreten, aber am Theater herrschen zumeist eigene Gesetze – und oft ist es so, daß die Tänzer jeden Gedanken an die eigene Zukunft, sofern sie sich nicht in überschaubaren Grenzen hält, konsequent verdrängen. Sie sind vielfach so auf ihre Kunst konzentriert, sind so darauf bedacht, in der permanenten Konkurrenz das Beste zu leisten, daß kaum Zeit für anderweitige Interessen bleibt. Sie tanzen tatsächlich wie in einem Elfenbeinturm.
In der DDR beispielsweise wird nach dem 15. Berufsjahr eine Mindestrente gewährt, die ungefähr 50 % der letzten Gage beträgt und damit Anreiz zu weiterer Beschäftigung gibt. In anderen Ländern kennt man vergleichbare Regelungen, wenngleich sie meist eine längere Berufstätigkeit voraussetzen. In der Bundesrepublik ist soziale Sicherheit hingegen nur dann voll gewährleistet, wenn der Tänzer oder die Tänzerin 15 Jahre lang ein- und demselben Theater angehört hat. Dann muß sich das Theater um eine angemessene Weiterbeschäftigung kümmern – was häufig dazu führt, daß man ehemalige Tänzer als Kassierer, als Bibliothekar, Inspizient, Souffleur oder Bühnenmaler wiederfindet. Seltener dagegen wachsen sie problemlos in Berufe hinein, die man als adäquate Fortsetzung ihrer bisherigen Tätigkeit ansehen kann – einfach deshalb, weil es viel zu wenig Vakanzen für Ballettchefs oder Choreographen, Ballettmeister, Trainingsleiter oder Pädagogen gibt.
Mancher eröffnet eine Ballettschule. Andere wiederum, die aufgrund von Krankheit, Alter oder zwingenden privaten Gründen ihren Beruf aufgeben müssen, bleibt nur der Weg zum örtlichen Arbeitsamt oder zur Zentralen

Bühnen-, Fernseh- und Filmvermittlung in Frankfurt. Finanziell unterstützt, können sie sich dort auf einen verwandten Beruf umschulen lassen. (Das Arbeitsamt steuert nach Rücksprache mit der ZBF unter bestimmten Voraussetzungen zwei Jahre lang 80% des bisherigen Einkommens als Übergangsunterstützung bei und übernimmt auch alle anfallenden Unkosten). Die ZBF nennt in ihrem Merkblatt als geeignete „Umschulungsberufe für Tänzer" den Gymnastiklehrer, den Sportlehrer, den Heilgymnasten, den Kranken- und Versehrtengymnasten sowie den Masseur und führt als Gründe die guten Kenntnisse der Anatomie, der Muskelfunktionen sowie der körperlichen Bewegungsabläufe an.

Für die meisten freilich bedeutet das Umsteigen auf einen anderen Beruf in jedem Fall einen sozialen Abstieg. Die eigenen Ansprüche müssen erheblich reduziert werden. Der Zwang, zu einer Zeit noch einmal von vorne anfangen zu müssen, da andere gerade in ihrem Metier die Höchstleistung erbringen, demoralisiert. Und die Unselbständigkeit, in der man jahrelang in Training und Proben gehalten wurde, macht mutlos.

Es fällt schwer, selbst die Initiative zu ergreifen, und es scheint nahezu aussichtslos, mit 40 noch einmal neue Interessen zu entwikkeln, wenn man zuvor nie einen Anstoß dazu erhalten hat. So wichtig die Hilfe der Münchner Heinz-Bosl-Stiftung auch sein

mag, die ergänzend zu ihrem Förderprogramm für junge Talente eine Art Altersvorsorge-Versicherung für jeden angehenden Tänzer einzuführen beabsichtigt; wichtiger ist die rechtzeitige Vorbereitung auf die Zukunft. Und die beginnt, wie gesagt, bei der Ausbildung. Wird schon in diesem Stadium des Berufs die „Früherkennung" wirksam, wie das Rainer Woihsyk in *Ballett 1979* einmal genannt hat, können den Tänzern und Tänzerinnen in ihrem späteren Leben soziale Schwierigkeiten und Härten erspart werden. Nur dadurch kann der Tänzerberuf zusätzliche Attraktivität gewinnen. Nur dadurch kann die Diskrepanz zwischen Wunsch und Wirklichkeit endlich abgebaut werden.

Hartmut Regitz

SOCIAL ASPECTS OF DANCE AS A PROFESSION

There are few professions in which the disparity between desire and reality is as great as in dance. Then, the impression that each ballet evokes, in so far as it meets the performers' own demands – the impression of apparent lightness, cultivated movement, and physical beauty – seems to mark permanently the image of the profession for all those who cannot imagine the strain which hides imperceptibly behind each performance, the strength-sapping preparations which make it possible, not to mention, the drudgery of physical discipline, increasing continuously over the years. And just this false impression seems, as paradoxical as it may sound, to attract newcomers to the dance profession. Without this false assessment, however, there would hardly be so many boys and girls willing to sacrifice their lives to this impression.

But the dancer's profession is, in any case, richer in paradoxes than others. This is primarily due to the fact that one has to choose this profession, if possible, at the age of eight or ten years, a time when one is not yet mature enough to make a decision of such great consequences.

If one does not attend a good ballet school from childhood on, it is hardly possible to attain sufficient mastery of the technique which, after all, is the prerequisite for all dance. It remains, come what may, fragmentary and defective.

It is for this reason that training must begin early – and thus it is primarily the parents who articulate the desire for this career. Often enough, it is they who wanted to become dancers, but, now being too old for that, delegate their goals to their daughter or – far less often – to their son. These are the parents who wish to realize in their child that which they themselves missed. Anne Woolliams' highly recommendable book *Ballettsaal* (1973) describes them most graphically – those parents who want to see their off-

spring living beyond the world of vacuum cleaners and washing machines, pampered by a life full of glamor and glory, treasure and travel.

And if Anne Woolliams, adding to her opinion, observes that no other profession "attracts more disciples at the age of ten, and turns out more disappointments ten years later", it is surely the fault of this vicarious role which the children are frequently expected to fulfill. The greater part of the blame can doubtlessly be traced back to the biological development which takes place during puberty. A great number of difficulties could be spared in the course of a later career if precautions had been taken at the appropriate time, which is, of course, in the ballet school. Then, if one sees the career of a future dancer not simply as a gamble, as an uncontrollable constellation of talent, luck, and chance, the risks which it hides could be reduced: For example, by arranging training in such a way that career corrections are possible at any point along the way, should declining interest or physical changes necessitate such a move. Training "to the bitter end", when the prerequisites are no longer present, would be the last thing which one should desire.

It is not difficult to imagine the form of this "prophylaxis". An education so comprehensive and multifaceted that new directions could be taken at any time should be a matter of course in the interest of preventing social problems. Every good ballet institute,

both here and abroad, which is not satisfied with the momentary successes of training, has developed a pluralistic educational program, with precautionary measures built in for every eventuality, giving the student a store of knowledge with which he could begin a new career – at least in a related profession.

The importance of this "prophylaxis", not only for the "drop-out", but particularly for the professional dancer, can be seen at the very beginnings of a career. Even such recognized institutions as the John Cranko School in Stuttgart can in no way guarantee employment. The Stuttgart Ballet can take on a maximum of two academy graduates per season. Others leave for Hamburg, Munich, or Ulm. The majority, however, is faced with years of search for a position – whether at the monthly "ballet market" of the Zentrale Bühnen-, Fernseh- und Filmvermittlung, ZBF (Central Placement Division of Theater, Television, and Film) of the Employment Office in Frankfort, or at individual auditions for the larger and smaller companies. Competition, and to no small degree from outside the country as well, is fierce and the capacity of the 53 opera houses in West Germany is limited. Even with the security of a contract, this sort of precaution can do no damage. The short-term contracts common in West Germany, due in part to artistic considerations, can as a rule be cancelled in the first half of the season without particular difficulties. And although salaries have in fact now risen considerably, they have certainly not been raised to the extent that one can accumulate great riches within the 20 years which is the maximum for pursuing this career: Even a member of the ensemble at the Deutsche Oper Berlin seldom enjoys a monthly gross salary of more than 3,000 German Marks (approx. $ 1,200).

It is quite apparent that under these conditions it is barely possible to think of setting anything aside for the future. And it is just such security which is indispensable in a profession which draws to a close at the age of 35 or 40. Moreover, who has ever heard of "continuing education" or a "sabbatical" in conjunction with ballet? This demand may well have found a place in the negotiating position of the Bühnengenossenschaft (Stage Actors Association), the union responsible for this profession, but actual theater practice adheres exclusively to its own rules – with the frequent result that dancers tend to consistently put out of mind thoughts about their own future, in so far as they do not remain within measurable limits. They are, in many cases, so involved in their art, concentrating so intensely upon giving their best in a situation characterized by permanent competition, that there seldom remains time for other interests. They truly dance as if in an ivory tower.

In the German Democratic Republic (East Germany), for example, a minimum pension is guaranteed following 15 years in the profession, this pension amounting to about 50 % of the last salary, thus providing stimulation to continue working. In other countries, there are comparable arrangements, though they usually demand a longer period in the profession. In West Germany, this social security is guaranteed only when a dancer has been engaged in the same house for 15 years. Then the theater must take care of finding suitable subsequent employment – which often leads to the situation that former dancers are found as cashiers, librarians, stage managers, prompters, or set painters. It is much less common that they achieve a trouble-free transition of professions which can be deemed adequate continuations of their previous career – rare simply because there are far too few positions for ballet directors or choreographers, ballet masters, coaches or teachers.

Some open a ballet school. Others who, due to illness, age, or pressing personal reasons, are forced to give up their profession, have no other path except to the local employment office or to the ZBF in Frankfort. There they can be retrained for a related occupation while drawing financial support. (Under certain conditions the Employment Office, after consultation with the ZBF, will award grants amounting to 80% of previous income over a period of up to two years for retraining programs, while assuming all the costs associated with the training itself.) In its information leaflet, the ZBF lists as "occupations suitable for retraining dancers" those of the gymnastics teacher, sports teacher, physical therapist, rehabilitation therapist, and masseur, basing this evaluation on a good knowledge of human anatomy,

muscle function, and general body movement.

For most, however, the transition to another occupation means, in any case, a step down the social and economic ladder. One's own demands have to be lowered considerably. The constraint of having to start all over again – while others are at the same time approaching the peak of their careers – is demoralizing. And the fact that one has been kept dependent in years of training and rehearsals leads to a certain feeling of helplessness. It is difficult to take the initiative and it seems nearly futile to try to develop new interests again at 40, if there had been no earlier impulses in that direction. As important as the assistance of the Heinz Bosl Foundation in Munich may be, which, as a supplement to its promotional program for young talent, intends to introduce a sort of social security insurance for every beginning dancer, more important is timely preparation for the future. And this begins, as is well known, during training. If early detection, as Rainer Woihsyk once called it in *Ballet 1979*, is effective at this stage, dancers could be spared social difficulties and hardships later in life. Only in such a way can dance as a profession gain in attractiveness. Only in such a way can the discrepancy between desire and reality finally be bridged.

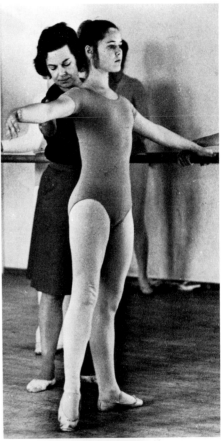

links/left
KURT JOOSS,
Foto: Annelise Löffler

Kurt Peters

25 JAHRE INTER-NATIONALE SOMMER-AKADEMIE DES TANZES KÖLN

EIN HISTORISCHER RÜCKBLICK

Viel bewundert, viel besucht, viel nachgeahmt – diese seit 25 Jahren bestehende Sommerakademie des Tanzes: erst in Krefeld, dann in Köln, in Deutschland, in Europa. International von Anfang an. Wie eine Bastille steht sie unter ihren heutigen europäischen Nachahmern, unzerstörbar. Von Revolutionären nicht zu erstürmen, denn ehe es soweit kommt, hat sie die Fahne der Neuerer längst gehißt, strömen die Adepten der Post-Moderne aller Richtungen zu Hunderten zusammen. Zu Hunderten die Klassiker, die Folkloristen, die Stepper, die Schuliker, die Meditativen und Sensitiven. Keine Kultursprache, die nicht gesprochen und getanzt würde. Grenzvorhänge öffnen sich, keine Nation schließt sich aus – und keine Epoche, so ist man versucht zu sagen, angesichts der Elevation der „Historiker".

Angefangen hatte alles mit der Idee eines Ballettomanen in der Seidenstadt Krefeld. Unter dem Vorsitz von Kurt Jooss und dem ehemaligen Chefdramaturgen Hans-Robert Doering-Manteuffel lud Heinz Laurenzen am 14. April 1955 zur öffentlichen Gründungsfeier der Gesellschaft zur Förderung des künstlerischen Tanzes ein. Der erste deutsche Ballettpapst, Otto-Friedrich Regner, und Kurt Peters sprachen über Situation, Aufgaben und Ziele des künstlerischen Tanzes. Eindringlich stellten beide Referenten die Mißstände dar, die zur Gründung der Gesellschaft geführt hatten. Einen „Eiertanz" nannte die Frankfurter *Abendpost* damals diesen Vorgang, der sich unter dem geschäftsführenden Initiator Heinz Laurenzen zu einem die gesamte schulische und theatralische Entwicklung in Deutschland beeinflussenden Unternehmen auswachsen sollte.

Nach zwei Jahren des Anlaufs und der Erprobung gewann unter vielen ambitionierten Projekten jene Idee Laurenzens Profil, die unter dem Namen Internationale Sommerakademie des Tanzes Weltgeltung erringen sollte und schließlich alle Vorhaben in sich vereinigte.

174 Teilnehmer, bereits in internationaler Zusammensetzung, meldeten sich im August 1957 zur ersten Sommerakademie in Krefeld. Unter der Präsidentschaft des 1980 verstorbenen Bühnenbildners Heinrich Wendel, der zusammen mit dem Choreographen Erich Walter die Wuppertaler Ballett-Epoche verkörperte, zeichnete sich von vornherein das hohe Niveau der Akademie ab. Zu den ersten Dozenten (Peggy van Praagh, Rosalia Chladek, Boris Kniaseff, Victor Gsovsky) gesellten sich unversehens aus den Reihen der Gäste Tatjana Gsovsky, Lia Schubert, Erich Walter und Marcel Luipart. Vorträge von Heinrich Lindlar, Georges Chapowalenko, Helmut Kluge, O. G. de St. Andrée behandelten Strukturprobleme, Symbolik, Systematik, Tanzschrift und Welt-

deutung des Tanzes. Ausstellungen und Büchertische ergänzten den geistigen Rahmen. Abschluß wurde ein öffentlicher Demonstrationsabend mit Choreographien der Dozenten.

Es soll hier nicht die Aufgabe sein, die gesamten Vorgänge der bisherigen Sommerakademien nachzuzeichnen, alle bedeutenden Namen (die in den Registern nachzulesen sind) zu nennen, die ständige Vermehrung der Unterrichtsfächer aufzuzeigen, die bald alle bedeutenden Pädagogen der Welt auf Köln konzentrierten, und die wachsenden Teilnehmerzahlen abzuschätzen, die die offiziell Gemeldeten oft weit überschritten. Versuchen wir also, Tendenzen und Veränderungen in den Entwicklungsjahren aufzuspüren, die den wachsenden Erfolg der Sommerakademie und ihren Einfluß auf das Zeitgeschehen mitverursacht haben.

Es war Heinrich Wendels Absicht, mit dem in die erste Sommerakademie hineingenommenen deutschen Tänzerkongreß sowohl an die früheren Kongresse anzuschließen, als auch den „machtlosen Sklavenverband", als den er die deutsche Tänzerschaft bezeichnete, zu sozialem Engagement zu bewegen. Über Jahre hin hielt dieser Kongreß die Presse wach, unterstützte das Bestreben der Bühnengenossenschaft zur Erreichung eines Tarifvertrages für Tänzer.

Eine tanztechnische Innovation bildete die Methode Boris Kniaseffs, das klassische Training „auf den Kopf zu stellen", d. h. das Exercise auf den Boden zu verlegen, mit dem am Boden liegenden Tänzer zu arbeiten. Bedeutende ausländische Tänzer hatten sich dieser Methode verschrieben; also holte sich Laurenzen Kniaseff. Und über Jahre hin sah man in den deutschen Schulen und Trainingssälen der Theater von nun an die Tänzer am Boden liegend trainieren. Einige Pädagogen kombinierten allerdings von vornherein die liegende und stehende

Praxis, wußte man doch, daß die bei Kniaseff „liegenden" Etoiles ihre Kondition bereits stehend erworben hatten. Immerhin entspann sich damals schon eine geistige Auseinandersetzung um Grundsätzliches.

Schon die zweite Sommerakademie brachte eine Bereicherung für die gesamte deutsche Tanzszene durch José de Udaetas Spanisch-Unterricht. Umgehend begann das verflachte Bühnenspanisch sich zu originalisieren. Über die gesamten Akademiejahre hinweg hat de Udaeta auch deutsche Tänzer zu perfekten Könnern des spanischen Tanzes gemacht und damit nicht zuletzt auch der bei uns nicht minder verwaschenen Folklore anderer Nationen aufgeholfen. Glücklicherweise zeigte Laurenzen immer das richtige Gespür, dort aufzugreifen, zu erweitern und zu verbessern, wo in der Tat etwas verbesserungswürdig war.

Doch es gab auch Zores. Manche Kollegen dachten zu „deutsch" und mißverstanden Laurenzens Bemühen, die deutsche Tanzszene mit möglichst vielen internationalen Anregungen zu befruchten. Daß die deutsche Machart darunter nicht litt, bewiesen später Hans Kresnik, Helmut Baumann, Jochen Ulrich, Jürg Burth, Pina Bausch, Gerhard Bohner, Reinhild Hoffmann, Susanne Linke und andere junge Choreographen, die sich zur gleichen Zeit entwickelten. Victor Gsovsky stellte den deutschen Tänzern in ihrer Ballettrenaissance das beste Zeugnis aus, obwohl sich Elvira Roné mit ihrer Pas de deux-Klasse damals recht schwertat. Noch haperte es an Methode und Stil. Die Akademie begünstigte die Gründung von Ballettmeister- und Pädagogenverbänden, doch dafür war die Zeit noch nicht reif. Die Verbände spalteten sich, kamen und gingen, doch immerhin als Zeichen, daß alles in Bewegung geraten war.

Und so blieb es, denn die nächste Sommerakademie kam bestimmt. Horst Koegler bezeichnete sie „als für die ganze deutsche Tanzwelt verbindlich". Exklusive Dozentennamen zierten wiederum das Programm. Der Jazz-Tanz weitete sich aus. Nach der spanischen entdeckte man die ungarische Seele (Emma Lugossy), die sich bisher hinter albernster Operettenhaftigkeit verbarg. Aber auch Kritik wurde laut. Stärkere qualitative Auslese der Teilnehmer (die bis heute problematisch geblieben ist) und die Herabsetzung der Stundenbelegung der sich selbst überfordernden Tänzer wurden gewünscht. Die theoretischen Exkurse von Max Niehaus, Gerhard Zacharias und Horst Koegler magerten sichtlich am Schweiß der Praxis. Begegnungen am Rande elektrifizierten das Arbeitsklima jener Jahre, während sich Leistung und Qualität durch immer strengere schulische Methodik auf allen Gebieten steigerten. Kontinuierlich blieb die Hinwendung des Folklore-Tanzes zur Originalität.

Alexandra Danilovas Charme und Vitalität zogen 1960 in die Akademie ein; Marianne Vogelsang, von der Basis der deutschen Moderne ausgehend, wußte zu faszinieren, Gerhard Zacharias' mythologische Themen fanden ihren Zuhörerkreis. Erstmals versuchte Laurenzen mit Erich Walter und Gise Furtwängler einen choreographischen Arbeitskreis aufzubauen, der später, unter sich ständig wandelnden Vorzeichen, das Unternehmen des Choreographischen Wettbewerbs nach sich zog. Ein Unternehmen, das mit den verrücktesten Themen und Praktiken immerhin Choreographen und Ballettleiter gebar, die sich mit Phantasie den vielen neuen großen und kleinen Schwänen querstellten, aber auch dem Dilettantismus in den eigenen Reihen.

1961. Die Krefelder Akademie war zu klein geworden, man war nach Köln in die alte Sporthochschule umgezogen. Die Intimität der früheren Jahre war auf der Strecke geblieben, um größere Ansprüche befriedigen zu können. Äußerlich schien alles beim alten geblieben zu sein, doch der deutsche Tänzer war nun über seine Elementarschulung hinausgediehen. Ein neues technisches Bewußtsein brachte das akademische Training zum Triumph. Der „akademische" Tanz wurde klassisch, beziehungsweise der klassische „akademisch". Der amerikanische Modern Dance pflügte den Boden für die Graham-Technik, die Jazzer Walter Nicks und Claude Thompson räumten mit den bis dato kümmerlichen deutschen Musical-Manieren auf. Die Theorie schrumpfte sichtlich, soweit sie sich nicht in den – nun von Aurel von Milloss geleiteten – choreographischen Arbeitskreis hineinrettete, in dem Wissen und Erfahrung, Ballettgeschichte und Technik das zusammenfaßte, was von Anfang an von den klassischen Dozenten hätte ausgehen sollen: Ihr Hinweis, ihre Hinführung zu Theorie und Kulturgeschichte hätte als Abfallprodukt dem geistigen Teil der Sommerakademie Rückenstärkung geben können. Indes, die physische Belastbarkeit der Tänzer hatte ihre Grenze erreicht.

Neue Balancen versprach man sich durch die von Laurenzen angekündigte ständige Akademie, die im Oktober 1961 als Institut für Bühnentanz ins Leben gerufen wurde. Doch den immer größer werdenden Anteil der ausländischen Tänzer berührte das wenig, und Schüler müssen bekanntlich erst einmal heranwachsen. Unbestritten blieb die organisatorische Leistung Laurenzens, der nun mit der Internationalen Sommerakademie, der Institutsschule und den folgenden Wettbewerben im Zusammenhang mit der Woche des modernen Tanzes der Kölner Oper ein schulisches Zentrum geschaffen hatte, wie es in Deutschland bisher einmalig zu verzeichnen ist.

Im folgenden Jahr waren ganze sieben, vornehmlich aus der Diaghilew-Ära und ihrer Nachfolge stammende Klassiker am Werk – unter ihnen Todd Bolender, der Rhythmiker unter den Choreographen. Er übernahm auch das Choreographische Kolloquium und führte die Ansatzpunkte von Milloss fort – weniger intellektuell, dafür großzügiger im freien Phantasiespiel. Weder in diesem Fach noch in anderen ästhetischen Bereichen ließ Laurenzen locker. Man muß ihm hoch anrechnen, daß er Randgebiete im besten schulischen und erzieherischen Sinne durchboxte, obwohl sich manche kritischen, ästhetischen, sozioästhetischen Themen selbst an den Rand drängten, als Folge einer „Friß-oder-stirb-Methode", wie Heinz-Ludwig Schneiders sie karikierte. Im übrigen wurde dem Verlangen nach Pantomime und historischem Tanz Raum gegeben. Beide Fächer wirkten noch reichlich abgesondert, was nichts mit dem immer sehr kollegialen Verhalten der Dozenten untereinander zu tun hat, sondern mit dem fehlenden historischen und geistigen Bezug, der alle tänzerischen Erscheinungen verbindet – und in den Schulen auf den Geschichtsunterricht isoliert bleibt. Immerhin, weltoffener als mit den Vertretern der ehemaligen Ballets Russes als Dozenten konnte die Danse d'école der Akademie nicht sein. Die Tänzer unterhielten sich über die Vor- und Nachteile pädagogischer Methoden, die Pädagogen über die Qualität der inzwischen 650 Tänzer, andere Sachverständige über Sinn und Unsinn der Veranstaltung überhaupt. Bei einem Podiumsgespräch bewunderten die ausländischen Dozenten (immer noch durch die Lupe des im Ausland nachgeehrten historischen deutschen Tanzes) die deutsche Theaterprovinz mit ihren 50 Opernhäusern; sie hatten keine Vorstellung vom Operetten-, Abstecher- und Statisterieverschleiß dieser Ensembles. Ein Anlaß für Wilfried Hofmann und Alphons Silbermann, sich für Nationalballett und -schule stark zu machen. Unter dem Titel „Ballettwoche" lief die gehabte Jahresproduktion im „Allegro" Bolenderscher Choreographien ab, die Auftritte Yurikos und der Merce Cunningham Company in ein unverhältnismäßiges Licht setzend.

Viel Hintergründiges spielte die Akademie nach vorn, denn das Ballett in Deutschland war noch keineswegs sonderlich beliebt. Die Provinzballette begannen zwar kräftig, sich zu rühren, ihre Güte bestand jedoch noch vornehmlich in der Benutzung moderner Musik, während auf internationaler Ebene das absurde Theater den Neo-Dadaismus ablöste – mit bleibender unbe-

fangener amerikanischer Musikalität, die uns so schwer zu schaffen macht.

Die inzwischen neunte Akademie wäre dem Zusammenbruch der Massen erlegen gewesen, hätten sich die Teilnehmer nicht so ausnehmend diszipliniert verhalten. Die fatale Fülle aller Kurse dämmte kein Aufteilungsversuch nach Leistungsgraden mehr. Abhilfe schaffte eine Art Festival der Dozenten-Assistenten. Paul Taylor wurde durch Norman Walker ersetzt, John Cranko durch Harald Lander, Katherine Dunham durch Christiane de Rougemont, Charlotte Sevelin durch Maria Surowiak, was insgesamt zwar keine Leistungsminderung bedeutete, wohl aber einen Verlust an kontinuierlicher Arbeit.

Die Woche des modernen Tanzes führte Altbekanntes zu neuen Höhepunkten: mit Paul Taylors *Aureole,* Maurice Béjarts *Reise* (mit Tilly Söffing und Lothar Höfgen) und *Sinfonie für einen einsamen Menschen* und auch Todd Bolenders *Still Point.* Die Sonderveranstaltung der Dozenten bot Beachtliches. Im übrigen hatte es wochenlang Bindfäden geregnet, doch kein Akademie-Teilnehmer war in die Flucht zu schlagen. Trotzdem meinte man, so ginge es nicht weiter. Man hatte neue Einsichten gewonnen, aber was ist schon vorherzusehen?

Unerwartet wurde die zehnte Akademie doch zum Wendepunkt. Der Zustrom der Tänzer wurde gebremst, Qualitätsstufen errichtet. Alvin Ailey bekam „nur" 100 von 170 der für seine Klasse Angemeldeten. Andere Klassen wurden aufgeteilt. José de Udaeta und Ursula Knaflewsky hatten längst drei Leistungsstufen aufgebaut, dort zeichneten sich auch am deutlichsten Fortschritte ab. Peter Appel, Edite Frandsen, Frank Wagner, Yuriko, Henryk Tomaszewski, um nur einige zu nennen, arbeiteten Hand in Hand; Lia Schubert leitete das choreographische Kolloquium. Manches Neue wurde ausprobiert, doch das Gebot der Stunde hieß Kontinuität. Und welch ein Wandel seit Wendel! Nach der damaligen „Grundsteinlegung eines Krankenhauses", wie Wendel die erste Sommerakademie genannt hatte, enthüllte Heinrich Lindlar mit seiner Eröffnungsrede zur zehnten ein Denkmal. Die Intendanten wurden zu Ballettomanen, von denen einer, Walter Erich Schäfer, sich nach seiner Ansprache auf das mit den Initialen der Sommerakademie versehene Schild der deutschen Ballettrenaissance gehoben sah. Seine Solistin Birgit Keil tanzte mit Bernd Berg die klassischen und doch verwirrend modernen Enchaînements Crankos in idealtypischer makelloser Schönheit.

Die Kontinuität garantierte weiterhin das nur wenig veränderte Pädagogenteam. Endgül-

tig konnte sich Brigitte Garski mit dem historischen Tanz durchsetzen, von dem einmal alles ausging, nur nicht im schulischen Geist unserer Zeit. Garski ist es zu verdanken, daß sie diesen Geist erfolgreich unterlaufen hat, nicht zuletzt dank Laurenzens Beharrlichkeit, in seinem (Teilnehmer-) Zahlenrausch auch Minderheiten in Kauf zu nehmen und am Leben zu erhalten, bis sie lebensfähig wurden.

Die „Elfte" konnte einmal durchatmen. Das durfte sich Laurenzen leisten, denn längst war „Cologne a well-known place in the world", wie Donald McKayle es ausdrückte. Bei aller Problematik, die dieser Institution auch Pfeffer gab, war neben der technischen Schulung auch „der Rang der Sommerakademie als (tanz-) gesellschaftlicher Kristallisationskern" (Hartmut Regitz) wichtig. Wo sonst auch konnte man auf nationaler und internationaler Ebene so zuhauf kommen, diskutieren, Engagements vereinbaren, Verbindungen anknüpfen, Freundschaften schließen?

Es hatte die „Zwölfte" geschlagen. – Wer auch nur etwas zu spät kam, stand vor den verschlossenen Türen Valentina Pereyaslavecs. Laurenzen höchstpersönlich stand dort wie Zerberus vor dem Eingang zum Hades und verscheuchte ahnungslose Zutrittsuchende. Hinter diesen Türen vollzogen sich „die furchtbarsten Exercise-Stunden, die ich bisher gesehen habe" (Jens Wendland). „Angefeuert und getriezt von feldwebelstarker Kommandogewalt" wurde – niveauvoll und stimulierend – trainiert. Zu Pereyaslavecs Bedingungen gehörten Auswahl und störungsfreies Arbeiten. Allgemein aber schien sich das Leistungsniveau durch überwiegend neue Teilnehmerschichten nicht gehoben zu haben. Für die Theaterensembles hatte die Sommerakademie inzwischen Maßstäbe gesetzt, die nun – selbst an mittleren und kleineren Theatern – von eigenen Trainingsmeistern bewahrt wurden. Die „Woche" wurde durch eigenwillige Tanzpoeme John Neumeiers, Gerhard Bohners originale Spitzfindigkeiten und Hans Kresniks Polit-Ballett-Anfänge gekennzeichnet. Die wirklich Jungen der Choreographie setzten sich mit Individualität und Masse auseinander. Lärmmontagen, Schreckensmärsche, Absurdes und Verrücktes blieben, obwohl alle choreographischen Erfahrenswerte streng vermieden wurden, immer noch „interessant" genug, denkt man an die zunehmende Verödung späterer preissuchender Kompositionen. Die Choreographie der Jungen zerlegte Körper- und Raumteile und kroch sich selbst durch die Beine. Es war ein einziges schöpferisches Tohuwabohu. Gepflegter ging es auf der Ballettwoche zu, wo Glen Tetley (Mythical Hunters), Job Sanders und Hans van Manen die Bretter beherrschten,

durch Gehabtes aus dem Repertoire der Kölner Kompanie ergänzt.

In der Spielzeit 1968/69 liest man von den jungen Choreographen John Neumeier, Gerhard Bohner, André Doutreval und den in Köln tätigen Jürg Burth, Helmut Baumann, Gray Veredon und Jochen Ulrich Aufsehenerregenderes als von den gestandenen Meistern. Pina Bausch setzte mit Im Wind der Zeit (erster Preis) ein Signal für ihre eigenwillige Zukunft. „Die traditionelle Ästhetik in der Choreographie hat(te) ausgedient" (Horst Koegler), während die Akademie durch Peter Wright einen englischen und durch Henning Kronstam einen höchst feinsinnigen dänischen klassischen Akzent hinzugewann.

Man kann auch nicht sagen, daß die 14. Sommerakademie eine Starschau abgab, obwohl sich Kenner und Könner Hector Zaraspe als wahrer Showmaster des klassischen Trainings in Szene setzte und Kronstam seine Klasse in erlauchteste Technik hüllte. Glen Tetleys Werkfragmente dominierten im Choreographischen Kolloquium; der Wettbewerb diesmal ohne Preise! In der Akademie hatte sich im Prinzip nichts geändert. Wenn auch Antony Tudor nicht sehr glücklich über seine durchschnittlich bemittelten Teilnehmer zu sein schien, prägten auf der anderen Seite Matt Mattox, Donald McKayle und Lynn Simonson ein ganz präzises Jazzbewußtsein. Und alle Klassen waren voll!

Da war ja noch so viel anderes! Kleine, glitzernde Randveranstaltungen hatten sich zwischen die Kurse gemogelt. Brigitte Garski erläuterte und demonstrierte mit ihrem historischen Ensemble den Tanz in der Renaissance, Ernö Pesovár kommentierte in der Bibliothek Stocktänze und Urtümliches in ungarischen Folklore-Filmen, einige im Wettbewerb nicht zum Zuge gekommene junge Choreographen erfanden hier mit Witz und körpereigener Rhythmik Mini-Kompositionen unter Aufsicht von Patricia Christopher. Zu erwähnen auch die fotokünstlerische Ausstellung Pieter Kooistras, die in alle Gänge der Akademie hineinquoll. Geradezu sensationell aber war José de Udaetas Arrangement spanischer Tänze des 19. Jahrhunderts in der Einrichtung von Juan Magrina mit den Solisten des Teatro Liceo, Barcelona. Spanischer Tanz auf der Spitze! Wie handkolorierte Holzschnitte der alten L'Illustration in den zauberhaften Farben der alten spanischen Ballettröcke und Tutus, mit den Inclinés und Ports de bras der romantischen Schule. Welch lieblicher Fluß spanischer Tanzfreude. Bournonville hätte das choreographiert haben können.

Gesamtergebnis dieser angeblich „verkorksten" Sommerakademie: pädagogische und psychologische Vertiefung bei allen Erlebnisfähigen.

„Fünfzehn Jahre lang hat die alljährliche Sommerakademie des Tanzes Hunderte und Aberhunderte von Tänzern vierzehn Tage lang auf Trab gebracht, sie gewalkt und geschmeidigt, weitergebildet, ihnen die vortrefflichsten Lehrer aller Kontinente zur Seite gestellt und beharrlich in Kauf genommen, daß man dem tänzerischen Massenbetrieb im Kölner Stadion nicht gerade das glücklichste Horoskop stellte. Heinz Laurenzen, der Organisator der Akademie, kann nun triumphieren. Denn aus dem Geknäuel der Ambitionen, der Drängelei des Talents, der Verfilzung der künstlerischen Wege, der sektiererischen Einigelei ist eine riesige Garküche der Begabung geworden, die nun mit einem Schlage den Deckel vom Topf sprengt." So schrieb Klaus Geitel treffend zur „Fünfzehnten" in der Welt.

Laurenzen kümmerte sich wenig um die ewig Reformationssüchtigen und engagierte sich Bill Hamilton, der mit feinster Bewegungskultur und höchster persönlicher Distinktion die choreographischen Figuren des Scottish Country Dance für ganze zwölf Teilnehmer unterrichtete. Kaum je zuvor hatte man einen Tanz und einen Tänzer von solcher Würde gesehen. Natürlich hatte Laurenzen andererseits die Techniker befriedigt. Mary Hinkson setzte der Graham-Technik den i-Punkt auf, Scott Douglas erfand die rhythmisch raffiniertesten klassischen Kombinationen, und viele machte schon der Name Tatjana Grantzeva trunken.

Prompt hatte Laurenzen auch die in der Luft liegenden Schulprobleme aufgegriffen. Vorträge wie Die private deutsche Ballettschule – Bestätigung und Warnung (Peters), Pas de deux-Technik (Luipart) und Historische Choreographie (Garski) wurden über alle Maßen besucht.

Trotz bleibender struktureller Kinderkrankheiten der Choreographie hatte der vierte Wettbewerb manch skulpturale Qualität und Musikalität in der Bewegungsfindung aufzuweisen, die aber von der Jury merkwürdigerweise nicht honoriert wurde. Berechtigt aber ging der erste Preis an die mit persönlichem Charme durchwirkten Volkslied-Collagen von Gigi-Gheorghe Caciuleanu, getanzt mit Ruxandra Racovitza. Tihana Skrinjariks Klänge Istriens bestachen durch faszinierende Formklarheit und an Mary Wigman gemahnenden Stil. Auch die Arbeiten anderer führten zu einem plötzlichen Niveauanstieg des Wettbewerbs.

Mit reiner Tanzfreude, Jugendlichkeit und Vitalität kam das Harkness-Ballett zur Woche des modernen Tanzes, mit kalkuliertem Virtuosentum in Time out of Mind und Percussion for Six. Das Ballettstudio Köln mit seinem Choreographen-Kollektiv schien durch seine Umbenennung in Tanz-Forum ein Versprechen einlösen zu wollen. Jochen

Ulrichs *Lewis C*, Christopher Bruces *Wings* und Helmut Baumanns *Die Sonate und die drei Herren* waren von höchster charakteristischer Qualität. Talentbeweise lieferten die Arbeiten von Jürg Burth und Gray Veredon.

Ohne Schwund der anderen Fächer brach im folgenden Jahr ein ungewöhnlicher Trend zur Graham-Technik aus, obwohl sich in den USA die Gewichte längst schon wieder in Richtung „informelle" Technik und Thematik verschoben hatten. Indische Tanztechnik unterrichtete erstmals Madhavi Mudgal, und es war Agnes Roboz, die für den ungarischen Tanz die exakten schulischen Grundlagen zu entwickeln begann. José de Udaeta, der sich nun schon 16 Jahre lang immer wieder neue, Begeisterung erweckende Beiträge hatte einfallen lassen, hielt einen unwiederbringlich erlebnisreichen Flamenco-Vortrag, zu dem er selbst mit der bezaubernden Marcela einen alternden Zigeuner tanzte: in hellster spanischer Sonnenlandschaft und in tiefsten Lorca-Schatten durch das Leben wandernd, durch Erinnerungen an Lust und Qual, in Einsamkeit endend. Erschütternd – und doch unbeschreiblich schön. Alle Wettbewerber hinter sich lassend, hatte auch Caciuleanu ein überzeugendes spanisches Thema aufgegriffen. Hans van Manen fesselte wieder mit seiner Choreographie-Klasse, und was er in seiner „Jury-Sprechstunde" den Wettbewerbern an Erläuterungen gab, verdiente auf Bütten festgehalten zu werden. Kurt Jooss' *Grüner Tisch* beherrschte das Tanz-Forum, aber das Forum auch den nun 40jährigen *Tisch*.

Die 17. Akademie vollzog sich bei tropischer Hitze, trotzdem wurde geschuftet wie nie. Unter den 21 Dozenten (es sollten schon bald 28 und mehr werden) bewährten sich seit je die Lehrkräfte des Instituts für Bühnentanz mit ungewöhnlichem Zuspruch. 24 Kurse, drei Lecture-Demonstrations, Wettbewerb, Filmabende, vier Vorträge wiesen eigentlich ein Festival von besonderem Ausmaß aus. Dazu kam die „Woche" mit einem unvermuteten Tiefpunkt der Batsheva Dance Company, die nur Rina Schenfeld als Tänzerin faszinierend herausstellte. Den nicht ganz geteilten Spaß an der Dollerei der Louis Falco Dance Company fing die Sternstunde eines Spiels beglückender Musenkinder der Lar Lubovitch Company auf. Letztere hatten denn auch die akademischen Vorgänge im Stadion in Euphorie versetzt, wo Hans van Manen, Alexandra Radius und Han Ebbelaar mit zusätzlichen Teilen die Abschlußveranstaltung krönten. Hier auch frenetischer Beifall für Marta Metzger (Staatsoper Budapest), die in allen künftigen Pas de deux-Klassen mitarbeitete. Aus der Öde stereotyper Fertigteile und des Ideenklaus im Wettbewerb ragten diesmal

nur Susanne Linke mit einer Groteske und das japanische Duo Takashi Koma und Eiko Otake hervor, das, die traditionelle Kultur in die Gosse zerrend, in wenigen Minuten das ganze asiatische Elend zusammendrängte. Entsetzlich großartig! Hier irrte die Jury gewaltig in ihrer Preisverweigerung. Nicht nur Wilfried Hofmann setzte sich mit seinem anspruchsvollen Thema gegen die brütende Tageshitze durch, auch Kurt Peters' Vortrag *Ballettschule – heute* fand – in Fortsetzung seines Schulthemas, das auf der vorigen Sommerakademie zur Konferenz der staatlichen Ballettschulleiter geführt hatte – reges Interesse; nicht zuletzt auch durch die in Rundfunk und Presse ausgeschlachteten Schulverhältnisse (die so lange problematisch bleiben werden, wie der Beruf des Ballettpädagogen vogelfrei bleibt). Die Schulleiter, bisher Anhängsel der Akademie, wurden nun mehr und mehr in den allzu eng gezogenen Begriff der Professionalität einbezogen. Der erwähnte Filmabend zeigte neben historischen Rückblicken *Dancers in School*. Da saß der geistreiche Choreograph und Tänzer Murray Louis, auf eine Pauke hauend, singend und erzählend, inmitten hüpfender, spielender, sich kugelnder, rhythmisch improvisierender Kinder, deren Augen funkelten, ihn anblitzten. Einige darunter wurden später seine Solisten. Das gab zu denken.

Als alles vorbei war, am Ende dieses Festivals der Kurse, zog Luigi im Hof der Akademiegebäude eine explosive Jazz-Show ab. Er selbst ein ekstatischer Gummischlauch mit hellem Strohhut.

Wer geglaubt hatte, nach 17 Sommerakademien habe „Heinzens Pillow" das tanzpädagogische Angebot in seiner ganzen Bandbreite erschöpft, der sah sich von neuen Eindrücken überwältigt. Der historische Touch der Limón-Technik durchdrang die Modernen, und der Jazz zeigte kraß seinen Show-Drive im rhythmischen Geschäft. Die ungarische Folklore wurde endgültig neben der spanischen etabliert. Da rief ein neuer Folklore-Mann, der Russe Anatoli Borsow, das pausenlose Entzücken aller hervor. Drahtig, in lässiger Eleganz, mit Schalk im Nacken gab er seinem Publikum ein kapriziös-historisches Quadrille-Gefühl zurück. Und ein bewegungsintelligenter Outsider, Karl Heinz Taubert, Professor an der Berliner Musikhochschule, begeisterte mit historischem Tanz in seinem spektakulären theoretisch-musikalisch-historischen Kulturbild. Sofort tat sich zwischen Taubert, de Udaeta, Roboz und Borsow eine einzigartige Geistesgemeinschaft auf, die einen des anderen Gedanken in die Praxis seiner Stunden aufnehmen ließ.

Auch die Woche des modernen Tanzes hatte wieder ihre Sternstunden mit Judith Jamison, mit Alvin Aileys und Murray Louis'

Truppe. Herrliche historisierende Verrücktheiten von Emily Frankel, persönliche von Gigi-Gheorghe Caciuleanu, Problematisches vom Ballet Rambert, Extremes vom Tanz-Forum, Rahmenprogramme und Abschlußveranstaltung machten die Masse des Gebotenen nicht mehr aufzählbar. Aber jeder hatte von jedem profitiert.

Das Mammut-Unternehmen Sommerakademie rollte dahin, in nun schon –für deutsche Verhältnisse – biblischem Alter, überrollte alle Einwände, im Akademischen oder Unakademischen, im Zuviel oder Zuwenig. Ein Koloß hatte seine eigene Dynamik entwickelt und war nicht mehr aufzuhalten. Und doch kam es zu restriktiven Verfeinerungen. Agnes Roboz gab in ihrem Vortrag der Akademie-Arbeit neue Einsichten: „… die schwerste Aufgabe in der Kunst, einfach zu bleiben und doch künstlerisch." Von Gisela Peters-Rohses Kinderklasse bis zu Hans van Manens Kompositionskurs, dessen „einfaches" Ergebnis mit 50 Teilnehmern zum überwältigenden Erlebnis wurde, machte sich diese Tendenz geltend. Fritz Lüdins wunderbare Ruhe in der Limón-Technik und Zena Rommetts „Placement"-Klasse, in der sich auch die Dozenten in Bewegungsversenkung übten, machten die technikbesessenen Tänzer zu Choreosophen. Kein rasender Steptanz, dessen Wiedergeburt Heinz Laurenzen in die Kurse eingebettet hatte, kein Crescendo des von José de Udaeta dirigierten Kastagnettenkonzerts vermochte dieses Zurück zur Einfachheit hinwegzuklappern.

Das Kölner Tanz-Forum und vornehmlich die Schwedenhappen Birgit Cullbergs überschwemmten die Woche des modernen Tanzes, doch die Wellen Cullbergs hatten ihre Brandung längst hinter sich. Es war Het Nationale Ballet mit seinen drei „vans" (Hans van Manen, Toer van Schayk, Rudi van Dantzig), das Furore machte, insbesondere mit *Twilight* und *Adagio Hammerklavier*. Dagegen hatten die Jungchoreographen diesmal so gar kein rechtes Vertrauen zur Musik, umso mehr dagegen in das Sitzfleisch der Jury.

Die Abschlußveranstaltung verlegte Laurenzen erstmalig unters Volk. Auf dem Kölner Roncalli-Platz kultivierte Garski ihre historischen Tänze, José de Udaeta und Emma Maleras schleuderten ihre Kastagnetten-T(h)riller aus dem Handgelenk ins Mikrofon und vor ein begeistertes Publikum. Die wahre – bereits zum Markenartikel gewordene – „una bomba di José" aber explodierte wieder im Stadion, wo Mary Hinkson („einmal die Erfüllung meines Lebens" nach dem Motto: einmal eine große Dame sein) im Flamenco ihre schwarzleuchtenden Augen an José auf und ab und um ihn herum blitzen und leuchten ließ, in schwingenden Rückbeugen ihn umgirrend, funkenstiebend assistiert von den Jazz-Dozentinnen Annette Plotten und Lynn Simonson. Da brach der Jubel schlicht in Raserei aus.

Zum 20. Male hatte Laurenzen eine Weltelite der Dozenten eingeladen. Trotz wieder brüllender Sommerhitze bestätigte man sich eine ausgesprochen angenehme Atmosphäre. Es wäre diesmal nichts Sonderliches zu vermelden gewesen, hätte nicht das amerikanische Jooss-Festival des Joffrey Ballet ein Echo beim Tanz-Forum gefunden. Sein Jooss-Abend wurde zu einem wunderbaren, die ganze deutsche Vergangenheit rehabilitierenden Erfolg. Der Wettbewerb hingegen, „auffallend die Flucht in philosophisch verbrämte Clowns-Allegorien", wurde zum reinsten „Festival des Meublements" (Horst Koegler).

Keine Partylücke mehr, kein Aufatmen, kein laisser faire ließ die 21. Akademie zu. Die Randveranstaltungen, Ausstellungen und Werkstattaufführungen drängten sich und der Wunderglaube, die Masse der Enchaînements großer Meister könne die Qualität der eigenen Leistung steigern, überschlug sich. Elena Schemtschuschinas Moskauer Stil stand gegen den englischen von Eileen Ward, der amerikanische gegen den französischen. Step, Spanisch und Historischer Tanz waren von neuen oder gar zusätzlichen Dozenten besetzt, Labanisches und Kinetographisches wurden von Lisa Ullmann in Erinnerung gebracht. Eine absolute Neueinführung war Gisela Peters-Rohses Kinderpädagogik, die im Sinne einer zeitgemäßen Bewegungserziehung versuchte, mit improvisatorischen Mitteln auf ein späteres Technikbewußtsein hinzulenken. Eine methodische Vertiefung neu-alter Erkenntnisse für die Ballettschulpädagogik.

Den Gongschlag zur Halbzeit gab wieder Hans van Manen mit einer chorischen Suite. Eine andere Werkstatt zeigte Eva Campianus historische Schau, und das Kamizawa Modern Dance Ensemble erschreckte mit Choreographien im psychischen Bereich des japanischen Gruppenmenschen.

Der inzwischen neunte choreographische Wettbewerb war mit Schwachstrom geladen. Veraltete Stadttheaterballette, gelackte Divertissements und unmusikalische ausländische Klassik mußten die Jury derart irritiert haben, daß ein Kölner Beitrag von musikalischer und choreographischer Substanz (Ballade von Krisztina Horvath) gleich mit unter den Tisch fiel. Einen grandiosen Ulk-Knüller tanzten dafür Anatoli Borsow und René Bon zur Abschlußveranstaltung: zwei russische Marktweiber, die sich, nach technisch verblödelten Schimpfkanonaden mit schiefen und krummen klassischen Posen, wieder ein Herz und ein Seele, in die Arme fallen. Und unvergessen die balladesken

Flamenco-Tänze der Meisterin Flora Albaicin.

Die Woche des modernen Tanzes ließ einen schmunzelnden Rückblick auf The Spirit of Denishawn der Joyce Trisler Dance Company genießen; Jennifer Muller and the Works waren unter anderem mit Beach beteiligt.

Werkstätten bestimmten des Gesicht der 22. Sommerakademie nach außen hin. Allerlei Gruppen und Grüppchen hatten sich inzwischen aufgetan, die nun ihr reflektierendes Heil in der Sommerakademie suchten. Die Frage, Werkstatt oder Wettbewerb, wurde danach mit der Spannung entschieden, die die Überraschung eines Dennochpreises auslöst. Eine Entdeckung auf weiter, öder Flur war Maguy Marin mit ihrem Théâtre de l'Arche. Ansonsten holten sich Reinhild Hoffmann und Carlos Orta Bestätigungen ihrer Begabung; mit Sternchen: Susanne Linke. Van Manens Seminar, natürlich einer ganz besonderen Kategorie angehörend, und „offene" Stunden reicherten die Werkstätten an.

Wesentliche Varianten im Akademie-Plan ergaben sich durch Anatoli Borsows Einführung in Moissejews Folklore-Exercise, Eva Campianus Rückgriff auf die Biedermeierzeit, Agnes Roboz' Zigeunertanz, Doris Rudkos Tanzkomposition und Gisela Peters-Rohses Motivfindung und Pädagogik im Vorschulalter. Deren Grundzüge der Pädagogik stellten eine neue Geistesgemeinschaft zwischen Rudko, Roboz (ungarischer Kindertanz), Borsow, Hinkson und de Udaeta her und glichen das etwas ins Hintertreffen geratene geistige Angebot der Akademie aus.

Das Akademie-Ende werteten dann Samy Molcho und José de Udaeta zu klassischem, historischem, folkloristischem, jazzigem und pantomimischem Hallodrio auf. Den Vogel schossen Three Women vom Nederlands Dans Theater ab, die sich selbst mitsamt dem Publikum in aufregenden weiblichen Exzessen verschlangen. Una bomba aber feuerte diesmal Lynn Simonson ab mit einer nie je so pointiert-verrückt gesehenen Groteske für Molcho, Bon, de Udaeta und Borsow. Vier Meister aller Meister waren in einer Jazzquadrille, zum Auswachsen komisch, außer Rand und Band geraten. Unwiederholbar einmalig.

Auf dem theatralischen E-Sektor zeigte Youri Vámos mit seiner Rhapsodie, was Ausdrucksakrobatik und was eine technische Harke ist, gebärdete sich Joseph Russillos Truppe mit luziferischem Gerangel wie in einem konfessionellen Nachtklub (Requiem), zeugte Caciuleanus Mozart-Messe von formalen Fähigkeiten.

Im Tanz-Forum hatten sich Jochen Ulrich und Joachim Freyer verbündet. Auf der Bühne, im Orchester, in den Rängen und

hängend in der (Zirkus-)Theaterkuppel wurde schlicht gesponnen, das Publikum mit richtigen Fäden eingesponnen (Dreiklang). Rufe wie „Schwachköpfe", „Und sowas lassen sich die Deutschen (!) gefallen" entfuhren den ratlosen Unspinösen. Wären die Stücke in einem Museum of Modern Art gelaufen, hätte man am Ende Ralf Harster (Re-Aktion) auf die Schultern genommen oder ihn auf den Schwarzen Schwan gehoben, der sowieso zusammenbrach. Die Reihe endete phantastisch, geheimnisvoll und meditativ mit Carolyn Carlsons Jahr des Pferdes.

Und wieder eine Sommerakademie! Ruth Currier und Pearl Lang verbreiteten die moderne Richtung, Brigitte Garski spürte drei Jahrhunderten deutscher Tanzgeschichte nach, die meditativ-philosophische Linie setzte Gia-fu Feng mit Tai Chi Chuan fort, Jerry Ames den Step und – über Jahre erwartet – Susana, die frühere Partnerin José de Udaetas, den spanischen Tanz neben der Grundlagenbewahrerin Ursula Knaflewsky. Gerhard Zacharias sah im Wirken Gia-fu Fengs („aus taoistischem Ursprung") die „Vereinigung des Apollinischen mit dem Dionysischen", bemerkte zu Susana: „Sie wird mit den Jahren immer mehr zum Zeichen. Duende." Und es war nicht nur Zacharias, der seine „bewundernde Liebeserklärung an Marta" (Metzger) abgab, an die Verkörperung der Zärtlichkeit und Schönheit des Tanzes. (Pas de deux-Klasse von Carlos Gacio).

Die Woche des modernen Tanzes stand ganz im Zeichen der José Limón Dance Company. Was tanzen diese Tänzer nicht mit delikatestem Gespür! There is a Time gehörte sogar zum Repertoire des Tanz-Forum. Pina Bauschs Blaubart ergänzte ihre Frühlingsopfer-Version aus dem Vorjahr. Ebenso außergewöhnlich auf anderer Ebene Jiři Kyliáns Nederlands Dans Theater-Werke Psalmensinfonie, Kinderspiele und Sinfonietta. Susanne Linke (Satie, Ballade) überragte die Studios und den Wettbewerb bei weitem, ausgenommen die Kurz-Ideen Bill Crattys und Ralf Harsters und das Werk Nils Christes. „tanz & talk" mit den Dozenten und Choreographen war der letzte Schrei Laurenzens in der Musikhochschule.

Die 24. Akademie, die zugleich die siebte Woche des modernen Tanzes und den elften Choreographischen Wettbewerb einschloß, hatte ein so gewaltiges Angebot, daß man wie bei Karstadt am Wühltisch ziehen und zerren mußte, um das Passende für sich herauszufinden. Was man auch fand, es war für jeden das Schönste. Das tat man sich, wie nach jeder Sommerakademie, um und an und ging damit ein Jahr lang spazieren, in dem Bewußtsein, man habe gut und billig eingekauft. Die Kölner Fachzeitschrift Das Tanzarchiv mußte in aufeinanderfolgenden Ausgaben ergänzende Berichte bringen, um den Vorgängen auch nur halbwegs gerecht zu werden.

Ein neuer Ekstatiker seit Luigi, Nat Horne, war im Jazz am Werk; Jerry Ames wußte den Step zu feinstem Diminuendo zu „steigern"; für den Modern Dance kamen die letzten Avantgardisten oder Post-Modernen: Trisha Brown und – in *Zwiesprache mit dem All* – Mariko Sanjo. Der Hüne Clay Taliaferro gab sich differenziert als Limón-Fortsetzer, Sandor Timar brachte, mit dem Munde gepfiffen und gemalt, urtümliche Improvisationstechniken in die ungarische Atmosphäre. Ein noch unbestelltes Feld beackerte Ruth Ashkenasi mit israelischen Tänzen. Die Fächer der „akademischen" Technik bereicherte Ursula Borrmanns Methodik-Kurs, der die von Gisela Peters-Rohse demonstrierte Kindertanz-Pädagogik auf klassischer Basis für die Vorberufsausbildung fortsetzte.

Vorweggenommener Höhepunkt der Woche des modernen Tanzes war wieder ein Nederlands-Programm von Kylián-Werken (*Dream Dances, Feldmesse*). Jochen Ulrich fand für die Knete-Kompanie (Kölner Sporthochschule) originelle Ideen und Bewegungsabläufe (*Kontra-Danse, Lesestunde*), für das Tanz-Forum jedoch nur *à la*

Jacques; Jennifer Muller lehrte nachsichtig und heiter, über der allgemeinen Misere nicht die Lust am Leben zu verlieren: Jennifer Muller and the Works.

Die Juroren wußten außer drei zweiten Preisen nur Anerkennungen und Ermutigungen auszusprechen. Hilfestellungen für die nur im Ansatz erkennbaren inszenatorischen Konzepte, wo nicht Abhängigkeit von Vorbildern überwog. Immerhin gab sich bei der Abschlußveranstaltung noch eine hervorstrebende Nachwuchs-Choreographin zu erkennen: Marilén Breuker. Und wieder war es der spanische Tanz, nun von Susana choreographiert, von Antonio Robledo komponiert, von Nina Corti getanzt – ein einfaches Übungsstück, das die Kunst im Einfachen aufleuchten ließ.

Zu kurz gekommen sind in diesem Rückblick die „akademischen" Klassiker. Sie bildeten jahraus jahrein den konstanten Schwerpunkt der Akademie. Die klassische Tanztechnik ist in ihren Grundlagen die breite Strömung, die heute alle Tanzarten trägt und verfeinert. Hier gibt es keine wechselnden Tendenzen, sondern nur Methoden und Persönlichkeitsstile, die allerdings epochale Auswirkungen haben können. Nicht einmal der Initiator Heinz Laurenzen ahnte, daß er mit der in Krefeld gegründeten

Sommerakademie einen 25 Jahre währenden Kraftakt bewältigen würde, der sich aus dem allgemeinen Vorhaben der Fördergesellschaft ergab, „die Tanzkunst auf breiter Basis zu pflegen und zu fördern". Die so bewirkte Kultivierung der Unterrichtsmethoden und schulische Durchdringung des Unterrichtsmaterials auf allen Gebieten der Tanzkunst entsprachen dem deutschen Nachholbedarf und nahmen den deutschen Tänzern – gegenüber den ausländischen Entwicklungen – ihren historisch bedingten Minderwertigkeitskomplex, gaben den jungen Tänzern und Choreographen Starthilfen. Über das Trainingszentrum hinaus war es das Anliegen Laurenzens, schöpferische Kräfte anzuregen. So entwickelten sich aus choreographischen Kolloquien und Studio-Veranstaltungen die Wettbewerbe, die – trotz aller, bei solchen Unternehmungen zu erwartenden Tiefpunkte – ihre Preisträger der Theaterballettszene empfahlen.

Die Kölner Sommerakademie des Tanzes ist weltumspannendes Modell geworden. Sie bleibt die große Anregerin, der große internationale Umschlagplatz der pädagogischen und theatralischen Strömungen. Ein 25jähriges deutsches Wunder.

SUMMARY

THE INTERNATIONAL SUMMER-ACADEMY OF DANCE COLOGNE

25 YEARS' HISTORICAL RETROSPECTIVE

Much admired, well attended, often imitated – this the International Summer Academy of Dance, existing for 25 years, first in Krefeld, then in Cologne – in Germany – in Europe. Hundreds of professionals representing every post-modern trend congregate each year: the classicists, the folklorists, the tap dancers. No nation excludes itself – and no epoch, either, one is tempted to note, in view of the increasing significance of the "historians".

The beginnings are to be found in an idea of Heinz Laurenzen who sent invitations for April 14, 1955, to the public founding of the Society for the Promotion of Artistic Dance in Krefeld. Ceremonies were chaired by Kurt Jooss and former chief dramaturgist Hans Robert Doering-Manteuffel. The first great German ballet critic, Otto-Friedrich Regner, and Kurt Peters discussed the situation, task and goals of artistic dance. Both speakers made clear the deplorable state of affairs which had prompted the formation of the Society. After a two-year period of organization and trial, Laurenzen's idea began to crystallize, taking precedence over numerous other ambitious projects. Under the name International Summer Academy of Dance it was to achieve world recognition, ultimately unifying all these plans under one roof.

One hundred and seventy-four participants,

already international in their composition, registered for the first Summer Academy at Krefeld in August, 1957. Under the presidency of set designer Heinrich Wendel (who died in 1980), the high level of the Academy made itself clear from the very start. The first instructors (Peggy van Praagh, Rosalia Chladek, Boris Kniaseff, Victor Gsovsky) were joined by guests Tatjana Gsovsky, Lia Schubert, Erich Walter, and Marcel Luipart. Lectures by Heinrich Lindlar, Georges Chapovalenko, Helmut Kluge, O. G. de St. Andrée treated structural problems, symbol-

ism, systematics, dance notation, and the social ranking of dance. Boris Kniaseff's method established an innovation in dance technique by transferring the exercise to the floor. Some instructors, however, combined the standing and reclining practice from the very first, knowing that Kniaseff's "recumbent" etoiles had already achieved their conditioning in standing positions. In any case there developed as early as that an intensive discussion concerning basic questions of technique. Exhibitions and bookstalls rounded out the intellectual framework. The first Academy was closed with a public demonstration evening featuring choreographies by the instructors. The dancers participating (Ulla Paulsen, Helga Held, Hella Troester, Judith Dornys, Boris Trailine, Karl-Heinz Hermes, Winfried Krisch) were to return for future classes.

It is not the task here, however, to list all the activities of the previous Summer Academies, to name all the significant names, to note the continuous expansion of the subject matter (soon to amass in Cologne a concentration including every ranking international teacher), or to estimate the ever growing numbers of participants, often far exceeding the number officially registered. Instead, one should attempt to trace the trends and changes in the developmental years, which brought about the growing success of the Summer Academy and its influence on the ballet scene.

By integrating the German dancers' congress into the first Summer Academy, it was Heinrich Wendel's intention not only to carry on jointly the work of earlier congresses, but to move the powerless "slaves' union", as he called the German dancers, to social commitment as well. Throughout the years, this congress occupied the attention of the press, supporting the efforts of the Stage Actors Union to establish contractual pay scales for dancers.

Already the second Summer Academy brought about an enrichment of the entire German dance scene with José de Udaeta's instruction in Spanish dance, whereby Spanish stage dance began to appear original. Throughout the years of the Academy, de Udaeta also trained German dancers to be perfect interpreters of Spanish dance. Laurenzen always had a fine sense for initiating, expanding, and improving just in the exact area which was in fact sorely in need of improvement. Some German colleagues were too "provincial" in their thinking, misunderstanding Laurenzen's efforts to enrich the German dance scene with as much international stimulation as possible. That German dance did not suffer from this was proven later by Hans Kresnik, Helmut Baumann, Jochen Ulrich, Jürg Burth, Pina Bausch, Gerhard Bohner, Reinhild Hoffmann, Susanne Linke and other young choreographers who developed parallel. Victor Gsovsky gave highest estimation of the German dancers at the beginning of their ballet renaissance, although Elvira Roné had to overcome initial difficulties with her pas de deux class. There were still deficiences in method and style.

The Academy supported the founding of professional associations for ballet masters and teachers although the moment proved to be not yet ripe. The associations parted ways, were dissolved, were refounded – nonetheless, a sign that things had begun to move.

In the years following, the Summer Academy continued to supply decisive impulses. Horst Koegler characterized the Academy as being "binding for the entire German dance scene". The names of exclusive instructors embellished once again the program; jazz dancing expanded. Following the Spanish, Hungarian folklore (Emma Lugossy) was discovered, which had previously been hidden in the silliest of operetta affectations.

Problems were encountered in effecting a more stringent qualitative selection of the participants and a reduction in the number of classes which could be taken, as the dancers tended to overtax themselves. The theoretical excursuses of Max Niehaus, who

died in 1981, of Gerhard Zacharias, and Horst Koegler showed themselves wanting in their relation to dance practice.

Encounters on the periphery of the sessions played a role which must not be underestimated. They electrified the working climate of those years, while performance and quality rose as a result of ever more stringent methods of schooling in all areas. The reversal of folk dancing towards originality remained constant.

Alexandra Danilova gave classes at the next Academy session, 1960; Marianne Vogelsang taught on the basis of the German modern dance; Gerhard Zacharias' mythological themes found their audience. In the same year Laurenzen, in cooperation with Erich Walter and Gise Furtwängler, attempted, for the first time, to form a choreographic working committee, which later developed into the Choreographic Competition. This undertaking, with the most extraordinary subjects and practices, brought forth choreographers and ballet masters who resisted with imagination not only the stagnating classical tradition, but also incompetence within their own ranks.

1961: Since the Krefeld Academy no longer offered sufficient space, a move was made to the former College of Physical Education in Cologne. In satisfying rising demands on the Academy, however, the intimacy of earlier years was lost. Outwardly everything seemed to have remained the same, but the German dancers had in the meantime grown beyond their elementary schooling. A new technical awareness pushed academic training into a new importance. American modern dance laid the groundwork for Graham technique; jazz dancers Walter Nicks and Claude Thompson cleared out the meager musical affectations which had existed in Germany to that date. Theory, on the other hand, receded into the background in so far as it was not continued by the choreographic working committee, now led by Aurel von Milloss. Here knowledge and experience, ballet history and technique amalgamated everything which should have originally emanated from the classical instructors; their commentary, their guidance towards theory and cultural history would have complemented the Summer Academy with necessary reflection. The dancers, though, had reached the limits of their capacities.

Relief was promised by the "permanent academy" announced by Laurenzen, which as the Institute for Stage Dance, was founded in October, 1961. But the continuously rising ratio of foreign participants was untouched by this development. In spite of these problems, Laurenzen had created, in the International Summer Academy, the school of the institute, and with the Choreo-

graphic Competition, in conjunction with the Modern Dance Week sponsored by the Cologne Opera, an educational center which, to this day, remains unique in Germany.

In the following year, instruction was offered by seven classicists, emanating primarily from the Diaghilev era and its progeny. The danse d'école could not have been represented in a manner more open to the world than with the representatives of the former Ballets Russes. Among them was Todd Bolender, who also assumed the leadership of the choreographic colloquium, carrying on less intellectually but instead more generous in the free play of fantasy. Heed was also paid to the desire for pantomime and historical dance. Both subjects seemed, however, to remain isolated in dance, due to the lack of historical and intellectual reference. The number of participants had, in the meantime, grown to 650. In a panel discussion, the foreign instructors expressed their undivided admiration for the German theater scene with its 50 opera houses.

Doing so, the visitors overlooked the numerous problems faced by the smaller houses, reason enough for Wilfried Hofmann and Alphons Silbermann to renew their advocacy of a national ballet with an associated school. The Modern Dance Week presented the annual production in the "allegro" of Bolender choreographies, which placed the performances of Yuriko and the Merce Cunningham Company in a disproportionate light.

Had the participants not been so disciplined, the next Summer Academy 1965, by now the ninth, would have been overcome by their own numbers. No attempt at dividing the participants according to their levels could cope with the fatal overcrowding of all courses. Help came from a "festival" of assistants, who substituted for the teachers engaged for only short periods. Paul Taylor was replaced by Norman Walker, John Cranko by Harald Lander, Katherine Dunham by Christiane de Rougemont, Charlotte Sevelin by Maria Suroviak. Although that caused no decline in quality, there was indeed a loss of continuity.

The Modern Dance Week brought familiar pieces to new heights: Paul Taylor's *Aureole*, Maurice Béjart's *The Journey* (with Tilly Söffing and Lothar Höfgen) and *Symphony for a Lonely Man*, Todd Bolender's *Still Point*.

Unexpectedly, the tenth Academy session 1966 became a turning point. The influx of dancers was checked, classes were organized according to qualifications. For Alvin Ailey's class, only 100 of the 170 applicants were accepted, other classes were divided. José de Udaeta and Ursula Knaflewsky had already established three levels, in which progress was most evident. Peter Appel, Edite Frandsen, Frank Wagner, Yuriko, Henryk Tomaszewski, to name only a few, worked hand in hand. Lia Schubert led the choreographic colloquium.

In his opening speech, Heinrich Lindlar "unveiled the monument" of the tenth Summer Academy, as Wendel had "laid the cornerstone for a hospital", his name for the first Academy session. Walter Erich Schäfer found himself, following his speech, elevated to the position of protagonist for the German ballet renaissance. His soloist, Birgit Keil along with Bernd Berg, danced Cranko's classical and yet perplexingly modern enchaînements with an ideal and faultless beauty.

Finally, Brigitte Garski succeeded in establishing herself with historical dance from which once everything had emanated, though not in the technic-oriented spirit of our time. It is to Garski's credit that this spirit was successfully undermined and not to a small degree thanks to Laurenzen's persistence on accepting and supporting minorities in his program, pending development of their own independence.

With the eleventh Academy Laurenzen could afford to take a breather, for he had long since made "Cologne a well-known place in the world", as Donald McKayle expressed it. With all the problems which also impelled this institution forward, there existed, in addition to the technical training aspect, "the position of the Summer Academy as a (dance-) societal crystallization nucleus" (Hartmut Regitz). Where else could one enter into discussion of this sort, on both national and international levels, arrange engagements, make contacts, forge friendships?

Anyone who came late during the twelfth Academy session was left standing before Valentina Pereyaslavec's closed doors. Behind these doors took place "the most horrifying exercise classes which I have ever seen.... Fired and badgered with a drill sergeant's power of command" (Jens Wendland), training was conducted at a high level and was stimulating as well. Pereyaslavec's conditions included the right to select her students and work absolutely free of disturbances. The Summer Academy had in the meantime set new standards for the theater ensembles, standards which were now being passed on by the ballet masters even in companies of medium and small size.

The Academy distinguished itself with the strong-willed dance poems of John Neumeier, Gerhard Bohner's original subtleties, and Hans Kresnik's germinal political ballet. The avant-garde choreographers analyzed the problems of individuals and masses. Noise collages and horror marches still supplied more interesting subjects for discussion than did the increasing flatness of later compositions. The choreography of the young analyzed the movement and dissected space, opposed tradition. The tenor of the ballet week was more civil, where Glen Tetley *(Mythical Hunters)*, Job Sanders and Hans van Manen dominated the boards, complemented by pieces from the repertoire of the company at Cologne.

In the 1968/69 season, young choreographers John Neumeier, Gerhard Bohner, and André Doutreval, along with those active in Cologne, Jürg Burth, Helmut Baumann, Gray Veredon, and Jochen Ulrich, aroused more interest than the established masters. Pina Bausch with *In the Wind of Time* (first prize) set a signal for her highly individual future. "The traditional aesthetic in choreography has (had) served its time" (Horst Koegler) while the Academy gained classical accents from England through Peter Wright and from Denmark through Henning Kronstam.

At the 14th Summer Academy Hector Zaraspe entered the scene as a true showmaster of classical training and Kronstam imparted to his class well-founded technique. Tetley's fragments dominated the choreographic colloquium; and the Choreographic Competition remained without prizewinners! Even when the average abilities of his participants disappointed Antony Tudor, Matt Mattox, Donald McKayle, and Lynn Simonson were able to develop a highly precise jazz consciousness.

Brigitte Garski explained and demonstrated Renaissance dance with her historical ensemble. Ernö Pesovár held forth on the subject of stick dances and used film to illustrate his comments on Hungarian folklore. Under the guidance of Patricia Christopher, a few of the young choreographers not represented in the competition invented small compositions characterized by humor and the body's own sense of rhythm. An exhibition of photographs by artist Pieter Kooistra in the Academy hallways rounded out the supplementary information offered. But positively sensational in its effect was José de Udaeta's arrangement of 19th-century Spanish dances (taught by Juan Magrina), with the soloists of the Teatro Liceo, Barcelona – Spanish dance on point.

For the 15th Summer Academy in 1971, Laurenzen engaged Bill Hamilton, who instructed his twelve participants in the choreographic figures of Scottish country dance. The offering also took the technicians into consideration, of course: Mary Hinkson offered Graham technique in perfection; Scott Douglas invented classical combinations worked out in rhythmic versions. With surety of instinct, Laurenzen attacked the pending school problems – as the great interest in speeches, such as *The Private German Ballet School – Affirmation and Warning* (Peters), *Pas de deux Technique* (Luipart), and *Historical Choreography* (Garski), proved.

In spite of abiding structural deficiencies in the choreography, the fourth Choreographic Competition exhibited certain qualities, which, nonetheless, went unhonored by the jury. With justification, however, the first prize went to the folk-song collages of Gigi-Gheorghe Caciuleanu. Tihana Skrinjarik's *Tones of Istria* impressed with fascinating clarity of form, reminiscent of the Mary Wigman style. These and other pieces contributed to a general rise in level.

The Harkness Ballet made a guest appearance in the Modern Dance Week, showing virtuosity in *Time Out of Mind* and *Percussion for Six*. The Cologne ballet studio, henceforth the Tanz-Forum, kept a promise of highest characteristic quality with Jochen Ulrich's *Lewis C.*, Christopher Bruce's *Wings*, and Helmut Baumann's *The Sonata and the Three Gentlemen,* which in no way took second place to the talent shown by Jürg Burth and Gray Veredon.

Without impairing other subjects, an unusual trend towards Graham's technique made itself apparent in the following year, although within the U.S.A. emphasis had long since shifted in the direction of "informal" technique and thematics. For the first time Madhavi Mudgal instructed in the techniques of Indian dance, and it was Agnes Roboz who began to lay exact groundwork for training in Hungarian dance. José de Udaeta, who for 16 years had conceived ever new, exciting contributions, gave a presentation on the art of flamenco, in which he himself, together with Marcela, danced an ageing gypsy. Leaving all the competitors far behind, Caciuleanu, too, was convincing in his handling of a Spanish theme. Hans van Manen fascinated once again with his choreography class and provided valuable explanations to the competitors in his "jury consultations".

Among the 21 instructors at the 17th Academy (and it was soon to become 28), the teachers at the Institute for Stage Dance proved themselves anew. Twenty-four courses, three lecture demonstrations as well as the Choreographic Competition, film evenings and four lectures marked a festival of particular dimensions. In addition to this came the Modern Dance Week with a surprising low point for the Batsheva Dance Company, which was only able to present Rina Schenfeld as a fascinating dancer. The not totally shared fun of the Louis Falco Dance Company was outshone by the guest appearance of the Lar Lubovitch Company; the crowning point: Hans van Manen, Alexandra Radius and Han Ebbelaar in the closing spectacle.

gegenüber/opposite page
THAT IS THE SHOW,
Ch: Norman Morrice,
Heide Tegeder und/and
James Saunders,
Tanz-Forum Köln/Cologne,
Foto: Annelise Löffler

Above the wasteland of plagiarism and stereotypical, pre-fab components in the Choreographic Competition rose in this year only Susanne Linke with a grotesque and Japan's duo, Takashi Koma and Eiko Otake, to whom the jury incomprehensibly refused to award a prize.

Not only interested Wilfried Hofmann with his demanding subject, Kurt Peters, too, was met with an enthusiastic audience for his lecture, *Ballet Schools Today*. Thus, he took up his main theme, that of training, which at the previous Summer Academy had led to calling a conference of the directors of state-supported ballet schools. The directors, up to that point barely represented at the Academy, were now included more and more in the all too narrowly drawn definition of professionalism. The film evening previously mentioned showed, in addition to historical retrospectives, *Dancers in School* with choreographer and dancer Murray Louis. At the end of this festival of classes, Luigi presented an explosive jazz show in the courtyard of the academy building.

Anyone who had believed that the Summer Academy – after 17 Summer Sessions – would have exhausted the entire range of offerings in the field of dance education found himself overcome by new impressions in 1974. The historical orientation of the Limón technique permeated the moderns, and jazz put on a bold display. A position had just been established for Hungarian folklore, next to the Spanish, when a new specialist, the Russian Anatoli Borsow, expanded the field. He gave his audience a capricious-historical feeling for the quadrille. Karl Heinz Taubert, professor at the College of Music in Berlin, enthused his listeners with historical dance, based on his well-founded concept of historical culture. Between Taubert, de Udaeta, Roboz and Borsow there developed a unique intellectual connection, which allowed one to incorporate the other's thoughts into the practical side of instruction.

The Modern Dance Week presented Judith Jamison, Alvin Ailey's and Murray Louis' companies. In addition, there was the historical from Emily Frankel, the personal from Gigi-Gheorghe Caciuleanu, the problematic from Ballet Rambert, the extreme from the Tanz-Forum. The peripheral program and the closing presentation added even more to the sheer magnitude of that which was offered.

The mammoth undertaking of the Summer Academy marched on, having reached a biblical age – at least by German standards – and having developed its own dynamics. In her lecture Agnes Roboz gave new insights for the Academy's work: "…the most difficult job for art, is to remain simple and yet artistic." This tendency asserted itself, from Gisela Peters-Rohse's children's classes to Hans van Manen's composition course, the "simple" result of which became an overwhelming experience with 50 participants. Fritz Lüdin's serenity in the Limón technique and Zena Rommett's placement class, in which the instructors, too, participated, impressed many.

The Cologne Tanz-Forum and primarily the pieces by Birgit Cullberg set the tone for the Modern Dance Week, but Cullberg's works were, however, no longer current. It was Het Nationale Ballet with its three "vans" (Hans van Manen, Toer van Schayk, and Rudi van Dantzig) which proved to be most exciting, in particular with *Twilight* and *Adagio Hammerklavier*. In contrast, the young choreographers this time showed no real trust in the music, but all the more in the jury's powers of concentration.

For the first time Laurenzen opened the concluding program to the public. On Roncalli Square in Cologne Brigitte Garski cultivated her historical dances, de Udaeta and Emma Maleras presented their Spanish dances to an enthusiastic audience.

For the 20th session Laurenzen again invited a world elite of instructors. The high point would have been missing, however, if the American Jooss Festival of the Joffrey Ballet had not found an echo in the Tanz-Forum. Its Jooss evening rehabilitated the entire German dance of the past. The Choreographic Competition, in contrast, "conspicuous for the flight into philosophically veiled clown allegories", was, to a purest, "a festival of furniture" (Horst Koegler).

The 21st Academy left no room for catching one's breath, no laissez faire. The peripheral events, exhibits and workshop performances multiplied, and the belief spread that the quantity of great masters could raise the quality of one's own performances. Elena Jemchuchina's Moscow style competed with the English style of Eileen Ward, the American with the French. Tap, Spanish and historical dance were taught by new or additional instructors, Laban technique and kinetographics were recalled by Lisa Ullmann. Gisela Peters-Rohse introduced new training methods for children which, in the spirit of contemporary movement training, attempted to use improvisational means to direct towards a later awareness of technique.

Once again it was Hans van Manen who led off the activities with a choral suite. Eva Campianu presented a historical workshop and the Kamizawa Modern Dance Ensemble shocked with its psychic studies of the Japanese mentality.

The choreographic competition, by now the ninth, brought forth only dated municipal-theater ballets, glossy divertissements and, from abroad, unmusical classics, which so muddled the jury that a contribution from Cologne, exhibiting musical as well as choreographic substance (*Ballade* by Krisztina Horvath) was left unrewarded. With polished irony, Anatoli Borsow and René Bon danced two Russian market women. Unforgettable were the balladesque flamenco dances of masterful Flora Albaicin.

The Modern Dance Week allowed for an amused glance back to *The Spirit of Denishawn* by the Joyce Trisler Dance Company; Jennifer Muller and the Works contributed with *Beach*, among others.

The face presented to the outside world by the 22nd Summer Academy was characterized by workshops. Various larger and smaller groups had formed in the meantime, which now sought their well-being in the Academy. An unparalleled discovery was Maguy Marin with her Théâtre de l'Arche. Moreover, Reinhild Hoffmann and Carlos Orta received confirmation of their talent; worthy of particular mention was Susanne Linke. In addition, van Manen's seminar and consultation enriched the workshops.

Essential variations in the Academy schedule resulted from Anatoli Borsow's introduction to Moisseyev's folklore exercise, Eva Campianu's excursion back to the Biedermeier period, Agnes Roboz's gypsy dance, Doris Rudko's *Dance Composition*, and Gisela Peters-Rohse's lecture on *Determination of Motives and Pedagogy for Preschoolers*. Her educational thesis produced a new intellectual connection between Rudko, Roboz, Borsow, Hinkson, and de Udaeta, balancing to some extent the underrepresentation of intellectual offerings in the Academy.

Samy Molcho and José de Udaeta brought to the Academy's finale climaxes in the classical, historical, folk, jazz and pantomime, finally overtrumped by *Three Women*, by the Nederlands Dans Theater. Lynn Simonson excelled with a grotesque, barbed as had never been seen before, in which she molded four masters (Molcho, Bon, de Udaeta and Borsow) to form a grotesque-comic jazz quadrille.

In the theatrical sector, Youri Vámos showed in his *Rhapsody* what acrobatic expression can be; Joseph Russillo's company reflected on religion in *Requiem*; Caciuleanu with his Mozart mass demonstrated formal abilities. Jochen Ulrich and Achim Freyer had created a special piece *(Triad)* for the Tanz-Forum: on the stage, in the orchestra pit, the balconies, and hanging from the ceiling of the theater, the performers wrapped the audience in strings, provoking massive protest. The Modern Dance Week drew to a mysterious and meditative close with Carolyn Carlson's *The Year of the Horse*.

Ruth Currier and Pearl Lang broadened the

DER WANDELBARE GARTEN/
THE MOVEABLE GARDEN,
Ch: Glen Tetley,
Tanz-Forum Köln/Cologne
oben/above
Foto: Stefan Odry
unten/below
Monika Montiva,
Jürg Burth, Jochen Ulrich,
Foto: Detlef Dorn

emphasis on modern dance at the following Summer Academy in 1979. Brigitte Garski worked through three centuries of German dance history; Gia-fu Feng carried on the meditative-philosophical line with Tai Chi Chuan; Jerry Ames continued with tap, and Susana – de Udaeta's former partner – continued the Spanish series, as did Ursula Knaflewsky. In Gia-fu Feng's effects, Gerhard Zacharias saw the "amalgamation of the Apollonian with the Dionysian", and noted that Susana ". . . with years is becoming more and more of a sign. Duende." And he was not alone in pronouncing a "declaration of love for Marta" (Metzger), the embodiment of tenderness and beauty of dance.

The Modern Dance Week was wholly dominated by the José Limón Dance Company. *There is a Time*, in fact, had become a part of the Tanz-Forum repertory. Pina Bausch's *Bluebeard* supplemented her version of *The Rite of Spring* from the preceding year. On another level but just as extraordinary: Jiří Kylián's Nederlands Dans Theater works *Symphony of Psalms*, *Children's Games* and *Sinfonietta*. Susanne Linke *(Satie, Ballade)* stood head and shoulders above the studios and the Choreographic Competition, with the exception of the works of Bill Cratty, Ralf Harster, and Nils Christe. Drawing the instructors into *dance & talk*, Laurenzen attempted a new form in the College of Music.

The 24th Summer Academy, including at the same time the seventh Modern Dance Week and the eleventh Choreographic Competition, surpassed preceding ones. Nat Horne knew how to instill enthusiasm in his jazz students; Jerry Ames "raised" tap dancing to the finest diminuendo; postmoderns such as Trisha Brown or Mariko Sanjo *(Dialogue with the Universe)* enriched the modern dance field. Clay Taliaferro instructed a differentiated further development of the Limón technique; Sandor Timar integrated primeval improvisation techniques into Hungarian folklore; Ruth Ashkenasi presented as yet unknown Israeli dances in her guest appearance. The offerings of the Academy in technique were expanded by Ursula Borrmann's course, Methodology, continuing the classical-based children's dance pedagogy demonstrated by Gisela Peters-Rohse for pre-professional training.

Once again the Nederlands Dans Theater program with works by Kylián *(Dream Dances, Fieldmass)* represented the premature highpoint of the Modern Dance Week. Jochen Ulrich invented original ideas and movement sequences *(Contra Dance, The Reading Hour)* for the Knete Company (Cologne College of Physical Education), but only *à la Jacques* for the Tanz-Forum.

Forbearing and cheerful, Jennifer Muller and the Works admonished not to lose touch with the essential lust for life in the face of all-encompassing misery.

The jurors, aside from awarding three second prizes, were able to express only recognition and encouragement: advisory help for concepts, recognizable only in an embryonic form, in which the dependency on models still predominated. Promising choreographic progeny was found in the closing performance in the person of Mari-lén Breuker. It was again Spanish dance – choreographed by Susana, composed by Antonio Robledo, and danced by Nina Corti – which illuminated the art of simplicity.

Too little attention has been devoted to the classicists in this retrospective. Through the years, they represented the constant focal point of the Academy. Today the foundations of classical dance technique form the broad current which underpins and refines every other dance form. It is subject to no changing trends; it is characterized only by methods and personal style, which can nonetheless have epochal effects.

Not even initiator Laurenzen could have imagined that with the founding of the Summer Academy in Krefeld he would persevere a strong-man's act for 25 years, arising from the generally stated intention to "nurture and support the art of dancing on a broad basis". The cultivation of training methods and the penetration of teaching material into schools in all fields of dance thus brought about, satisfied a pent-up German need for regeneration, freeing German dancers of their historically conditioned inferiority complex, giving the younger dancers and choreographers a starting boost. Beyond the goals of the training center, Laurenzen was always interested in stimulating creative forces. Thus, there developed out of choreographic colloquia and studio seminars the competitions which – in spite of occasional lows – commended its prizewinners to the world of the ballet theater.

The Cologne Summer Academy of Dance has become a world-encompassing model. It remains the great initiator, the vast international marketplace for the interaction of educational and theatrical currents.

oben/above
TUB,
Ch: Jennifer Muller,
Jennifer Muller and the Works,
Foto: Annemarie Heinrich
unten/below
BEACH,
Ch: Jennifer Muller,
Jennifer Muller and the Works,
Foto: Jorge Fatauros

gegenüber/opposite page
DER GRÜNE TISCH/THE GREEN TABLE,
Ch: Kurt Jooss,
Tanz-Forum Köln/Cologne,
Fotos: Gert Weigelt

links/left
SUITE OTIS,
Ch: George Faison,
Maxine Sherman (links/left),
Donna Wood,
Alvin Ailey American Dance Company,
Foto: Jack Vartoogian

diese Seite/this page
oben/top
SPEEDS,
Ch: Jennifer Muller,
Jennifer Muller and the Works,
Foto: Gert Weigelt
Mitte/middle
SALTIMBOCCA,
Ch: Louis Falco,
Louis Falco Dance Company,
Foto: Jack Vartoogian
unten/bottom
CAVIAR,
Ch: Louis Falco,
Louis Falco,
Louis Falco Dance Company,
Foto: Martha Swope

gegenüber/opposite page
oben/above
ERRAND INTO THE MAZE,
Ch: Martha Graham,
Bühnenbild von/set by
Isamu Noguchi,
Kostüme von/costumes by
Edythe Gilfond,
Elisa Monte, David Brown,
Martha Graham Dance Company,
Foto: Graham Company
unten/below
DIVERSION OF ANGELS,
Ch: Martha Graham,
Bühnenbild von/set by
Isamu Noguchi,
Martha Graham Dance Company,
Foto: Martha Swope

diese Seite/this page
LIGHT,
Ch: Kei Takei,
Kei Takei's Moving Earth,
oben/above
LIGHT Teil/Part 13
unten/below
LIGHT Teil/Part 12,
Fotos: Lois Greenfield

Fotos in diesem Artikel,
falls nicht anders angegeben/
Photos in this article,
if not otherwise credited:
Annelise Löffler

diese Seite/this page
oben links/top left
LISA ULLMANN, KURT JOOSS (1977)
oben rechts/top right
HANS VAN MANEN (1979)

Mitte links/middle left
SIMON MOTTRAM (1979)
Mitte rechts/middle right
HANS VAN MANEN (1979)

unten links/bottom left
CARMEN DE LAVALLADE (1977)
unten rechts/bottom right
MARY HINKSON (1976)

MARTA METZGER,
JONATHAN WATTS (1977)
Mitte/middle
Klasse von/class of
GEORGES SKIBINE (1968)
unten/bottom
(v.l.n.r./left to right)
HEINZ LAURENZEN,
JOSE DE UDAETA,
HECTOR ZARASPE

FRITZ LÜDIN (1977)
Mitte/middle
CARLOS GACIO (1979)

Mitte/middle
NAT HORNE(1980)
unten/bottom
CHARLES KELLEY (1976)

Klasse von/class of
MARY HINKSON (1976)
unten/below
Klasse von/class of
MARY HINKSON (1971)

Klasse von/class of
MARTA METZGER,
JONATHAN WATTS (1977)
unten/below
Klasse von/class of
MARY HINKSON (1977)

Jochen Schmidt

DIE PHANTASIE AN DIE MACHT!

DER CHOREOGRAPHISCHE WETTBEWERB VON KÖLN UND DIE FRAGE, WIE MAN JUNGE BALLETTSCHÖPFER AM BESTEN FÖRDERT

Die bekannteste, schönste und wohl auch folgenreichste aller Parolen, die Unbekannte während der Studentenunruhen im Mai 1968 auf die Häuserwände im Quartier Latin in Paris gepinselt haben, lautet: „Die Phantasie an die Macht!" Es ist das ideale Motto nicht nur für jede utopische Gesellschaft, sondern auch für jede bestehende künstlerische Institution, wie erdacht für einen Wettbewerb, der sich die Anregung, Förderung und finanzielle Unterstützung junger Choreographen zur Aufgabe gemacht hat.

Natürlich gibt es keinen direkten Zusammenhang zwischen dem Pariser Mai (und überhaupt der Studentenrevolte des Jahres 68) und dem Choreographischen Wettbewerb der Internationalen Sommerakademie des Tanzes in Köln. Aber eine entfernte verwandtschaftliche Beziehung ist unübersehbar. Nicht nur, daß gleich der erste Choreographische Wettbewerb im Sommer 68 seine Solidarität mit der Studentenbewegung bekundete, indem er ihr – mit Hans Kresniks Tanzstück O Paradies – seinen meistdiskutierten Beitrag widmete. Der Choreographische Wettbewerb entstammt demselben geistigen Klima, derselben kulturell-gesellschaftlichen Aufbruchsstimmung wie das weltweite Aufbegehren der Studenten. Nichts liegt hier ferner, als die große, tragisch gescheiterte Studentenrevolte und den kleinen ästhetischen Fortschritt des Kölner Choreographischen Wettbewerbs in eins zu setzen und damit die Studentenbewegung zu verharmlosen. Aber es ist nicht zu leugnen, daß es einen gemeinsamen Mißmut gegenüber dem Bestehenden und seinen alten, nicht aufzulösenden Verkrustungen, ein gemeinsames Unbehagen an einer Ausbildung gab, die ganz auf Drill und stures Lernen setzte (und bei den Tänzern mehr noch als bei den Studenten), und daß dieser Mißmut die Gegenbewegung auslöste. Die Propagierung der Phantasie erschien hier wie dort als probatestes Mittel zur Neubelebung und Humanisierung erstarrter Traditionen.

In der Praxis allerdings gelang es dem Choreographischen Wettbewerb beinahe genauso schlecht, die Phantasie an die Macht zu bringen (oder sie zumindest an der Macht zu beteiligen), wie der Studentenrevolte. Die nunmehr 13jährige Geschichte des Wettbewerbs liest sich keineswegs als eine Kette strahlender Siege von Phantasie und Kreativität, sondern als ein ständiges Auf und Ab der Vorstellungen, Projektionen und Qualitäten.

Gleich der erste Wettbewerb endete im Grunde mit einer Panne. Die Organisatoren hatten über den Grundsatz, daß gleiches Recht für alle Teilnehmer gelten müsse, nicht sehr intensiv nachgedacht und den Stars des Wettbewerbs – den Choreographen John Neumeier, Gerhard Bohner und Hans Kresnik und den Ensembles der Opernhäuser von Stuttgart, Berlin und Köln – das Schauspielhaus mit seinen technischen Möglichkeiten zur Verfügung gestellt, den übrigen Konkurrenten aber nur einen kahlen Raum der Tanzakademie im Müngersdorfer Stadion. Daraufhin disqualifizierte die Jury (mit John Butler als Sprecher) die Bevorzugten, fand danach aber keinen ersten Preisträger mehr.

Erst der zweite Wettbewerb im Jahre 1969 verlief unter regulären, für alle gleichen Bedingungen und erbrachte auch ein Ergebnis, das seine Repetition für eine Weile sicherte: Pina Bausch (mit ihrem frühen Stück Im Wind der Zeit) vor Gerhard Bohner. Doch gleich im folgenden Jahr geriet der Wettbewerb erneut in Schwierigkeiten, für die diesmal die hochbesetzte Jury (Antony Tudor, Glen Tetley, Donald McKayle, Peter Wright, Patricia Christopher) sorgte. Sie ließ nämlich von den eingereichten Arbeiten nur zwei zur öffentlichen Vorführung zu, die damit unterblieb; statt im Schauspielhaus für die Öffentlichkeit wurden die verbliebenen zwei Choreographien in den Räumen der Akademie für die Akademieteilnehmer aufgeführt (und die Preise und Preisgelder eingespart).

Die Jahre 1971 und 1972 verliefen ohne Mißhelligkeiten, mit Gigi-Gheorghe Caciuleanu – heute Direktor des Théâtre Chorégraphique im französischen Rennes – als überragendem Preisträger beider Konkurrenzen. Eigentlich zum erstenmal konzentrierten sich die Berichterstatter auf die rein ästhetische Erörterung; diskutiert wurden nicht Jury-Entscheidungen oder technische Pannen, sondern stilistische Trends und künstlerische Qualitäten. Allgemeiner Eindruck: Der Wettbewerb habe in diesen Jahren an handwerklicher Qualität gewonnen und an künstlerischer Originalität eingebüßt – ein Urteil, das ein Jahr später schon wieder von den Umständen überholt war.

Wieder siebte die Jury (Mary Hinkson, Kurt Jooss, Christopher Bruce, Helmut Baumann, der Autor dieser Zeilen) die Mehrzahl der intern vorgeführten Choreographien aus und sparte die Preise ein, ließ die verbleibenden drei Stücke allerdings doch öffentlich im Schauspielhaus vorführen; es gab, mit 37 Minuten reiner Spielzeit, das kürzeste Wettbewerbsprogramm aller zwölf Konkurrenzen.

Es war nur logisch, nach dem erneuten künstlerischen Einbruch die Aussetzung des Wettbewerbs für ein Jahr zu diskutieren und zu beschließen und generell zu der Auffassung zu kommen, ein Zwei-Jahres-Rhythmus stünde dem Choreographischen Wettbewerb besser an, weil dann in jedem Fall die Auswahlbasis größer sei. Doch nachdem der achte Choreographische Wettbewerb des Jahres 1976 – mit 27 eingereichten Balletten, Stücken von, unter anderem, Reinhild Hoffmann, Carlos Orta und Krisztina Horvath, einem starken Hang zum Modern Dance und einer Tendenz zum Rätselhaften und Irrationalen – vergleichsweise glücklich verlaufen war, vergaß man alle schlechten Erfahrungen und richtete den Wettbewerb wieder im jährlichen Rhythmus aus.

Das Prinzip wurde nur noch einmal unterbrochen, als Heinz Laurenzen, Leiter der Wettbewerbe wie der Sommerakademie, im Jahre 1978 zwischen den neunten und zehnten Choreographischen Wettbewerb eine Choreographische Werkstatt einschob, die sich gegenüber dem Wettbewerb letzten Endes jedoch als die schwächere Lösung erwies; der Verlust an Spontaneität und künstlerischer Offenheit wurde durch kein Qualitätsplus wettgemacht.

Wer die in Schlangenlinien verlaufene Geschichte des Wettbewerbs derart hat Revue passieren lassen, wird auf die Frage nach dem Erfolg kaum eine eindeutige Antwort geben können – und eine eindeutig positive schon gar nicht. Gewiß, fast alle jüngeren Choreographen, die für die bundesdeutsche Ballettszene wichtig sind, haben an diesem Wettbewerb irgendwann einmal teilgenommen: Pina Bausch, Reinhild Hoffmann, Susanne Linke, Gerhard Bohner, Hans Kresnik und John Neumeier. Einige von ihnen haben in Köln Preise gewonnen, und mindestens für Pina Bausch war der erste Preis von Köln eine wichtige Ermutigung für ihre weitere Arbeit und auf dem Weg zu internationaler Beachtung; sie gewann ihn, 1969, lange ehe die deutsche Öffentlichkeit und das deutsche Stadttheatersystem auf sie aufmerksam wurden.

Doch international bedeutende Teilnehmer an der Konkurrenz sind eher rar; außer Caciuleanu und Alejandro Witzmann-Anaya, der 1975 einen Preis gewann, waren es vorwiegend in deutschen Ensembles beschäftigte Ausländer (wie Carlos Orta oder Zoltan Imre), die in Köln auffielen. Und eine Karriere – zumindest die Beschleunigung seiner Karriere – verdankt dem Choreographischen Wettbewerb eigentlich nur der zwei-malige Sieger Caciuleanu, den Talent und Witz gewiß auch ohne die Kölner Bestätigung rasch nach oben gebracht hätten.

Unter solchen Umständen wird den Nutzen des Choreographischen Wettbewerbs in seiner bisherigen Geschichte niemand überschätzen. Doch seine Notwendigkeit zu bezweifeln, wäre ebenso falsch; gewisse – und nicht einmal geringe – Meriten, über die Funktion eines Barometers für ästhetische Trends und Modeströmungen hinaus, lassen sich kaum bestreiten. Um sie zu beschreiben, muß man weit ausholen und die Grundbedingungen choreographischer Ausbildung erörtern.

Das Tischlern von Möbeln und das Reparieren defekter Autos oder Fernsehgeräte, die maßgerechte Anfertigung eines Anzugs, das Abschmecken einer delikaten Sauce und die fachmännische Zerlegung eines toten Rindviehs: alles das und noch viel mehr kann man erlernen in exakt reglementierten Ausbildungsgängen, angeleitet von erfahrenen, sachkundigen Meistern. Sogar für die meisten künstlerischen Berufe sind Studiengänge eingerichtet. Es gibt Akademien und Hochschulen für Orchestermusiker und Klaviersolisten, für Sänger und Tänzer, Bildhauer und Maler, Schauspieler und Architekten. Das Filmen ist ebenso (hoch-) schulmäßig erlernbar wie das Komponieren. Es gibt Dirigentenlehrgänge und Klassen für Schauspielregie, und selbst das Schreiben von Romanen, Gedichten und Stücken – als die neben dem Malen und Komponieren einsamste kreative Tätigkeit – wird mancherorts akademisch gelehrt.

Nur Choreographen sind in jedem Fall Autodidakten. Für sie gibt es nirgendwo in der Welt Lehrgänge oder Ausbildungsstätten. Was sie lernen – selbst in den Kompositionsklassen der Sommerakademie –, lernen sie nicht durch Unterweisung, sondern nur durch Erfahrung und Beobachtung, allenfalls dadurch, daß sie einem Seniorchoreographen als Assistenten über die Schulter schauen, eventuell auch, indem sie die Stücke anderer einstudieren. Doch letztlich ist durchs Assistieren noch kein Choreograph groß geworden. Wirklich lernen und sich entwickeln kann man nur, indem man seine eigenen Stücke herausbringt, wie fehlerhaft und epigonal sie zunächst sein mögen.

Choreographen sind in jedem Fall Autodidakten; der Satz gilt auch noch in einem anderen Sinn. Zwar sieht es gelegentlich so aus, als wüchsen Choreographen besonders dort heran, wo bereits ein arrivierter Ballettschöpfer tätig ist, der Jüngeren Vorbild und Maßstäbe liefert. Als Beispiel könnte man auf den amerikanischen Modern Dance verweisen, dessen bedeutende Choreographen der zweiten Generation fast

alle aus der Schule von Martha Graham stammen, auch auf Stuttgart und John Cranko, der in gewissem Sinn als künstlerischer Vater so verschiedener Choreographen wie Jiři Kylián und John Neumeier anzusehen ist. Doch solche Beispiele kennzeichnen eher eine Minderheit und die Ausnahme von der Regel, wonach bedeutende Choreographen weniger oft im Sog eines anderen heranwachsen als auf einer künstlerisch gleichsam kahlen Fläche.

Choreograph wird man entweder aus Nachahmungstrieb oder aus Mißvergnügen an der jeweils herrschenden Ballettästhetik – und die wirklich schöpferischen Choreographen, jene, welche die Kunstform Ballett oder das Tanztheater weiterbringen, kommen durchweg aus der zweiten Kategorie. Sie choreographieren, weil sie sich als Tänzer – und es gibt keine Choreographen, die nicht als Tänzer begonnen hätten – nicht begnügen mochten mit dem, was das Repertoire und der Ballettmeister für sie und ihre Freunde an Tanz und Rollen bereithielten. Solches Mißvergnügen an der herkömmlichen Ästhetik und am überlieferten choreographischen Angebot tritt, merkwürdigerweise, häufig kollektiv auf. Es waren nicht nur Maurice Béjart und Roland Petit, die im Nachkriegs-Frankreich Serge Lifars blutleeren Neoklassizismus überwanden, nicht nur John Cranko und Kenneth MacMillan, die das Londoner Tanztheater der späten 40er Jahre revolutionierten. In Holland brachte die Unlust, sich mit dem traditionellen Ballett zufriedenzugeben, in den späten 50er Jahren nicht nur die Choreographen Rudi van Dantzig und Hans van Manen hervor, und auch in Köln war es um das Jahr 1968 – als Tanz-Forum und Choreographischer Wettbewerb fast parallel entstanden – eine ganze Gruppe junger Tänzer, die ihre eigene Vorstellung eines zeitgenössischen Tanztheaters verwirklichen wollte: Helmut Baumann und Hans Kresnik, Jürg Burth und Jochen Ulrich. Praktisch gleichzeitig begannen in der Bundesrepublik Pina Bausch (damals noch an der Essener Folkwang-Schule) und Gerhard Bohner (noch als Solist der Deutschen Oper Berlin) ihre Choreographenkarrieren.

Das könnte so klingen, als sei Choreographieren etwas, das sich dank eines dunklen künstlerischen Triebs der Choreographen auf jeden Fall ereigne und in seiner Qualität dann allein vom Talent des jeweiligen Choreographen definiert sei, der öffentlicher Förderung folglich nicht bedürfe. Wer es so sähe, ginge allerdings allzu naiv und blauäugig an die Sache heran.

Anders als Malen, Schreiben oder auch Komponieren ist Choreographieren nämlich etwas, das nicht im stillen Künstlerkämmerchen und isoliert von jeglicher Umwelt geschehen kann. Das choreographische

Pendant zu Spitzwegs einsamem Poeten existiert nicht. Ein Maler benötigt nichts als Leinwand (oder Pappkarton, Holz, Papier) sowie Pinsel und Farben, ein Schriftsteller nichts als Papier und Schreibutensil, ein Komponist darüber hinaus nur noch ein Instrument, auf dem er die erdachten Klänge zur Überprüfung in reale umsetzen kann. Ein Choreograph dagegen benötigt Menschen, Tänzer, die ihn inspirieren und mit denen er seine Bewegungssequenzen erarbeiten kann, darüber hinaus einen Raum, in dem diese Arbeit stattfindet.

Choreographenarbeit ist also immer Arbeit mit einem Ensemble – und sei dieses Ensemble noch so klein und bestehe etwa nur aus einem oder einigen Tänzerkollegen, die sich dem choreographierenden Anfänger aus Freundschaft oder Interesse für seine Arbeit zur Verfügung stellen. Die erste und wichtigste Förderung eines jeden jungen Choreographen erfolgt in der eigenen Gruppe und durch diese. Wenn die Ensembleleitung vernünftig (und nicht etwa auf neue Talente eifersüchtig) ist, unterstützt sie solche Prozesse und zieht sich dadurch den eigenen Choreographennachwuchs selbst heran. Doch in naheliegenden historischen Beispielen war solche Vernunft nicht immer am Werk. Der holländische Aufbruch vor gut 20 Jahren war eher ein Aufstand gegen das Ballett-Establishment, und auch die Anfänge des Kölner Tanz-Forums erfolgten nicht innerhalb der Hierarchie der Kölner Bühnen, sondern neben ihr, auf einer Plattform, die Mäzene – damals die Gesellschaft für künstlerischen Tanz e.V., die auch hinter den Anfängen der Sommerakademie steht – den jungen Choreographen bereitgestellt hatten.

Um die Bereitstellung solcher Plattformen, und sei es als temporäre Einrichtungen, geht es bei der Förderung junger Choreographen in erster Linie. Dabei ist natürlich keine zeitlich limitierte Maßnahme in der Lage, die kontinuierliche Förderung in der eigenen Gruppe zu ersetzen. Nur der ständige Umgang mit (immer denselben) Tänzern, das ständige Ausprobieren tänzerischer Ideen, die permanente Möglichkeit zu choreographischer Arbeit garantiert die kontinuierliche Entwicklung eines Choreographen – wie überhaupt bedeutende Choreographien immer nur im engen Miteinander von Choreographen und Gruppen und nie auf kurzfristigen Stippvisiten von Freelance-Choreographen bei noch so bedeutenden Ensembles entstanden sind. Die Kombinationen Balanchine/New York City Ballet, Cranko/Stuttgarter Ballett, van Manen/Nederlands Dans Theater oder Béjart/Ballet du XXe Siècle (im 19. Jahrhundert Bournonville/Königlich Dänisches Ballett, Petipa-Iwanow/Ballett des Maryinsky-Theaters) haben gemeinsam den künstlerischen

194

Erfolg verbürgt und stehen für viele andere, auch weniger prominente Verbindungen dieser Art.

Wer als Choreographen-Anfänger das Glück hat, in der eigenen Gruppe kontinuierlich schöpferisch tätig werden zu können, benötigt im Grunde keine andere Plattform – es sei denn, zur Bestätigung der eigenen Leistung und als öffentliches Siegel darauf. Die Bestätigung einer künstlerischen Leistung durch einen Preis bei einem internationalen Wettbewerb macht keinen Choreographen, vermag ihn aber zu fördern, indem sie ihm – möglicherweise – zu besseren Arbeitsbedingungen daheim oder bei einem neuen Ensemble verhilft, das durch den Preis auf ihn aufmerksam geworden ist.

Natürlich können choreographische Wettbewerbe wie der von Köln die Förderung junger Talente durch ihre einheimischen

Kompanien selbst dann nicht ersetzen, wenn ihre Preise nicht aus Geldsummen, Pokalen oder Diplomen, sondern aus Arbeitsstipendien bestehen (die gewiß die richtigsten Preise für choreographische Wettbewerbe sind). Aber sie sind in der Lage, die Förderung am Heimatort in verschiedener Hinsicht zu ergänzen. Neben den Preisen, die wenigen ein bißchen mehr Ansehen verleihen und im günstigsten Fall — wir erwähnten den des zweimaligen Kölner Preisträgers Caciuleanu - eine Karriere günstig beeinflussen können, bieten die Wettbewerbe die Möglichkeit eines künstlerischen Vergleichs im größeren Rahmen.

Dabei mag auch die Abschreckung eines Choreographiewilligen ein Erfolg für die Tanzkunst sein. In Köln kann jemand, der zu Hause vielleicht schon als kleines Genie gefeiert wird, aus dem Spruch einer kompe-

tenten Jury und – bei einiger Fähigkeit zur Selbsteinschätzung – aus dem Vergleich mit den Stücken anderer, ebenfalls noch namenloser Choreographen, auch ermessen, wo er tatsächlich steht: am Kopf, in der Mitte oder eher am Ende der Talentschlange. Und wenn jemand in Köln auf den Boden der Wirklichkeit zurückgeholt würde und feststellte, daß er zum Choreographieren vielleicht doch nicht geboren ist, wäre auch das kein geringer Erfolg des Wettbewerbs.

Zwar sind Choreographen äußerst dünn gesät; unter 500 Tänzern, hat John Cranko einmal gesagt, habe vielleicht einer das Zeug zu einem Choreographen. Doch darf das keineswegs heißen, daß man jedes Miniaturtalent um jeden Preis ermutigen solle, bei der Stange zu bleiben. Denn schlechte Choreographen gibt es, weltweit, wirklich mehr als genug.

Jochen Schmidt

POWER TO FANTASY!

THE CHOREOGRAPHIC COMPETITION OF COLOGNE AND THE QUESTION OF HOW BEST TO PROMOTE NEW TALENT IN BALLET

The best known, most appealing, and certainly the most momentous of all the slogans painted on the house walls by unknown authors in Paris' Latin Quarter during the student revolts in May of 1968 read, "Power to fantasy!" It is the ideal motto not only for a utopian society, but also for every existing artistic institution, as though formulated for a competition which has taken as its mission the stimulation, promotion and financial support of young choreographers.

There is, of course, no direct connection between the May demonstrations in Paris (or the 1968 student revolts in general) and the Choreographic Competition at the International Summer Academy of Dance in Cologne. But a distant relationship is unmistakable. It was not only that the very first Choreographic Competition in the summer of 1968 manifested solidarity with the student movement by dedicating to that movement its most widely discussed contribution – Hans Kresnik's composition *O Paradise*. The Choreographic Competition arose from the same intellectual climate, from the same socio-cultural mood of departure as the world-wide student protest. Nothing would be further from reality here than to equate the widespread and tragically unsuccessful student revolts with the minimal aesthetic advances of the Cologne Choreographic Competition, thus making the student movement appear harmless. But it cannot be denied that a common discontent with existing structures and their encrustation which showed no signs of loosening underlay both movements, a common uneasiness believed due to an education which was based only on drill and rote learning (for the dancers even more

than for the students), and that this discontent triggered the countermovement. Propagation of fantasy appeared in both spheres to be the most potent means of revitalizing and humanizing rigid traditions.

In practice, however, the Choreographic Competition was almost just as unsuccessful as the student revolts in elevating fantasy to a position of power (or at least to allow it to play a role in the exercise of power). The history of the Competition, now 13 years long, in no way reads like a chain of triumphal victories for fantasy and creativity, but rather as a continuous rise and fall for concepts, projections and qualities.

The very first Competition ended after all as a mishap. The organizers had not devoted a great deal of thought to the principle that all competitors should be given the same rights. The stars of the Competition – choreographers John Neumeier, Gerhard Bohner and Hans Kresnik and the ensembles of the Stuttgart, Berlin and Cologne opera houses – were booked into the Municipal Theater with its manifold technical possibilities, while the other competitors were assigned to a bare Dance Academy room in the Müngersdorf Stadium. As a result the jury (with John Butler as its spokesman) disqualified the privileged but,

nonetheless, found no first prize winner after this correction.

Only the second Competition in 1969 operated under egalitarian rules and brought about results which insured its repetition for a while: Pina Bausch (with her early piece *Im Wind der Zeit/In the Wind of Time),* followed by Gerhard Bohner. But in the very next year the Competition ran into new problems, generated this time by the highly qualified jurors (Antony Tudor, Glen Tetley, Donald McKayle, Peter Wright, Patricia Christopher). Of the works submitted, they authorized only two for public performance, which was thus dropped; instead of appearing in the Municipal Theater for the public, the two remaining compositions were performed in the Academy's rooms for the participants at the Summer Academy (the prizes and prize money were spared).

The years 1971 and 1972 passed without incident, with Gigi-Gheorghe Caciuleanu – currently director of the Théâtre Chorégraphique in Rennes, France – as the paramount prizewinner in both competitions. For the first time actually, the commentators concentrated on the purely aesthetic discussion; jury decisions or technical hitches were not discussed, but rather stylistic trends and artistic qualities. General impression: The Competition in those years gained in craftsmanship while losing in artistic originality – a judgement which was made obsolete by circumstances a year later.

Again the jury (Mary Hinkson, Kurt Jooss, Christopher Bruce, Helmut Baumann and this author) sifted out the majority of the choreographies presented and spared the prizes, while, however, having the remaining three pieces shown publicly in the Municipal Theater; it was, with 37 minutes of net performance time, the shortest Competition programm of all twelve Competitions.

It was only logical that after the renewed artistic slump the Competition should be suspended for a year, to discuss, to decide, and to reach the general opinion that a two-year rhythm would be better for the Choreographic Competition, as the basis for selection would, in any case, be greater. But after the eighth Choreographic Competition in 1976 – with 27 entries, among which were pieces from Reinhild Hoffmann, Carlos Orta and Krisztina Horvath, demonstrating a marked inclination towards modern dance and a tendency for the puzzling and the irrational – had run relatively free of problems, all the unpleasant experiences were forgotten and an annual rhythm for the Competition was reinstated.

The principle was broken only one other time, when Heinz Laurenzen, director of the Competitions as well as of the Summer Academy, inserted a choreographic workshop between the ninth and tenth Choreographic Competitions, which finally proved to be the weaker solution in comparison to the Competitions. The loss of spontaneity and artistic openness was not balanced out by any qualitative improvement.

If anyone had ordered the serpentine history of the Competition to pass in review, he would not have been able to give an unequivocal answer to the question of its success – and certainly not a clearly positive answer. It is true that virtually all of the new choreographers who are of importance to the German ballet scene have at one time or another taken part in the Competitions: Pina Bausch, Reinhild Hoffmann, Susanne Linke, Gerhard Bohner, Hans Kresnik and John Neumeier. Some of them have won prizes in Cologne and at least for Pina Bausch the first prize in Cologne was an important encouragement for her further work and on the path to international recognition; she won this prize in 1969, long before she had attracted the attention of the German public and the German municipal theater system.

Competition participants of international stature are more rare than not; except for Caciuleanu and Alejandro Witzmann-Anaya, who in 1975 garnered a prize, the most conspicuous participants in Cologne are foreigners employed in German ensembles (such as Carlos Orta or Zoltan Imre). Actually the only one whose career – or at least the acceleration of his career is indebted to the Choreographic Competition is the two-time winner Caciuleanu, although his talent and humor would certainly have

brought him to the top even without the confirmation of the Cologne awards.

Under such circumstances no one will be likely to overestimate the usefulness of the Choreographic Competition in its hitherto history. But to doubt its necessity would be just as incorrect; certain – and not minor – merits, over and above the function of a barometer for aesthetic trends and styles, can hardly be disputed. To describe them, one must make a wide detour and discuss the basic requirements of choreographic training.

Building furniture, repairing defective autos or televisions, tailoring a suit, spicing a delicate sauce, and professional butchery of an animal carcass – these and many other skills can be learned in exactly designed training curricula under the tutelage of experienced, knowledgeable craftsmen. Courses of study have even been laid out for most of the artistic professions. There are academies and colleges for orchestral musicians and piano soloists, for singers and dancers, sculptors and painters, actors and architects. The cinematic arts, just like composition, can be learned at an institution of higher education. There are directors' courses for both orchestra and theater, even writing novels, poems and plays – next to painting and composing, the arts with the greatest measure of solitude during creation – are taught on an academic level in some places.

Only choreographers are, in every case, self-taught. Nowhere on earth are there training courses or institutes for them. What they learn – even in the composition classes of the Summer Academy – they learn not through instruction, but only through experience and observation, in any case, by looking over the shoulder of a senior choreographer while working as assistant, and eventually also by studying the compositions of others. But in the last analysis no one has ever become a choreographer only by being an assistant. Real learning and development are possible only by creating one's own pieces, however defective and imitative they may initially be.

Choreographers are, in every case, self-taught. This claim also has validity in another sense. It may, from time to time, seem that choreographers arise in particular numbers in an atmosphere where an established creator of ballet is working, providing a model and guidelines for younger aspirants. As an example one can take American modern dance, whose significant second-generation choreographers almost all have passed through the Martha Graham school, or Stuttgart and John Cranko, who can in a certain sense be seen as the artistic progenitor of such diverse choreographers as Jiři Kylián and John Neu-

meier. But such examples characterize more a minority and the exception to the rule, according to which choreographers of stature are less often found to have arisen in the wake of another than in an artistic vacuum.

One becomes a choreographer either from an imitative drive or out of displeasure with the ballet aesthetic currently prevalent – and the really creative choreographers, those who advance the ballet art form or dance theater, come, without exception out of the second category. They choreograph because they, as dancers – and there are no choreographers who did not begin as dancers – are not satisfied with that which the repertoire and the ballet master may have in stock for them and their friends in the way of dance and roles.

Remarkably enough, such displeasure with conventional aesthetic and with the traditional range of choreographic options offered often appear collectively. It was not only Maurice Béjart and Roland Petit who overcame Serge Lifar's neoclassicism, drained of all life, not only John Cranko and Kenneth MacMillan who revolutionized the London dance theater of the late '40s. In Holland in the late '50s the aversion to traditional ballet brought forth not only choreographers Rudi van Dantzig and Hans van Manen; and in Cologne around 1968 – as the Tanz-Forum and the Choreographic Competition arose almost parallel – it was a whole group of young dancers who wanted to realize their own concepts of a contemporary dance theater: Helmut Baumann and Hans Kresnik, Jürg Burth and Jochen Ulrich. At virtually the same time Pina Bausch (then still studying at the Folkwang-Schule in Essen) and Gerhard Bohner (still a soloist at the German Opera in Berlin) began their choreographic careers in West Germany.

It might sound as though the art of choreography is something that will arise in any case, thanks to some dark artistic drive in the choreographer, the quality of which will be defined only by the talent of the particular choreographer, which as a result will not require any public promotion or support. Anyone who sees the situation in this way is all too naive in his approach to the matter. Different from painting, writing or even composing, choreography cannot arise in the artist's quiet loft, isolated from every environment. There exists no choreographic counterpart to Karl Spitzweg's lonely poet. A painter requires nothing more than canvas (or cardboard, wood, paper) along with brushes and paints, a writer nothing more than paper and a writing utensil, a composer, in addition, only an instrument on which he can test in reality the tones which he has thought out. A choreographer, on the other

QUARTETT,
Ch: Nils Christe (1979)

hand, requires people – dancers – who inspire him and with whom he can work out his sequences of movements – and further, a space in which the work can take place. Choreographic work is thus always work with an ensemble – and be this ensemble ever so small, consisting perhaps of only a single or a few fellow dancers who have placed themselves at the disposal of the beginning choreographer, either out of friendship or interest. The first and most important promotion of any young choreographer takes place in and because of his own group. If the leaders of the ensemble are reasonable (and not jealous of new talent), they will support such processes, helping to promote their own choreographic new generation. But in recent historic examples such reason was not always predominant. The Dutch "uprising" a good twenty years ago was more an uprising against the ballet establishment, and the beginnings of the Cologne Tanz-Forum were found not within the hierarchy of the Cologne theater system but parallel to it, on a platform which patrons – at that time the Society for Artistic Dance, which also backed the beginnings of the Summer Adademy – had provided.

In supplying such platforms, even as temporary institutions, the primary purpose is the promotion of young choreographers. Of course, no institution covering such limited periods of time is in a position to substitute for continuous promotion within one's own group. Only constant work with dancers (and always the same dancers), constantly trying out new dance ideas, the permanent chance for choreographic work, can guarantee the continuous development of a choreographer – as in all cases significant choreography can arise only out of a close association between choreographers and the groups, and never in short-term visits by free-lance choreographers, no matter how good the ensemble may be. Combinations such as Balanchine/New York City Ballet, Cranko/Stuttgart Ballet, van Manen/Nederlands Dans Theater or Béjart/Ballet du XXe Siècle (and in the 19th century Bournonville/Royal Danish Ballet, Petipa-Ivanov/Ballet of the Maryinsky-Theater) have confirmed artistic success through mutual efforts and are representative of many other, though perhaps less prominent, constellations of this type.

Anyone who, as a choreographic beginner, has the good fortune of being able to pursue continuous, creative work within his own group requires, in fact, no other platform – unless for the confirmation of his own achievement and as a public "seal" for his efforts. Confirmation of an artistic achievement with a prize in an international competition does not make a choreographer,

but may promote him by – perhaps – boosting him into better working conditions at home or into a new ensemble which has become aware of him through the prize.

Of course, choreographic competitions such as that at Cologne cannot replace the promotion of young talent through their home companies even then when the prize consists not of monies, cups or diplomas, but rather of work scholarships (which are certainly the most appropriate prizes for choreographic competitions). They are, however, in a position to supplement promotion in the local company in various ways. In addition to the prizes, which may lend a bit more prestige to a few competitors and in the most favorable case – we have mentioned Caciuleanu's repeated honors in Cologne – may have a salutary influence on a career, the competitions offer the possibility of artistic comparison on a larger scale.

To deter, thereby, a would-be choreographer may represent a success for the art of dance. In Cologne someone who might at home be acclaimed as a minor genius can – from the decision of a competent jury and, with some ability for self-estimation, based on a comparison with works by other equally unknown choreographers – also measure where he actually stands: at the head, in the middle or closer to the end of the talent queue. If in Cologne one is brought back to the solid footing of reality and determines that he or she perhaps was not born to choreograph, after all, then this would be no minor success for the Competition.

Choreographers are, in fact, sown extremely thin; among 500 dancers, John Cranko once said, perhaps one has the prerequisites necessary for a choreographer. But that must in no way mean that one should encourage at all costs every mini-talent to continue his work. Then world wide, there is certainly no dearth of second-rate choreographers.

SCHRILL/SHRILL,
Ch: Robert Solomon (1975)

HEITER BIS WOLKIG/
PARTLY CLOUDY,
Ch: Marilén Breuker (1977)

gegenüber/opposite page
QUATRES ELEMENTS, MOINS UN
A LA RECHERCHE DU SENS DE L'HISTOIRE,
Ch: Cathérine Morelle (1977)

diese Seite/this page
oben/top
ELVIRA,
Ch: Margaret Hurd (1976)
Mitte/middle
UPTIGHT,
Ch: Julio Padilla (1975)
unten/bottom
BALLADE,
Ch: Krisztina Horvath (1977)

gegenüber/opposite page
oben/above
UPTIGHT,
Ch: Julio Padilla (1975)
unten/below
IM WIND DER ZEIT,
Ch: Pina Bausch,
Pina Bausch (1969),
Foto: Pieter Kooistra

diese Seite/this page
oben/above
APRES-MIDI D'UN FAUNE,
Ch: Jorge Sansinanea (1976)
unten/below
WHITE DANCE,
Ch: Takashi Koma,
Eiko Otake (1973)

diese Seite/this page
oben/top
ODE,
Ch: Diane Broman (1979)
Mitte/middle
FROM „FORGOTTEN HORIZON" DALI,
Ch: Marcela Aguilar (1976)
unten/bottom
DIE BEGEGNUNG DES CORNELIUS,
Ch: Ernesto Hirt (1976)

gegenüber/opposite page
CREPUSCULE,
Ch: Jean-Marc Forêt (1977)

gegenüber/opposite page
oben/top
EMPTY MOUNTAIN,
Ch: Hsueh-Tung Chen (1979)
Mitte/middle
A LA CHARME DES JEUNES FILLES EN FLEURS,
Ch: Jürg Aebersold (1976)
unten/bottom
PRIERE,
Ch: Pascale Messager (1976)

diese Seite/this page
HELIX,
Ch: Gael Alma Stepanek (1979)

Internationale Sommerakademie des Tanzes
International Summer Academy Of Dance

Jahr/Year	1957	1958	1959
Ort/City	Krefeld	Krefeld	Krefeld
Dauer/Duration	5.–19. August	4.–17. August	26. Juli–9. August
Leitung/Direction	Laurenzen/Wendel	Laurenzen/Wendel	Laurenzen/Wendel
Teilnehmerzahl/Number of Participants	174	253	349
Ausländische Teilnehmer/Foreign Participants	35/20%	59/23%	148/42%
Klassischer Tanz/Classical Dance	Victor Gsovsky Boris Kniaseff Peggy van Praagh	Victor Gsovsky Boris Kniaseff Elvira Roné	Victor Gsovsky Nadine Nicolaeva Legat Lia Schubert Charlotte Sevelin
Moderner Tanz/Modern Dance	Rosalia Chladek	Rosalia Chladek Laura Sheleen	Dore Hoyer
Folklore-Tanz/Character Dance	–	José de Udaeta	Emma Lugossy José de Udaeta
Jazz-Tanz/Jazz Dance	–	–	Walter Nicks
Historischer Tanz/Historical Dance	–	–	–
Pantomime/Mime	–	–	–
Komposition/Composition	–	–	–

Jahr/Year	1965	1966	1967
Ort/City	Köln	Köln	Köln
Dauer/Duration	10.–25. Juli	9.–24. Juli	8.–23. Juli
Leitung/Direction	Bolender/Laurenzen	Laurenzen/Lindlar	Laurenzen/Lindlar
Teilnehmerzahl/Number of Participants	578	525	463
Ausländische Teilnehmer/Foreign Participants	208/35%	204/38%	185/40%
Klassischer Tanz/Classical Dance	Peter Appel Marika Besobrasova Todd Bolender Anton Dolin Charlotte Sevelin Maria Tallchief	Peter Appel Sonia Arova Edite Frandsen Charlotte Sevelin Maria Surowiak Jonathan Watts	Peter Appel Sonia Arova Roland Casenave Edite Frandsen Rosella Hightower Charlotte Sevelin Maria Surowiak Jonathan Watts
Moderner Tanz/Modern Dance	Yuriko Kikuchi Paul Taylor	Yuriko Kikuchi	Yuriko Kikuchi
Folklore-Tanz/Character Dance	Katalin Balogh Ursula Knaflewsky Csaba Palfi José de Udaeta	Ursula Knaflewsky José de Udaeta Boguslav Wolczynski	Ursula Knaflewsky José de Udaeta Boguslav Wolczynski
Jazz-Tanz/Jazz Dance	Jeanna Belkin Christiane de Rougemont	Alvin Ailey Frank Wagner	Walter Nicks Frank Wagner
Historischer Tanz/Historical Dance	–	Brigitte Garski	Brigitte Garski
Pantomime/Mime	Samy Molcho	Henryk Tomaszewski	–
Komposition/Composition	John Cranko	John Butler	John Butler

1960	1961	1962	1963	1964
Krefeld	Köln	Köln	Köln	Köln
31. Juli–14. August	30. Juli–15. August	29. Juli–12. August	14.–28. Juli	19. Juli–2. August
Laurenzen/Wendel	Laurenzen/von Milloss	Laurenzen/von Milloss	Bolender/Laurenzen	Bolender/Laurenzen
402	548	551	568	591
165/41%	218/39%	233/42%	221/38%	214/36%
Alexandra Danilova Victor Gsovsky Nora Kiss Lia Schubert Charlotte Sevelin	René Bon Anton Dolin Victor Gsovksy Nora Kiss Charlotte Sevelin	René Bon Anton Dolin Nora Kiss Charlotte Sevelin Léon Woizikowski	Marika Besobrasova René Bon Anton Dolin Felia Doubrovska Charlotte Sevelin Léon Woizikowski	Marika Besobrasova Anton Dolin Felia Doubrovska Nora Kiss Charlotte Sevelin Léon Woizikowski
Marianne Vogelsang	Jean Cébron Joseph Gifford Anna Sokolov Marianne Vogelsang	Anna Sokolov Marianne Vogelsang	Yuriko Kikuchi Marianne Vogelsang	Yuriko Kikuchi Marianne Vogelsang
Branko Marković José de Udaeta	Louis Gromaz Annemarie Hoth Branko Marković José de Udaeta	José de Udaeta Léon Woizikowski	Ursula Knaflewsky José de Udaeta Léon Woizikowski	Ursula Knaflewsky Csaba Palfi José de Udaeta
Walter Nicks	Walter Nicks Bob de Witt	Walter Nicks Claude Thompson	Jean Mattox Frank Pietri	Talley Beatty Frank Wagner
–	–	–	Marianne Vogelsang	Marianne Vogelsang
–	–	Samy Molcho	Samy Molcho	–
Gise Furtwängler Erich Walter	–	Aurel von Milloss	Todd Bolender	Todd Bolender

1968	1969	1970	1971	1972
Köln	Köln	Köln	Köln	Köln
30. Juni–14. Juli	6.–20. Juli	2.–16. Juli	4.–18. Juli	2.–16. Juli
Laurenzen/Lindlar	Laurenzen/Lindlar	Laurenzen/Lindlar	Laurenzen/Lindlar	Laurenzen/Lindlar
494	477	559	524	573
242/49%	229/48%	313/56%	273/52%	315/55%
Peter Appel René Bon Edite Frandsen Valentina Pereyaslavec Charlotte Sevelin Georges Skibine Marjorie Tallchief Jonathan Watts	Peter Appel René Bon Edite Frandsen Henning Kronstam Valentina Pereyaslavec Charlotte Sevelin Peter Wright	Peter Appel Edite Frandsen Henning Kronstam Charlotte Sevelin Antony Tudor Peter Wright Hector Zaraspe	Peter Appel Scott Douglas Edite Frandsen Eva Géczy Tatjana Grantzeva Henning Kronstam Hector Zaraspe	Peter Appel Edite Frandsen Eva Géczy Tatjana Grantzeva José Pares Hector Zaraspe
Yuriko Kikuchi	Yuriko Kikuchi Anna Mittelholzer	Patricia Christopher Yuriko Kikuchi Anna Mittelholzer	Mary Hinkson Anna Mittelholzer Glen Tetley	Brigitte Garski Mary Hinkson Anna Mittelholzer Norman Walker
Ursula Knaflewsky José de Udaeta Boguslav Wolczynski	Zsuzsa Horváth Ursula Knaflewsky Ernö Pesovar José de Udaeta	Zsuzsa Horváth Ursula Knaflewsky Ernö Pesovar José de Udaeta	Bill Hamilton Ursula Knaflewsky José de Udaeta	Ursula Knaflewsky Branko Marković Madhavi Mudgal José de Udaeta
Frank Wagner	Frank Wagner	Donald McKayle Lynn Simonson	Donald McKayle Lynn Simonson	Fred Benjamin Jay Norman Lynn Simonson Yoe Lan Tjoa
Brigitte Garski	Brigitte Garski	Brigitte Garski	Brigitte Garski	Brigitte Garski
–	–	–	Samy Molcho	Samy Molcho
John Butler	Gise Furtwängler Lucas Hoving	Glen Tetley	Patricia Christopher Glen Tetley	Hans van Manen

Internationale Sommerakademie des Tanzes
International Summer Academy Of Dance

Jahr/Year	1973	1974	1975	1976
Ort/City	Köln	Köln	Köln	Köln
Dauer/Duration	24. Juni–8. Juli	14.–28. Juli	13.–27. Juli	4.–18. Juli
Leitung/Direction	Laurenzen/Lindlar	Laurenzen/Lindlar	Laurenzen/Lindlar	Laurenzen/Lindlar
Teilnehmerzahl/ Number of Participants	536	627	644	668
Ausländische Teilnehmer/ Foreign Participants	284/53%	351/56%	348/54%	341/51%
Klassischer Tanz/ Classical Dance	Peter Appel René Bon Edite Frandsen Eva Géczy Kirsten Ralov Maria Surowiak Patricia Wilde Boguslav Wolczynski	Peter Appel Edite Frandsen Eva Gugel Melissa Hayden Viktor Rona Marian Sarstädt	Peter Appel Edite Frandsen Alan Howard Ulrich Köster Márta Metzger Viktor Rona Jonathan Watts	Peter Appel Una Kai Ulrich Köster Márta Metzger Lia Schubert Eileen Ward Jonathan Watts
Placement	–	–	Zena Rommett	Zena Rommett
Moderner Tanz/ Modern Dance	Christopher Bruce Richard Gain Brigitte Garski Mary Hinkson	Brigitte Garski Mary Hinkson Betty Jones Anna Price	Viola Farber Mary Hinkson Betty Jones Fritz Lüdin	Brigitte Garski Mary Hinkson Don Redlich
Folklore-Tanz/ Character Dance	Ursula Knaflewsky Agnes Roboz José de Udaeta	Anatoli A. Borsow Ursula Knaflewsky Agnes Roboz José de Udaeta	Andrei Klimov Ursula Knaflewsky Agnes Roboz José de Udaeta	Anatoli A. Borsow T. N. Gayathri Ursula Knaflewsky Emma Maleras Agnes Roboz José de Udaeta
Jazz-Tanz/Jazz Dance	Luigi Matt Mattox Yoe Lan Tjoa	Matt Mattox Lynn Simonson Jo Jo Smith	Helena Högberg Matt Mattox Lynn Simonson	Charles Kelley Donald McKayle Lynn Simonson
Step-Tanz/Tap Dance	–	–	Karen Rabinowitz	Karen Rabinowitz
Historischer Tanz/ Historical Dance	Brigitte Garski	Karl-Heinz Taubert	Brigitte Garski	Brigitte Garski
Kinder-Tanz/ Children's Dance	–	–	–	–
Tai Chi Chuan	–	–	–	–
Pantomime/Mime	Samy Molcho	Samy Molcho	Samy Molcho	Samy Molcho
Komposition/ Composition	Hans van Manen	Hans van Manen	Hans van Manen	Nina Fonaroff Hans van Manen

1977	1978	1979	1980	1981
Köln	Köln	Köln	Köln	Köln
26. Juni–10. Juli	25. Juni–9. Juli	24. Juni–8. Juli	22. Juni–6. Juli	5.–19. Juli
Laurenzen/Lindlar	Laurenzen/ von Rautenstrauch	Laurenzen/ von Rautenstrauch	Laurenzen/ von Rautenstrauch	Laurenzen/ von Rautenstrauch
684	676	697	724	709
328/48%	335/49,5%	359/51,5%	356/49%	364/51,3%
Joelle Mazet Márta Metzger Robert Poujol Jelena N. Schemtschuschina Michael Simms Eileen Ward Jonathan Watts	Ursula Borrmann Maria Fay Attilio Labis Joelle Mazet Simon Mottram Christiane Vlassi Eileen Ward Jonathan Watts	Ursula Borrmann Renita Exter Edite Frandsen Carlos Gacio Márta Metzger Simon Mottram Robert Poujol Eileen Ward	Peter Appel Ursula Borrmann Carlos Gacio Joelle Mazet Márta Metzger Simon Mottram Ruxandra Racovitza Eileen Ward	Peter Appel Dinna Björn Ursula Borrmann Joelle Mazet Simon Mottram Sergiu Stefanski Eileen Ward
Zena Rommett	Zena Rommett	–	–	–
Brigitte Garski Mary Hinkson Betty Jones Carmen de Lavallade Fritz Lüdin	Ruth Currier Brigitte Garski Mary Hinkson	Ruth Currier Brigitte Garski Mary Hinkson Pearl Lang	Trisha Brown Louis Falco Brigitte Garski Mary Hinkson Mariko Sanjo Clay Taliaferro	Brigitte Garski Mary Hinkson Clay Taliaferro Clive Thompson
Flora Albaicin Anatoli A. Borsow Ursula Knaflewsky Agnes Roboz José de Udaeta	Anatoli A. Borsow Ursula Knaflewsky Agnes Roboz José de Udaeta	Anatoli A. Borsow Ursula Knaflewsky Madhavi Mudgal Agnes Roboz Susana	Ruth Ashkenazi Anatoli A. Borsow Ursula Knaflewsky Susana Sándor Timár	Ruth Ashkenazi Anatoli A. Borsow Ursula Knaflewsky Susana Sándor Timár
Alvin McDuffie Donald McKayle Lynn Simonson	Alvin McDuffie Donald McKayle Michael Owens Lynn Simonson	Gus Giordano Matt Mattox Alvin McDuffie Michael Owens	Nat Horne Matt Mattox Alvin McDuffie Michael Owens	Matt Mattox Alvin McDuffie Lynn Simonson Bruce Taylor
Hildie Woode	Hildie Woode	Jerry Ames	Jerry Ames	Jerry Ames
Eva Campianu	Eva Campianu	Brigitte Garski	Brigitte Garski	Brigitte Garski
Gisela Peters-Rohse	Gisela Peters-Rohse	–	–	Gisela Peters-Rohse
–	–	Gia-fu Feng	–	–
Samy Molcho	Samy Molcho	–	Elie Levy Samy Molcho	Samy Molcho
Hans van Manen Lisa Ullmann	Hans van Manen Doris Rudko	Hans van Manen Doris Rudko	Hans van Manen	Hans van Manen

Choreographischer Wettbewerb Köln
Choreographic Competition Cologne

Jahr/Year	1968	1969	1970	1971
Jury/Jury	**John Butler** René Bon Yuriko Kikuchi Georges Skibine José de Udaeta Frank Wagner	**Lucas Hoving** René Bon Gise Furtwängler Yuriko Kikuchi Peter Wright	**Glen Tetley** Patricia Christopher Donald McKayle Antony Tudor Peter Wright	**Glen Tetley** Patricia Christopher Mary Hinkson Donald McKayle Hector Zaraspe
Preisgekrönte Werke/ Prizewinning works 1. Preis/1st prize		**Im Wind der Zeit** Pina Bausch, Essen Musik: Mirko Dorner	Preise wurden nicht vergeben/ Prizes were not awarded.	**Stimmen** Gigi-Gheorghe Caciuleanu, Bukarest Musik: Collage
2. Preis/ 2nd prize	a) **Metamorphosis** Zoltan Imre, Budapest Musik: Endre Szervansky b) **Lamento** Diana Isabel Obedman, Buenos Aires, Musik: Janko Jezovsek	**Silvia frustriert Anspannen – abschlaffen** Gerhard Bohner, Berlin Musik: Jannis Xenakis		**Fantasy** Saeko Ichinohe, New York Musik: Toru Takemitsu
3. Preis/ 3rd prize		**Summer Music** Suzanne Hywel, London Musik: Samuel Barber		
Anerkennungspreise/ Honorable mentions	**Volutes** Aline Roux, Paris Musik: Johann Sebastian Bach	**Zinctum** Kenneth Rinker, Berlin Musik: S. Cervetti **Verschuivingen** Helene Thémans, Rotterdam Musik: Gustave Charpentier		**Klänge Istriens** Tihana Skrinjaric, Zagreb Musik: Matetić Tonjgev **Ballet Six** Ricardo Nunez, Marseille Musik: Béla Bartók
Zuschauerpreise/Prizes awarded by spectators				

1972	1973	*1975	1976	1977
Hans van Manen	**Hans van Manen**	**Horst Koegler**	**Jochen Ulrich**	**Kurt Jooss**
Helmut Baumann	Helmut Baumann	Mary Hinkson	Nina Fonaroff	Mary Hinkson
Kurt Jooss	Christopher Bruce	Betty Jones	Mary Hinkson	Kurt Peters
Horst Koegler	Mary Hinkson	Hans van Manen	Jiři Kylián	Jochen Schmidt
	Kurt Jooss	Jochen Ulrich	Donald McKayle	Lynn Simonson
	Jochen Schmidt	Jonathan Watts	Kurt Peters	Jochen Ulrich
			Jens Wendland	Jonathan Watts
Kerzenschatten	Preise wurden	2 gleichrangige Preise/	2 gleichrangige Preise/	**Crépuscule**
Gigi-Gheorghe	nicht vergeben/	2 equal prizes	2 equal prizes	Jean-Marc Foret, Nancy
Caciuleanu	Prizes were	**Entre Tonnerre et**	**Fin al Punto**	Musik: Richard Strauss
Musik: Maurice Ravel	not awarded.	**Oiseau**	Reinhild Hoffmann, Essen	
		Alejandro Witzmann-	Musik: Wilhelm Killmayer	
		Anaya, Mexiko-City	**Der Fehler**	
		Musik: Walter Carlos/	Carlos Orta, Köln	
		Karl-Heinz Stockhausen	Musik: Hector Campos	
		Puppe?	Parsi	
		Susanne Linke		
		Musik: Wolfgang		
		Amadeus Mozart		
Equivalence				Zwei 2. Preise wurden
Zoltan Imre, Köln				vergeben für:
Musik: Collage				Two 2nd prizes were
				awarded for:
				Opus Vivaldi
				Aimé de Lignière,
				Antwerpen
				Musik: Antonio Vivaldi
				Tip of the Iceberg
				Sjoerd Schwibbetus,
				Amsterdam
				(ohne Musik)
Game Over				
Antonius Lutgerink,				
Rotterdam				
Musik: Collage				
Individuum		a) **Men's Trio** und	a) **La Chaise**	**Images on a Meadow**
Bernd Berg, Stuttgart		b) **Bovary**	Robert Thomas, Straßburg	Daryl Gray, Brüssel
Musik:		Patrice Regnier, New York	Musik: Ch. Chaynes	Musik: Franz Liszt
Witold Lutoslawski		Musik: 12. und 13.	b) **Rêve d'enfant**	
		Jahrhundert	Robert Thomas	
			Musik: George Crumb	
		1. **Serenata de un**		
		passente		
		Carlos Orta, Köln		
		2. wie Anerkennungspreis		
		like honorable mention		
		3. **Regards**		
		Robert Thomas, Straßburg		

* 1974 wurde kein Wettbewerb durchgeführt/In 1974, no competition was organized.

Choreographischer Wettbewerb Köln
Choreographic Competition Cologne

Jahr/Year	1978	1979	1980	1981
Jury/Jury	1978 wurde statt eines Wettbewerbs eine Choreographische Werkstatt durchgeführt. In 1978, a Choreographic Workshop was organized instead of a competition. Ensembles/Companies: Rush Dance Company, New York; Moving Visions, London; Folkwang-Tanztheater, Essen; Tanzforum Köln; Bayerische Staatsoper München; Junction Dance Company, London; Le Cercle, Paris; Théâtre de L'Arche, Paris; Ensemble Reinhild Hoffmann, Essen; Ensemble Jean-Marc Foret, Nancy; Ensemble Carlos Orta, Köln	**Hans van Manen** Gigi-Gheorghe Caciuleanu Harro Eisele Martin Kazmeier Pearl Lang John Percival Doris Rudko Jochen Ulrich	**Bengt Häger** Gigi-Gheorghe Caciuleanu Harro Eisele Brigitte Garski Susanne Linke Mariko Sanjo Heinz Spoerli	**Bengt Häger** Gigi-Gheorghe Caciuleanu Brigitte Garski Manfred Gräter Clay Taliaferro Clive Thompson Lenny Westerdijk
Preisgekrönte Werke/ Prizewinning works 1. Preis/1st prize		**Quartett** Nils Christe, Den Haag Musik: Dimitri Schostakowitsch **3-Way with Ethyl** John Goodwin, New York; Musik: Camille Saint-Saëns	Der 1. Preis wurde nicht vergeben/1st prize was not awarded.	**Anima** Rhys Martin, London (ohne Musik)
2. Preis/2nd prize			Drei 2. Preise wurden vergeben für: Three 2nd prizes were awarded for: **The Knife against the Wave** Doris Seiden – Wendy Shankin, New York; Musik: Johannes Brahms/ Ludwig van Beethoven **Anillos sin Dedos** Avelina Arguelles Miranda, Barcelona; Musik: The Dead Boys **Passacaglia** Gilberto Agustin Ruiz-Lang, Barcelona; Musik: Georg Friedrich Händel	(Ohne Titel/Untitled) Bruno Jacquin, Paris; Musik: Krysztof Penderecki
3. Preis/3rd prize				
Anerkennungspreise/ Honorable mentions		**Ode** Diane Broman, Brüssel; Musik: Johann Sebastian Bach/ Egberto Gismonti/ Musik aus Zentralafrika	Drei Anerkennungspreise für: Three honorable mentions for: **Passatges** Elisa Huertas Pantaleón, Barcelona; **Kindertotenlieder** Ralf Dörnen, Köln; **Suite** Jean-Claude Gallotta, Grenoble	Zwei Anerkennungspreise für: Two honorable mentions for: **Running Into Color** Darlene L. Stevens, London; Musik: Anders Nordmark; **Kein Lächeln für Alice** Christine Brunel, Essen; Musik: Limonaire/ Johann Sebastian Bach
Zuschauerpreise/ Prizes awarded by spectators			Eine lobende Anerkennung für/An acknowledgement for: **I am a Motherless Child** Alexander Klayman, Köln	Einen Sonderpreis für/ A special prize for: **Ildiko Pongor,** Budapest, in **Equinoxe** von Laszló Péter

Fotos in diesem Artikel,
falls nicht anders angegeben/
Photos in this article,
if not otherwise credited:
Annelise Löffler

diese Seite/this page
oben/top
IMAGES ON A MEADOW,
Ch: Daryl Gray (1977)
Mitte/middle
Klasse von/class of
URSULA BORRMANN (1980)
unten/bottom
EVA CAMPIANU,
Abschlußdemonstration/
closing presentation (1977)

gegenüber/opposite page
oben links/top left
SILVIA FRUSTRIERT,
Ch: Gerhard Bohner (1969)
oben rechts/top right
SONATE FÜR VIOLONCELLO
UND ORCHESTER,
Ch: André Doutreval,
Eröffnung der 13.
Internationalen Sommerakademie/
Opening of the 13. International
Summer Academy, 1969
Mitte links u. unten links/
middle left and bottom left
IM WIND DER ZEIT,
Ch: Pina Bausch (1969)
Mitte rechts/middle right
ZINCTUM,
Ch: Kenneth Rinker (1969)
ANSPANNEN – ABSCHLAFFEN,
Ch: Gerhard Bohner (1969),
Fotos: Pieter Kooistra

Fotos auf dieser
und der gegenüberliegenden Seite/
Photos on this
and the opposite page
LOUIS FALCO DANCE COMPANY
bei einer/during a
lecture demonstration (1980)

220

gegenüber/opposite page
oben/top
THE KNIFE AGAINST THE WAVE,
Ch: Doris Seiden, Wendy Shankin,
Calck Hook Dance Theater (1980)
Mitte/middle
ANILLOS SIN DEDOS,
Ch: Avelina Arguelles Miranda (1980)
unten/bottom
Preisverleihung des
11. Choreographischen Wettbewerbs 1980/
Awarding of prizes,
11. Choreographic Competition 1980,
(v.l.n.r./left to right)
ALEXANDER KLAYMAN,
ELISA HUERTAS PANTALEON,
GILBERTO RUIZ-LANG,
AVELINA ARGUELLES MIRANDA,
RALF DÖRNEN, WENDY SHANKIN,
DORIS SEIDEN,
JEAN CLAUDE GALLOTTA,
Fotos: Archiv Sommerakademie

diese Seite/this page
von oben nach unten/
top to bottom
Klasse von/class of
ALVIN MCDUFFIE,
Abschlußveranstaltung
der 24. Internationalen
Sommerakademie/
Closing presentation
of the 24. International
Summer Academy, 1980,
PASSACAGLIA,
Ch: Gilberto Ruiz-Lang (1980),
Teilnehmer des 12. Choreographischen Wettbewerbs/
Participants of the 12. Choreographic Competition, 1980,
ELASTICITY,
Ch: Patrice Regnier (1980)
alle Fotos dieser Seite/
all photos on this page:
Detlef Herchenbach

Fotos in diesem Artikel,
falls nicht anders angegeben,/
Photos in this article,
of not otherwise credited:
Annelise Löffler

oben/top
MARY HINKSON, ALFRED BIOLEK
Mitte/middle
HSUEH-TUNG CHEN, ALFRED BIOLEK
unten/bottom
KATALIN CSARNOY,
DANIEL LOMMEL,
HELMUT SCHEIER
in „Tanz & Talk",
Abschlußveranstaltung
der 23. Internationalen
Sommerakademie/
Closing presentation
of the 23. International
Summer Academy 1979

Die künstlerische Leitung und Dozenten des Instituts sind ein Team von Pädagogen, deren überwiegend internationales Renommee eine qualifizierte Tanzausbildung garantiert.

Durch Beschäftigung der Studenten in Aufführungen der Kölner Oper und des Kölner Tanz-Forums wird von der Schulleitung ein praxisbezogener Unterricht angestrebt.

Praktische Erfahrungen bieten auch die innerhalb des Instituts bestehenden Ensembles. So etwa eine Gruppe für Spanischen Tanz und die Corona di Danza, ein Ensemble für Historischen Tanz.

Eine weitere Gruppe wird für Tanzdemonstrationen in allgemeinbildenden Schulen eingesetzt. Ihr Ziel ist es, Tanz als künstlerisches Medium einem breiten Publikum zugänglich zu machen.

Ähnliche Aufgaben erfüllen auch die dem Institut vorgeschalteten Kinderballett- und Vorbereitungsklassen. Kinder ab fünftem Lebensjahr kommen hier in den Genuß tänzerischer Früherziehung.

Für Tanzpädagogen aus dem Bereich der privaten Ballettschulen werden an der Akademie Seminare und Wochenendlehrgänge zur beruflichen Weiterbildung durchgeführt. Die Kurse beinhalten hauptsächlich methodische Lernziele der Tanzpädagogik.

Ein spezielles Unterrichtsangebot besteht für Laien, die am tänzerischen Geschehen interessiert sind. Ihnen bietet das Institut in mehreren Kursen Einblick in die Techniken der verschiedenen Tanzstile.

Mit diesem breitgefächerten Angebot erfüllt das Institut für Bühnentanz als staatliche und kommunale Ausbildungsstätte einen umfassenden kulturellen Auftrag.

Während der jetzt 20jährigen Arbeit unter der künstlerischen Leitung von Aurel von Milloss, Todd Bolender, Peter Appel und Kurt Peters wurden an diesem Institut zahlreiche bekannte Tänzer, Tanzpädagogen und Choreographen ausgebildet.

Das Institut für Bühnentanz ist eine Abteilung der Rheinischen Musikschule der Stadt Köln sowie der Staatlichen Hochschule für Musik Köln. Es umfaßt folgende Abteilungen:

DAS INSTITUT FÜR BÜHNENTANZ KÖLN

NACHDEM DIE INTERNATIONALE SOMMERAKADEMIE DES TANZES IHR DOMIZIL IN KÖLN ERRICHTET HATTE, WURDE IM JAHRE 1961 AUF INITIATIVE VON HEINZ LAURENZEN UND AUREL VON MILLOSS DAS INSTITUT FÜR BÜHNENTANZ — BALLETTAKADEMIE — ZUR AUSBILDUNG PROFESSIONELLER TÄNZER UND TANZPÄDAGOGEN GEGRÜNDET.

I. KINDERBALLETT

a) Vorschulklassen: 5. bis 7. Lebensjahr
Die Vorschulklassen haben vornehmlich musischen Charakter: rhythmisches Spiel, Improvisation, Entfaltung der Kreativität.
b) Schulklassen: 7. bis 16. Lebensjahr
(Bitte Sonderprospekt *Kinderballett* anfordern.)

II. VORBEREITUNGS- UND AUSBILDUNGSKLASSEN

a) Vorbereitungsklassen: 7. bis 9. Lebensjahr
b) Ausbildungsklassen: 10. bis 16. Lebensjahr
c) Theaterklassen

Unterrichtsplan der Ausbildungs- und Theaterklassen:

1. Jahr: 3 x wöchentlich

1 Std. Klassischer Tanz
1 Std. Improvisation

2. Jahr: 3 x wöchentlich

1 Std. Klassischer Tanz
1 Std. Improvisation

3. Jahr: 4 x wöchentlich

1 Std. Klassischer Tanz
1 Std. Kastagnetten
1 Std. Moderner Tanz
Klavierunterricht

4. Jahr: 4 x wöchentlich

1 Std. Klassischer Tanz
1 Std. Folklore-Tanz
1 Std. Moderner Tanz
Klavierunterricht

5. Jahr: 5 x wöchentlich

1,5 Std. Klassischer Tanz
1 Std. Folklore-Tanz
1 Std. Moderner Tanz
Klavierunterricht, Musik- und Tanzgeschichte

6. Jahr: 6 x wöchentlich

1,5 Std. Klassischer Tanz
1 Std. Folklore-Tanz
1 Std. Moderner Tanz
Klavierunterricht, Musik- und Tanzgeschichte

Der Unterricht in den Ausbildungsklassen findet parallel zum Unterricht in den allgemeinbildenden Schulen statt. Als Abschluß wird Mittlere Reife bzw. Abitur angestrebt. Es schließen sich zwei Theaterjahre mit Ganztagsunterricht an:

7. Jahr: 2 x täglich Klassischer Tanz

1 x wöchentlich Repertoire
1 x wöchentlich Pas de deux
3 x wöchentlich Moderner Tanz
3 x wöchentlich Folklore-Tanz
Klavierunterricht, Musik-, Tanz- und Kulturgeschichte, Musiktheorie

8. Jahr: 2 x wöchentlich Klassischer Tanz

1 x wöchentlich Repertoire
1 x wöchentlich Pas de deux
3 x wöchentlich Moderner Tanz
3 x wöchentlich Folklore-Tanz
Klavierunterricht, Musik-, Tanz- und Kulturgeschichte, Musiktheorie

Unterricht in Historischem Tanz, Jazztanz, Anatomie und Schminktechnik wird in Kursform erteilt.

Die ersten zwei Semester gelten als Probesemester. Aufnahme und Versetzung erfolgen nach besonderen Prüfungen.

III. BERUFSFACHKLASSEN

Das Studium bis zur Bühnenreife dauert für extern aufgenommene Studierende mindestens acht Semester. Der Unterricht findet ganztägig statt.

Studienfächer

Technik des Klassischen Tanzes
Pas de deux
Repertoire
Technik des Modernen Tanzes
(Graham-Technik)
Rhythmik
Improvisation
Komposition
Folklore-Tanz
Kastagnetten-Technik
Historischer Tanz
Jazz-Tanz
Musiktheorie
Musikunterricht (Klavier)
Tanz-, Musik-, Kultur- und Theatergeschichte
Anatomie
Schminktechnik

Nach jedem zweiten Semester finden Zwischenprüfungen statt, die über das weitere Studium entscheiden.

IV. PÄDAGOGISCHES SEMINAR

Das Studium für den Beruf des Tanzpädagogen dauert mindestens vier Semester.
Voraussetzung zur Zulassung ist die Büh-
nenreifeprüfung und eine mehrjährige
Theaterpraxis.

Studienplan:

1. Semester:
Praktische Fächer – Hospitieren

Vorschulklassen: täglich
(Kinderballettschule)
Klassischer Tanz: täglich
Unterstufe: Moderner Tanz
Unterstufe: Folklore-Tanz

Theoretische Fächer
Pro Woche 2 Stunden Kindertanz
Pro Woche 2 Stunden
Moderne Tanz-Technik
Pro Woche 2 Stunden Folklore-Tanz
plus Klavierunterricht/Musikgeschichte/
Tanzgeschichte

2. Semester:
Praktische Fächer – Hospitieren

Vorbereitungs- und Ausbildungsklassen
(Unterstufe)
Klassischer Tanz täglich
Unterstufe: Moderner Tanz
Unterstufe: Folklore-Tanz

Theoretische Fächer
Pro Woche 2 Stunden Klassischer Tanz
Pro Woche 2 Stunden Moderner Tanz
Pro Woche 2 Stunden Folklore-Tanz
plus Klavierunterricht/Musikgeschichte/
Tanzgeschichte

3. Semester:
Praktische Fächer – Hospitieren

Ausbildung Unterstufe und
Ausbildung Oberstufe
Klassischer Tanz: täglich
(Repertoire – Pas de deux)
Unterstufe: Moderner Tanz
Unterstufe: Folklore-Tanz

Theoretische Fächer
Pro Woche 3 Stunden Klassischer Tanz
(1 Std. Unterstufe, 2 Std. Oberstufe)
Pro Woche 2 Stunden Moderner Tanz
(Unterstufe)
Pro Woche 2 Stunden Folklore-Tanz (Unter-
stufe)
Pro Woche 2 Stunden Folklore-Tanz (Unter-
stufe)
plus Klavierunterricht/Musikgeschichte/
Tanzgeschichte

4. Semester:
Praktische Fächer – Hospitieren

Oberstufe: Klassischer Tanz
(Repertoire – Pas de deux)
Moderner Tanz
Unterstufe: Folklore-Tanz

Theoretische Fächer
Pro Woche 2 Stunden Klassischer Tanz
(Oberstufe)
Pro Woche 2 Stunden Moderner Tanz
Pro Woche 2 Stunden Folklore-Tanz
(Unterstufe)
plus Klavierunterricht/Musikgeschichte/
Tanzgeschichte

Kurse: Anatomie, Jazz-Tanz, Historischer
Tanz. Zusätzliche Studienfächer: Pädagogik, tanzbezogene Psychologie, Terminologie, Methodik, Lehrproben.

DOZENTEN DER AKADEMIE

Ursula Borrmann
Klassischer Tanz (Leitung)

Renita Exter
Klassischer Tanz

Brigitte Garski
Moderner Tanz (Graham-Technik),
Rhythmik, Improvisation, Komposition,
Historischer Tanz

Eva Gugel
Klassischer Tanz
Moderner Tanz

Ursula Knaflewsky
Folklore-Tanz
Kastagnetten-Technik

Gisela Peters-Rohse
Kinderballett, Vorschulklassen,
Vorbereitungsklassen

Helmut Scheier
Tanzgeschichte, Theatergeschichte,
Kulturgeschichte

Hans-Joachim Schütz
Klavier, Musiktheorie

Ulrich Steiner
Kinderballett

Peter Vondruska
Klassischer Tanz (Pas de deux, Repertoire)
und Gastdozenten

AFTER THE INTERNATIONAL SUMMER
ACADEMY OF DANCE MADE ITS PERMA-
NENT HOME IN COLOGNE, THE INSTITUTE
FOR STAGE DANCE – BALLETT ACADEMY
– WAS FOUNDED ON THE INITIATIVE OF
HEINZ LAURENZEN AND AUREL VON MIL-
LOSS IN 1961, ITS AIM BEING THE TRAIN-
ING OF PROFESSIONAL DANCERS AND
DANCE TEACHERS.

The artistic direction and teachers of the Institute make up a team of pedagogues
whose international reputation guarantees
a qualified dance education.

By engaging the students in performances
of the Cologne Opera and Cologne Tanz-
Forum, the direction of the Institute aims at
practical training.

Practical experience is offered through
ensembles existing within the Institute:

THE COLOGNE INSTITUTE OF DANCE

Spanish Dance Group and the Corona di
Danza, an ensemble for Historical Dance.

Another group gives dance demonstrations
in public schools, its aim being to make
dance as an artistic medium accessible to a
wider public.

Preparatory and children's classes fulfill
similar tasks. Children from five years of age

onwards benefit from early dance training.

The Institute organizes seminars and week-
end conferences for dance teachers from
private ballet schools in order to provide
them with advanced training. They deal
mainly with methodical aims of dance
education.

Special courses are offered for laymen interested in dance in which the Institute aims to
give insight into the techniques of different
dance styles.

Under the artistic direction of Aurel von Milloss, Todd Bolender, Peter Appel and Kurt
Peters, many well-known dancers, dance
teachers and choreographers have been
trained during the last two decades.

The Institute of Stage Dance is a division of
the Rhenish Music School of the City of
Cologne.

Kurzbiographien der Autoren
Short Biographies of the Authors

URSULA BORRMANN

Ursula Borrmann, geboren 1937 in Dresden. Erster Ballettunterricht mit acht Jahren. 1949 bis 1958 Studium an der Opernballettschule, der Palucca-Schule (beide Dresden) sowie dem Leningrader Choreographischen Institut. 1958 bis 1960 Engagements an der Staatsoper Dresden (Solistin) und am Theater für Oper und Ballett Duschanbe (UdSSR). 1960 bis 1967 Dozentin bzw. Trainingsmeisterin an der Palucca-Schule, Staatsoper Berlin und im Ensemble der NVA. 1967 bis 1976 künstlerische Leiterin der Staatlichen Ballettschule Leipzig. Seit 1978 Dozentin am Institut für Bühnentanz Köln, dessen Leitung sie 1980 übernahm.

Ursula Borrmann, born in Dresden in 1937, received her first ballet training at the age of eight; from 1949 to 1958 studies at the Opera Ballet School and Palucca School (both in Dresden) as well as the Institute of Choreography in Leningrad. From 1958 to 1960 she was engaged at the State Opera in Dresden as a principal dancer and at the Theater for Opera and Ballet, Duschanbe (USSR). From 1960 to 1967 she was teacher and ballet mistress at the Palucca School, State Opera in Berlin and the NVA ensemble. From 1967 to 1976, artistic direction of the State Ballet School in Leipzig. Since 1978 teacher at the Institute of Stage Dance Cologne, the direction of which she assumed in 1980.

ROLF GARSKE

Rolf Garske, geboren 1952 in Lehrte, Niedersachsen. Studium der Theater-, Film- und Fernsehwissenschaft, Germanistik und Kunstgeschichte in Köln. Vorsitzender der Fördervereine für Ballett und Tanztheater der Deutschen Ballett-Bühne e. V. und Gründer des Ballett-Bühnen-Verlages. Herausgeber der Monatszeitschrift Ballett-Info.

Rolf Garske, born in Lehrte, Lower Saxony, West Germany in 1952, studied theater history and criticism, film, art history and German at the University of Cologne. He is the chairman of the Deutsche Ballett-Bühne e. V., an organization which fosters and promotes interest in dance theater and founder of the Ballett-Bühnen-Verlag which publishes the monthly magazine Ballett-Info, of which he is also the editor in chief.

HANS WERNER HENZE

Hans Werner Henze, geboren 1926 in Gütersloh. Zahlreiche Kompositionen für Ballett: u. a. Anrufung Apolls (Dritte Sinfonie, 1949), Jack Pudding, Ballett-Variationen (beide 1949), Rosa Silber (1950), Die schla-fende Prinzessin (1951), Der Idiot (1952), Maratona di danza (1957), Undine (1958), Des Kaisers Nachtigall (1959), Tancredi (1966), Tristan (1974), Orpheus (1979).

Hans Werner Henze, born in Gütersloh in 1926, has written many compositions for ballet: among others Anrufung Apolls (Third Symphony, 1949), Jack Pudding, Ballett-Variationen (both 1949), Rosa Silber (1950), Die schlafende Prinzessin (1951), Der Idiot (1952), Maratona di danza (1957), Undine (1958), Des Kaisers Nachtigall (1959), Tancredi (1966), Tristan (1974), Orpheus (1979).

DEBORAH JOWITT

Deborah Jowitt, geboren 1934 in Los Angeles. Begann 1953 ihre Tanzkarriere, tanzte in Stücken mehrerer Modern-Dance-Choreographen. Begann 1960 zu choreographieren. Aufführungen ihrer Stücke in New York wie auch in anderen Städten der USA. 1967 begann sie für Village Voice über Tanz zu schreiben, seitdem zahlreiche Artikel in anderen Zeitschriften und Zeitungen. Ein Buch ihrer gesammelten Artikel, Dance Beat, erschien 1977. Sie lehrt Tanzgeschichte und -kritik an der New Yorker Universität.

Deborah Jowitt, born in Los Angeles, 1934, began to dance professionally in 1953, performing in works by a number of major modern dance choreographers. She began to choreograph in 1960, and her works were seen both in New York and around the USA. In 1967, she began to write a dance column for the Village Voice. She has also published articles in many other magazines and newspapers. A book of her collected articles, Dance Beat, was published in 1977. She teaches dance history and criticism at New York University.

HORST KOEGLER

Horst Koegler, geboren 1927 in Neuruppin/ Mark Brandenburg. Studium der Germanistik, Musikwissenschaft und Kunstgeschichte in Kiel, dann auch Theaterwissenschaft. Ausbildung als Dramaturg und Regisseur an der Theater-Hochschule Halle/ Saale. Opernregisseur und -dramaturg in Görlitz. Freischaffender Publizist für Tanz- und Musiktheater in Westberlin und Köln. Seit 1977 Musikredakteur der Stuttgarter Zeitung. Buchveröffentlichungen u. a.: Friedrichs Ballettlexikon von A–Z (1972), The Concise Oxford Dictionary of Ballet (1977), Mitherausgeber des deutschen Ballettjahrbuches (seit 1965).

Horst Koegler, born in Neuruppin, Mark Brandenburg in 1927, studied German, musicology and art history in Kiel, as well as theater history. Training and professional work as dramaturgist and director in Halle and Görlitz; free-lance journalist for dance and music theater in West Berlin and Cologne. Since 1977, music editor of the Stuttgarter Zeitung. Publications among others: Friedrichs Ballettlexikon von A–Z (1972), The Concise Oxford Dictionary of Ballet (1977), co-editor of the German ballet yearbook (since 1965).

JIŘI KYLIÁN

Jiři Kylián, geboren 1947 in Prag. Tschechischer Tänzer und Choreograph. Studium am Prager Konservatorium und der Royal Ballet School. Ab 1968 Tänzer beim Stuttgarter Ballett, begann 1970 zu choreographieren u. a. für das Nederlands Dans Theater, dessen künstlerische Leitung er 1976 übernahm.

Jiři Kylián, born in Prague in 1947, is a Czechoslovakian dancer and choreographer. He studied at the Prague Conservatory and Royal Ballet School, London. In 1968, he joined the Stuttgart Ballet as a dancer, started to choreograph in 1970 for the Nederlands Dans Theater, the artistic direction of which he assumed in 1976.

JOHN PERCIVAL

John Percival, geboren 1927 in London, studierte am St. Catherine's College, Oxford. Seit 1965 Ballettkritiker der Times, seit 1950 für Dance & Dancers, dessen Mitherausgeber er seit 1965 und dessen Herausgeber er seit 1981 ist. Veröffentlichungen: Antony Tudor (1963), Modern Ballet (1970, neue bearbeitete Auflage 1980), The World of Diaghilev, Experimental Dance (beide 1971), Nureyev – Aspects of the Dancer (1975), The Facts about a Company (1979). Zur Zeit arbeitet er an einer Biographie über John Cranko.

John Percival, born in London, 1927, studied at St Catherine's, Oxford. He is ballet critic of The Times since 1965, writer for Dance & Dancers since 1950, associate editor 1965, editor 1981. Author of Antony Tudor (1963), Modern Ballet (1970, new edition 1980), The World of Diaghilev, Experimental Dance (both 1971), Nureyev – Aspects of the Dancer (1975), The Facts about a Company (1979). He is now writing a biography of John Cranko.

KURT PETERS

Kurt Peters, geboren 1915 in Hamburg. Deutscher Tänzer, Tanzpädagoge und -publizist. Gründer des Tanzarchivs, zunächst als Sammlung von Büchern und Dokumenten zum Tanz, von 1953 bis 1980 Herausgeber der Monatszeitschrift *Das Tanzarchiv,* Köln.

Kurt Peters, born in Hamburg in 1915, is a German dancer, teacher and dance journalist. He is the founder of *Tanzarchiv,* which started as a collection of books and documents on dance. From 1953 to 1980 he was editor in chief of the monthly magazine *Das Tanzarchiv* in Cologne.

KIRSTEN RALOV

Kirsten Ralov, geboren 1922 in Baden/Österreich. Trat 1929 in die Königlich Dänische Ballett-Schule ein; studierte darüber hinaus in Paris, London und New York. Von 1940 bis 1962 Mitglied des Königlich Dänischen Balletts, seit 1942 als Solistin. Choreographierte und inszenierte in Kanada, den USA, Neuseeland, Schweden, Deutschland, der Schweiz und Dänemark. Sie ist Dozentin am Königlich Dänischen Ballett, häufig Gastdozentin im Ausland. Seit 1978 ist sie Kodirektorin des Königlich Dänischen Balletts.

Kirsten Ralov, born in Baden, Austria, 1922, entered the Royal Danish Ballet School in 1929. She also studied in Paris, London and New York. She danced with the Royal Danish Ballet from 1940 to 1962, as principal dancer from 1942. She has staged and choreographed ballets in Canada, USA, New Zealand, Germany, Sweden, Switzerland and Denmark. Ms. Ralov is a teacher with the Royal Danish Ballet and is frequently a guest teacher abroad. Since July 1978, she has been Associate Director of the Royal Danish Ballet.

HARTMUT REGITZ

Hartmut Regitz, geboren 1943 in Bad Cannstatt. Studium der Germanistik, Geschichte, Wissenschaftlichen Politik, Volkskunde und Musik an der Universität Tübingen. Erste Arbeiten über Ballett in der Zeitschrift *Das Tanzarchiv.* Von 1963 an regelmäßiger Mitarbeiter mehrerer in- und ausländischer Zeitungen. 1970 Film über das Nederlands Dans Theater für das ZDF. Seit 1978 Herausgeber der im Friedrich-Verlag Velber erscheinenden Ballettjahrbücher. Von 1978 bis 1980 Redakteur beim Hessischen Rundfunk. Seitdem Redakteur der *Stuttgarter Nachrichten.*

Hartmut Regitz, born in Bad Cannstatt in 1943, studied German, history, political science, ethnology and music at the University of Tübingen. First works on ballet in the magazine *Das Tanzarchiv.* Since 1963 regular contributor to several German and international journals. In 1970 he produced a film of the Nederlands Dans Theater for the ZDF. Since 1978 he is editor in chief of the ballet yearbooks, published in Friedrich-Verlag Velber. From 1978 to 1980 he was editor at the Hessian Radio and Television. Since then, he is editor of the *Stuttgarter Nachrichten.*

HELMUT SCHEIER

Helmut Scheier, geboren 1926 in Remscheid. Studium der Theologie, Literatur- und Kunstgeschichte an den Universitäten Bonn und Heidelberg, anschließend dort wissenschaftliche Tätigkeit. Seit 1974 freier Publizist – vorwiegend im Bereich Ballett und Pantomime – bei Presse und Rundfunk. Dozent für Tanz-, Theater- und Kulturgeschichte am Institut für Bühnentanz, Köln.

Helmut Scheier, born in Remscheid in 1926, studied theology, literature, and art history at the Universities of Bonn and Heidelberg, where he also worked as a research assistant. Since 1974 he is a free-lance journalist for radio and press – primarily in the field of ballet and mime. He teaches history of dance, theater and civilization at the Institute for Stage Dance in Cologne.

JOCHEN SCHMIDT

Jochen Schmidt, geboren 1936 in Borken/Westfalen. Studium der Wirtschaftswissenschaften in Münster, München und Köln. Lebt in Düsseldorf als Kritiker der *Frankfurter Allgemeinen Zeitung.*

Jochen Schmidt, born in Borken, Westfalia, 1936, studied economics at the Universities of Münster, Munich and Cologne. He is currently critic for the *Frankfurter Allgemeine Zeitung.*

MARCIA B. SIEGEL

Marcia B. Siegel, geboren 1932 in New York, Tanzkritikerin der *Soho Weekly News* in New York und der *Hudson Review.* Sie hat bislang zwei Sammlungen über Tanzbesprechungen herausgegeben: *At the Vanishing Point* und *Watching Dance Go By,* sowie eine Studie über amerikanische Choreographie, *The Shapes of Change.* Sie erhielt ein Diplom über Labans Bewegungsanalyse.

Der in diesem Buch veröffentlichte Artikel basiert auf dem dritten von acht Vorträgen über Tanz im 20. Jahrhundert, die Marcia B. Siegel im Herbst 1980 als Teil eines Dreijahresprogramms über *The Meanings of Modernism* am Walker Art Center, Minneapolis, Minnesota, hielt. Diese Reihe wurde vom National Endowment for the Humanities finanziert.

Marcia B. Siegel, born in New York, 1932, is dance critic for the *Soho Weekly News* in New York and the *Hudson Review.* She has published two books of collected dance reviews, *At the Vanishing Point* and *Watching Dance Go By,* and a study of American choreography, *The Shapes of Change.* She holds a certificate in Laban's movement analysis.

The article published in this book is based on the third of eight lectures on 20th century dance that were given by Marcia B. Siegel during the fall of 1980 as part of a three-year-program on *The Meanings of Modernism,* at the Walker Art Center, Minneapolis, Minnesota. The series was funded by the National Endowment for the Humanities.

ULRICH TEGEDER

Ulrich Tegeder, geboren 1935 in Wismar/Mecklenburg. Studium der Kunstgeschichte und Tanzwissenschaft an der Hochschule für Musik, Köln. Danach Produktionsleiter für politische Fernsehsendungen der ARD. Seit 1975 Fernsehreporter und -autor für Kulturberichterstattung für Sendeanstalten der Dritten Welt und des Public Broadcasting System (PBS) der USA und Kanadas. (Serien: *The Art of Mime, Dances of the World.*) Er ist Mitglied des Tanzrates der UNESCO.

Ulrich Tegeder, born in Wismar, Mecklenburg in 1935, studied history of art and dance at the College of Music in Cologne. After that, he became production manager for political programs of the ARD. Since 1975, he is a TV reporter and TV author for cultural events for radio and television stations in the Third World and the Public Broadcasting System (PBS) in Canada and the United States. (Series: *The Art of Mime, Dances of the World.*) He is a member of the dance council of UNESCO.

GLEN TETLEY

Glen Tetley, geboren 1926 in Cleveland, Ohio. Amerikanischer Tänzer und Choreograph. Studium bei Hanya Holm, Antony Tudor und Martha Graham. Von 1946 bis 1961 Tänzer in verschiedenen amerikanischen Kompanien u. a. von Holm, Graham, Butler, Robbins sowie dem American Ballet

Theatre (ABT). Ab 1962 als Tänzer und Choreograph beim Nederlands Dans Theater (NDT), von 1969 bis 1970 (zusammen mit Hans van Manen) künstlerischer Leiter des NDT. Von 1974 bis 1976 Direktor des Stuttgarter Balletts. Seitdem freier Choreograph u. a. für NDT, ABT, Boston Ballet, Ballet Rambert, Royal Ballet, London sowie die Mailänder Scala und das italienische Aterballetto.

Glen Tetley, born in Cleveland, Ohio in 1926, is American dancer and choreographer. Studied with Hanya Holm, Antony Tudor and Martha Graham. From 1946 to 1961 dancer in various American companies, among others those of Holm, Graham, Butler, Robbins as well as the American Ballet Theatre (ABT). Since 1962 dancer and choreographer at the Nederlands Dans Theater (NDT), from 1969 to 1970 (together with Hans van Manen) artistic director of NDT. From 1974 to 1976 director of the Stuttgart Ballet. Since then free-lance choreographer, among others for NDT, ABT, Boston Ballet, Ballet Rambert, Royal Ballet, London, as well as La Scala in Milan, Italy, and the Italian Aterballetto.

dent der *Süddeutschen Zeitung.* 1973 bis 1976 Lehrauftrag am Institut für Bühnentanz Köln, 1980 an der Universität Göttingen für Medienrecht und Rundfunkorganisation. Publikationen: Beiträge für die Ballettjahrbücher seit 1967.

Jens Wendland was born in 1944 in Bad Polzin. Following his studies of law and economics, he began 1966 on his journalistic hobby: ballet, opera and theater criticism among others for the *Frankfurter Allgemeine Zeitung* and West German Radio and Television. He joined Hessian Radio and Television in 1971 where he was named director of the division for journalism and media planning in 1980. He is ballet critic and correspondent for the *Süddeutsche Zeitung* (Munich). From 1973 to 1976 he taught at the Institute for Stage Dance, Cologne; since 1980 in the department of media law and radio organization at University of Göttingen. Publications: articles for ballet yearbooks since 1967.

DAVID VAUGHAN

David Vaughan, geboren 1924 in London. Tänzer und Tanzschriftsteller, Autor von *Frederick Ashton and His Ballets* und – neben Mary Clarke – Mitherausgeber der *Encyclopedia of Dance and Ballet.* Er ist Mitarbeiter bei *Ballet Review* und Kritiker für *Dance Magazine.* Derzeit arbeitet er an einer Studie über die Arbeiten von Merce Cunningham, für die er ein Guggenheim Stipendium erhalten hat.

David Vaughan, born in London, 1924, is dancer and dance writer, author of *Frederick Ashton and His Ballets* and co-editor with Mary Clarke of *The Encyclopedia of Dance and Ballet.* He is a contributing editor of *Ballet Review* and a senior critic of *Dance Magazine.* He is currently working on a study of the choreography of Merce Cunningham, for which he received a Guggenheim Fellowship.

JENS WENDLAND

Jens Wendland, geboren 1944 in Bad Polzin. Nach dem Studium der Rechts- und Volkswirtschaft Konzentration auf das journalistische Hobby: Ballett-, Opern- und Theaterkritik u. a. für *Frankfurter Allgemeine Zeitung* und WDR seit 1966. 1971 Eintritt in den Hessischen Rundfunk, seit 1980 Leiter der Abteilung Publizistik und Medienplanung des HR. Ballettkritiker und Korrespon-

Ausgewählte Bibliographie
Selected Bibliography

von/by NORBERT SERVOS

Arséne Alexandre, *The Decorated Art of Léon Bakst, Notes on the Ballets by Jean Cocteau,* London, 1913; New York, 1972

George Amberg, *Art in Modern Ballet,* Washington, 1946

Gasparone Angiolini, *Lettere di Gasparo Angiolini a Monsieur Noverre sopra i balli pantomimi,* Mailand, 1773

Lettre d'un des petits Oracles de Monsieur Angiolini au Grand Noverre, Mailand, 1774

Reflessioni di Gasparo Angiolini sopra l'uso dei programmi nei balli pantomimi, London, 1775

Thoinot Arbeau, *Orchesographie,* Paris, 1888

Merle Armitage (ed.), *Martha Graham: The Early Years,* Los Angeles, 1978

George Balanchine, *Complete Stories of Great Ballets,* New York, 1954

Sally Banes, *Terpsichore in Sneakers: Post-Modern Dance,* Boston, 1980

Georges Barbier, *Design and the Dance of Vaslav Nijinsky,* London, 1913

Herbert Bayer/Walter Gropius/Ise Gropius (ed.), *Bauhaus 1919–1928,* New York, 1979 (Reprint)

Cyril W. Beaumont, *Ballet Design, Past and Present,* London, 1946

The Romantic Ballet as Seen by Théophile Gautier, London, 1932

Vaslav Nijinsky, London, 1932

Walter Benjamin, *Das Kunstwerk im Zeitalter seiner technischen Reproduzierbarkeit,* Frankfurt a. M., 1963

Alexandre Benois, *Reminiscences of the Russian Ballet,* London, 1941

Fritz Böhme, *Der Tanz der Zukunft,* München, 1926

Fritz Böhme/Curt Moreck, *Der Tanz in der Kunst, Die bedeutendsten Tanzbilder von der Antike bis zur Gegenwart,* Stuttgart, 1924

Max von Boehn, *Der Tanz,* Berlin, 1925

August Bournonville, *Etudes Chorégraphiques,* Paris, 1861

My Theatre Life, Middletown, 1979

Hans Brandenburg, *Der moderne Tanz,* München, 1921

Inge Brunner, *Jazztanz, Training, Technik, Taktik,* Reinbek bei Hamburg, 1978

Richard Buckle, *Costumes and Curtains from the Diaghilev and the Basil Ballets,* London, 1972

Nijinsky, New York, 1971

In Search of Diaghilev, London, 1955

John Cage, *Notations,* New York, 1969

Silence, Middletown, 1963

A Year from Monday, Middletown, 1963

Calouste Gulbenkian Foundation (ed.), *Dance Education and Training in Britain,* London, 1980

Dolores Kirton Cayou, *Modern Jazz Dance,* Palo Alto, 1971

Gay Cheney, *Modern Dance,* Boston, 1969

Mary Clarke/Clement Crisp, *Ballet in Art: From the Renaissance to the Present,* London, 1978

Design for Ballet, London, 1978

Making a Ballet, London, 1974; New York, 1975

Selma Jeanne Cohen (ed.), *Dance as a Theatre Art,* New York, 1974

Selma Jeanne Cohen, *Doris Humphrey: An Artist First,* Middletown, 1972

Selma Jeanne Cohen (ed.), *The Modern Dance: Seven Statements of Belief,* Middletown, 1965

Merce Cunningham, *Changes: Notes on Choreography,* New York, 1969

Ted Dalbotten, *Louis Horst,* New York, 1970

Tai F. Deharde, *Tanz-Improvisation in der ästhetischen Erziehung,* Bern und Stuttgart, 1978

Rudolf von Delius, *Mary Wigman,* Dresden, 1925

François Delsarte, *Mimique, Physionomie et Geste,* Paris, 1895

Friderica Derra de Moroda, *Die Ballettmeister vor, zur Zeit und nach J.G. Noverre,* o.O., o.J.

Georges Detaille, *Les Ballets de Monte Carlo 1911–1944,* Paris, 1954

Paul Draper, *On Tap Dancing,* New York, 1978

Irma Duncan, *Duncan Dancers: An Autobiography,* Middletown, 1966

Irma Duncan/Allan Ross MacDougal, *Isadora Duncan's Russian Days,* New York, 1929

Isadora Duncan, *The Art of the Dance,* New York, 1928

Memoiren, Zürich, 1928

Der Tanz der Zukunft, Leipzig, 1903

The Technique of Isadora Duncan, London, 1950

Robert Dunn (ed.), *John Cage,* New York, 1962

S. Enkelmann, *Tänzer unserer Zeit,* München, 1937

Angna Enters, *On Mime,* Middletown, 1978

Elfriede Feudel, *Rhythmik, Theorie und Praxis der körperlich-musikalischen Erziehung,* München, 1926

Raoul Feuillet, *Chorégraphie,* Paris, 1701

Michail Fokine, *Gegen den Strom – Erinnerungen eines Ballettmeisters,* Berlin, 1974

Loie Fuller, *15 Years of a Dancer's Life,* London, 1913

Théophile Gautier, *Histoire de l'Art dramatique en France depuis vingt-cinq Ans,* Paris, 1959

Théâtre – Mystère, Comédie et Ballets, Paris, 1872

Gus Giordano, *Anthology of American Jazz Dance,* New Rochelle, 1966

RoseLee Goldberg, *Performance: Live Art 1909 to the Present,* New York, 1979

Nathalie Gontcharova/Michel Larionov/Pierre Vorms, *Les Ballets Russes, Serge de Diaghilev et la Décoration théâtrale,* Belvés, 1955

Martha Graham, *The Notebooks of Martha Graham,* New York, 1973

Manfred Grimmer/Helmut Günther, *Tap Dance – Aus der Praxis für die Praxis,* Stuttgart, o. J.

Tap Dance – Geschichte, Technik, Praxis, Stuttgart, o. J.

Theorie und Praxis des Jazz Dance, Stuttgart, 1975

Walter Gropius, *Die Bühne im Bauhaus,* München, 1925

Dorothee Günther, *Der Tanz als Bewegungsphänomen – Wesen und Werden,* Reinbek bei Hamburg, 1962

Ivor Guest, *The Romantic Ballet in Paris,* London, 1980

The Ballet of the Second Empire, Middletown, 1974

Kay Hamblin, *Pantomime, Spiel mit deiner Fantasie,* Weidgarten, 1979

Barbara Haselbach, *Improvisation, Tanz, Bewegung,* Stuttgart, 1976

Arnold Haskell, *Diaghilev: His Private and Artistic Life,* London, 1935

Hans Werner Henze, *Undine, Tagebuch eines Balletts,* München, 1959

Moira Hodgson, *Quintet: Five American Dance Companies,* New York, 1976

Louis Horst, *Pre-Classic Dance Forms,* New York, 1979

Louis Horst/Caroll Russel, *Modern Dance Forms in Relation to the Other Modern Arts,* San Francisco, 1961

Doris Humphrey, *The Art of Making Dances,* London, o.J.

Anna Ivanova, *The Dancing Spaniards,* London, 1970

Eleanor King, *Transformations – The Humphrey – Weidman Era,* New York, 1978

Claude Kipnis, *The Mime Book,* New York, 1976

Michael Kirby, *The Art of Time,* New York, 1969

Lincoln Kirstein, *Movement and Metaphor,* New York, 1970

Heinrich von Kleist, *Über das Marionettentheater und andere Schriften,* München, o.J.

James Klosty (ed.), *Merce Cunningham,* New York, 1975

Boris Kochno, *Le Ballet par Boris Kochno,* Paris, 1954

Diaghilev and the Ballets Russes, New York, 1970

Boris Kochno/Maria Lutz, *Le Ballet,* Paris, 1954

Svend Kragh-Jacobsen, *The Royal Danish Ballet,* Copenhagen, 1955

Vera Krasovskaya, *Nijinsky,* Leningrad, 1974; New York, 1979

M. Krüger, *Jean Georges Noverre und das Ballet d'action,* Emsdetten, 1963

Rudolf von Laban, *Choreographie,* Jena, 1926

Deutsche Tanzfestspiele 1934, Dresden, 1934

Gymnastik und Tanz, Oldenburg, 1926

Ein Leben für den Tanz, Dresden, 1935

Mastery of Movement on the Stage, London, 1950

Modern Educational Dance, London, 1948

Die Welt des Tänzers, Stuttgart, 1920

Rudolf von Laban/Mary Wigman, *Die tänzerische Situation in unserer Zeit,* Dresden, 1936

Jacques Lassaigne, *Marc Chagall, Dessin et Aquarelles pour le Ballet,* Paris, 1969

Joan Lawson, *Mime, The Theory and Practice of Expressive Gesture,* London, 1957

The Principles of Classical Dance, New York, 1980

The Teaching of Classical Ballet, London, 1973

Karl Leabo (ed.), *Martha Graham,* New York, 1962

Fernand Léger, *Conférence über die Schau-Bühne, Vortrag an der Pariser Sorbonne 1924, Rolf de Maré, dem Leiter der Ballets Suédois gewidmet,* Frankfurt a.M., 1968

André Levinson, *Bakst, The Story of the Artist's Life,* London, 1923

L'Oeuvre de Léon Bakst, Paris, 1921

Serge Lifar, *La Musique par la Danse de Lully à Prokofiew,* Paris, 1955

Serge Diaghilev: His Life, His Work, His Legend, New York, 1940

Anne Livet, *Contemporary Dance,* New York, 1978

György Lörinc (Hg.), *Methodik des klassischen Tanzes,* Berlin, 1964; Wilhelmshaven, 1978

Roger M. Louis, *Steptanz,* Basel, 1979

Nesta MacDonald, *Diaghilev Observed,* New York and London, 1975

Paul David Magriel (ed.), *Chronicles of the American Dance,* New York, 1948

John Joseph Martin, *America Dancing,* New York, 1936

The Modern Dance, New York, 1933

Colette Masson/Jean–Louis Rousseau/Pierre Faucheux, *Béjart by Béjart*, New York, 1980

Olga Maynard, *The American Ballet*, Philadelphia, 1959

American Modern Dance: The Pioneers, Boston, 1965

Joseph H. Mazo, *Dance Is a Contact Sport*, New York, 1974

Prime Movers: The Makers of Modern Dance in America, New York, 1977

Joan McConnell, *Ballet as Body Language*, New York, 1977

Don McDonagh, *Martha Graham*, New York, 1973

The Rise and Fall and Rise of Modern Dance, New York, 1970

Asaf Messerer, *Classes in Classical Ballet*, Moskau 1967; New York, 1975

Agnes de Mille, *America Dances: A Personal Chronicle – in Words and Pictures*, New York, 1980

Dance to the Piper – The Life Story of America's Greatest Creative Dancer, New York, 1954

Barbara Morgan, *Martha Graham*, New York, 1941 and 1980

Ebbe Mørk (ed.), *Salut for Bournonville*, Copenhagen, 1979

Hedwig Müller/Norbert Servos, *Pina Bausch – Wuppertaler Tanztheater*, Köln 1979

Ruth Lovell Murray, *Dance in Elementary Education*, New York, 1953

Myron Howard Nadel/Constance Gwen Nadel (ed.), *The Dance Experience: Readings in Dance Appreciations*, New York, 1970

Paul Nettl, *Tanz und Tanzmusik*, Freiburg i. Br., 1962

Max Niehaus, *Ballett-Faszination, Ein Kompendium der internationalen Ballettszene*, München, 1980

Romola Nijinsky, *Nijinsky, Der Gott des Tanzes*, Frankfurt a.M., 1974

Jean Georges Noverre, *Lettres sur la Danse et sur les Ballets*, Stuttgart/Lyon, 1760; deutsche Ausgabe: Hamburg und Bremen, 1769 (Reprint München, 1977)

Lettres sur les Arts Imitateurs en général et sur la Danse en particulier, Paris, 1807

Claes Oldenburg, *Raw Notes*, Halifax, 1973

Store Days, New York, 1967

Marius Petipa, *Meister des klassischen Balletts, Selbstzeugnisse, Dokumente, Erinnerungen*, hg. v. Eberhard Rebling, Berlin, 1975

Emil Pirchan, *Harald Kreutzberg, Sein Leben und seine Tänze*, Wien, 1941

Yvonne Rainer, *Work 1961–1973*, Halifax and New York, 1974

Kirsten Ralov (ed.), *The Bournonville-School (4 vols.)*, New York und Basel, 1979

Pierre Rameau, *Le Maître à Danser*, Paris, 1725

Brian Reade, *Ballet Designs and Illustrations 1581–1940* (Catalogue), London, 1967

Henning Rischbieter (ed.), *Art and the Stage in the 20th Century*, New York, 1969

Henning Rischbieter/Wolfgang Storch, *Bühne und bildende Kunst im XX. Jahrhundert*, Velber bei Hannover, 1968

Harvey Rochlein, *Notes on Contemporary American Dance*, Baltimore, 1964

John Schikowski, *Geschichte des Tanzes*, Berlin, 1926

Oskar Schlemmer, *Briefe und Tagebücher*, hg. v. Tut Schlemmer, München, 1958

Oskar Schlemmer/Laszlo Moholy-Nagy/Farkas Molnar, *The Theater of the Bauhaus*, Middletown, 1979

Christine Schlundt, *The Professional Appearances of Ruth St. Denis and Ted Shawn*, New York, 1967

The Professional Appearances of Ted Shawn and His Men Dancers, New York, 1967

Günther Schmidt-Garre, *Vom Sonnenkönig bis Balanchine*, Velber bei Hannover, 1966

Rolf Schrade, *Sowjetisches Ballett*, Berlin, 1977

Ernst Schur, *Der moderne Tanz*, München, 1910

Nona Schurman, *Modern Dance Fundamentals*, New York, 1972

Arthur Seidl, *Die Hellerauer Schulfeste und die Bildungsanstalt Jaques-Dalcroze*, Regensburg, 1912

Nikolai Serebrennikow, *Pas de deux im klassischen Tanz*, Berlin, 1976

Victor Seroff, *The Real Isadora*, New York, 1971

Ted Shawn, *The American Ballet*, New York, 1926

Every Little Movement: A Book about François Delsarte – The Man and His Philosophy, New York, 1974

Gods Who Dance, New York, 1929

Ruth St. Denis: Pioneer and Prophet, San Francisco, 1920

Juri Slonimsky, *Soviet Ballet*, New York, 1947

Walter Sorell. *Hanya Holm: The Biography of an Artist*, Middletown, 1969

Walter Sorell (ed.), *The Mary Wigman Book*, Middletown, 1973

Ruth St. Denis, *An Unfinished Life*, New York, 1939 and 1969

Francis Steegmuller (ed.), *Your Isadora*, New York, 1974

Ina Stegen, *Die Ecole de Paris und das Theater*, (Diss.), Wien, 1966

Virginia Stewart/Merle Armitage, *Modern Dance*, New York, 1935

Igor Strawinsky, *Leben und Werk – von ihm selbst*, Mainz, 1957

Nikolai J. Tarassow, *Klassischer Tanz – Die Schule des Tänzers*, Berlin, 1974

Gottfried Taubert, *Rechtschaffener Tanzmeister oder gründliche Erklärung der französischen Tanzkunst*, Leipzig, 1717 u. 1976 (Reprint)

Karl Heinz Taubert, *Höfische Tänze, Ihre Geschichte und Choreographie*, Mainz, 1968

Walter Terry, *The Dance in America*, New York, 1956

Frank Thiess, *Der Tanz als Kunstwerk*, München, 1920

Mabel Elsworth Todd, *The Thinking Body*, New York, 1972

Fred Traguth, *Modern Jazz Dance*, Bonn und New York, o.J.

Pierre Tugal, *Jean Georges Noverre, Der große Reformator des Balletts*, Berlin, 1959

Paul Valéry u.a., *Le Ballet au XIX. Siècle.*, Paris, 1921

Agrippina Waganowa, *Grundlagen des klassischen Tanzes*, Leningrad, 1934; Berlin, 1954

Larry Warren, *Lester Horton: Modern Dance Pioneer*, New York, 1977

Grete Wehmeyer, *Erik Satie*, Regensburg, 1974

Mary Wigman, *Deutsche Tanzkunst*, Dresden, 1935

Die Sprache des Tanzes, Stuttgart, 1963

Helen Wingrave/Robert Harrold, *Spanish Dancing: A Handbook on Steps, Style, Castanets and Dancing*, Speldhurst, 1972

Marian Hannah Winter, *The Pre-Romantic Ballet*, London, 1974

Lydia Wolgina/Ulrich Pietsch (Hg.), *Die Welt des Tanzes in Selbstzeugnissen*, Berlin, 1977

Anne Woolliams, *Ballettsaal*, Stuttgart, 1973

Gerhard Zacharias, *Ballett – Gestalt und Wesen*, Köln, 1962

Les Ballets Russes de Serge Diaghilev, Katalog zur 2. Exposition européenne d'art moderne, Strasbourg, 1969

Les Ballets Suédois dans l'art contemporaine, Paris, 1931

Royal Academy of Arts (ed.), *Bauhaus 50 Years* (Exhibition catalogue), London, 1968

Royal Academy of Dancing London Syllabi, *Abhandlungen über Balletterziehung und Examensvorbereitung*, o. O., o. J.

Register/Index